It was Frank who spotted the first corpse: a limp wet lump of clothing floating face down less than fifty feet from *Vagabond*'s course. Frank's first instinct was to alter course to retrieve the body, but then he quickly realized that the last thing they needed aboard was a corpse. There would be more.

The two ships coming towards them remained close to the western shore and soon disappeared past them heading up the Chesapeake to God-knew-where. That they had survived at all was a surprise. The boat on the same course as *Vagabond* disappeared into a cove or river on the western shore. By late morning they seemed to be all alone on the vast expanse of the Bay.

The fallout still fell.

By the same author

The Dice Man
Matari

LUKE RHINEHART

Long Voyage Back

GRANADA
London Toronto Sydney New York

Published in paperback by Granada Publishing Limited in 1983

ISBN 0 586 05624 6

First published in Great Britain by
Granada Publishing 1983
Copyright © Luke Rhinehart 1983

Granada Publishing Limited
Frogmore, St Albans, Herts AL2 2NF
and
36 Golden Square, London W1R 4AH
515 Madison Avenue, New York, NY 10022, USA
117 York Street, Sydney, NSW 2000, Australia
60 International Blvd, Rexdale, Ontario, R9W 6J2, Canada
61 Beach Road, Auckland, New Zealand

Made and printed in Great Britain by
Collins, Glasgow
Set in Baskerville

Granada ®
Granada Publishing ®

Signalling the new attitude over a year ago, George Bush spoke of emerging a 'winner' in a nuclear exchange – and more recently, Administration officials have talked of surviving a limited war in better shape than the other side. Many critics believe that mere discussion of 'winnable' nuclear war increases the chance of one occurring and inevitably escalating into full-scale conflict. The Bulletin of the Atomic Scientist agrees: at the end of 1980 its famous 'doomsday clock' was moved up three notches to just four minutes before midnight . . .

Newsweek, 5 October 1981

The Bulletin of Atomic Scientists, in an unusual action, declared today that their 'doomsday clock' was now at thirty-seven seconds to midnight. It was the first time the scientists have used seconds rather than minutes in their periodic assessments of the probable proximity of nuclear war . . .

A.P. Bulletin, 9 January 1985

Behold, the day of the Lord comes,
  cruel, with wrath and fierce anger,
to make the earth a desolation and
  to destroy the sinners from it.
For the stars of the heavens and
their constellations
  will not give their light;
the sun will be dark at its rising
  and the moon will not shed its light . . .
Therefore will I make the heavens
tremble,
  and the earth will be shaken out
of its place . . .

Isaiah, 13:9–10, 13

Preface

This is not a ship's log nor an official report. Although notes we have taken over the last year have certainly helped, it's also not our diaries and journals. What we've tried to do, for ourselves primarily, for some future readers if there are any, is to re-create what it was like for those we knew and for us, for this small family of people who are still survivors.

We make no effort to take a global view, nor have we pretensions to being historians. We have no thesis. We are interested in people, in those who survived the initial holocaust, whom we met, knew, tried to save, in some cases failed to save; how we all, the remnants, coped with the aftermath; how we were dragged down by it, so often failing.

Yet some of us survive. At this point that alone gives our story significance.

Part One

FIRE

The room was crowded, its occupants scurrying from place to place in organized chaos. A gigantic videoscreen filled the north wall, showing a map of the earth with lighted and blinking symbols indicating weapons, forces, counterforces. A second, smaller screen high on the east wall spewed forth printed messages, with an inventory of warheads, explosive power, probable targets, number of casualties. Along the south wall were ten desk-size computers, each with a uniformed man watching it as ancient priests watched moiling entrails. Along the western wall was a long table at which sat thirteen men, all but one of them uniformed, listening to the man at the head of the table speak to them in a sullen, lugubrious tone of the intentions of the enemy, the probability of surviving various war scenarios.

There was no joy or humour in the room. The seriousness had a disjointed, alienated quality as of men working hard at a job they don't quite understand, discussing alternatives they don't quite believe in. The sullenness that marked many of the faces was the expression of men doing what was expected of them, but doing things they didn't want to be doing. Their voices were sometimes high-pitched, close to cracking. A few of the eyes seemed wild. When one general burst out passionately in favour of one course of action, a few looked at him as if he were mad; others looked at him gloomily, nodding. When an admiral spoke for the opposite course of action, a few looked at him as if he were mad; others looked at him gloomily, shaking their heads,

The words spoken, whether coolly or in anger, sadness or nervous panic, all had about them a scientific detachment as consistent and codified as the uniforms most of them wore.

11

They were eminently reasonable words, and they poured out across the table with the sporadic urgency of a teletype machine rolling out its messages: nullify evasive evacuation . . . no more than eighty million . . . reduce counterstrike potential by forty-two per cent . . . state of belligerency inherent in . . . dilute the economic infrastructure . . . diversification of missile response . . . reduced military options necessitated by the higher kill ratio . . . the incidental effects of maximizing radiation . . . nullifying recuperative capacity . . .

Behind the ten desks the ten uniformed men stared at the ten computers. On the north wall the giant screen blinked out its kaleidoscope of pulsating lights like a pinball machine; a few uniformed men stared up at it as if waiting for it to tally the final score.

Eventually the men at the long table seemed to reach some sort of decision. A telephone was brought to one of them. With the receiver at his ear he waited patiently for the proper connection. The others watched, some smoking, others staring at the table. None spoke. None bothered to look at either of the videoscreens. None smiled.

The man with the phone began speaking respectfully to the party at the other end, paused, listening, then spoke again. After less than two minutes he hung up. The others looked at him. Two orderlies began placing cups and saucers in front of the officers and pouring out a hot steaming liquid. The man cleared his throat and uttered a simple declarative sentence indicating that the man he had spoken to had decided to adopt the course of action they had just recommended. None spoke. None leapt to action. None smiled. One man sipped at the hot steaming liquid; then another man sipped. At the end of the table opposite the presiding officer a man began to cry. The officer opposite him glared angrily; two other men looked away, tightlipped.

The presiding officer began to speak again in a tense, gloomy voice, addressing first one man and then another

12

down the table. One by one the men rose to depart. Most hurried. None spoke. None smiled.

Left at the table finally were the presiding officer and the man who was crying. The first, sullen and gloomy, rose and left. Only one man was left.

1

Her three white hulls slicing quietly through the water, her giant genoa bellying out to starboard, *Vagabond* sailed into the Bay. Neil Loken sat in the port cockpit of the large trimaran watching the causeway of the Chesapeake Bay Bridge–Tunnel, through which they had just passed, recede behind them. At the wheel Jim Stoor was peering ahead and shifting his weight excitedly from one foot to the other. Although his father owned *Vagabond*, this was the first time Jim had made a landfall after a long ocean passage, and his boyish face, haloed by the rays of the early morning sun, showed it. He appeared to Neil at that moment – his slender broad-shouldered body bronzed by their five days at sea – like a seagoing Pan.

But Neil didn't share Jim's excitement and joy. Sailing up into the huge mouth and throat of the Bay depressed him. He was an ocean sailor; he rarely enjoyed leaving the clear deep waters of the open sea for the mud and shallows of ground-enclosed bays and inlets.

And it didn't help that the Chesapeake was a sort of home. Neil had attended the US Naval Academy at Annapolis for four years and, after serving in Vietnam for three, captained a forty-six-foot sloop based in Norfolk for several summers. Sailing down the Bay out to sea had often meant adventure, freedom, escape. Sailing into it meant land, civilization, the complications of returning home.

As he looked forward to examine the set of the mainsail and genoa and check Jim's course towards the next buoy, Neil was troubled too by the quite mundane fact that *Vagabond*'s propeller shaft had been struck and bent by a submerged log off Cape Hatteras and the big trimaran thus

15

had no auxiliary engine power. How long it would take to sail her the next seventy-five miles up to Point Lookout to pick up Frank Stoor and his guests now depended on the wind, a notoriously unreliable friend, especially in the Chesapeake.

'Hey, look!' Jim suddenly said, pointing past Neil towards Norfolk. 'Warships. Three of them.'

Turning, Neil saw low on the horizon three long grey vessels steaming out of Hampton Roads heading out of the southern channel to the bridge and the ocean. Two were destroyers, the third a ship the Navy must have designed since he'd resigned his commission. A supply ship maybe – but since when was a supply ship accompanied by two destroyers?

'I wonder where they're going,' Jim went on, looking past Neil now through binoculars, holding the large stainless steel wheel in place by the pressure of his bare chest. Like Neil he was wearing only a pair of blue jean cut-offs.

'There are always a few ships from the Norfolk Naval Base either coming or going,' Neil said quietly, but even as he spoke he recognized yet another reason he was depressed: the slow, awkward, terrifying way the US and Russia seemed to be trying to frighten each other into war. For the last three days, the radio news reports had been increasingly disturbing. On Wednesday an American reconnaissance plane downed by an Iraqi missile, probably fired from a launcher manned by Russians; yesterday the US rejecting the Soviet mutual troop withdrawal proposal, labelling it extortionate; today the US government reinforcing its marine units in Saudi Arabia. Neil had listened to these radio reports alone.

'You ever serve in ships like those?' Jim asked, lowering his binoculars and smiling with his general excitement.

'No, I was lucky,' Neil replied, turning back to Jim. 'They put me in the smallest combat vessels the Navy had – coastal patrol boats.'

16

'You ever get sunk?' Jim asked next.

Neil smiled, his usually stern face suddenly lit, his blue eyes crinkling. Jim's boyish curiosity about things always redeemed for Neil some otherwise annoying habits: listening to loud rock music at every opportunity; leaving food, towels, dishes, clothing strewn about the boat as if they were precious jewels he was magnanimously bestowing upon the poverty-ridden ship; his penchant for pot . . . But Jim's enthusiasm redeemed him; that, and the important fact that he'd turned out to be an excellent sailor.

'No, I can't say I did,' Neil replied, standing up and watching the distant warships. 'In fact, most of the war I and some of my men were thoroughly depressed that no one ever fired at us.'

'But Dad said you were wounded,' Jim said.

'Oh, yes,' Neil agreed. 'Occasionally we got lucky.'

'And you sank a lot of ships?'

'So they say.' Neil could feel himself tensing over the direction the conversation was taking. He walked towards Jim and began doing chin-ups from the edge of the wheel-house roof. He had a muscular gymnast's body, browned from the sun like Jim's, but thicker, more mature; that of a well-conditioned athlete in his thirties. Like Jim he held his six foot height with military erectness. But his face, unlike Jim's, was weathered and lined, a light scar running into his hairline at his right temple. His blue eyes often pinned people with distracting coldness, but could suddenly lighten and crinkle with the warmth of his smile. His shock of thick brown hair was uncombed and stiffly awry from the saltwater and wind.

'Well?' insisted Jim.

Neil lowered himself from the last chin-up and moved into the wheelhouse and stood beside the eighteen-year-old. Two empty glasses sat on the wheelhouse shelf, reminders of the whisky they'd drunk at dawn when they'd sighted land for

17

the first time since northern Florida. Neil picked up one and drained it.

'It was a pushbutton war, even for the smallest ships,' he said slowly. 'We killed at long range. If we ever happened to see what havoc we had fashioned it was always a little disconcerting to find that the "enemy gunboat" or "'Cong supply ship" looked suspiciously like a fishing boat, and the dead and dying like bony fishermen.' Neil paused, staring through the windows of the wheelhouse forward past *Vagabond*'s wide white deck and mainmast to the grey bay stretching out ahead.

'Some of them must have been . . . 'Cong,' said Jim.

'Oh, sure,' said Neil.

'Is that why you resigned your commission?'

'That and a dozen other reasons.'

He didn't go on. He walked back out of the wheelhouse to end the conversation. He knew he'd been the wrong man for the job. When he'd graduated from Annapolis he'd been fully prepared to stand on the poopdeck of his ship and fight to the last man. But he wasn't prepared to stand and blast away not knowing whether he was killing good guys or bad guys, rarely being fired at in return, and being forbidden by standing orders to pick up the wounded survivors.

Resigning his commission had been both a protest against a specific war, and an acknowledgement that for him, even were the war 'justified', the technological and impersonal means of fighting it were not. For years after resigning he'd been a loner, unfit for either the unregimented chaos of civilian life or companionship with his old Navy friends. A woman had brought him back to life, but after a year and a half, with the abrupt arbitrariness of battle, she'd been killed in an auto accident. Since then he'd found a healthier aloneness as professional captain of wealthy men's yachts, re-establishing some of the order that he'd liked in military life, and finding a closeness with the sea and sky that seemed to heal.

18

Staring upwards at the set of the mainsail he noticed two trails of jet vapour inching across the sky, the thin cotton lines tinged with pink and seeming to emerge from nowhere in the west and to be disappearing nowhere to the east. The planes themselves were invisible. When a loud sonic boom broke the stillness of early morning, Jim turned quickly towards Neil.

'What was *that*?' he exclaimed.

Neil pointed to the vapour trails in the sky.

Jim seemed momentarily frightened, but then grinned. 'I thought the destroyers had opened fire on us,' he said.

Neil watched the cotton trails disappear into the brightness towards the east.

'Welcome back to civilization,' he commented.

Throughout the morning *Vagabond* sailed up the bay at a little over seven knots and Neil went about the boat, making sure it would be ready for its owner's inspection that night. *Vagabond* was a fast, roomy trimaran that moved through the water like a strange three-legged insect skipping from wave to wave. You entered the cabins of the side hull from the two side cockpits and went down steps to the long, narrow floor area. The berths were up in the 'wing' area over the water separated from the main cabin by a plywood and veneer partition. *Vagabond* was steered from the enclosed wheelhouse that was between the main cabin with its galley and dinette area and Neil's aft cabin. On either side of the wheelhouse were the open cockpits with seats and the sliding hatchway leading down into the side cabins. All this space meant that people could get away from each other at sea and Neil, being a private man, found that important, almost as important as *Vagabond*'s ability to go fast, without heeling, in almost any kind of weather.

At noon he relinquished the helm to Jim in order to put through a call to Frank at his office in New York City. Jim turned on the transistor radio to listen to the noon news, a rarity, since he usually preferred music or his cassette tapes.

Neil's aft cabin contained only twelve square feet of standing space between his double berth dead aft and the bulkhead that separated his cabin from the ship's engine compartment. Although not as spacious as the cabins in the two side hulls Neil preferred it to anywhere else aboard. The radio-telephone, a shortwave radio, and a chart table had all been installed here; his books were crammed along two long shelves. With the large grey radio, the navigational equipment and the sparse furnishings, it was a very masculine room, 'about as pretty as the inside of a tank' as one woman had described it.

When the marine operator got the call through to New York Neil was glad to hear Frank's husky voice.

'This stupid war stuff is screwing up everything,' Frank announced loudly. 'I can't get a flight to Washington; they're booked solid. You think you could meet me today in Crisfield? I can get a flight to Salisbury, Maryland, and then rent a car.'

Crisfield, Neil knew, was a small fishing town about twenty-five miles across the bay from Point Lookout.

'Sure,' he replied. 'That's as easy as Point Lookout. What about the Foresters?'

'We'll sail *Vagabond* across the bay and pick them up as soon as you get me. What time you figure you'll make it to Crisfield?'

'If the wind holds or improves we'll be there by six tonight. But if it drops or we're headed . . .'

'Well, do your best,' Frank said into the pause. 'I know you must be beat. *Vagabond*'s a lot of boat for just two men, especially when one of them's a goof-off.'

'Your son's a good sailor,' Neil commented quickly.

'Yeah?' Frank replied, seeming surprised at the news.

'In that blow off St Augustine,' Neil went on, 'Jim went up the mast when the mainsail jammed. He also took the helm for almost four hours, letting me sleep through half my watch.'

'At home I can't get him to do five straight minutes of any kind of work, much less four hours.'

'Neil!' Jim's voice broke into the conversation from the deck just outside the cabin hatchway. 'I've got to talk to Dad. There's going to be a war!'

'What are you talking about?' Neil asked, looking up at Jim.

'I just heard the news,' Jim went on. 'We rejected the Russian offer. Let me speak to Dad.'

'Uh, Frank, Jim wants to talk to you,' Neil said. 'We'll meet you tonight in Crisfield unless we're becalmed. If we are, I'll try to get a message through to Carter's Bluewater Marina. Got it?'

'What? Sure. Good.'

Neil hopped up the cabin steps and hurried to the wheel as Jim took over the radiophone's mike.

'Holy Jesus, Dad,' Jim said. 'We're going to be fighting the Russians. There's going to be a *war*!'

For a moment there was silence on the other end, then Frank's voice replied slowly and huskily. 'Don't worry about it, Jimmy,' he said. 'This is just another *scare*. Just like three months ago. Just like two years ago. This is international poker and the secret is never to call, just keep raising.'

'The radio said we rejected their offer of mutual troop withdrawals,' Jim went on. 'Why?'

'If we withdraw any troops now,' said Frank, his husky voice again coming in only after a pause, 'we'd be seen as giving in. Our President may be a jerk, but he's a *macho* jerk, so we can be sure that now that our troops are in Arabia they're going to stay, even if no one's around to kill.'

'Dad, we ought to take the boat back south,' said Jim, gripping the mike in both hands. 'When the war starts—'

'Now cut that crap,' Frank interrupted with abrupt

21

annoyance. 'This is just another game of international brinkmanship and neither their assholes nor our assholes are stupid enough to go to war. The Russians don't really care about Saudi Arabian nomads and we don't really care about Asian democracy.'

'But we care about oil!'

'Not enough to blow up the world,' said Frank. 'Now give me Neil. No, don't bother. Just hang up and get your ass up to Crisfield.' The line went dead.

Jim stood alone in the aft cabin. He was angry. He hated the way his father dealt with him. Since he'd been only an average student and never held a job, his father had always made him feel he was something of a good-for-nothing. He enjoyed rock music, playing his guitar, getting high with his friends and partying, and making it with Celia or an occasional other girl. None of these qualified in Frank's eyes as anything but being a waste of time. The three or four occasions he'd sailed with Frank on *Vagabond* there'd been a lot of older people aboard who'd helped Frank handle the boat. Jim had ended up retreating to his cabin to get stoned and listen to music. His father had inevitably come to shout at him to turn it down and to criticize him for not helping more with the sailing. It had been a downer. He didn't even think he liked sailing much until this sail from Florida alone with Neil.

He climbed slowly up the ladder from the aft cabin and went back into the wheelhouse. Neil, who'd heard Jim's end of the conversation and its abrupt termination, stared forward.

'There's going to be a war,' Jim stated angrily. 'And Dad doesn't care.'

Neil glanced at Jim and then back forward. 'I don't know,' Neil replied. 'I suppose it's possible our troops and theirs may be killing each other in a month or two. But maybe the world will pretend everyone's a guerrilla and we won't have to call it a war.'

'But that retired general says we ought to hit Russia before they attack us,' said Jim. 'And those Protestant ministers said the same. If the Russians read that then *they'll* have to strike first. Don't you see?'

'No, Jim . . .'

'They're going to do it,' Jim insisted, his long hair falling down his forehead so that when it obscured his left eye he tossed it back angrily. 'I know they are. I can feel it!'

Neil looked forward, reminded of a young sailor on his last patrol who had panicked from watching B-52s bomb the coast two miles away. He knew from Frank that when Jim was fifteen he'd had a bad acid trip, hallucinated a nuclear holocaust about to occur and kept insisting to his family that they leave the country and fly to Australia. He'd had to be sedated for most of three weeks, and since then, according to Frank, Jim tended to become upset whenever there was news of nuclear power plant accidents or nuclear test explosions or the threat of war. There'd been a lot to be upset about in the last three years.

'The Russians aren't going to start a nuclear war,' Neil said softly.

'Then *we* are!' he shot back. 'There's no way the two sides can go on this way. It's going to happen!'

'Take it easy, Jim,' Neil rejoined sharply, putting his hand on Jim's shoulder. 'Shouting isn't going to stop anything.'

'Damn it! You don't care either.' Jim stood facing Neil defiantly, but Neil didn't look at him.

'Look,' Neil persisted softly, 'it's no more appropriate to panic about this international storm than it is in a storm at sea. You just do what has to be done when it has to be done.'

'We should find a fallout shelter, stock up on food. We . . .'

'Right now,' Neil interrupted firmly, 'our job is to sail *Vagabond* to your father.'

'Oh, Neil,' Jim responded. 'It's so sad. It's so . . .'

'Drop it,' said Neil. He was still staring forward. 'Here, take the helm,' he went on. 'It's still your watch.' He walked away into the port cockpit and stood with his back to Jim.

The shore was only dimly visible far off.

He was feeling distinctly uneasy. Jim's fears struck a responsive chord; he could feel fear vibrating in his own gut. A part of him also wanted to return and run back out the mouth that he felt closing now behind them. His instinct was to get out to sea, away from the mess that men might make on land. He turned to Jim.

'We're meeting Frank in Crisfield instead of Point Lookout,' he said quietly. 'Our course is changed to zero one zero. You got it?'

'Zero one zero,' Jim answered, glancing once at the compass and beginning to turn the wheel to starboard.

As Neil stared ahead he was surprised to find himself wondering anxiously whether *Vagabond*'s charts of the West Indies were still aboard. Annoyed at his irrationality, he held himself firmly standing in the port cockpit staring at the great expanse of bay lying before him. His course was zero one zero, ten degrees east of north. Getting to Crisfield without an engine was worry enough for one day.

2

Frank felt good. His adrenalin was really flowing. All morning he'd been marching in and out of his office ordering Rosie and Jason to phone here, phone there, get this, send for that, then marching back to telephone someone himself. It was one of those days that when he stared out his office window overlooking lower Manhattan and New York Harbour he felt like a king.

He loved this war crisis. He loved the way it was driving the stock market down, just as he'd known it would; loved the way it made people edgy, nervous, scared shitless.

A few things had gone wrong for him during the day – Neil's report of the bent propeller shaft, the booked flights to Washington, Jim's panic, a real estate deal falling through . . . but he shook them off like so much dandruff. He was making thousands of dollars an hour on his short selling of stocks and by tonight he'd be aboard *Vagabond* in the Chesapeake and the whole world could blow up and he wouldn't give a damn.

After he'd talked to Neil and Jimmy at noon and eaten the lunch Rosie brought into him, he'd put in a call to his stockbroker. As he waited he leaned back in his huge leather chair, the phone at his ear, his long lanky body stretched out comfortably. He was a good-looking man in his mid-forties with thinning grey hair, warm dark eyes and an easy grin.

'Hi, Al,' he said when he got through. 'Selling panic still in full swing? . . . Down thirty-four points! Jesus, that's even worse than I thought it would be. Or better than I thought.' He laughed briefly, then listened. 'Okay, good. Look I think there's going to be a turnaround sometime late today – this

25

thing can't look any worse than it does right now – so I want to take my profits in most of my shorts. Give me the quotes ... Right. Okay. I want to cover the US Home at ... what'd you say it was at now? ... at twenty-four then; the Datapoint at fifty-five, and the Microdyne at thirty. Got it? All the shares ... Yeah, I'll hold the other two short positions ...

'I'm flying down this evening ... I've got the radio-telephone on the boat but I don't like to think about stocks or real estate while I'm at sea. I'll phone you later today if I haven't left and we'll see what we did ... Yeah? Thanks. I'm no genius. I just know that with the jerks who end up running countries, things have to get very bad before anyone can figure out a way to make 'em better ... Okay, Al, thanks.'

Well well well: even Al seemed worried about a war, poor bastard. Hell, New York City didn't have anything to worry about. It was such an archetypal centre of capitalist decadence that the Russians would probably want to preserve it as an historical park for their tourists: porno shops here, Harlem there, Wall Street next ... They wouldn't nuke New York; hell, it would destroy itself in just a few more years.

Frank got up and paced back and forth across the deep rust-coloured carpet and then buzzed Rosie to see if Jason had returned yet with the propeller shaft from Hempstead. No, but he was on his way. Let's see, what else for the boat? The new charts for the Chesapeake – he had them. And the bag of specialities that Norah had got for him from Flynn's delicatessen: caviar, cashews, some of Flynn's incredible cheeses, two loaves of good bread, and Norah's own fantastic pies: the sort of stuff Neil never got aboard no matter how many commands he was given. It was Neil's one great flaw: he shopped and cooked as if he were feeding a reform school.

But Jesus, was he lucky to have got him as Captain. Imagine, a Navy officer! The guy sails a couple of thousand miles with as little fuss as most men go to the corner drugstore. He loses his engine to a freak accident and still probably will make it on schedule.

Oh oh. He hadn't got through yet to Jeannie Forester about the change of plans.

He returned to his big chair, buzzed Rosie, and waited for her to place the call. He felt a warm anticipation for that throaty, sexy voice of hers, sexy especially because she didn't really *mean* to be sexy. For two years now Jeannie had become the only thing that ever took his mind off business, and he was aware that whenever he thought of her he fell victim to an almost adolescent melancholy and longing. They'd been friends for five or six years and he knew she must be aware that he'd developed feelings for her beyond friendship. But she wasn't so much rejecting his feelings as kind of ducking and letting them slide past her.

'Frank, hi. Everything still on for the sailing?'

'Hi, Jeannie. Sure,' he replied, smiling at nothing. 'Only I've had to change my travel plans about getting to the boat.'

'Are you still coming here this evening?'

'No, that's just it. I can't get a flight into Washington, but I got one to the Eastern Shore, to Salisbury, and I'm meeting the boat at Crisfield – that's just across the bay on the eastern side.'

'I know. You want us all to meet you there?'

'No no. We'll sail over to Point Lookout and pick you up. Unless something goes wrong we should still get there late this evening.'

'That's great. I'm sorry you're not going to be here though.'

Frank felt himself flush with pleasure. 'We'll see so much of each other in the next ten days you'll probably remember with great fondness your last evening without me.'

Jeanne laughed. 'I like *you*, Frank,' she countered, 'but I

27

confess I'm a little nervous about spending that much time on the Bay. I prefer water in a glass or a bathtub.'

'Baloney.'

'No, it's true. Now that you've finally got me to sail with you I'm going to be the worst sort of landlubber.'

'You're a terrific swimmer,' said Frank.

'Only when I can see both the bottom and other end of the pool,' she commented. 'Hold it a sec,' she added, and her next words were spoken to someone in the room with her. 'What's that, Rita? No. In the second drawer, I think. With the clippings from the *Post* . . . Sorry, Frank, where were we?'

'What was all that about?'

'My anti-nuke group is meeting here today,' she answered. 'Emergency meeting because of the Arabian mess.'

'Oh, yeah, right,' said Frank, made uncomfortable by the subject. Jeannie became too emotional about any kind of war scare. He thought of making a joke about her group's being sure to stop the war for at least ten more days so they could finish their cruise, but stopped himself. 'It's a tough situation,' he finally said lamely.

'I've lost heart,' she replied with unexpected weariness. 'We haven't achieved anything in these four years. And now it's really hopeless. I feel like a fool for even trying.'

'Well, maybe that's good,' Frank said. 'Shows you need a vacation.'

'I suppose so,' she replied after a pause. 'Some of my friends think I'm going off to fiddle while Rome burns.'

'No, you don't,' he said firmly. 'You've promised me. Let Rome burn.'

'I know, Frank, I'll be there. Tonight I hope, or tomorrow morning at the latest.'

'At Point Lookout.'

'Fine. What, Rita? . . . Okay. Frank, look, I guess I've got to go. I'm looking forward to the sail and . . . I've got to go.'

'Sure, Jeannie. See you soon.'

28

'Bye, Frank.'

Frank lowered the receiver slowly back into its cradle and sighed, feeling that ridiculous tingling she somehow created in him. Then he shook his head and grunted. Why did she bother with that stuff? Peace groups had been marching and protesting for five years but they'd never stopped a war and never would. They only weakened the poor nation that let them get too influential.

Sighing, he leaned back in his chair, rocking slightly, looking out at the sky above the harbour past the Twin Trade Towers. He had finally got her to go sailing with him, though. In the past he'd invited her and her husband Bob and always ended up being stuck with just Bob. It was strange. An outdoorsy woman like her, good swimmer, tennis player, hiker – why the resistance to water? Was it her way of resisting him? He knew that he liked her a lot more than was probably wise for either of them, but he wasn't *doing* anything about it. And now for ten days they'd be together on *Vagabond*.

His intercom buzzed and Rosie's crisp voice informed him that his wife was on the line. He remembered he'd promised to call her.

'Hi, sweetheart,' he boomed out when he heard her soft musical voice on the phone. 'Yep. Everything's go for this afternoon. I . . . What? . . . Oh, don't be silly, it's just a war scare. Like the last time. A lot of sound and fury signifying . . .' Frank frowned and grimaced as he listened.

'No, no, no,' he finally interrupted. 'It's going to be all right. Bob Forester says it's all just a big bluff, the Pentagon and the Russians know exactly what they're doing . . .' Again he listened for a while, and then broke in.

'Hey, more good news. You should be proud of me. I made over eight thousand dollars on my shorts today . . . No . . . no, not that kind of shorts . . . stocks, selling stocks short, you know . . . He's *fine*. Captain Loken just told me he was a great sailor. Brought the ship single-handed through a

29

terrific storm. When the sail . . . What? . . . No no no, there was no storm . . . I was just exaggera . . . He's fine I tell you. I bet he looks like a bronze Greek god. He's so good-looking, he's obscene. Girls will be in heat all over the Chesapeake . . . Damn it, no. If there was going to be a war they would have told me in the *Wall Street Journal* . . . Yeah, yeah, right, sweetheart. Look, I got to get going to the airport . . . Ten days . . . Oh sure, don't worry . . . Goodbye, honey . . . Right . . . You too . . . So long.'

Frowning, Frank hung up. In the last year or two Norah seemed to be all fears, mostly about Jimmy, her 'baby', but sometimes about everything. Maybe that's where Jimmy got *his* panic from. He was glad Susan was home from college and staying there while he and Jimmy were off cruising. Norah needed company these days but couldn't join them in the Chesapeake until the last weekend.

Rosie buzzed again.

'Mr Tyler on the line.'

'Put him on,' said Frank, reaching for the phone to speak to George Tyler, a partner on several real estate ventures.

'Well, Frank, it was no go,' Tyler's voice announced loudly as if all important news had to be shouted. 'I'm afraid Mulweather called and gave me a cock-and-bull story which boils down to the fact that his clients are considering backing out on the West 80th Street deal.'

'What the hell. Why?' Frank countered.

'My guess is that his clients decided that an apartment house, no matter how attractive, tends to lose its cash flow when reduced to rubble.'

Frank didn't reply, stunned by the sardonic comment.

'Well,' Frank said after a pause, 'I don't think cash or stocks sitting at Chase Manhattan are going to retain much value either when they're drifting down over the Atlantic in a million pieces.'

'I know,' said Tyler with incongruous cheerfulness, 'but what are we going to do? Mulweather found a clause in our

30

preliminary agreement and he can back out. In this climate I think everyone's more interested in vacationing in Tierra del Fuego than in conducting any new business.'

Frank could feel himself becoming unreasonably angry at Mulweather and his clients for being panicked out of a deal that would make both parties good money. He stared gloomily at his desk.

'Okay, George, keep after it,' he said finally with a sigh. 'Make them feel like they're being chicken or something. Maybe they'll change their minds next week.'

After Tyler had hung up, Frank felt depressed. Worse, it was getting late. What time was it? Almost four. Jesus, he had to be at La Guardia by five for his flight to Salisbury, so he'd have to hurry it.

He made one last call to his broker and learned that the Dow Jones Industrial Average was down something like fifty-one points, the high speed ticker still almost twenty minutes behind. When he hung up, even though he'd made good money on his short selling, he was even more depressed. As he rose and began to gather his things for the boat he remembered his own favourite axiom with a strange sense of irritation . . .

'*The stock market never lies . . .*'

3

By late afternoon the Chesapeake had become as still as a pond. Only the tiniest breaths of wind occasionally hinted at movement, while Captain Olly and his son Chris worked steadily in the clear sunshine, enjoying the luxury of the calm water. They were working their last oyster bed, using the long wooden shafts of their rake-like metal tongs with practised ease. Both Captain Olly, a small wizened old man, wrinkled and bald, and his twenty-year-old son, a thickset, husky youth, had huge forearms and biceps from their years of working the oyster beds. Their twenty-six foot fishing smack, the *Lucy Mae*, with only a small deckhouse forward and a huge area aft for depositing the oysters, was old and paint-chipped and heeled groggily as both men worked.

The two men had been at the beds since one o'clock that afternoon, starting a couple of hours before the three P.M. low tide and planning to quit a couple of hours after the tide turned. In all that time their work proceeded in a casual persistent rhythm, Olly talking away occasionally in seemingly free-association monologues, Chris, quiet, steady, always puffing on a cigarette, now and then grunting a comment or asking a question. When Olly would lapse into silence or lean on his rake, Chris would continue his oystering, working the heavy long tongs until he could feel them full, then raising them to the surface and depositing the contents on to the aft deck. Most of the sorting would come later. Olly's monologues and silences succeeded each other in a mood as relaxed as the becalmed bay. Chris would occasionally down a bottle of beer, his father a glass of water, sometimes 'coloured' with a dash of whisky. They never had

32

to speak about their work; they knew their routine so thoroughly they could have oystered efficiently from dawn to dusk and not uttered a word. Smith Island, their home, lay to the east of them, Tangier Island to the south and Point Lookout and the wide mouth of the Potomac River to the west.

As Captain Olly neared the end of his working day he was feeling depressed at how tired he felt. After less than four hours work his back ached, and if he didn't stop and lean on his rake handle every five minutes or so he got winded. It embarrassed him, and he knew that even if he tried to pretend to be so fascinated with his own monologues that he couldn't work, Chris could tell he was shirking.

Ever since Ellen had run off to Florida two years ago with Cap'n Smithers, his life had been downhill. It was the first time since he was fourteen he hadn't had a woman reg'lar and he felt his health was deteriorating fast as a result. The main reason he went oystering with Chris most every day was so he wouldn't be stuck alone in his house watching the TV. A man could go nuts watching those game shows and soaps.

'I don't know, son,' he found himself saying in an effort to cheer himself up, 'seems to me some of these oysters must have meningitis. Seem sorta stunted. We may have to sell 'em to the circus as midgets.' He had deposited a load of oysters and muck on to the deck and was staring at it with exaggerated gloom. 'Though I s'pose midgets ain't in fashion any more even in the circus. People these days want things big: big money, big boats, big tits.'

As he wiped the sweat from his bald top he squinted south at a couple of sailboats sitting like cement monuments in the bay. That'll teach 'em, he thought vaguely, the rich playboy good-for-nothings.

'They even seem to want their wars bigger these days,' he went on, turning back to his work, 'sittin' up there in Moscow and Washington calculatin' how they can build a real big elephant-like war that'll flatten the earth like a pancake so the gods can use it as a frisbee . . .'

As Olly lowered his tongs back into the water, Chris made an unaccustomed halt to his work.

'There ain't gonna be a war, is there, Pop?' he asked.

'Well now you know I never predict what the rake'll bring up,' Olly snapped back automatically, 'but I got to say that imagination ain't created the stupid terrible thing which man ain't fool enough to up and do.'

'They ain't fightin' yet,' Chris commented, pausing to light a fresh cigarette.

'The way I figure it is the only reason they ain't made a frisbee of Earth before this is that they got a lot of *smaller* terrible things they want to do first.' Olly spat over the side of the boat into the bay. That's my great hope for mankind, he thought: man's got so many little sins he's got the hots for, he'll never get around to the big one.

'You think so?' his son asked after a pause.

''Course I don't think so,' Olly snapped back irritably, again wiping his sweaty forehead with his thick-veined right arm. 'You know I don't like to do any thinking.' He chuckled. 'Whenever I think – get a really deep thought, you know? – I always have to take a crap.' He paused and glared at his son, his eyes twinkling. 'Standing at the helm alone in a blow I gotta watch my mind like a cat, be sure no deep thoughts come, 'cause taking a crap on a bouncy ship when you're alone at the helm and havin' all you can do just standing much less squatting over a pail on a roller coaster while watching the compass and sail and handling the wheel is a trick I done once but don't hanker to do again.'

He paused and frowned in concentration.

'The deep thought I had that time was, "Time will tell." See? Deep thoughts just ain't worth the fuss and bother.'

As he looked with mock severity at his son, who grinned back at him, Olly remembered that sail: in his old Chesapeake Bay skipjack that he'd owned and captained, dragging for oysters in those days instead of fiddling around with these tiny rakes. But he couldn't afford a skipjack now and couldn't pull his weight as crew so he'd settled for the *Lucy Mae*. It kept him alive, but barely.

Shit, he thought, as he had to pause again, I wish to hell I'd just get it over with and croak. Not much sense in living if you can't work and can't fuck. Nowadays whenever he went into restaurants or bars and flirted with the cute little taut-butted waitresses they'd either be shocked at him or treat him like a harmless child. When a man couldn't turn a woman on it was time to cash in his chips. Women used to always be pestering him, first for his cock and then for his deep thoughts; he wished one were pestering him now.

'Women are always asking what I'm thinkin',' he began saying aloud, watching three seagulls fly noisily around the stern of the *Lucy Mae* and then plop expectantly in the water. 'But after four wives I finally figured how to handle 'em. I always say I'm thinking about the wind and weather and repairing my dinghy and how much I love her ass. Well, every woman I've known will frown and frown and frown until I get to my deep thoughts about her ass and then everything's jolly. A man who limits his deep thoughts to his woman's ass is a sober man, trustworthy and true, and likely to stay out of trouble.'

Chris was smiling as he worked but Olly's face was as stern as a Baptist preacher. He paused and took a long drink of water from his glass on the deckhouse shelf. He damn well wished he had a lady these days whose ass he could praise, even if the ass were flatter than an ironing board.

'Gettin' late, Pop,' Chris said to him, making him abruptly aware he was leaning on his rake again.

'Late?' Olly snapped back. 'We just begun.' But he began to haul in his rake with a sense of relief. 'I been talkin' so much today I'm pooped,' he added.

I do love talking, he thought as he emptied his last load into the boat. Especially my own talking. As Chris's mother

35

once said, I think it was his mother, could've been someone else's, 'Olly I never know'd a man who listened to hisself as good as you do.' He smiled to himself.

'Cal Markham said this morning the radio makes it sound like war,' Chris said suddenly, as if it had been on his mind much of the day.

Olly looked at him in surprise. 'Son, you got to stop listening to people who babble,' he said firmly. ''Course there's gonna be a war. They ain't keepin' all those jets dancing across the sky just for skywriting forever, you know. A gov'ment is a business, and sooner or later the gov'ment is gonna want its money's worth.'

His son looked at him with youthful seriousness. 'What you gonna do, Pop, when that happens?' he asked.

Olly tossed his empty tongs into the forward cabin with a sense of relief and then stared out across the water. 'I'm gonna run, son,' he said with a sigh. 'That's why I'm gonna take up jogging. I would've taken it up years ago but I ain't learned how to do it on the water yet. Christ knows the Chesapeake's got enough mud in it to support a man three times my weight but somehow I just can't get the hang of it.'

He wouldn't run, though. He would almost welcome it if it came, especially if the war would just take him and let Chris live to enjoy asses for another forty years as he had done. He'd always hated seeing old geezers sitting around in front of the general store, useless and unneeded. Although he was probaly now a geezer, he wasn't gonna be a sitter.

No, he wouldn't run – unless he figured there was a live lady up the road aways, or a solid bit of honest work he could do. Then maybe he'd stick around. Take up jogging.

4

Lethargically Jeanne gathered and packed clothing and sleeping bags for the cruise aboard *Vagabond*. She had no heart for the trip, no heart, really, for anything these days. She was packing only for herself, Lisa and Skip, since Bob had telephoned at three that afternoon to tell her that the Defense Department had asked everyone above the level of clerk to work over the weekend. He couldn't sail with them in the Chesapeake. He would be coming home only to eat and get a change of clothes.

As she moved around first Skippy's bedroom and then her own, Jeanne was close to tears. It was anger and frustration at the insane way the Americans and Russians were stumbling towards war; frustration at her own incapacity to do anything; anger at Bob's failure even to *see* what was happening; anger that she was married to him. Normally lithe, catlike, and intense, now she moved dully, her long dark hair hanging limply down her back instead of bouncing as it usually did. She felt she had married the wrong man and was living only half a life. As she closed her suitcase carefully she imagined Bob's superior ironic smile at such a cliché about her life. He would assure her that of course she had married the wrong man, everybody did, but that was no reason to be miserable.

Lisa came into her bedroom to ask if she could go visit her girlfriend Nancy before dinner and Jeanne had to focus in on her daughter. Framed in the doorway, Lisa held her tall, budding fifteen-year-old body with that strange stiff dignity she'd adopted over the last two years to show she was no longer a child. It irritated Jeanne, reminding her of the worst of the Forester family stuffiness. Compared to Lisa, round, energetic, happy-faced Skippy still seemed, at five spontaneous and free.

'Have you finished your packing?' she asked.

'I did it last night,' Lisa replied. 'But don't forget to pack the lotions and towels you promised.'

'I will, I will. But look, honey. I need your help here. We'll be eating as soon as your father gets home, and I'd like you to go downstairs and begin heating the leftover stew. I'll be down soon.'

'Oh, Mother,' Lisa replied. 'Can't you do that?'

'Go,' said Jeanne.

And she went, with a promptness that never ceased to amaze Jeanne – was that Bob's doing? A moment later she was alone again with her two suitcases and sleeping bag.

Living with Bob wasn't working any more and she knew why: the war thing had grown too big and was too important to both of them. The whole world was divided into two groups, those desperately trying to avoid a war and those desperately preparing to see that their side won it. She and Bob were on opposite sides and the tension between them was becoming too much.

The tension often tempted her just to give up. The cause she worked for seemed so hopeless. For close to three years she'd been active in a Washington-based group called SMN, Stop the Madness Now, an eclectic collection of feminists, political radicals, pacifists, scientists, doctors and even a few former high-ranking military officers, all of whom agreed on only one issue: the necessity of taking drastic actions to reverse the momentum towards nuclear war. She'd begun as a volunteer, in effect an unpaid secretary, but a year ago had been put on the part-time staff as a fundraiser and occasional speechwriter and editor for one of the retired admirals.

But her promotion had, in the last six months, only made her increasingly depressed. The admiral spoke to the same audiences; the fundraising events raised the same piddly amounts of money – their yearly total budget would barely finance a single jet fighter; their letters got published in the *Washington Post* and *New York Times* and sank out of sight like pebbles in the sea; the marches got marched – and forgotten; and the great masses of Americans, vaguely worried about war, remained quite precisely and strongly worried about how they were going to meet their mortgage payments or feed their children. The prolonged worldwide economic crisis, which was so exacerbating the international tensions, also made reducing nuclear armaments or creating a United Nations superforce very low items on most people's agenda. The United States and Soviet Union argued and manoeuvred for power; Bob and she argued and manoeuvred for – for what she didn't know – and both sets of sides became increasingly alienated.

Bob came home at six, gave a big hug to Skippy, a dignified kiss to Lisa, several words and caresses to their terrier Banjo, and a cheerful 'Hi, honey' to her. He went straight upstairs to change his clothes and pack an overnight bag. Ten minutes later they were all having dinner together.

Jeanne's scruffy jeans and open-necked cotton blouse and long dark hair falling wildly about her face and shoulders contrasted sharply with her husband's neat three-piece suit, neatly combed dark hair and chiselled good looks, but she sensed that their moods were aligned: they were both subdued and anxious, hoping to control their conflict. They sat at opposite ends of the table with Lisa on Jeanne's left and Skip, propped up on two cushions, on her right. Lisa, with her erect posture and adult-sounding precise speech patterns, looked to Jeanne that evening like a young governess in some Victorian melodrama. Her husband was the villain. And she . . . ?

Jeanne certainly no longer felt like a heroine. Now that her sporadic idealistic efforts to promote disarmament and peace were so clearly ineffective she felt as weak and foolish as Bob had always accused her of being. Yet as she watched him so meticulously eating his dinner and talking with such total seriousness with Lisa about the clothing she planned to wear in the Chesapeake, she could feel herself becoming angry. It was her anxiety being transmuted into anger, anger at those who were causing her fear: the Russians and the Pentagon and people like Bob who could so coolly calculate and contemplate the probabilities of various world catastrophes.

'And what are you going to be doing, Daddy?' Jeanne heard Lisa say, and saw Bob start in surprise that the forbidden subject had been broached.

'Just playing with Mars,' he replied with a soft smile. He poured himself more wine and awkwardly signalled with the bottle to ask her if she wanted some more. She shook her head.

'Is that all you ever do?' Lisa asked a little impatiently.

'I suppose so,' he replied. 'But the situation these days has been changing so fast we have to feed our monster new food five times a day instead of once or twice a week.' She noticed his eyes flash as he said this.

'It still sounds boring,' said Lisa.

'Calculating the probability of various war scenarios is many things, some of which your mother has strong feelings about,' Bob told Lisa, 'but one thing it never is is boring.'

'You enjoy this crisis, don't you?' Jeanne said quietly as she leaned forward to wipe some spilled gravy from Skip's shirt. 'I suppose for you it's like playing in the Superbowl.'

Bob put down his fork and took a sip of wine. 'People are rather interested these days in our calculations,' he said, smiling nervously. 'I'm human enough to enjoy using my capabilities to the fullest and knowing I'm needed.'

'That's fine,' Jeanne said slowly. 'But are you also human enough to be scared?'

He looked startled, then laughed.

'As a matter of fact, yes,' he replied. 'The world is in a

40

measurably dangerous situation. I'm rather proud that our department, probably more than any other, is responsible for determining just *how* dangerous.'

'Why "proud"?' she asked quietly. Whenever they began to argue, their voices would get softer and softer, a trait that she realized she had adopted from him. Their civility went with the French Provincial dining-room furniture, but she once told him that if he ever really got mad at her, his voice would get so low no one could hear it.

'Because it is we who can warn the President which of his policy decisions are *most* dangerous,' Bob answered. 'Without us he might do something that we could have predicted would provoke the Soviets into attacking.'

Jeanne took a last spoonful of the stew and wiped her mouth. 'And does your computer tell you what happens if they do attack?' she asked next.

'No, Jupiter does,' Bob replied, absently pushing Skippy's hand away from the plate of chocolate chip cookies. 'Jupiter calculates who will probably win once a war starts. We on Mars just calculate the chances of a war starting.'

'And what are the chances?' she asked with a coolness she didn't feel. 'Pretty high, aren't they?'

He looked at her sombrely and shook his head. 'You know better than that,' he replied. 'Obviously to one definitely knows, not even Mars, and if it did, I wouldn't tell you.'

'Thanks,' she said.

'But if I thought I knew, I'd bundle you and the kids off to the South Pacific. I certainly wouldn't be chatting with you ten miles from the White House with a glass of wine in my hand.'

'Instead you send me off to the Chesapeake,' she countered, feeling even as she spoke that it was a childish rebuttal.

'I *do* want you to go, Jeanne,' he said to her with unusual seriousness.

'Why?' she answered, frowning. 'You know I'm not fond

of being on the water, and it's no safer there than any place else.'

'Because I want you and the children to get away and have a good time,' he replied. 'Lisa's always had a crush on Jimmy,' he went on, smiling at his daughter, 'and Neil Loken's a hunk, if you like the type.'

'Give me back my cookie!' Skippy said abruptly.

'What's the type?' Jeanne asked, remembering that the previous summer Bob had described the captain as officious and remote.

'You've had enough,' announced Lisa.

'Horatio Hornblower,' Bob replied. 'The quiet he-man always standing tall on the poopdeck and squinting into the salt spray letting everyone know he's in command.'

'I have not,' Skippy whispered in his squeaky voice. 'I've had six, same as you.'

'Well, we've had enough.'

'You make him sound like a pain in the neck,' said Jeanne.

'I have not,' Skippy said firmly. 'Give me . . .'

'Let go!' Lisa hissed as Skippy's little body sprawled across the tablecloth, lunging for the plate of cookies.

'Ouch! You shit!' said Skippy.

'Skip!' Bob Forester exclaimed. 'Don't swear like that, and sit down!'

'She pinched me.'

'Lisa, leave the punishment of Skippy to us,' Jeanne said wearily.

'He was stealing a cookie,' Lisa insisted with dignity.

'I was not!' Skippy exclaimed.

Bob erupted finally from his chair and pulled his son firmly back into his seat, striking him twice sharply on the hand, Jeanne wincing with each slap. As the boy pouted and fought back tears, Bob resumed his seat and looked selfconsciously back at Lisa and Jeanne.

'Yes, now, where were we?' he said.

42

'At sea,' said Jeanne ironically.

'Oh, yes, Neil,' Bob went on, adjusting his cloth napkin in his lap, his narrow eyes scowling. 'He's too quiet to be a pain in the neck.' His eyes crinkled into a smile. 'You have to be *aware* of his loud quietness in order to be annoyed. Some people like him. Women, I imagine, would find him attractive.'

'Not if he never leaves the poopdeck,' Jeanne commented.

Bob glanced at his watch and stood up, smiling awkwardly. 'Oh, Frank tells me he's perfectly willing to come down to . . . shall we say, ride frailer vessels?'

Jeanne glanced over at Lisa.

'Daddy means he can be a makeout artist,' she explained to her mother.

Jeanne laughed for the first time that day.

'Thank you, sweetheart,' she said.

'Mommy?' said Skippy.

'Yes, dear?'

'If there's going to be a war I think we should eat *all* the cookies now.'

And this time they all laughed.

But when Bob left to return to the Pentagon twenty minutes later Jeanne wasn't laughing.

He called her over to him and took her in his arms and said simply, 'I love you.' It was years since he had used those words, their separations being marked by parting comments such as 'Where did you leave the keys to the Rabbitt?' or 'I hope you left the refrigerator well-stocked.' But that evening, just when she felt herself most alienated from him and their lives together, he said 'I love you.'

She looked across at him, her large dark eyes widening in both surprise and attention. 'All right,' was all she could say.

'Go down to Point Lookout tonight,' he went on. 'Get on the boat. Forget the mess the world's in.'

Again at first she could only stare at him. 'You come too,'

she said impulsively, feeling fear flooding through her.

'I've got my job,' he said.

'Leave it,' she countered desperately.

He smiled softly, a tinge of sadness in it. 'I like my job,' he replied.

And she felt the wall rise between them again. As he started to turn, though, she grasped his arm and held it. 'You're a good man,' she said.

'Really?' he said, with that same half-sad smile.

They looked at each other and for the first time she saw that he was afraid too. Then she saw the emotion click off and the computer come back on. He frowned.

'Did you remember to get some frozen dinners into the freezer?' he asked.

'Yes,' she answered.

'Good,' he said, pecked her cheek, and was gone.

5

With *Vagabond* becalmed, Neil finally got Jim to put the seven horsepower outboard on the inflatable dinghy to tow the trimaran into the docks of Tangier Island. Earlier, even after the wind had fallen to mere puffs in the late afternoon, they'd been able to ride the incoming tide northwards towards Crisfield. But as the sun set and the tide was about to turn against them they were still almost fifteen miles short. Being only a mile off the little village of Tangier and needing to let Frank know what had happened to them, he had *Vagabond* towed in with the dinghy.

He moored her at the end of the fuelling dock, which was closed for the night. With her three white hulls gleaming under the glow of the dock lights, the strange fifty-foot trimaran lay among the old fishing boats and conventional stinkpots like a futuristic fighter plane among World War II relics. But towing her in was a joke; like pulling a space satellite with a tricycle.

While Jim secured and adjusted the spring lines and fenders Neil went into his aft cabin to change his clothes for going ashore. He was tired now, the dull fatigue of trying for six hours to nurse a sailing vessel towards her goal in winds that sometimes wouldn't ruffle a feather on a flea. He poured himself a shot of brandy from the bottle he kept in his cabin and switched on the short wave radio. After he had pulled off his blue jean cut-offs, he stood naked for a moment trying to tune into the BBC frequency. He finally located it and, after pulling on a pair of trousers, sat back on his bunk with the brandy and listened. The cultured English announcer reported with the usual stylized indifference that a fleet of thirty private boats had left England for Ireland or the Azores, that international flights out of the country were booked solid, with near hysteria at Heathrow. The exodus because of the war scare was stirring up a national outcry and debate. One MP labelled those fleeing as 'no better than rats fleeing a sinking ship', an analogy that made Neil smile sardonically: 'sinking ship' was a devastating allusion to Great Britain on the eve of a possible nuclear war.

When the BBC announcer began to discuss more parochial local events, Neil turned the set off.

He was tired and he was depressed, a combination he knew from experience often went together. He felt a restless need for a woman, a feeling he knew was often associated with low-level anxiety. It was the world scene, of course, but also the fact that in a few hours Frank would be joining them and Neil would lose his freedom. He always resented it at first when an owner rejoined a boat that he'd been living aboard as captain and king. The owner inevitably liked to run the ship differently, and he hated to relinquish the control which was his when he was sailing with just crew. Frank was just about the only owner he'd sailed with who consistently shared Neil's exhilaration at the gruelling joys of ocean passages. Frank genuinely loved sailing, loved being out on the water, and wasn't aboard simply to impress clients or make a few women, but Neil was still a little depressed at his coming.

Jim interrupted his gloom by shouting down the hatchway that he was going to change and spruce up. Neil stood and searched for a clean sportshirt. Jim might be a sailor like his father, but this trip north had been too easy a passage to be a true test. In the last four hours of their crawling with the tide, Jim had given up on the sailing and spent the time with his guitar and cassette player. Well, that was cool. He himself had read half a novel.

Glancing at his watch he saw that it was nine-ten. He quickly switched on the short wave radio again and tried

46

tuning it to a radio ham operator he'd discovered on the trip north who broadcast sometimes at nine. After the news from the BBC, listening to a farmer from East Tennessee might be a welcome relief. Soon he had located the farmer's gruff voice, speaking as usual in a casual folksy monologue as if he were chatting with neighbours around a hot wood stove in mid-winter:

'. . . not everyone so happy. Mel Hutchins says the rain we got last night was too much for his spring rye and not enough for his tomatoes. 'Course, Mel wouldn't be satisfied unless God rearranged the whole upper atmosphere every day to re-route the right weather patterns over each one of Mel's seventy acres. Last time I known Mel to praise the weather was when the remains of a hurricane struck here one October after he'd harvested everything, but Jack Pillitson had half his crops still in the ground. Mel and Jack don't get along too well and Mel said the hurricane rains showed good timing.

'It's getting towards sign-off time. I sure hope the Russians stop their messing around over there in Arabia. Izzy Klein says people thinking there may be a war cleaned out half his A & P this morning – and that was *before* he opened. Just joking, friends. He did say it appeared that everyone in town seemed to be expecting guests this weekend and had to stock up on triple the normal amount of food. Well, for me, if *I* thought there was going to be a war you wouldn't catch me buying canned baked beans, and you wouldn't catch me sitting in a fallout shelter next to anyone who'd just stocked up on 'em. That's sure enough not the way *I* want to go. But I don't expect to die for awhile yet so I'll be talking to you again on Sunday. This is Charlie Wittner signing off.'

When the radio became silent, Neil smiled and stood up. At least there was *one* man who was showing no panic.

Up on deck, under the star-studded sky, Jim was waiting for him, dressed like Neil in jeans, sportshirt and boatshoes. Jim hadn't shaved since they'd left Fort Lauderdale, and his slight beard, longish hair – salt- and sun-streaked – and bronzed skin tone gave him precisely the salty air he probably was trying to achieve. He looked as pleasantly excited as he had when they'd entered the Chesapeake sixteen hours earlier.

The only bar in Tangier was a fishermen's hangout rather than a tourist place, so there were no fishing nets on the walls or stuffed fish, but instead dart boards, electronic games, pool tables and a television set. There were half a dozen men sitting at the bar and two old men playing chess at a table. Neil led Jim to a booth next to the bar where through their window they could see *Vagabond*'s masts and cabin top above the docks and pilings.

'Where you fellas in from?' a large bearded man with a pot belly asked them from his seat at the bar.

'Fort Lauderdale, Florida,' Jim answered proudly. 'We made it in five and a half days.'

'That's pretty good,' the bearded man replied promptly. 'That must be one helluva powerful dinghy engine.'

While Jim looked startled and uncertain, Neil and the men along the bar all burst out laughing. Jim, realizing they'd seen *Vagabond*'s entrance, soon joined in.

'Once or twice we cheated and used sails,' Neil said, and remembered he had to phone to get a message to Frank.

'Don't blame you,' said the man.

Neil stood up and went to the bar to order two beers and then went on to the payphone. The wife of the marina owner answered and Neil explained to her the situation and told her to tell Frank to take the ferry to Tangier. When he returned to his table he was glad the television set wasn't on to remind Jim of the outside world.

'Well, mate,' he said to Jim after he'd taken a long swallow of beer. 'I'd say we'd made a damn good passage, even if we did fall a little short.'

'*Vagabond*'s a great boat, isn't she?' Jim said.

'She even tows well,' Neil replied with a smile.

'I like crewing for you,' Jim went on. 'It's a lot better when there are only two of us. With Dad and his friends I feel like a passenger. I never get to *do* anything. But being alone at the helm, especially at night, or when she's surfing down a big swell . . .' He stopped, smiling, flushed with the pleasure of the memory. 'Anyway, I really enjoyed your putting me to work.'

'I wish all my crew would say that,' Neil commented, smiling.

'Blast 'em, I say. Hit 'em first,' came a voice from the bar.

'You tell 'em, Charlie,' another voice countered. 'And don't forget to duck.'

'Hey, my friend,' Neil said to the large man at the end of the bar, hoping to change the subject. 'Are there any women on this island?'

'Oh, yes, there's women all right.'

'You keep them locked up?'

'Don't have to,' the bearded man replied. 'We keep 'em so tired from screwin' they ain't got no energy to go out.'

Laughter tumbled along the length of the bar.

'Must be all the oysters you fellas eat,' Neil commented.

'Eat oysters?' the bearded man exclaimed, grinning. 'Shit, we Bay men can't afford to eat oysters. Too expensive.'

A few men laughed.

'Still,' said Neil, 'it's too bad you don't have a few women in especially good shape to greet tired sailors returning after a long stint at sea.'

'We got two or three ladies like that,' a little man next to the bearded man said. 'But they always get themselves laid by tourists in speedboats from the eastern shore, men who tell 'em they're all pooped from motoring 'cross the bay.'

The quick burst of laughter at this remark made Neil think it was an allusion to some women they all knew. He finished his beer and went to the bar to order two more. As he was standing there, a pudgy woman came in and complained to the bartender that 'The TV don't work.'

49

Could he fix it? After handing Neil two bottles of beer and his change the bartender followed her through a doorway into what were probably living quarters.

'See what we mean?' the little man at the bar said, turning to grin at Neil. 'Ol' Jake's going back there now to give her a quick one. That TV business is all a front.'

But Jake returned almost immediately with a frown on his face. He went to the television set raised up behind the bar and turned it on. Neil and the others along the bar were all watching him. The screen remained dark for a few seconds, but the voice of the face that emerged on the screen began intoning immediately in a tense, hurried voice:

'. . . I repeat, this is not a test, this is not a test. The Emergency Broadcasting System announces a national war alert. All precautionary measures should be taken immediately to prepare for the possibility of an enemy attack. This is not a test. Civil Defence workers are to report immediately to their assigned posts. Police, Fire and Emergency Medical personnel on standby for national war alert should also report to their assigned posts. I repeat, this is not a test, this is not a test. The Emergency Broadcasting System announces a national war alert. All precautionary . . .'

It was only when he became aware that the announcer was going to say nothing new that Neil became conscious of himself standing next to his table, still holding his beer bottle, his mouth open in stunned bewilderment. As the bartender lowered the volume and began switching channels and Neil could see that all the operating channels had the same announcer, he became aware of the total silence in the room.

Finally someone at the bar spoke:

'Oh, good Jesus,' a tired voice said. '*Now* what the fuck are the silly bastards trying to prove?'

Then the television picture disappeared, the lights in the bar went out, and the whole room was in total blackness.

6

Frank flung his lanky body back and forth across the end of the ferry dock at Crisfield with an impatience unusual even for him. Everything was running late. Traffic had been so bad going out to La Guardia that afternoon that the twenty-five minute drive had taken over an hour, and he'd arrived ten minutes after his plane had supposedly left. But La Guardia was a madhouse and his plane had been delayed forty minutes so he'd made it. Then it was delayed another half-hour on the runway awaiting takeoff, the long line of taxiing planes reminding him of sailors outside a Bangkok whorehouse.

So he'd arrived in Salisbury almost an hour late, taken an agonizing thirty minutes to rent a car and finally made it to Crisfield after nine o'clock in the evening.

And no *Vagabond*. When he'd inquired at the marina it had taken Frank so long to find someone with a message from Neil that he figured he'd missed the last ferry to Tangier Island. The damn woman said only that Neil was becalmed at Tangier and to take the ferry. But there was now a light breeze blowing; would Neil try to sail on to Crisfield?

Then it turned out he hadn't missed the last ferry because the last ferry hadn't even returned from Tangier. So he was pacing back and forth across the dock, a half-dozen locals sitting on the waiting benches staring at him as if he were a performing acrobat. He didn't care. He had the new propeller shaft; he had his fishing gear and swimsuits and scuba equipment; and he was impatient to be out on the bay. The smell of the salt water and of dead fish had even eased his annoyance at first, such a stab of joy did it give him

51

after nothing but the smells of Manhattan for three months, and the insane hysteria of the streets and airports of civilization.

Finally the lights of the tiny ferry appeared in the distance. Frank placed himself at the edge of the dock, leaning, as if he were a magnet capable of drawing the stupid thing in faster. The local fishermen and their families simply sat there smoking and joking and generally behaving with a calm that drove Frank crazy – until he'd been aboard *Vagabond* for a few days and began to re-create it for himself.

The ferry was a big launch with a long deckhouse roof and six or seven benches that would probably seat forty people during the height of the tourist season. There were only four people coming off the island.

Some of the locals came up as the boat approached the dock and took the two mooring lines. A skinny little man was at the wheel and a young kid put out the fenders. When the launch was secured, the little man came out of the wheelhouse, puffing on a pipe. After Frank had walked back to where he had set his dufflebags and then transferred himself and his stuff on to the ferry, the captain helped a woman he apparently knew to climb on board.

'You folks heah about the woah?' he asked her and the two men with her.

'What war is that, Cap?' one of the men boarding asked in return.

'I don't know as whether they've named it yet,' he answered, a quizzical frown on his round face. 'But it's another one of *our* woahs.'

'What do you mean?' the woman asked nervously, seating herself next to Frank on a middle bench.

'My radio says theahs going to be a woah. With the Russians.'

'Oh, that,' said Frank, feeling the tension that the captain's vague statements had created beginning to lessen.

'When'd you hear this?' another man asked.

'Five minutes ago, I'd guess,' the captain said. 'Made it seem pretty important. National emergency or something. Like an air raid wahning.'

'Air raid warning for where?' Frank asked irritably.

'Well, I guess for just about the whole country,' the little man replied.

'What are you going to do about it, Cap?' the first man asked.

'Not much I can do till I finish this last ferry trip,' he said, motioning to the young kid to free the mooring lines.

'Has anyone been killed yet?' the woman asked.

'Not that they mentioned,' the captain replied as he went through to the wheelhouse. He turned back to them halfway to the wheel. 'They just kep' saying emergency,' he concluded.

The forty-five foot ferry swung out of the dock area and began its hour and a half trip through the darkness to Tangier. Frank leaned back on the bench, hugging his right knee for balance, and sensed the anxiety rising within him. It was one thing to have a war scare but quite another to declare some sort of national emergency so that people began telling their neighbours there was a war.

He stared unseeingly off to his right and began to consider the effect an escalation of the panic might have on his business fortunes when something caught his attention.

There was a strange increasing glow across the bay like the lights of a huge city being slowly turned on. It didn't seem to him to be a fire; the light was too diffuse, too much just a glow. Unless it were a long way off.

'What's that?' the woman next to him asked the man on her other side. Along with the seven or eight other passengers Frank watched in fascination as the light, like the slowly rising head of a deadly cobra, gradually rose with increasing intensity. He felt a stab of horror and stood up.

'Looks like a fire,' someone said.

Frank pushed past the knees of the two people next to him and strode forward to the wheelhouse.

'What's our heading?' he asked the little captain in the dimly lit wheelhouse.

'Heading?' the little man asked, squinting up at him.

Frank looked at the compass binnacle lit with a soft reddish light. Their course was southwest. The glow then was to the northwest, perhaps a little north of northwest. He tried to visualize the map of the Chesapeake which he'd been studying the day before, then looked back at the spreading and intensifying glow.

Washington. There were no cities along the Chesapeake northwest of Crisfield. The first city northwest of Crisfield was way inland – Washington. A hundred miles away.

A hundred miles away. Holy Sweet Jesus. The light glowed more brightly. Frank staggered out of the wheelhouse.

7

Captain Olly was dozing in his faded and worn overstuffed chair, the television set gleaming in front of him, the sound turned down low, though still audible. Hours before, his son had gone out to a Smith Island bar, but Olly had decided to stay home, bushed as usual.

The face of a newscaster on the screen was intoning in tense, anxious tones but Olly didn't hear. Then with a gentle popping sound the screen went dark and the lights Olly had left on behind the set and in the kitchen also went out.

Olly stirred, awakened by the change, and opened his eyes.

'Chris?' he said into the darkness.

He began feeling for the thin blanket that Chris sometimes put over him when he'd fallen asleep in his chair and Chris didn't want him to wake up. But his lap was bare. It didn't *feel* like he'd been sleeping that long but if Chris were home and had turned out all the lights it must be damn late.

He shuffled slowly to the bathroom and, without bothering to turn on the light, pissed into the sink – no problem with aiming at such close range. Then he shuffled off to his small bedroom at the rear of the house. He hesitated for a moment at his bedroom door, a vague feeling of uneasiness nagging at him. In years at sea and in the bay he'd learned to be responsive to such intuitive twinges of concern, but he was in his own little house, anchored solidly to Smith Island which was anchored less solidly to Chesapeake mud. It was the moonlight streaming in the bedroom window that bothered him, but he couldn't tell why.

He was old and he was tired. He fell on to his bed fully

clothed and closed his eyes. Something was wrong but damned if he could think of anything that wouldn't wait till morning. Soon he was asleep in the empty house, the half-moon not yet risen in the east, but light streaming in his window from the northwest.

8

Jeanne was driving the stationwagon through the darkness on Route 5 south towards Point Lookout, having already travelled more than forty of the seventy miles from Washington. Lisa was sitting silently beside her in front, Skippy sprawled asleep in the rear with the dog, when a flash of bright light filled the car from the rear as if a vehicle with its headlights on had suddenly come up fast behind them. When Jeanne glanced in her rear-view mirror the brightness was more like a gigantic diffuse searchlight on the horizon aimed at her. Lisa turned to stare back out the rear window, and then, her face glimmering in the light, looked fearfully at Jeanne.

'What *is* it, Mother?' she asked.

Jeanne, following fifty yards behind a blue pickup truck, didn't reply. The inexplicable and terrifying brightness had numbed her mind.

Then her car was suddenly out of control, picked up by an invisible giant hand and flung forward at ten or fifteen miles faster than she'd been going, the rear end swinging sickeningly to the left then gliding back as if they'd hit a patch of ice. The pickup truck had swerved into the ditch on the right, then careened back on to the two-lane highway and across it until finally, wobbling as if all four tyres had gone flat and still speeding forward at sixty miles per hour, it steadied in the centre of the highway. Jeanne followed it, almost oblivious of what was happening to her own car. When the pickup's brakelights glowed, she began to brake her wagon, both vehicles quickly slowing to fifty, then forty, then driving on at that speed.

Jeanne glanced at Lisa who was staring speechlessly at her in wide-eyed horror. Still not thinking, she slowed her car, letting the pickup disappear ahead of her into the eerily lit night. When she saw a pulloff space in front of a fruitstand she pulled the car off the road and stopped.

I'm trembling, was the first thought she had, and she gripped the steering wheel more tightly, trying to control her shaking hands. Yes, 'trembling' was what it was called, she thought stupidly.

'Oh, Mommy, Mommy, what's happening?' Lisa cried and Jeanne felt her daughter press against her, clutching her arm, her face against Jeanne's shoulder. The rear-view mirror was filled with light. Two cars sped by, lit by the eerie brightness from behind. Then Jeanne turned to look back: a light was ballooning outwards and upwards into the sky, the central brightness becoming dimmer, but the area of light growing. Lisa's fingers dug into her still trembling arm and Jeanne thought simply: *A nuclear bomb has struck Washington.* There was no conscious terror or fear, only the bland fact. *And this is what it's like forty miles away.*

Two more cars sped past towards Point Lookout. No one was now travelling back towards Washington. She closed her eyes and slowly lowered her head to the wheel.

'Mommy . . . Mommy . . .' Lisa pleaded beside her, but Jeanne couldn't seem to function, couldn't seem to *think* anything. She had a sudden image of the house in Alexandria being shattered into tiny pieces by some blast but she felt nothing. The wheel was cold against her forehead. From the back seat the dog barked twice nervously, apparently disturbed by the light.

Jeanne raised her head and straightened up, staring forward. She turned the car's engine back on. She shifted into forward, swung the car in a U, and began to drive back towards Washington.

Beside her Lisa began to whimper. 'Where are we going, Mommy?' she gasped out between low moans.

Ahead of them a bell-shaped clump of light expanded into the sky, its upper parts rising but growing dimmer, the lower parts spreading out horizontally and retaining their brightness. When the car headed straight towards it Jeanne had trouble seeing the road. When an oncoming car honked its horn at her and she swerved to the right, her right wheels slid off the shoulder, skidded, then climbed back on to the road.

'Oh, Mommy, Mommy!'

How long it's been since Lisa has called me Mommy, she thought, driving unthinkingly onwards.

And then she saw a fire: two cars tangled off the opposite side of the road, one of them engulfed in flames. She slowed as she passed them and then after a minute brought her car to a halt off the side of the road. They were on a slight rise overlooking miles of land ahead. She could see several other small fires burning in the half-darkness of this night, whether cars or houses she couldn't tell. Off to the right a whole village seemed to be burning. The landscape was otherwise dark.

You're in shock. Get the children to safety. You're in shock, get the children to safety, you're in shock . . . Her mind was like some alien machine functioning mechanically and improperly, she herself dumb, helpless.

'Mommy, let's go the other way,' Lisa whispered against her shoulder.

'Yes, sweetheart,' she found herself saying calmly, her arm still trembling. 'We'd better get down to Point Lookout.'

She swung the car a second time in a U, almost colliding with a van that was already speeding southwards and which she had seen and yet not seen. Then she was in line with the other vehicles, speeding through the night away from Washington.

9

Neil ran down the dock and began untying *Vagabond*, feeling vulnerable, naked. Leaving the Tangier bar he'd seen the glow to the northwest and known what it meant, but had not broken stride towards the boat. As Jim leapt on to *Vagabond* and ran aft to descend into the inflatable dinghy tied off between the hulls, Neil could sense that now that Jim's nightmare had come true he was acting with unpanicked calm. With the wind still light out of the east Jim would have to tow them out to the bay before the ship would have a proper slant to sail to Crisfield and pick up Frank. But even as Neil acted to get the boat one way, a part of his mind was focused on getting the boat south, out of the Chesapeake into the open sea.

When Jim came sliding between the hulls in the dinghy Neil dropped him the towline. The glow to the northwest was worse, and a surge of panic forced Neil to steady himself, holding on to the forestay and staring at the glow on the horizon.

'Get going,' he said sharply and ran aft to raise the sails.

Five minutes later *Vagabond* was out of the cove and sailing northward behind her dinghy at almost four knots. Neil knew Frank might be on some late ferry coming to Tangier, so he was keeping his boat in the buoyed channel. As they moved through the night he became aware of the total darkness on Tangier and Smith Islands and on the eastern shore. The battery-operated buoy lights were working but the rest of the world was in darkness.

Some twenty minutes out into the bay he spotted the ferry, the lighted launch closing on them fast and bearing away. He put the spreader lights on so that Frank, if aboard, would be certain to recognize his trimaran. When he trained his glasses on the passengers, some of whom were visible in the launch lights, he saw Frank standing on the stern waving his arms at them like a drowning man.

Neil signalled Jim to drop the towline and get over to the launch. When he looked back through the binoculars he saw Frank standing on the ship's side, a dufflebag in each hand; after staring dubiously at the widening gap between the ferry and *Vagabond* and then at the water, the tall, gangly figure stepped awkwardly off the boat and disappeared into the blackness, the ferry speeding on to Tangier. While Neil watched – feeling both fear and admiration for Frank – it took Jim only a half-minute to reach Frank and another two to bring them both back to the trimaran. As Neil let *Vagabond* come up into the wind and rushed over to the port cockpit, Frank tossed his two wet bags aboard and prepared to swing himself up.

'Thank God we found you,' Neil said, grabbing Frank's hand to pull him aboard.

'There's a war, did you know?' Frank shot back.

'Yes,' Neil answered.

'You got a towel for me? I'm freezing to death.'

Neil carried the two dufflebags into the wheelhouse and found a towel Jim had left on a settee. As Frank began undressing and vigorously drying his body, Neil went back to speak to Jim.

'Come back aboard,' Neil shouted to him. 'We'll tow the dinghy and sail.' As Jim began to obey, Neil went back to the wheel to get *Vagabond* turned around and headed down the bay towards the Atlantic Ocean.

'Where the hell are you going?' Frank asked, pausing in drying his legs to look up at Neil winching in the mainsail.

'We've got to escape this madness,' Neil said, taking *Vagabond* off the wind on a starboard tack. 'The Chesapeake will soon be nothing but a saltwater burial ground. The whole east coast is probably doomed.'

61

Frank stared at him.

'We've been at war less than an hour,' he snapped back to Neil. 'Are you surrendering already?'

The question startled Neil. He *was* ready to surrender in some sense, not to an invading army – that he'd be willing to fight – but to the invisible anonymous destruction which he knew was being unleashed.

Jim had made the dinghy fast and now appeared in the wheelhouse, looking uncertainly at the confrontation.

'*You* may want to run immediately,' Frank went on angrily. 'But I've got a wife and daughter thirty miles outside of New York City who may still be alive. I've got Jeannie and Bob to pick up.'

'The Foresters can't have survived what happened to Washington,' Neil said.

'They may have come down to Point Lookout earlier this evening,' Frank explained. 'In any case it's damn certain it's our job to go over and see.'

'All right,' said Neil. 'But then we've got to get out into the Atlantic – before we're blown up or buried in radioactive ash.'

'Don't give me any more crap about an ocean voyage,' Frank shot back. 'We're at war! We have to stay here!'

'There may not *be* a here much longer,' Neil insisted.

'Neil's right, Dad,' Jim broke in. 'We've got to get out of the Chesapeake.'

'Shut up! Both of you!' Frank shouted. He paced past Jim out into a side cockpit and then, after staring at the ballooning glow on the horizon, returned.

'Even if New York's already been hit, no one can be certain how wide the destruction is around each city.' He paused. 'I'm going to try to fly north. I've got to get to Norah and Susan.'

Neil stared at him in disbelief.

'I figure there's a chance they're still alive,' Frank

continued huskily. 'I can charter a plane in Salisbury to fly to Oyster Bay and bring them back.'

Neil searched Frank's anguished face.

'It's madness, Frank,' he said softly. 'That whole area has probably been hit. If your wife survived she's already fled out the island. There's no way . . .'

'I'm going,' Frank interrupted sharply. 'If there's only one chance in ten I've still got to try.'

'And what are Jim and I supposed to do?' Neil asked, brushing roughly past Frank to adjust the mainsheet. 'Sit here for two or three days waiting for the fallout or the next explosion?'

'You try to get the Foresters over at Point Lookout.'

'All right, we'll do that,' Neil said. 'But then what?'

'You pick me up in Crisfield tomorrow night.'

Neil grimaced and turned away, shaking his head.

'We'll sail to Crisfield now,' Frank went on, 'and I can get to Salisbury by eight or nine in the morning.' Both he and Neil watched *Vagabond* sail past a red buoy, both instinctively noting the ship's speed. 'I should be able to get a plane by ten or eleven. New York by noon. If I give myself six hours to find her and Susan that'll get me back at Crisfield by . . . nine tomorrow.'

Neil stared at him. 'Look, Frank,' he began, glancing at Jim who was listening with grim attentiveness. 'Not many people are going to survive what's happening. Those that do are those that act fast and . . . ruthlessly. Those that know enough to cut their losses and run. Don't go. We can go over to Point Lookout to check for the Foresters now and then ride the tide down out the bay later tomorrow morning.'

Frank flushed.

'I'm going,' he said. 'And you're not using my boat to escape your responsibilities.'

'*What* responsibilities?' Neil exploded. 'Tell me, what in God's name you think any of us can do now against incoming missiles except try to survive. Every second you delay us you're risking me and your son and the Foresters.'

'I have to try to save my family and there may be other things to do,' Frank went on. 'We can't just run.'

'We can't help anyone dead,' Jim blurted out.

'Jim's right,' Neil said.

Frank leaned against the wheelhouse shelf, put his face in his hands, and rubbed his forehead. When he looked up, much of his colour seemed to have drained away.

'I'm going to try,' he said softly. 'Get *Vagabond* turned around. If I'm not back by nine tomorrow tonight . . . by ten . . . that's when the tide's high . . . you can leave without me.'

As Neil stared forward past the mainmast and across the water he felt resentment at Frank's putting him in the villain's role of running. During the last crisis three months before, he'd considered what he would do if a nuclear war broke out and decided he'd probably have it easy because he'd be on a boat at sea or on the coast and thus could flee the explosions and fallout. But the holocaust had actually found him becalmed without an engine seventy-five miles up a bay in the middle of dozens of prime targets, owner and guests and family scattered to the winds. Frank's effort to find his family in the north complicated things further and was insane: every moment they remained in the Chesapeake decreased their chances of survival.

'Don't go, Dad,' Jim said after a long silence. 'Please don't go. We can't help Mom now.'

'I've got to go,' Frank replied, turning to walk out into the port cockpit. 'I could never forgive myself if . . . I didn't try . . .'

Neil turned the wheel over to Jim, told him to bring *Vagabond* about, and walked after Frank.

'All right,' he said, standing near him and looking at Frank's frightened, determined face. 'If you've got to go, so be it. We'll take you to Crisfield and then go to Point

64

Lookout to try to help the Foresters, then back into Crisfield tomorrow.'

'And you can leave without me at ten,' Frank concluded.

'I plan to sail south at no later than ten, tomorrow night,' Neil agreed without expression.

Frank nodded gloomily. As *Vagabond* swung about to take Frank back to Crisfield they all stared forward at the terrifying glow on the horizon. On every other side the world was dark.

'Be back on time, you fool,' Neil said softly to Frank. 'We need you.'

'Yeah,' said Frank huskily. 'I can't let you steal my boat.'

10

By the time Jeanne was within a few miles of Point Lookout she was out of her state of shock. Point Lookout, she knew, was a dead end: a small town at the end of the huge V-shaped peninsula bordered on one side by the wide Potomac River and on the other by the Chesapeake. The nearest bridges were almost fifty miles away and might have been destroyed by the blast over Washington. She would meet *Vagabond* in Point Lookout or have to get herself and the children on to another boat. Hundreds, thousands of survivors from the destruction to the north would be funnelled south to this tiny town, and everyone would be seeking a boat.

She knew that *Vagabond* might not come for her, that Frank might conclude that she and her family had been killed. She could only hope the trimaran was already *in* Point Lookout and would wait a few hours at least.

Lisa too had regained control. She seemed to need to talk, so Jeanne nodded and grunted while her mind worked along in its own channels. Mostly Lisa recited what she could remember from reading pamphlets about radioactive fallout, a subject Jeanne already knew well. Neither of them mentioned her father, dead, Jeanne assumed dully, in Washington. Her strongest emotion when she emerged from shock was anger: anger at the Russians and Americans who had created this war that had killed Bob and was threatening to kill Lisa and Skip.

As they neared Point Lookout it struck Jeanne as strange that she could see other drivers, like herself reacting to the largest crisis of their lives, yet say nothing to them. Each vehicle was its own separate island, its occupants shipwrecked alone.

And something else was strange: there didn't seem to be anyone at home along the road. The area was deserted. Then she realized: there's no electric power. The lights are out. Forever.

The thought 'forever' chilled her even as she recognized it as melodrama; she shook her head to get rid of it. But she felt her anger rising again to see on either side of the road the dark houses, as if already everyone inside of them were dead. The stupid, thoughtless life-haters were doing it: they were blowing up the world.

When she entered the village of Point Lookout it too was dark. By the time she arrived at the waterfront it was a little after eleven. The only lights were from the cars and the glow to the northwest. She drove past a place called 'Kelly's Marina', but turned in when she saw a sign saying 'Municipal Marina'.

The parking lot was not crowded, and she chose a spot at the end next to a small saltwater creek and parked. For a moment she sat there staring down at the barely visible black flowing waters of the creek and ignoring Lisa's question of 'What are we going to do now?' Then, after watching someone running through the yard carrying a kerosene lantern, she turned to her daughter.

'I want you to stay here with Skippy,' she said quietly. 'Lock the car doors. Don't let anyone in. I'm going to see if Frank is here yet.'

'Yes, Mother.'

'If he's not here,' she went on, 'we'll have to wait. Maybe we'll go to the motel or perhaps we'll stay here. But *you* stay here no matter how long it takes me to get back.'

'I will, Mother,' Lisa answered. 'You be careful.'

When Jeanne leaned over to give Lisa a kiss she found herself being hugged strongly by Lisa's long arms.

'It's going to be all right, honey,' she said softly as she

67

loosened herself from the embrace. 'The bastards haven't killed us yet.'

After getting out of the car Jeanne waited until Lisa had locked the doors and then hurried through the parking lot towards the docks. In the darkness she noticed clusters of people gathered quietly in the parking lot and along the dock. She felt alone and vulnerable, then frightened as some car's headlights would suddenly sweep over her like some new nuclear blast. She knew what a trimaran looked like – thank God Frank had such a strange-looking boat – but in the darkness it was difficult to tell if three boats together were three boats or one large trimaran. Several boats were lit up and most people hurrying along the waterfront had flashlights.

How she wished she could talk to someone. There was a war, a war, and everyone just hurried past, ignoring her.

The dock was a giant 'T', but after searching along both its arms she had not found *Vagabond*. Finally she stopped someone hurrying towards her to land.

'Excuse me, do you know if there's a trimaran . . .'

'Can't help you, lady,' the man replied, not even slowing his pace.

Closing her eyes Jeanne moved over to a piling and held on to it to steady herself. She noticed several boats dimly visible anchored out and wondered if *Vagabond* were among them. She could feel her arms trembling again and thought of Skippy and Lisa in the car, depending on her.

Okay. Eleven-twenty and the trimaran's not at the municipal dock. It might not get here until dawn. She'd check with the dockmaster and motel for messages; she'd take a look at any other marinas here in the heart of town; and then all she could do was wait.

There was no dockmaster on duty and when Jeanne finally got a man to listen to her question about Frank's boat he said he knew nothing about any trimaran. She returned wearily to the car.

Lisa, wide-eyed, lowered the window on the passenger's side.

'Frank's not here yet,' Jeanne said with exaggerated nonchalance. 'He may not arrive until dawn. I'm going to check the motel down the street to see if maybe he got a message through to us before the . . . I'll be gone another half hour,' she concluded. 'Why don't you climb in back beside Skippy and try to get some sleep.'

'I'm not sleepy.'

'You need some rest.'

'I've been keeping an eye out for Frank.'

Jeanne examined her frightened, eager-eyed daughter. 'I'll be back,' she said, and walked away.

In the darkness the motel was difficult to locate. Lit only by the glow from the northwest the place seemed like a ghost town in some horror film, the main street like a path through a dark canyon.

There was no message at the motel and they had no room for her, having given it to some 'personal friends'. Sorry.

She searched Porter's and Kelly's and then the municipal docks again but there was no trimaran. As she returned to her car she realized that in an hour and a half she hadn't heard a friendly word.

Lisa was still in the front seat, slumped sideways asleep. When Jeanne unlocked the driver's door she stirred but slept on. Jeanne decided that she herself should sleep. If Frank arrived now he'd certainly wait until morning before leaving again. She relocked the driver's door and climbed over the seat to arrange herself on the sleeping bag beside Skippy. After pulling the light blanket up over herself and Skip, she stared up at the dark ceiling of her stationwagon. A strange sense of unreality flowed through her. Was she really lying here in her car three hours after the start of a nuclear war? The warm softness of Skippy's body beside her seemed so human, so nice, so reassuring. She lifted her head to look out the window: figures with lanterns and flashlights moved in the darkness along the dock. Someone shouted. The war was real.

After a while Jeanne slept. She was awakened once in the night by a scream but when she sat up saw nothing. There was then only one light moving in the darkness. Near dawn she was awakened again by someone shaking her foot and then pulling her whole body out of the back of the stationwagon. When she sat up she banged her head on the car roof and, awake, saw two men, one of whom had hold of her feet and was dragging her out the back of her own car. Banjo was growling.

'Stop it!' she shouted, but the man dragged her to the edge of the stationwagon's rear and then took hold of her arm and pulled her roughly out.

'Give us the car keys,' he said, his fingers digging into her upper arm, his face, tensely expressionless in the early light of pre-dawn, only a foot away from hers. Fully awake, but still groping for reality, she looked speechlessly back at him.

'Yes . . . yes, of course,' she finally said. 'But let us get our stuff out.'

When she tried to turn back to the car the man held her fast.

'I found them,' she heard the other man say, and saw he had her handbag and now the keys.

The man holding her then flung her off to the side, sending her stumbling over the small embankment and down on to her face, rolling towards the shallow creek. The cold water struck her legs like a slap.

'Let's go,' she heard a voice say.

11

Vagabond was moving towards Point Lookout with agonizing slowness. The nightmare of the war was compounded for Neil by the more personal and immediate nightmare of running in place, being unable to move forward no matter how hard he tried. It had seemed an endless crawling toward Crisfield with Frank in the wee hours of the morning, and since leaving him off just before dawn, an endless crawling in light winds to try to cross the bay.

And as they struggled, the horror of the unfolding nuclear destruction was becoming more real. At the dock in Crisfield Frank had tried to telephone his wife and reported back dully to Neil and Jim: 'The operator didn't even try. She said – the operator said . . . "I'm sorry, Sir, New York State is disconnected." ' He'd laughed joylessly.

They had all listened in the darkness to the transistor radio and on the entire A.M. dial they were able to bring in only five stations where normally there would have been forty or so. Dribs and drabs of hurried, sometimes barely coherent news drifted out. It often took the reporters several repetitions of each frightened report before a piece of grim news could be accepted as confirmed and indisputable. The idea that Washington and New York and apparently fifty to a hundred other places had been destroyed and that twenty to eighty million people had already been killed; that almost all major radio and television stations were not operating; and that the war was continuing: all this was almost beyond their ability to handle. It seemed beyond some of the announcers' abilities to handle. A few read the news items as if they were reading a weather report and made it seem so absurd that at one point Frank giggled. Others would become emotional and be replaced by a more controlled voice.

One commentator pointed out that there was no way of knowing how many nuclear warheads had hit a given target, whether the target had been struck directly or peripherally, and whether the explosion had occurred on the ground or in the air. Knowledge that a place had been hit at all usually came only from that place's total silence. There were few eyewitness reports.

All United States military personnel had been ordered to report for duty. Where the home base was 'no longer a viable alternative' they were ordered to report to the nearest military base of their service.

The President issued a statement at 4.30 A.M. indicating that he and all cabinet members were safe, but that dozens, perhaps hundreds of US Congressmen had been killed in the blasts over Washington and other major cities. Offensive action had been commenced against the Soviet Union; nuclear war was occurring in Europe and Asia too. Although at least twenty major American cities had already been reported hit and twice that many missile and other military sites, the implication was that for some unstated reason the Russians hadn't unleashed as devastating an attack as might have been expected. To Neil it meant only that worse might yet come. One exchange between two announcers on the Norfolk radio station particularly depressed and frightened him.

'Is there anything new from the national news wire, Herb?' a man's tense, hurried voice asked.

'There's still no contact with NBC news in New York, John. All we've got, actually, are the items we're picking up from WTUV in Richmond, but they seem to have a direct connection with the Federal government.'

'What about WBZE here in Norfolk? Do they have access to the ABC news wire?'

'No. All three network news services are out.'

'What about the west coast centres?'

'Los Angeles and San Francisco were both hit, John. There's just no contact . . .'

'What about military targets here in the Norfolk area?'

'The mayor has ordered the evacuation of all non-essential personnel,' the other voice replied. 'I'm afraid that with the US Naval base here and the shipyards in Portsmouth, this would appear to be a prime target area . . .'

Neil knew that if Norfolk, at the mouth of the Chesapeake, were hit, they might never escape to sea.

By the time they were away from Crisfield and on their way to Point Lookout the net effect on Neil of listening to the frenzied preliminary reports of destruction was to produce a strange and unexpected emotion which, he realized after a moment, was shame. He felt like a child whose classmates have run amok: although he wasn't personally involved, the destruction was somehow his responsibility.

Yet the dawn and early morning hours almost belied the reports they were hearing. A third of the way across the bay the day was clear; the sun shone brightly on the still water. A mile away Smith and Tangier Islands lay lush and green and silent like some bucolic utopia. Land and houses on the now receding eastern shore lay gleaming with postcard-like clarity. There even seemed to be an oysterman up and working the oysterbeds to the southeast. It was as if the radio reports were an Orson Welles prank.

But to the northwest the nightmare of the new life was clear: a huge grey cloud spread over half the northwest horizon, quite dark low in the sky, but the greyness reaching quite high up. The mass had no shape but was diffuse. A second area of cloudiness to the northeast was merging with it. Philadelphia? Only from the east through south to due west was the sky still clear. Norfolk still lived.

By 8 A.M. the breeze began to pick up and Neil felt that if

73

it held or freshened further they would make Point Lookout by ten-thirty.

As their progress became routine and they ceased listening to the radio Neil was saddened that he felt no desire to try to rush northward to anyone's rescue. When he imagined his parents struggling to survive after an explosion over Boston and great damage to their town of Ocean Bluff he felt depressed and vaguely ashamed, but the idea that he could get there and become a rescuer simply had no reality. Frank's plan seemed insane. For Neil it was as if the war had created a new world, one which ended all previous relationships. One's family would now be defined by those one found oneself with. And the new world, for Neil, would survive only if they could make it out to sea.

'What do you know about nuclear fallout?' Jim asked from beside him, interrupting his thoughts.

'Enough,' Neil replied.

'That stuff we see ahead of us is radioactive fallout,' Jim said. He looked at Neil as if searching to see how horrible this fact was. The grey cloud cover to the northwest was more pronounced now that the sun was higher in the sky. It also seemed to be spreading slightly towards them.

'Yes,' said Neil. 'I expect it is.'

'It will spread,' Jim said.

'Yes,' Neil replied quietly. 'But we're almost a hundred miles away.'

'We won't be at Point Lookout,' Jim replied. 'And even so I think it's got closer since dawn.'

Neil squinted at it as if noting the fact for the first time.

'Maybe,' he said. 'But this northeast wind is helping us. It's moving the stuff away at right angles.'

'You told me earlier you think the wind will be shifting to the north,' Jim persisted.

Neil went out into the port cockpit to adjust the genny sheet, and then returned to the wheel.

'We do what we must do, Jim,' he said. 'Right now we're

74

sailing *Vagabond* to Point Lookout.'

'And when that stuff starts falling on deck?' Jim asked, still searching Neil's face for Neil's fear.

Neil hid it and looked back at him neutrally.

'Then we sweep it off,' he replied.

12

Jeanne and Lisa, with Skippy and the dog huddled around
them, blinked in bewilderment at the chaos that was now
the waterfront of Point Lookout. Two hours after they'd
been thrown out of the stationwagon by the two men, there
were several hundred people where the night before there
had been perhaps two dozen. In places along the docks and
on wooden picnic tables a thin layer of ash had been
discovered at dawn, a discovery that had increased the
panic. Jeanne had already seen people siphoning gasoline
from automibiles for boat engines or for another car; seen
men rush past with guns stuffed in their belts, rifles in their
hands. Along the dock milled people pleading with those on
boats to take them aboard, the women sometimes weeping,
the children silent. She had seen five or six people with
burned faces and arms and two people being carried on
makeshift stretchers. One of the cars that had driven into the
parking lot had most of its red paint blistered.

One by one over the two hours since she'd been up
searching for *Vagabond*, vessels had motored away from the
dock area, a few completely packed and low in the water,
others with only two or three people aboard. Some were
motor yachts, some sailing boats; most were open boats with
inboard and outboard engines. All wanted to get away from
Washington and the fallout.

Although many ships had already left, the waterfront was
still crowded. Several boats that had been anchored, were
now coming in to get fuel or to pick up passengers. Others
were arriving from down the Potomac.

Jeanne had recovered from the shock of being thrown out

of her car. The men had let Lisa and Skippy leave and had tossed out the children's dufflebags, her larger suitcase and a sleeping bag, but had driven off with her smaller suitcase, her handbag, and a lot of little stuff in the car, including snack food she'd tossed together. She had no money or credit cards and they hadn't eaten breakfast. When she'd rolled into the creek she'd wet her jeans through so had changed into white shorts and tee-shirt; her wet boat shoes she'd had to leave on since her other footwear was in the missing smaller suitcase.

As she stood with one arm around Lisa's waist and the other holding Skippy's hand, she was tremblingly considering other options. With every minute that passed the chances of the trimaran's arriving at Point Lookout grew smaller. She could conceive of no reason for Frank not to have arrived by now. He'd said he hoped to come at ten last night, early morning at the latest. What could possibly stop him from motoring across the bay? Her only conclusion was that Frank had decided that she and her family were dead. He wasn't coming.

So what could she do? She had no husband, no home, no car, no money, no friends, and no place to stay. Her isolation and powerlessness saddened and angered her. The burned faces, sightless eyes and the shuffling, numb way so many people moved frightened her. She had to focus on her alternatives but when she did she could see only one: she should try to get across the bay to Crisfield. Frank would probably not be there, but it seemed her only hope. At least it was movement. She should try to hitch a ride on some other boat.

Even as she decided, she could feel herself absorbing the alternating numbness and hysteria she saw all around her. The people were becoming more numerous and the remaining boats fewer. Two fistfights had broken out at the gas dock and just after ten a man there was shot. The absence of electric power had forced the marina to develop some sort of mechanical siphoning system and the dock-master's effort to ration the amount of fuel he pumped seemed to have initiated the shooting. Within two minutes of the gunshot everyone seemed to have forgotten about it. The wounded man had staggered off alone. There were no policemen.

When she went in search of a boatowner willing to take her and her family across the bay, she left Lisa next to the marina office to take care of Skippy and their two bags and went out on the docks alone. Each remaining boat was bounded along the dock by men and women either dully or passionately begging for a chance to board. Around the first boat were two families, two stony-faced mothers, their children cowering big-eyed around their legs, the husbands, angry, holding out money. She didn't see any sense in competing, so she moved on.

The second boat was a twenty-five-foot motor yacht with two men working on its engine. One of them looked up at the group accosting him from the dock. She saw the man stare appraisingly at an attractive blonde woman who was pleading with him to take her and her child, and then his gaze shifted to Jeanne herself, first her bare legs, then her breasts, and finally her eyes. She felt a sensual shock: from fifteen feet away and without uttering a word, the man seemed to have propositioned her.

She hurried on. The third boat was filled to overflowing, but as she passed it she had the feeling that people had boarded an empty boat and that no one really knew what was going on. Most of those looking for a vessel were women, children and older men. She was walking back from the end of one of the arms of the 'T' when a slender young man about thirty came up and stopped her.

'Are you looking for a boat?' he asked.

'Yes,' she replied eagerly. 'I want to get across the bay to Crisfield.'

'I might be able to help you.'

'Thank God. I've got two children too. Where's your boat?'

'Two children?' the man said, frowning. 'We've only got room for one more person.'

'They're only children . . .' Jeanne pleaded. 'They won't take up much . . .'

'I'm sorry, ma'am, we're just too full.'

When he brushed nervously past her and hurried away, she stared after him in shock. 'You BASTARD!' she shouted at his retreating back.

As she headed back down the docks towards where she'd left the children she realized how vulnerable she was, especially with two children. No one would want that additional burden.

Lisa and Skippy were where she'd left them, hot and hungry. Lisa had fished a half-eaten banana out of a trash can and Skippy, after first accusing it of being dirty, had finally eaten it. She grabbed Skippy's hand and they traipsed like the war refugees they were down the fifty feet of road to the entrance to Kelly's, but seeing that Porter's Boatyard seemed much less crowded she went on first to it.

At the gate two men with shotguns greeted her.

'Can we help you, ma'am?' one of them asked.

'Yes, I hope so,' Jeanne replied, thankful for the first politeness she'd experienced all day. 'I . . . I need to get a boatride across the bay.'

'Do you know anyone in here?' the man asked.

'No.'

'Our orders are that no one is permitted to enter the yard unless they're the friends or guests of owners of one of the boats here. I'm sorry.'

'Oh.'

She hurried back to Kelly's Marina, which was slightly less crowded than the town docks, but the situation was the same: boatowners nervously preparing their boats, refugees looking for rides. She halted in the yard before going out.

She had nothing to offer that the others didn't have but she had to try.

'Lisa,' she said to her daughter at her side. 'I want you to keep yourself and Skippy thirty or forty feet behind me and out of sight. Follow me, watch me, don't lose me, but stay away until I call you. Do you understand?'

'Yes, Mother,' Lisa replied. 'What are you going to do?'

'I'm trying to get us a ride across the bay where I hope to find Frank.'

Jeanne had noticed a sailing boat tied slightly off a small dock between the municipal marina and Kelly's, and now that a family of four was leaving, there was only one man on the nearby dock.

'Do you have a hairbrush?' she asked her daughter. 'Mine was in my handbag.'

'I think so.'

Lisa dug out her hairbrush from the dufflebag and Jeanne let down her hair which she had tied back earlier and brushed it out. She had no fresh makeup on but hoped that she didn't need it.

'How do I look?' she asked Lisa.

Lisa looked at her uncertainly. 'You . . . you look fine,' she answered.

'I mean no makeup running . . .'

'No . . . Mother, what are you going to do? Let me come with you.'

'No, honey, stay here,' she replied and walked away.

She moved without haste and without the desperation that she realized now had been with her all that morning. It was still with her, of course, but since she was acting, it was paradoxically under control. She was trying to walk like a beautiful woman out for a stroll on a lovely summer morning. A wave of horror at the image surged through her. She felt ridiculous. She kept walking.

She saw that the man on the dock was adjusting a line out to the sailing boat where two other men were working rapidly. They looked as if they were about to leave.

'Hi,' she said as the man watched her approach down the gentle embankment which led to the dock.

'Hello,' he said, glancing at her nervously. He was a muscular-looking man in his mid-twenties dressed in khakis and a polo shirt.

'I could use a boatride,' she said.

'You and half the rest of the world,' the man answered, his eyes flicking quickly over her, his expression neutral.

She tried to smile. 'There *are* a lot of us,' she agreed.

'What's *she* want?' an older man called from the boat tied twenty feet off the dock.

'Says she wants a boatride,' the first man answered.

When she turned to the sailing boat she saw that the two men had stopped whatever they were doing and were staring at her. There was no friendliness in their faces, only appraisal.

'I'd like to get a ride over to Crisfield,' she said, still smiling.

The older man, in his forties she guessed, greyhaired with glasses, looked her up and down. 'Can you cook?' he asked.

'Cook?' Jeanne echoed, then nodded. On a twenty-mile voyage?

'Come aboard then,' he said.

Jeanne hesitated. 'Are you going to Crisfield?'

'We haven't decided,' the man answered, still staring at her without smiling. 'If you want to come, come. We're leaving.'

She slowly let her eyes drift to her left and then attentively off to her right: Lisa was seated in the grass fifty feet away feeding Skippy something while watching Jeanne.

'I hope to find a friend on a big trimaran in Crisfield,' she went on to the man on the boat.

The two men in the cockpit whispered together urgently. The other was a round, heavy-set man in his twenties with a full black beard.

'We've got work to do. Come aboard and let's talk about it,' the older man repeated. 'Pull us up to the dock, Gary.'

The man next to her pulled on a line and the stern of the sailing boat eased towards the dock. The round, bearded man came to the back of the boat to assist her down.

She hesitated, half of her wanting to run, the other half knowing that this was probably her last chance to get a boat across the bay to find Frank. Then she felt the hands of the man on the dock take hold of her waist from behind.

'Ready?' he said.

'What?' she replied.

But he lifted her and held her out towards the big man in the stern who grabbed her under the armpits and slowly lowered her on to the deck, grinning in her face.

'Welcome aboard,' he said. 'I'm Carl.'

'Thank you,' she said, smiling at him uncertainly. She turned to the older man.

'I . . . I need a ride to Crisfield,' she said again, feeling stupid.

'Come down below and have a drink,' he said. 'Carl, warm the engine up.'

Again she wanted to run, but the children were safe and . . . she had to get them to Frank. After a five-second hesitation, she smiled again.

'Thank you,' she said. She moved past him to the cabin entrance and then down the steps. The two men followed her.

Inside was a pleasant galley and dinette area on one side and a long settee on the other. She sat down on the settee. The older man stopped to pour three drinks of bourbon while Carl got a key and returned on deck to start the engine. The older man handed her a glass with the whisky.

'Here's to survival,' he said.

'To survival,' she replied and they clinked glasses.

'You can come,' he said to her. 'We can use a female aboard the boat.'

'I just want to go across the bay,' she said.

'What if you don't find your friend?' the man countered. 'Then what are your plans?'

'Then I guess I'm open to . . . suggestions,' she replied slowly. 'My husband's dead and my chil . . .'

'If you sail with us,' the man said, 'you'd be expected to cook for us, clean up, and perform . . . all the duties a woman usually . . . performs.'

'If . . . if I don't find Frank . . . then that . . . will be fine.'

'She'll cook for all of us,' Carl said to the older man as he descended back into the cabin. 'And perform all her duties for all of us. Agreed?'

The man looked at Carl coldly but nodded.

'You understand?' he asked Jeanne.

'Yes,' she said after a pause. 'But if . . . if my friend is in Crisfield . . . ?'

'We'll leave you with your friend.'

'Oh,' she said, relief flooding through her. 'It sounds fair enough.'

'Good,' the man said. 'Let's see how good a cook you're going to be.'

'I beg pardon?'

The man put his glass of whisky down on the dinette table and came up close to her, still not smiling. He reached down with large hands and cupped her two breasts, squeezed them, then ran each thumb and first finger along until he was first squeezing and then rolling her nipples through the tee-shirt and bra.

'You should be an incredible cook,' he said, flushed and grinning awkwardly.

Jeanne suppressed the desire to leap away, but leaned back against the cushion of the settee and folded her arms in front of her.

'Yes, I can be,' she said steadily as the man let his hands fall away but stood in front of her still grinning. 'But there's one other element in the agreement,' she went on.

'What's that?'

'You have to bring my two children also.'

The older man was frowning.

'Children?' he said. 'Who said anything about children?'

'I just did,' Jeanne answered. 'If they don't go, I don't go.'

'We can't take kids,' Carl said sharply.

'Survival, my dear woman,' the older man said, stepping back and finishing his drink. 'We're low on food as it is.'

'Take it or leave it,' Jeanne answered firmly, now hoping just to get off the boat. 'Three of us or none. And a dog.'

'Your kids will be safer on shore,' the man said. 'If they come with us we might end up having to throw them overboard.'

'Or we might have to eat them,' Carl said. 'We only want to eat you.' Carl laughed, and the older man again smiled awkwardly.

'Just take us to Crisfield then,' insisted Jeanne.

'No, honey,' the older man said. 'A cook like you . . .'

'Then I'm leaving,' said Jeanne and she stood up and began walking to the entrance ladder, but Carl grabbed her by the arm.

'How about it, Ned?' he said to his friend. 'Shall we cast off?'

The older man looked at Jeanne, swallowed, then looked away.

'Yes,' he said. 'Tell Gary to untie the mooring lines, come aboard, and haul in the anchor.'

'Let me go,' said Jeanne, struggling.

'Take it easy, honey,' Carl said. 'We're not going to hurt you.'

She hit him in the face with her right hand and pulled away, but he simply grabbed her with both arms in a bear hug and held her close. He grinned down at her.

With all her strength Jeanne screamed for help.

13

It was ten-twenty when Neil and Jim sailed *Vagabond* in close to the municipal dock at Point Lookout. Earlier they'd noticed many boats on the water, especially coming down the Potomac. Two vessels had been close to foundering because of masses of people aboard, but those sights hadn't prepared them for the hysteria and chaos they now found at the docks.

'Bring her around into the wind, Jim,' Neil ordered from the cockpit. He'd already lowered the mizzen and genoa and was sailing now with just the main. 'We're going to anchor off. Swing her! Swing her!'

As Jim finally brought the boat around into the wind thirty yards from the dock Neil rushed forward and threw the thirty-five-pound CQR anchor into the water.

'Drop the mainsail!' he shouted back, and Jim rushed out of the wheelhouse to come forward and do it.

When they had the sail secured and the anchor well-hooked, *Vagabond*'s stern lay only about twenty-five feet from one end of the 'T' of the main dock.

'What do we do now?' Jim asked, looking with amazement at the scene before them. Already a dozen people had rushed down to their end of the dock and were shouting at them.

'Go get your .22,' Neil replied coldly. While Jim went below to get his rifle Neil considered the situation. He'd already decided during the sail over that if the Foresters didn't appear immediately – *Vagabond* was an easy object to see, even in this chaos – he would make one quick search around the docks and, after thirty minutes, get the hell back to Crisfield. Seeing the chaos ashore made him question whether he should risk even a brief trip off the boat. Certainly he would wait half an hour, but was there any sense in going ashore?

Jim emerged beside him with the .22.

'Is it loaded?' Neil asked.

'No.'

'Load it.'

While Jim loaded the .22, in full view of the crowd on the dock Neil noted with satisfaction, Neil decided he could risk sending Jim ashore.

'You know what the Foresters all look like?' he asked.

'Sure.'

Then Neil reconsidered. It was important to him to get more food aboard, and that he couldn't expect Jim to handle. Whether there would be any chance to buy, barter, or steal any food he didn't know, but it was worth a trip into the town to find out. Frank had shown him several photos of Jeanne and Lisa.

'I'm going ashore,' he said to Jim. 'I want you to shorten the anchor line twenty feet so we're further away from the dock. Don't let anyone aboard.'

'Aren't we going to help some of these people?' Jim asked.

'Yes,' Neil answered, still staring at the growing crowd. 'But not until I get back. Not until we know how many of our own people we'll be sailing with.'

'Okay,' said Jim. 'But what do I do if someone tries to board? I can't shoot them.'

'No, I guess not,' he said after a pause. 'Try to keep them off with bluff. If you fail, I'll be back and we'll take it from there.'

Neil climbed down into the inflatable dinghy and had Jim pay out its line so he would be blown slowly down on to the dock by the wind. When he was less than ten feet away he stood up in the dinghy and shouted for silence from the crowd.

'I'm coming ashore,' he announced loudly. 'In half an hour we're sailing across the bay to Crisfield. At that time we'll take passengers who want to get to Crisfield. Until then you all wait on the dock. Do you understand?'

A few nodded eagerly as if trying to please; others shouted. Neil ignored them all, signalled to Jim to pay out ten more feet of line and soon pulled himself up on to the dock. Still ignoring the people pressing in around him he watched Jim pull the empty dinghy back to *Vagabond*. Then he began pushing his way through them to get to land. He looked closely at the clusters of refugees along the docks for the Foresters, hoping that they had seen *Vagabond* sail in and would be here on the docks. But they weren't. If they were alive in Point Lookout they would have to be either at another marina or else away from the dock area for some reason. He couldn't conceive what such a reason might be.

When he reached the marina office on land he went in and questioned a harried and frightened teenager who was the only one there, but he knew nothing about anyone looking for a trimaran. Outside, Neil looked towards the two marinas to the north but decided he'd go into town first to check there and see if he could buy some food supplies.

He began walking to the street, automatically looking at everyone within sight, when he saw a figure running along the street shouting for help, a girl, a young girl. Trying to catch what she was screaming, Neil abruptly realized that she looked something like the picture he'd seen of Lisa. Passing him, she turned into the entrance of the municipal marina, still running and now moving away.

'Lisa!' he shouted.

The girl stopped and looked around. It *must* be her.

'Lisa Forester!' he shouted and ran over to her.

'Who . . . who are you?' she asked.

'Neil Loken, Frank Stoor's captain,' he answered quickly. 'I've come . . .'

87

'Come quick,' Lisa cried. 'I think they're stealing my mother!'

'What?'

'Some men took my mother on their boat and I heard her scream and they're leaving!'

'Show me,' said Neil.

Lisa began running back along the street with Neil running beside her. 'There!' she shouted while still running, and she pointed at a long low yawl that was easing away from a nearby dock. 'She's on that boat.'

'You're sure?' Neil asked, looking into the young stranger's eyes.

'Yes! Yes! Please save her!'

Neil ran down the embankment out on to the dock and in one motion dived into the water. A part of him felt uncertain and ridiculous, but it was no time for second thoughts. Where was Lisa's father?

As he surfaced from his first six strokes he realized that the yawl was easing up over its anchor and he was gaining quickly on it. There was one man in the cockpit and another handling the anchor line. They didn't seem to notice him. In another twenty strokes he was at the vessel's raked stern and, grabbing a cleat, he hauled himself up over the transom and on to the aft deck. When he stood up, the man in the cockpit, a man in his forties, saw him.

'Who the hell are you?' he asked.

Neil walked forward, stepped down into the cockpit, smiled at the man and walked down into the cabin. A huge man stood in the galley-way with his back to Neil and beyond him was a woman barely visible past the man's bulk. Carl swung around when he heard Neil and the two men confronted each other.

'Excuse me,' Neil said and walked up and past Carl. The woman, crouching at the far end of the cabin, had a butcher knife in her hand. It was Jeanne Forester. He was startled by the sudden impact of her tensed animal beauty, accentuated by her gleaming wide dark eyes and long black hair falling wildly across one side of her face.

'Hey, Ned!' Carl shouted up to the cockpit. 'Who is this guy?'

'Hand me up the gun!' Ned shouted back.

Neil had stopped three feet from Jeanne. What a beautiful woman, he was still thinking irrelevantly.

'Can you swim?' he asked her softly.

'What?' she said back. 'Who are you?'

As Neil walked again forward she raised the knife but he picked her up in his arms. She brought the knife down and held its point against his chest and stared at him. With her eyes only inches from his and the knife point pricking his skin Neil gazed at her.

'Can you swim?' he asked her softly.

'Yes,' she answered, still holding the knife tight against his chest, her eyes searching his.

He swung around and began to leave just as Carl handed a gun up to the man in the cockpit. Neil again brushed past Carl, climbed the stairs, went out into the cockpit, walked up to and past the man with the gun and in one unbroken motion threw Jeanne out into the water. She landed with an undignified splash, but began immediately swimming for shore.

'What the hell?' the older man said, rushing up beside Neil and looking down at Jeanne.

Neil hit him a crushing blow to the side of the head that sent him sprawling against the cockpit seat, the gun clattering to the deck. Neil picked it up and glanced back: the big, bearded man had been about to spring forward but stood frozen now in a crouch. Neil stuffed the gun deep into his trousers under the pressure of his belt and dived overboard.

He swam the first thirty feet underwater, and when he surfaced he looked back to see if the men on the yawl had other weapons, but they were hurrying their preparations to get out to sea. Neil began swimming after Jeanne.

He came up to her where she was resting with her two slender hands grasping the edge of a small boat dock at Kelly's, her head bowed, her wet black hair clinging in strands down her back. When she turned to him, she looked puzzled.

'Are you Neil Loken?' she asked.

'Yes, I . . .'

'Are you really Neil?' she persisted, suddenly smiling and crying both at once. 'Thank God. Is Frank here? The boat? I couldn't find it. We waited and waited. I was trying to get . . .'

'It's okay,' he interrupted, reaching out with his free hand and touching her shoulder. 'Let me help you up on to the dock.'

'At first I thought you were another member of their crew,' she went on, still crying and laughing at the same time. 'When you asked, "Can you swim?" I thought . . .' She shook her head. 'How did you find me?' she asked next, pulling her head back and smiling up at him, tears mingling with the salt water on her face.

'Lisa found me,' Neil answered.

'Oh my God, where are Lisa and Skip?'

When Neil pointed to Lisa standing on the dock watching them, she began trying to pull herself up on to the edge of the dock. Neil spread his right hand across her buttocks and lifted her up; she sprawled forward on to the dock. With a quick surge he pulled himself up beside her.

'Let's get to *Vagabond*,' he said, helping her up. They ran up the gangway to the main dock where Lisa and her mother hugged each other.

'Where's Skippy?' Jeanne asked as they all rushed on.

'Still on the grass,' Lisa said happily, pointing.

While Neil picked Skippy up into his arms, Lisa and Jeanne grabbed their bags. Together they hurried back along the street to the town dock, Neil already beginning to worry about *Vagabond*.

As he looked at the end of the dock Neil was surprised to note that the crowd had evaporated, but just as he was feeling reassured he saw trouble: seven or eight people had got aboard *Vagabond*, which had somehow drifted back to the dock. The stern of its starboard hull was banging periodically against a piling. People had thus been able to board directly.

Neil felt a flush of anger at Jim. When he went to board *Vagabond* he saw a man in a bright pink shirt and green pants standing on the hull facing him with a pistol.

'No more aboard,' the young man said to Neil.

Feeling an incongruous rush of mirth, Neil laughed. The man frowned, made uneasy both by the laugh and by the gun shoved in Neil's jeans.

'If you plan to try to sail this boat,' Neil said, 'you'd better let me aboard.'

'Neil!' he heard Jim shout and saw him standing in the side cockpit behind the man with the pistol.

'Okay,' the man said. 'You can come aboard. But you'll have to give me that gun.'

'Like hell I will,' Neil replied.

'He's the captain,' Jim said. 'No one can sail us out of here except him.'

The man stared at Neil and then shrugged.

Neil stepped down and then helped Jeanne, Lisa and Skip down after him. He could feel his body tense at the invasion of his boat and remained for the moment on the deck to steady himself. Lisa had rushed up to Jim and buried her head against his chest, clinging to him. Neil noticed a mother breast-feeding her child in the side cockpit, three suitcases scattered around her feet. As he went past Jim and Lisa into the wheelhouse he saw two men and a woman standing on one side looking nervously at a thickset man seated opposite them. In the far cockpit someone was sprawled on the deck with a woman bent over him weeping. Neil turned to Jim, who had followed him into the wheelhouse.

91

'How many people have guns?' he asked.

'Just that young guy guarding the starboard hull and *him*,' Jim replied, nodding towards the man sitting on the settee at the rear of the wheelhouse, one leg crossed over the other, dressed in a brown business suit, a large .45 and Jim's .22 cradled in his lap. The man met Neil's gaze with alert coldness.

'What happened?' Neil asked.

'The wind shifted a little,' said Jim earnestly. 'And *Vagabond* swung around closer to the docks. When I went forward to shorten the anchor a whole mass of people got aboard. The two guys with guns herded half the crowd back up on to the docks and . . . shot the man in the side cockpit when he refused to get off.'

Jeanne had passed them and was kneeling now beside the weeping woman. Lisa stayed with Skippy, listening. Neil turned to the man seated with the .45 on his lap. In his mid-thirties, thickset with dark, receding hair, he again gazed back at Neil with quiet confidence.

'We're sailing over to Crisfield to pick up a friend,' he announced. The man simply nodded. 'I don't appreciate people forcing themselves on to my boat at gunpoint,' Neil added coldly.

'These are tough times, Buddy,' the man said softly. 'And I didn't notice you or your friend selling tickets.'

'You had to shoot someone?' Neil asked.

'There were thirty people aboard,' the man replied quietly. 'Your young friend said this boat couldn't sail out of here with that much weight. Jerry and I kicked twenty of them off. A guy pulled a knife on Jerry and Jerry shot him. It's only a shoulder wound and I already patched it up. Nothing serious.'

'I'd like our .22 back,' Neil said quietly.

The man looked down at his lap as if surprised to find Jim's rifle lying there.

92

'Sure,' he said after a pause. 'Just borrowed it for a minute.' He handed it to Neil.

'Lisa,' said Neil, turning to the young girl, 'get Skippy and your mother down into the port cabin. Jim, get the sails back up.'

He turned back to the man with the .45.

'Do you know much about sailing?' he asked him.

'Not much,' he said.

'How about your friend Jerry?'

'He thinks he's standing on the front of the boat.'

Neil glanced at the pink-shirted Jerry who stood nervously on the stern of the port hull watching the dock.

'All right,' said Neil. 'This boat is motorless so I'll trust you're not stupid enough to get rid of Jim and me since we're the only ones who can sail it. I'd appreciate it, however, if you'd both put your guns away.'

'Sure,' said the man with a slight smile. 'You're the captain.'

Jim had raised the two sails forward and as Neil headed there to help him with the anchor Jeanne appeared.

'Where's Frank?' she asked.

'We're meeting him in Crisfield,' he answered.

'And then?'

'Out to sea,' he replied and, as he moved forward, frowned at how simple the three words made it sound. He doubted they'd ever see Frank again, and their chances of getting past Norfolk to the ocean in one piece were probably small. He'd be happy if they made it to Crisfield without the wind dying or one of the outlaws shooting someone. But one step at a time. Jim came aft after making the main halyard fast.

'Take the wheel, Jim,' he said, 'and put her on the port tack. I'll handle the anchor.'

'I couldn't stop them,' Jim burst out unexpectedly. 'The guy in the wheelhouse said he'd shoot me.'

Neil nodded and thought of the man in the wheelhouse. 'He would have,' Neil said. 'Now go.'

In five minutes *Vagabond* was labouring across the bay at six knots in a nice breeze. Neil found himself looking for Jeanne, but the wheelhouse remained empty except for Jim and the cold-eyed Buddha with the gun. With *Vagabond* moving again Neil felt almost content, even strangely happy. Then, looking aft, he saw that the cloud mass from Washington was still spreading; the sky directly above them was no longer blue. He looked at it a moment, feeling fear and anger both, then went back to work.

14

Although the traffic between Crisfield and Salisbury had been thin, at the airport the parking lot was overflowing. There were three Maryland State Police cars and eight or nine policemen, but they seemed unclear about what they were supposed to be doing.

Inside the drab terminal, people were strangely quiet. The room was crowded but what little movement there was occurred slowly as if everyone was moving through molasses.

As Frank walked directly towards the door marked 'Manager's Office', he had to push his way through two long lines that stretched far out into the room from the ticket counter.

'I want to buy or charter a plane,' he said to the small, spare man seated at a desk who had invited him in when he knocked.

After looking at Frank for a moment the man frowned down at the papers he'd been looking at.

'All the regular charter planes are filled,' he said. 'There are also twenty or thirty private planes operating out of this airport and a few are unofficially selling seats to passengers. The going rate is five thousand dollars a seat.'

'Any of them going to New York?' Frank asked eagerly.

'None going north,' the manager replied. 'Most are going to the Bahamas or West Indies. One or two of the bigger ones to South America.'

'Then I want to buy a plane and hire a pilot.'

'No one will fly you to New York.'

'Money talks,' said Frank.

'Not very loudly as far as heading north is concerned.'

The manager squinted up at Frank. 'May I ask why you're so hot to get to what's left of New York?' he asked.

'Family.'

'Ahhh,' the manager said and shook his head. 'Well, I can't help you. The private planes are housed in C and D Hangars at the west end of the field. If someone wants to sell a plane that's where they'd be.'

When Frank got to Hangar C there was a flurry of activity: two small planes being worked on, one being pushed out of the hangar, and three or four clusters of people talking. Frank began asking people who might sell him a plane to fly north.

'There's only one guy here I know of who said he'd let his plane go north if the money was right,' one man told him, 'and that's Tommy Trainer over in Hangar D.'

'How'll I find him?' Frank asked.

'Little guy. Wears a natty white suit,' the man answered. 'He owns the two-engine Beechcraft over in the back corner. But, Buddy, you don't think you're going to make it north and back through what's happening up there, do you?'

Frank wheeled and headed off to Hangar D. Tommy Trainer was a flashily dressed little man with dark, slicked-down hair and an absurdly large cigar. He was checking his Beechcraft with a mechanic when Frank found him. After listening to Frank explain what he wanted to do, the little man just continued to stare at him and chewed lightly on his unlit cigar.

'Well, suh,' he said in the dignified drawl of a southern gentleman completely in contrast to his bookmaker appearance. 'Ah'd like to help you, I really would. But I believe the general opinion is that it's dangerous travelling north these days. I believe there's just a bit of risk involved. Wouldn't you agree, suh?'

'A lot of risk,' Frank said. 'I'll pay accordingly.'

'That's right generous of you, suh, and I appreciate it. I'll tell you what,' he continued in his southern drawl, 'I can't

96

charter you my plane 'cause the *in*surance doesn't cover it, you know, but I'll sell you the plane. Let's see. One hundred thousand dollars. How does that sound, suh?'

'What about a pilot?'

'I believe I might be able to obtain you a pilot for . . . yes, for another twenty.'

Frank, who sometimes quibbled over the price of a twenty-five-cent sinker, felt a flash of anger. The beat-up plane couldn't be worth more than twenty-five thousand dollars and the pilot would be doing at the most a half-day's work.

'It's a deal,' he said.

'In cash, gold, or silver,' said Tommy Trainer.

Frank frowned, his forward momentum checked. He looked at Tommy Trainer. Where the hell could he get the money?

'Where's the nearest bank?' Frank finally asked.

'Bank!' Tommy Trainer exclaimed. 'It's a little late for banks, I'm afraid.'

Frank stared at him uncertainly.

'I'll be back,' he said.

On the short drive from the airport into Salisbury Frank realized that it wasn't going to work. He needed a plane this instant, and the banking system, even in the best of times, was not used to producing a hundred and twenty thousand dollars in an instant. In these times . . .

The situation turned out to be worse than he had imagined. Most banks hadn't even opened. The two that were, were mobbed with long lines outside their doors. And he realized, of course, that there was no phone or teletype contact with either of his New York City banks nor his bank in Oyster Bay.

'They're doing no banking business with any except their own customers,' a man told Frank. 'I doubt that there's a single bank in the country today that doesn't have the same policy.'

Giving up, Frank returned to his car and sat slumped in shock. He might be able to steal the plane, he thought, pay for it later. But he couldn't fly it.

He supposed he could kidnap a pilot . . . But gradually he realized that there was no way. He couldn't get there by car. He couldn't fly. He was stuck.

As he slowly drove back to Crisfield he felt himself disoriented from the succeeding shocks of the day. All his life he had been a doer, a man who faced problems squarely and set about solving them. His success in the world of New York City real estate was based partly on this ability to deal with problems as soon as they arose, make fast decisions and get the job done. It also helped that he wasn't afraid of risks. He enjoyed taking risks.

He had wanted to treat the unthinkable catastrophe of nuclear war as he would a disastrous cashflow problem, for the *challenge* of the war stimulated him, the challenge of the logistics of saving his wife, shoring up his financial position, surviving – all these got his adrenalin flowing, had him acting decisively, rationally, quickly.

But the experiences he'd had in his three hours in Salisbury had been for him the psychological equivalent of being bombed. He had begun to realize that all his paper wealth – his stocks, bonds, trust funds, treasury certificates – were probably worthless. And the more material assets he owned – the apartment houses in New York City, his home in Oyster Bay, the shopping centre in Englewood – had all, with the hopeful exception of his house in Oyster Bay, been destroyed. But worse, he realized that the 'problems' and 'challenges' presented by the holocaust were not something that could be dealt with. He couldn't buy a plane, or a car, or even, maybe, a tank of gasoline. He couldn't even *telephone* anyone. He was almost helpless. Suddenly, over-night, he was an unemployed pauper.

But alive. For as he drove back towards Crisfield with the car-radio tuned to the appalling news, cities with whom all communication had been lost, *countries* with whom all communication had been lost, a large part of him began to fear for his life and want to scurry for the nearest hole to survive. The numbing, incomprehensible, dreamlike list of American cities and defence installations that had been struck by nuclear missiles or bombs dazed him. He heard the Secretary of Defense urging people to stick to their jobs if their jobs were important, to report for service if they weren't. In one sentence the man warned against needless panic and in another advised people to evacuate fallout areas. He didn't list fallout areas. Frank learned that the United States had bombed Cuba, that Europe was being devastated; London wiped out, Moscow, Leningrad, numerous unpronounceable other Russian cities; Russian forces in Iraq attacked. China and Japan had been struck. Several countries in South America and Africa had loudly proclaimed their neutrality.

His fear for himself began to grow. He knew that part of his frantic activity to get back north to his wife was based on the simple fact that it was the expected thing to do. It was a man's job to protect his wife. The thought of her there in their house, helpless, confused, worried about Jimmy, worried about him too, huddled together with Susan, that thought made him sad, made him feel needed, made him want to find a way north. But the only thing left now was *Vagabond*. He was frightened: he pressed his foot further on the accelerator. All salvation lay in *Vagabond*.

15

With the wind shifting more to the north, *Vagabond* had one long tack across the bay to Crisfield. Despite the extra ton of weight from the new passengers and their luggage, she plugged along at six or seven knots until within two miles of the town when the wind fell. Then her speed dropped to two knots and she began to wallow and crawl. Neil hailed and bribed a small cruiser to tow them the last two miles into the dock.

The trip was uneventful. Although thin wisps of the dark cloud mass from Washington seemed to be stretching almost over them there was no sign of radioactive fallout. The ten passengers maintained a stunned and numb order which made the boat-handling easy. Jeanne had spent the first hour and a half below but, with Skippy napping and Lisa helping Jim at the helm, she came up and stood beside Neil in the port cockpit.

He was again aware of her as a woman, her bare brown legs and arms set off by the white shorts and shirt. Her long hair was now brushed and tied up on top of her head. She stared forward for a while without speaking.

'Do you think Frank will be there?' she finally asked.

'There's no way of knowing,' he answered. 'We'll just have to see.'

'And then what?' she asked.

'I suppose that will be mostly up to Frank,' he said after a pause.

'We should leave,' she said with unexpected force. 'Get out of this country.'

He glanced at her. She seemed more angry than fearful.

'I agree,' he said. 'But I'm afraid Frank doesn't.'

'I just listened to a radio down in the cabin,' she went on. 'The whole world is collapsing.'

Neil felt a fear, partly of what she said and partly of her intensity.

'I imagine it is.'

'And we've done it,' she continued, again staring forward. 'Our country and Russia are destroying the world.'

Neil was aware that two of the women seated in the wheelhouse were looking at her uneasily.

'If we live through this madness we have to create a new world,' she said, her eyes seeming to make a personal appeal to Neil. 'We have to create a family, support each other, end the selfish divisions that led to this horror.' She looked at him for confirmation.

Neil felt an unaccountable heaviness. He supposed it was because he didn't think the species that killed a hundred million of its own kind in one day was likely to be too great on its next go-round. If there was a next go-round.

'First we have to survive,' he replied.

'Yes,' she said, seeming to relax some of her intensity. 'But, my God, how cold-hearted this war is making us survivors. I think you're the only friendly face I've seen all day.'

'Cornered and fleeing animals aren't nice,' Neil said.

She nodded and frowned. 'Back before you rescued me I could have killed with that butcher knife,' she said softly, looking, Neil saw, quite puzzled and a little saddened by the knowledge. 'How depressing that is.'

Neil didn't comment. Two passengers were leaning out over the coaming in the port cockpit and he wondered why until he saw that one of them was being seasick.

'And that's the way of madness,' Jeanne went on and, pausing, she looked up at him. 'I'm glad I spared you,' she said. Suddenly and unexpectedly she was smiling up at him.

'I am too,' Neil replied, smiling back.

'My personal Captain Luck,' she said.

'How so?' he asked, puzzled.

'You said that before we can create a new world we have to find the luck to survive,' she said, strangely gay all of a sudden. 'I guess I found you.' She paused. 'Although I hope your style isn't always to throw me overboard.'

After the horror of Point Lookout, Crisfield was as quiet and relaxed as a tourist and fishing town should be. There were no mobs and few boats. Neil supposed survivors from the Philadelphia area had more options to flee to than did those south and east of Washington and Baltimore.

After *Vagabond* was tied up at the dock in front of a large green fishing trawler named the *Lucky Emerald*, he assisted his passengers ashore. Most were bewildered; it seemed to Neil that if someone had offered them a boatride back to Point Lookout many of them would have crowded aboard. As they were leaving, Jeanne came up beside him where he stood overseeing the exodus.

'Can't we invite some of them to stay with us?' she asked him.

'That's Frank's decision to make,' he replied, feeling something of a liar. 'When he comes we can reconsider it.'

'They have no place to go,' she said.

'And we have nothing to feed them with,' Neil explained.

'I was in their place four hours ago,' she said, looking away.

'I know,' he said gently, frowning. 'But we can't save everybody. We'll be lucky if we can save ourselves.'

'We should try to save as many as we can,' she said.

'We haven't enough food to last ourselves more than two or three days,' he went on. 'That's our job now: to try to get some supplies aboard.'

'I'd like to invite that woman with the nursing child,' Jeanne persisted.

Neil looked at the retreating passengers.

'All right, Jeanne,' he answered. 'But let her know the food situation.'

While Jeanne hurried forward to overtake the nursing mother Neil turned to Jim. When he did, he saw that the man with the .45 was still sitting on the settee and beside him the much younger man, Jerry, with the pink shirt and green pants. Neil went over to them.

'What are your plans?' he asked the older man.

'What are yours?' the man countered.

'We wait here until ten to pick up the owner, then we're heading out of the Bay into the Atlantic.'

'All right.'

'All right what?'

'We'd like to come along.'

Neil studied the man. His business suit seemed somehow inappropriate, fraudulent. The man's round, unshaven face never seemed to vary its placid expression. The young man beside him was morose-looking.

'Who are you?' Neil asked.

'Conrad Macklin,' he replied. 'This is my friend Jerry.'

'What do you do?'

The man shrugged. 'I used to be a marine,' he said. 'Paramedic. After Vietnam, I flew planes, freelancing. Now . . . I sail a trimaran.'

'We don't have much food,' Neil said.

Macklin shrugged again.

'We're going shopping,' Neil said, feeling irritated. 'Could you two contribute some cash to the cause?'

Macklin took out his billfold, removed two hundred-dollar bills and handed them to Neil.

'Jim,' said Neil, turning away. 'I want you and Jeanne to go into town to the nearest supermarket and buy everything you can carry. I'll give you three hundred dollars and don't hesitate to pay double for anything you can get. Triple, if you have to.'

Jeanne reappeared in the wheelhouse alone.

'What happened?' Neil asked.

'She'd hooked up with a man and he had a car,' she answered, looking saddened that her offer had been rejected.

Neil wrote out a brief list of basics for Jeanne and Jim and sent them off. Skippy had fallen asleep during the sail, so Neil had Lisa begin making an inventory of the cans and boxes of food already on hand. Although uneasy about the presence of Macklin and his friend, he decided Macklin already had what he wanted – namely a boat to escape in – so now there should be no worry.

He worked briefly setting up Lisa with the inventory and then went back up into the wheelhouse.

'I've got an important job I'd like you to do for us,' he said to Macklin.

'Yes?'

'We've got a bent propeller shaft and can't get it out,' Neil explained. 'We need a slide-hammer puller, it's a tool. I want you to try the boatyard over there and see if you can rent, buy or borrow the tool. How about it?'

'Why don't you go?' Macklin asked.

Neil met the man's cold gaze with equal coldness.

'You'll help when I ask you to help or you're not sailing with us,' he said, feeling absurdly for an instant like he was in some western in which both he and Macklin were about to go for their guns.

Macklin in fact looked down at his .45, again cradled in his lap, and caressed the barrel once with his left hand.

'That sounds reasonable,' Macklin said and, standing, put the gun into a shoulder holster beneath his suit jacket. He smiled for the first time. 'Relax, captain,' he went on. 'I'm just out to save my ass like the rest of you.'

'A slide-hammer puller,' Neil repeated coldly.

'Got it.' Macklin ambled off the boat.

'And I want you,' Neil said to the man named Jerry, 'to go

along the docks and see if there's a water outlet we can get water from.' The man – he seemed only a couple of years older than Jim – nodded and went off.

The other thing is fishing gear, Neil thought, as his mind immediately returned to the task of preparing the ship for a long survival voyage. It would help if they had extra nylon line and metal lures, another rod too, maybe. Those might actually be easier to pick up than food. He looked restlessly ashore: Jeanne and Jim were already returning, and emptyhanded. The two of them jumped down on to the side deck and came over to him.

'There was a line forty yards long outside the supermarket,' Jeanne explained. 'And then the manager came out, counted about twenty people and told the rest of us to go home. He was closing after those twenty.'

'Every other grocery store was closed,' Jim added. 'Half of them were boarded up and the others had an armed guard.'

Neil simply nodded.

'Give me the money, Jeanne,' he said. As Jeanne fished in her pocket for the cash he went on to Jim, 'We need to get water aboard. All we can get. I sent that guy named Jerry to locate an open tap. Fill the tank and all the plastic jugs.'

'How about that leaky ten-gallon container?' Jim asked.

'That too,' Neil replied. 'I sent Macklin – that's the man with the .45 – after the puller. I'm going to take a shot at getting us some supplies. Stay here, get your .22 out again, and don't let anyone aboard except Macklin. When he's back, have him stand guard.'

'You trust him?' Jim asked.

'I trust him to keep unnecessary people off the boat,' Neil explained.

'Okay.'

Neil hesitated, gauging Jim's character.

'This time . . .' he began, as Jim looked at him attentively, 'if you feel you have to shoot . . . shoot.'

'Macklin?' asked Jim.

'Anybody,' Neil replied.

The situation in Crisfield was as Jeanne and Jim had described it. Fortunately, the local hardware store was open.

'Cash only,' a clerk announced as he entered. 'All prices triple what's marked.'

Neil went to the fishing gear section and quickly picked out three lures, two wire leaders and 500 feet of 30 lb test line. As he walked to the cashier he grabbed two kerosene lanterns. The manager said he didn't sell kerosene, but Neil bought the lamps anyway.

Back on the main street he considered his tactics. He'd hidden his gun under a loose-fitting jacket and the bag of supplies he was carrying. He'd become aware throughout the day of a feeling he hadn't had for a long time: that he was ready and able to kill, had in the past killed, and that this readiness gave him a power and confidence in this situation, since the missiles had started flying, that was essential for survival. He felt he could sense when others lacked that readiness – as with the grey-haired man on the yawl who was holding Jeanne – and when they *did* have it, as with Macklin.

This feeling of power had always bothered him, ever since he'd first sensed it in Vietnam more than a decade ago, but he knew it was now one of his chief assets.

Neil passed a closed grocery store behind the door of which sat a fat man with a shotgun across his knees. Neil felt it would be easy enough to take such a store, but it didn't feel right and he walked on. Ahead he saw a line of about twelve people outside a large Foodtown store. He went around to the back. The first rear entrance was locked but at the other end of the back of the building he saw another. A man with a white apron was exiting with an armload of boxes. When Neil followed him back to the door the clerk turned.

'You can't come in this way,' the young man said.

Neil pulled out a hundred-dollar bill and held it out to the clerk.

106

'I'd like to go in and do a little shopping for my family,' he said casually.

The boy squinted at the bill, grimaced and shook his head.

'I just can't do it,' he said. 'The manager would know.'

Neil let the hundred flutter to the ground and pulled out his gun.

'Tell the manager I pulled a gun on you but that I promised to pay double for all my food.'

Neil pushed past him, restoring his gun to his pants, and entered the back of the supermarket.

Inside was frenzied order: it was a normal supermarket except that people were all moving twice as fast as usual and their trolleys were twice as full. The shelves were three-quarters empty. The room was noticeably unlit, the usual harsh glitter of a supermarket absent. Neil looked back at the aproned clerk – whom he noticed pocketing something, presumably the hundred – and patted his waist where the gun was. The boy smirked uneasily.

Neil took an empty metal trolley and, putting in the bag of fishing gear, entered the fray. He knew he'd have to take what he could get. Which wasn't much. He found six cans of pears in syrup and eight cans of mixed fruit: that was all that was left in the canned fruit section.

In the dried fruit section he was luckier. Since dried fruit was ridiculously expensive and not that necessary except to a starving man, there was a lot left. Neil took it all. There was still dried noodles and spaghetti and he threw a bunch of that in. A large bag of potatoes. Frozen and refrigerated foods he avoided and with that thought he became aware that Crisfield had no electricity. He wondered how much of the rest of the world also lacked it. There were dried crackers left and he grabbed some, but all the canned meats were gone.

Forty minutes later, his trolley overflowing, Neil headed again for the back door. There was now a man standing beside it with a rifle held awkwardly with its butt on the floor. Neil took out all of the rest of his money, a hundred and sixty

107

dollars, and held it out.

'To save time I'd like to leave this back way,' he said. 'Here's what I owe plus a tip.'

'What's the trouble, Calvin?' a man asked, coming up behind Neil.

'He wants to leave the back way,' said Calvin.

'Here's more than enough money to cover my purchases,' said Neil.

'How much money you got?'

'A hundred and sixty dollars,' Neil said, handing it to him.

'Shit, mister,' the manager said, taking the money. 'This don't cover much more than half what you've got there. Our prices are triple.'

'Then I'll go to my boat and bring back more money.'

'You do that.'

Neil pulled out his gun and pointed it at the belly of the man with the rifle.

'I'll take my food with me now, though,' Neil said. '*Won't I?*' he asked the manager sharply.

'Let him go,' the manager said, backing away.

And Neil left.

As he pushed the trolley across the bumpy backlot of the supermarket he felt relief. The food situation had been his greatest worry. Now, although what he'd bought normally wouldn't last six people more than a week at the most, rationed it might go a month. He'd even brought a large container of dog food for the meat content for humans.

He picked up speed when he hit the smoother sidewalk of the main street. It was almost five o'clock, and if Macklin had obtained the puller, he could start work on the propeller shaft before Frank got back. If Frank got back.

When he came around the corner to head to the dock Neil stopped. He couldn't believe what he was seeing. Ahead of him was the fishing trawler *Lucky Emerald*, and in front of it was nothing. *Vagabond* was gone.

16

Abandoning the food cart in the parking lot Neil ran to the edge of the dock, his eyes searching the water for the trimaran. It wasn't in sight. Even while the dread in his stomach told him the boat had been pirated he tried to think of why else it might have been moved. Frank had returned and taken it to a boat yard . . . But they would have left someone to tell him, and as he let his eyes search up and down along the docks he saw no sign of either *Vagabond* or a member of its crew.

He needed a boat he could use to give chase. But chase where?

'Ahoy, *Lucky Emerald*!' he shouted at the trawler. A big, red-faced man came to the door of the deckhouse and looked down.

'What happened to the trimaran?' he shouted up.

The man looked to where *Vagabond* had been, then out into the bay.

'Sailed out of here close to an hour ago,' he said.

'Was there any trouble aboard?'

'Not that I saw.'

'Where'd she head?'

The man stroked his chin and scowled.

'Southwest,' he said. 'Out the main channel.'

'Have you got a small boat I can borrow to give chase?' Neil asked. 'My boat's been stolen.'

The man shook his head.

Neil went back to his food trolley and wheeled it up to the dock next to the *Lucky Emerald*.

'Keep an eye on this for me,' he shouted up and went to

find a boat. Macklin had pirated *Vagabond*. Neil raged at his own stupidity. He'd assumed Macklin wasn't a sailor and wouldn't try anything with a motorless sailing boat, but if he found a puller he may have felt he should take *Vagabond* while the taking was good. Poor Jim.

Over the next forty minutes Neil went down the docks and to two marinas trying to buy, borrow or steal some craft with which he could pursue his trimaran. No one would help him. Twice he was turned away by someone with a gun. After he'd gone to the last dock in the village he turned back in fury. He stopped a young man walking along carrying a fuel tank and asked him for help but got another 'Sorry, fellow.' On the street again, a police car came towards him with its siren wailing and Neil tried to wave it down. It whizzed past.

At the dock where *Vagabond* had been tied he saw Frank standing with his hands in his pockets staring dull-eyed out at the water.

'Frank!' he called.

'Where are you hiding *Vagabond*?' Frank asked with a puzzled frown as Neil came up to him.

'She's gone, Frank,' he answered. 'Stolen. Close to two hours ago.'

Frank's already tired face looked stunned.

'Wh . . . what?'

'Two men, I think,' he went on. 'And as far as I know Jim and Jeanne Forester and her children are still aboard.'

'Stolen?' Frank repeated, looking bewildered. He walked past Neil to the edge of the dock to look out the channel towards the bay. Several gulls circled behind a small runabout but there was no sign of *Vagabond*.

'We've got to get a fast boat and catch *Vagabond* before she gets too far down the bay,' Neil said to him.

Frank looked at Neil with glazed eyes and didn't reply. He hadn't shaved and looked haggard. He turned back to the water.

'If *Vagabond* gets too far away there's no hope for any of us,' Neil persisted. 'I can't get through to the Coast Guard by phone. We've probably got to get *Vagabond* ourselves. In another few hours everything will be lost.'

Neil saw that Frank was in shock and he felt a similar helplessness beginning to flood his own body. A small fishing smack putted slowly by along the channel and the little old man standing stiffly at the wheel looked at Neil and smiled and winked. Neil, engrossed, didn't register anything at first and then came alive.

'Hey, captain! Ahoy there!' he shouted, and ran to the edge of the dock.

The old man was facing forward again and Neil thought he must not have heard. He felt his shoulders slump, but the fishing smack abruptly swung left away from them and kept circling until it was motoring back to the dock. As Neil watched and Frank came up beside him, the boat, the *Lucy Mae*, angled into the dock.

'That boat's too slow,' Frank said.

'Not with this light wind and rising tide,' Neil answered and watched as the *Lucy Mae* coasted forward, banging first one piling and then the next, and being stopped inches short of the *Lucky Emerald* only by the old fisherman's wrapping a line around a piling.

'Pretty neat, huh?' the bald old man on the *Lucy Mae* said, smiling a big grin. 'Ain't got no reverse. Makes docking a challenge. Help you, Cap?'

'Yes,' Neil said quickly. 'Pirates stole our trimaran about two hours ago and kidnapped four of our people, including a woman, two children.'

'You own that big three engine spaceship?' the old man interrupted.

'Yes.'

'Saw her sailing out of here about four-thirty,' the old man said. 'Thought I'd got trapped in a *Star Wars* movie. Nice ship though, if you don't mind looking like you just got

111

in from Mars. When I . . .'

'Our ship was stolen,' Neil interjected. 'We'd like your help.'

'You mean chase the pirates?' the old man asked, scowling.

'Just help us locate them,' Neil said. 'That's all.'

'I'll pay you five thousand dollars,' Frank said.

'These fellas got guns?' the old man asked, squinting up at Neil.

'Yes, but . . .'

'And you want me to take you in the *Lucy Mae* and go poking around after them?'

'Yes,' said Neil. 'But we . . .'

'Well, git aboard,' the man said. 'Sun's gonna be settin' pretty soon and I don't see so good at night.' With a flip of his wrist he released the line from the piling and went back to his engine controls. Frank stood doubtfully on the dock but Neil rushed away to get the groceries aboard.

When he was back at the edge of the dock he lifted the whole trolley and lowered it to Frank in *Lucy Mae*'s cockpit. Frank couldn't quite handle all the weight and the trolley smashed down on to the deck and tipped over, the groceries spilling out like a load of dead fish. Neil leapt aboard.

'Let's go, Cap,' he said.

'Push out my bow there, sonny,' the old fisherman said to Frank, 'so my bowsprit don't go and goose *Lucky Emerald*. Cap'n Rivers is partic'lar who gooses her.'

Frank pushed out the bow, the old man shoved the gear into forward, and the old smack putted noisily forward, swinging round to head out towards the bay.

'I don't have the five thousand dollars, uh, easily at hand,' Frank said into the ear of the old man, Captain Olly, almost having to shout over the noise of the engine.

'I don't want no money, Cap,' Olly said. 'I ain't had a chance to get involved with pirates since . . . back in seventy-four I think it was . . .'

112

He turned the *Lucy Mae* a little to starboard to follow the channel to the open bay. 'And then the pirate was me.' Neil began picking up the rolling food cans and other groceries and righting the trolley.

'What you fellas think of this *war*?' Olly went on to Frank, who stared back at him dumbly.

'I sort of like it,' the old man said. 'Hell, I was planning to die this year anyway what with depression and gall bladders and all, but this here war makes everything interesting again.'

'My wife may have been killed in this interesting war,' Frank shouted in angry reply.

'Well, I figure there were four or five million other wives killed today,' the old man countered. 'Probably two or three of mine. Still, nothing beats being alive now, does it?'

Frank looked at the grinning, grotesque face in stunned silence.

'You fellas got any idea where these pirates are headed?' he asked amiably.

'No,' Neil replied sharply. 'But we've got to assume they're heading south.' Olly nodded.

'How fast will this thing go?' Neil shouted. Frank was standing off to the right scanning the horizon for a sight of *Vagabond*. There was a big motor yacht anchored off to port and several runabouts within sight, but no *Vagabond*.

'She'll do eight knots in the morning,' the old man shouted back, 'but in the late afternoon she gets a little pooped.'

'How much fuel?'

'Ten hours worth. With you big fellas aboard maybe only eight.'

As they churned out the channel from Crisfield, there was a large low island to their left which blocked their view to the south, and Neil strained impatiently for them to be past.

'Do you have binoculars aboard?' Neil asked.

''Fraid not,' the captain replied. 'Don't need glasses to see fish.'

Neil had been gauging the wind and tide and could feel hope rising. The tide was coming in and thus *Vagabond* would be bucking it if she headed south. The wind, still light, was out of the north so it wasn't much help to them either. Would they try to hide in a cove or inlet to repair the shaft? Would they sail between Tangier and Smith Islands to get into the main part of the bay? He thought of his own tactics if he were Macklin and decided he'd just head south as fast as possible. They could work on the shaft while sailing and if they were to be attacked by someone trying to re-take the boat the further out in the water they were the easier it would be to see any approaching enemy.

He took out his pistol and examined it to see if it had been damaged by the salt water. He removed the clip, cleaned it and put it back in. There were five bullets. He hesitated, sighted on a drifting piece of styrofoam and pulled the trigger. The gun 'banged' and the styrofoam shattered.

'You have any weapons aboard?' Neil asked the old man.

'What?' Captain Olly said, cupping his ear.

'Weapons! You got weapons aboard?' Neil shouted.

'Gaff. Boathook. Two knives. A harpoon. I mostly hunt fish.'

'Hey, there's water coming in over your cabin sole,' Frank shouted from the entrance to the little cabin forward. He looked back at the captain and Neil in alarm.

'Well, if it worries you,' the old man answered, 'you can exercise that pump there you got your right hand on. I don't generally pump until my bait box floats aft. You know how to pump?'

Frank saw that he had his hand on an old-fashioned manual bilge pump and without replying he began pulling it up and pushing it down.

'You spaceship pilots don't get much chance to pump bilges I 'spect,' the old man said to Neil with a grin. 'But it

114

keeps the body in trim, it does, 'specially in a gale when you figure you're two inches from havin' more water inside your boat than out.'

They had emerged past the island to port and Neil searched the sea horizon to the south. He estimated that *Vagabond* could be making only four or five knots through the water, and they were being headed by a knot and a half tide. In two hours they would thus have at the maximum a five or six mile lead. With binoculars he could see that far. With the naked eye . . .

He climbed up on the foredeck and then up on to the wheelhouse roof, balancing uncertainly as *Lucy Mae* rhythmically hobbyhorsed through the water.

There were dozens of boats in sight. He knew they were pouring down the Potomac from Washington and probably from the northern parts of the Bay too. Patiently he focused in on one distant boat after another. He hoped some emotional vibration would permit him to recognize *Vagabond* even if it were only a white speck on the horizon. He got no hit. He saw nothing which registered.

As *Lucy Mae* motored due south and left more and more of Cobble Island behind to port Neil began to sweep the horizon off to the east-southeast. It might make a certain sense to get out of the tidal flow in Tangier Sound and into the quieter waters of Pocomoke Sound. He saw what appeared to be a sloop three or four miles off but almost nothing else. The only advantage Macklin might find there was that any boat approaching him out of the main channel would be highly suspicious. He stared hard at the sloop again and suddenly he saw it was *Vagabond* sailing without her mizzen sail.

'Hard to port,' he yelled down at the old fisherman, and leapt back on to the foredeck and then into the cockpit.

'Our boat's at about east-southeast,' he said.

Captain Olly squinted through his dirty wheelhouse window and scowled.

115

'I'll take your word for it,' he said.

'Get these groceries out of sight, Frank,' Neil said. As Frank began to manoeuvre the trolley down below, Neil could see to his right a spectacular wash of red spreading across the horizon, the great grey mass from the explosion now an incongruously glorious red. Only the undersides of a few cumulus clouds were still touched with light, and then they too turned to pink. *Lucy Mae* chugged forward at only about six knots.

'You fellas got a plan?' the old man asked.

Neil and Frank looked at each other and when Olly saw that they hadn't he shook his head.

'You ain't got a *plan*,' he said, frowning at them like a disappointed father.

'If they're becalmed, we can offer to give them a tow,' Neil mused aloud.

'I don't think they's gonna be too trustful when they sees the men whose boat they just stole.'

'The two of us will hide below,' Neil went on. 'Captain, you offer them a tow or to sell them some food and bring *Lucy Mae* alongside the trimaran. Make one of them come aboard your boat to make their tow line fast or to check your food supplies. It'll be fairly dark by the time we overtake them. When one comes aboard *Lucy Mae*, I'll go out the forward hatch and rush the man still on *Vagabond*. You and Frank jump the man who's here on *Lucy Mae*.'

'Sounds good, sonny.'

'Can we go any faster?' Neil asked.

'Maybe, but those fellas may have binoculars; you fellas better lie low.'

'Frank,' Neil said, 'fix a large bag of groceries and leave it in sight. Store the rest in the cabin.'

Neil looked forward. The sun had set, but in the early twilight there was still sufficient visibility to permit them to see almost a mile. *Lucy Mae* chugged steadily east-southeast. Neil could no longer see *Vagabond*.

116

'I don't see it,' Frank said from beside him.

'Where?' Neil asked urgently, misunderstanding what he'd said.

'I said I don't see anything,' Frank shouted at Neil.

Cobble Island was still to their left and some shoals to their right and dead ahead . . .

'There she is!' Neil said, pointing, and there, barely visible a mile away in the dusk, its three hulls indicating it was probably going directly away from them, was *Vagabond*. Captain Olly slowed his boat slightly and squinted forward. All three of them were straining forward in the dusk as *Lucy Mae* chugged ahead loudly.

'GET BELOW!' Olly shouted, and just then the bright white flash of a spotlight from *Vagabond* swept over *Lucy Mae*.

Frank and Neil lowered their heads and scrambled forward into the little cabin. The old man opened up the throttle some to increase speed back to eight knots. He switched on his running lights.

'What are you going to do?' Neil shouted over the hammering of the engine. He was peering up at the old man from the cabin entrance.

'Same plan, sonny,' the captain yelled back and then motioned with his free hand for them to be quiet. That hand was trembling, and Captain Olly's face was now pale. His lips were drawn back exposing his gums and his few remaining teeth, giving his face a slightly mad expression. He kept his little craft motoring steadily forward, and the strange three-hulled, insect-like trimaran grew glacially out of the darkness towards him. For ten minutes they motored thus, Neil and Frank straightening up the grocery mess below, Captain Olly eventually singing softly to himself.

'Ain't gonna sink her 'til the sun sets low,' he began in a low, sometimes cracking voice. 'Don't care how much the wind does blow, I got a few fishies still to stow, so . . . ain't gonna sink her 'til the sun sets low . . . AHOY SPACESHIP' he

117

suddenly shouted and Neil took out his pistol and crawled forward to undo the forward hatch.

The *Lucy Mae* was only fifty feet behind and slightly to port of the slowly moving *Vagabond* when the old man hailed her. He slowed his ship slightly as he waited for an answer. There were two men in the unlit wheelhouse of the trimaran and one of them moved into the port cockpit.

'What do you want?' Jerry shouted.

'You fellas want me to give you a tow?' Olly shouted back. 'Do it pretty cheap.' He slowed *Lucy Mae* so she was going at the same speed as the slowly sailing trimaran, now only thirty feet away.

Jerry turned back to the man at the helm. 'No thanks,' he finally shouted back.

'You fellas stay on this course and in another two minutes you'll run aground,' Olly said amiably. The two men looked at each other and Macklin went forward to the instrument panel.

'Our depthmeter shows twelve feet of water,' he said loudly.

'Well, then, I reckon I must be ten feet tall,' the old fisherman said. ''Cause I get in my high boots and go clammin' right here every Saturday low tide and four feet of me sticks outa the water.'

Macklin stared again at *Vagabond*'s instrument panel.

'Get the boat hook,' he ordered Jerry.

Olly slipped *Lucy Mae*'s throttle forward and eased the boat slowly ahead against the tide and towards the port side of the big trimaran. It was almost dark.

'Careful of the sharks,' Captain Olly suggested quietly.

'What sharks?' the young man who'd got the boat hook asked nervously as he approached the side of the trimaran to test the depth.

'School of small sharks feedin' here in the shoals. Better not put your hand too near the water.'

Lucy Mae was moving slowly ahead only a foot or two

118

from *Vagabond*. Jerry stood uncertainly with the boat hook and looked back at Macklin.

'You fellas sure you don't want me to give you a tow out of here? Only cost you fifty bucks an hour.'

'Who the hell *are* you?' Macklin burst out and turned the spotlight on, sweeping the length of the *Lucy Mae* and then holding steady for a moment on the old man.

'Cap'n Oliver Mann,' the old man answered, smiling a toothless grin up into the light. 'Cap'n Olly, they calls me. Just an old geezer tryin' to earn a crooked buck. You want some Colombian pot? Or I can sell you this here bag of groceries cheap, too. Cost only forty.'

'That's twice what it must have cost,' Macklin barked back, turning off the spotlight.

'Cost yesterday,' the old man replied, still smiling. 'Price tripled today. Be eight times tomorrow, I reckon.' *Lucy Mae* bumped the side of *Vagabond*. 'Hold this line, will ya, young fella?' Captain Olly went on and tossed a mooring line to the man with the boat hook, who instinctively grabbed it and made it fast to a cleat on the forepart of *Vagabond*'s port cockpit.

'Let's see your groceries,' Macklin said, coming over to stand beside Jerry, his big gun clenched in his right hand.

'It's right here, sonny,' the old man said amiably, turning on his flashlight and pointing it at the big bag of groceries.

'Hand it up here and let's have a look,' Macklin said.

'I ain't got enough strength in my back to lift a tea cup off a saucer,' Captain Olly said. 'One of you young fellas have to come aboard and haul it out.'

'Hand it up here,' Macklin repeated.

'I tell you, sonny, my back won't take it.'

'I'll get it,' said Jerry.

'No,' said Macklin, suddenly shoving Jerry away from where he had begun to board *Lucy Mae*. 'There's something wrong about all this. Get the .22.'

'Suit yourself, fella,' Captain Olly said indifferently,

switching off the flashlight and leaving everyone only barely visible in the darkness and the dim red glow of *Vagabond*'s portside running light. 'I've made a lot of money today towing sailing boats. If you . . .'

'Raise your hands and climb up here,' Macklin snapped, crouching with his gun aimed at Olly, his eyes flicking nervously over the length of the *Lucy Mae*. Jerry returned with Jim's .22 and stood beside Macklin.

'Now what you want me . . .' Olly began protesting when the forward hatch cover clattered on to the foredeck. Macklin swung his gun and fired past Jerry, and two shots exploded from Neil's gun. Macklin and Jerry disappeared behind the coaming of the cockpit.

After the three sudden explosions in the darkness, a silence descended on the two boats, which rocked gently side by side in the small swells. *Vagabond*, left untended, began swinging up into the wind, her sails fluttering as they luffed.

'Jerry?' Macklin called hoarsely from the other side of the trimaran.

The only answer was the rough hum of *Lucy Mae*'s idling engine and the gentle slapping of the sails. For twenty seconds, then thirty, no one spoke. Olly was crouched in his cockpit peering up at the vacant space where Macklin and Jerry had been standing. Neil stood with his head and shoulders out of the forehatch, his gun aimed at the wheelhouse entrance, which he could just make out in the darkness. A small stream of blood crept down his left arm – pierced by splinters from *Lucy Mae*'s shattered hatch opening.

'Your friend's dead, sonny,' Captain Olly finally shouted. 'Better come over here and give up.'

The silence resumed. Neil, feeling certain he had hit Jerry, pulled himself quietly out on to *Lucy Mae*'s deck and crawled over on to the foredeck of the trimaran; he felt Macklin must be in the opposite cockpit. He crawled swiftly across *Vagabond*'s entire width forward of the cabins and crouched on the foredeck on the opposite side from *Lucy Mae*.

Olly had felt his boat rock as Neil's weight shifted to *Vagabond* so he called out again to draw Macklin's attention.

'We got four men here with automatic rifles, sonny,' he shouted. 'Better get on over here with your hands held high.'

Macklin again didn't respond. Peering aft, Neil couldn't see any dim bulk crouched in the starboard cockpit as he had expected. Macklin must be close to Frank's cabin hatchway. He wondered where Jim and Jeanne were. If Macklin were to take them as hostages they were in trouble, but even so he didn't dare risk his life now by rushing him. He crouched and waited to see the effect of the old fisherman's propaganda campaign.

'Three to one, ain't good odds, sonny,' Olly's high-pitched voice called out through the darkness. 'If you're not over here in the next minute we're going to come after you.'

Neil could still see no sign of Macklin and suddenly had the unnerving conviction that Macklin wasn't there, that he, Neil, had again miscalculated. He glanced down behind him into the water, then to the other cockpit, but nothing moved. He strained his vision again to see some sign of Macklin in the starboard cockpit, strained his ears to pick up the slightest movement.

'I surrender.'

The words, spoken quietly, reached Neil from the area he'd been so desperately searching.

'I'm throwing my gun across the top of the cabin,' Macklin continued. Something clattered across the cabin top.

'Come over here with your hands behind your head,' Olly shouted. A flashlight suddenly lit the wheelhouse from *Lucy Mae*'s cockpit. Macklin abruptly appeared in the light, his empty hands behind his head, moving slowly. He had to step over something before emerging into the centre of Olly's light in the cockpit near the *Lucy Mae*. As Neil glided over the cabin tops Frank came up over *Vagabond*'s coaming and picked up the .22.

'We've got him, Neil,' he called, holding the .22 on Macklin.

When Neil arrived he saw Frank and Macklin staring down at Jerry, who lay in a pool of blood, his open eyes fixed.

'I told him not to do it,' Macklin said quietly. 'But he said you were going to kick us off.'

Frank and Neil stared at him.

'I got that puller tool you asked for,' he said to Neil.

As Frank broke away to throw back the port hatch to search for Jeanne, Neil watched Macklin.

'Are any of our people hurt?' he asked coldly.

'Your people are all a lot healthier than Jerry.'

'They'd better be,' said Neil and, as he heard Jeanne's voice, he began to feel relief: *Vagabond* was again theirs.

17

An hour and a half later *Vagabond* lay at anchor, *Lucy Mae* still tied to her port side. After the initial exhilaration and relief of being reunited, those aboard were in various states of disorientation and exhaustion. Jeanne, Jim and Lisa had all been hurt resisting the taking of *Vagabond*, and Neil during its rescue. Jim had bruised ribs, a bloody nose and cut and sore wrists where they had bound him. Jeanne's left cheek had a swollen and bluish bruise where Macklin had hit her when she'd tried to help Jim. When Lisa had begun pounding on Macklin's back, Jerry had struck her on the side of the head with the butt of his gun. Neil had a two-inch long, half-inch wide wood sliver lodged in his left arm. Conrad Macklin had examined Lisa's head right after her injury and again when *Vagabond* had been sailing away and told Jeanne that Lisa probably had a minor concussion but no fracture. He offered now to pull the splinters from Neil's arm, but after first refusing, Neil soon concluded that Jeanne and Frank were being too gentle in their probes. He finally let Macklin coolly butcher the splinters out.

Later, after tying Macklin's hands behind him and to the mizzen mast and placing Jim as guard, they buried Jerry at sea. Jeanne came up on deck and saw Neil, Frank and Olly standing in the dim light of the wheelhouse with Neil reading in a low voice from the Bible. She stood momentarily mesmerized by the weird scene, continuing on when Neil stopped reading and he and Olly lifted the body up and slid it overboard. The whole experience was so unreal, so disconnected from her previous life, that she staggered down the steps to the main cabin for the reassuring sight of pots, pans, a kitchen – anything to erase the horror of those three dim figures in the cockpit, like warlocks chanting some imprecation, and then throwing a body into the sea.

She prepared coffee not because anyone had asked her to but to ground herself, to re-establish everyday reality. When Frank came down he looked concernedly at Jeanne and came over to take her in his arms again. His white sports shirt was sweat-stained and grimy, his grey hair wet with sweat. He had embraced her after the initial rescue and she had clung to him as a brother or father, a haven in the insane chaos that was raining upon her.

'Coffee or scotch?' Jeanne now asked Frank. Captain Olly was already sipping at a cup of scotch – caffeine being 'bad for the teeth'.

'Both,' Frank replied and sat down with a great sigh on the settee opposite Olly, who was now slumped sideways and snoring.

When Neil appeared he stopped with uncharacteristic uncertainty at the foot of the steps. He accepted a cup of coffee from Jeanne with a mechanical smile, his severe face showing none of the warm attention to her it had shown so often throughout the day.

'We should be getting under way,' Neil said to Frank, who sat with his back to him. Frank stared into the bronze glow of his whisky and in a single swallow tossed it off. When Frank didn't reply Jeanne asked: 'Where are we going?'

'It's my judgement we should sail out the Bay to the ocean,' Neil replied, looking at Frank's back.

Frank turned on the transistor radio on the shelf above the dinette table and after a moment obtained a working station. As they all began listening to a radio report of the events of the day Jeanne exchanged a strangely conspiratorial glance with Neil and then sat down beside Frank, instinctively placing her hand on top of his.

The nuclear war was exactly one day old and already, although someone claimed both sides were showing 'restraint',

124

every European country and most regions of the United States had been hit. The US retaliation on the Soviet Union was described as if it were even more devastating than the blows the US had received. A statement from the President indicated that the war would be fought to the bitter finish, no matter what the consequences. The President said that he expected every citizen to do all he could to support the American effort against the world-destroying Soviet Union. A state of martial law had been declared, requiring everyone to obey the military as the law of the land.

Finally Frank reached up to his right and turned off the radio. 'I couldn't get to Norah,' he said to no one in particular.

'No planes available?' Neil asked.

'Nothing to pay with,' Frank replied. 'I have no money.'

In the silence that followed Jeanne became aware of Neil's unanswered call to get going hovering over the room.

'What are we going to do now?' she asked Frank gently.

'I don't know,' Frank answered.

'Macklin obtained a puller,' Neil said, 'and they loosened the old shaft. Jim and I should be able to put in the new one and get the prop on in less than an hour. Then we should sail south.'

Frank turned in his settee seat to look past Jeanne at Neil still standing at the foot of the companionway steps.

'What about Bob?' he asked. 'What about Captain Olly? What about the rest of the country?'

It seemed strange to Jeanne to hear someone asking about Bob. It was like an inquiry into another lifetime.

'Bob is dead,' she said automatically.

'The radioactive cloudbank from Washington is still spreading,' Neil went on. 'The fallout will get worse. I doubt we can survive unless we get east and south. Fast.'

With a wave of fear Jeanne suddenly saw in Frank's haggard face that he was in a state of shock, that he was barely there. She saw a vague irritation cross his features when Neil spoke, but no comprehension.

'Then . . . we should get under way,' she said softly and stood up. Looking back at Frank she saw him turning to pour himself another small glass of whisky.

'We've got new food supplies in Olly's smack,' Neil said to her. 'I'd like you and Olly to transfer them over to *Vagabond* and then you can begin storing them.'

'All right,' she answered, aware of how gently Neil was speaking to her.

'We're running away,' Frank announced in a low, husky voice.

'I hope so,' Neil snapped back.

'What else is there we can do?' Jeanne asked quickly.

Frank tossed off his second drink, slid himself sideways and stood up. 'When I know, we'll do it,' he said. 'HEY! YOU!' he shouted at the sleeping fisherman, who awoke, startled and blinking. 'You want to join us on an ocean cruise?'

Captain Olly squinted dazedly at Frank. 'I gotta son I want to see,' Olly replied, frowning.

'Well, then, you'll have to shove off,' Frank said. 'We're only taking cowards and deserters.' He brushed past Jeanne and Neil and up the companionway. Neil and Olly followed.

'What are we going to do with this load of filth?' Frank asked, stopping to stare at Conrad Macklin, who was seated bound to the base of the mizzen mast with his arms tied behind his back. Jim was seated on a settee seat guarding him, a bandaged forehead and bluish bruise on his lower rib cage indicating his wounds.

'I'm sorry we stole your boat,' Macklin said unexpectedly.

'I say we dump him overboard,' Frank went on fiercely, turning to Neil. 'I tried to get through to the Coast Guard to come arrest him, but the man on duty said we'd have to bring him in.'

'To where?' Neil asked.

'Their station at Crisfield.'

'We're not wasting time going back there.'

'Throw him overboard.'

A silence followed, Macklin looking expressionlessly at Frank. When Jeanne came up into the wheelhouse he looked at her.

'I'm sorry about your girl,' he said. 'Jerry didn't mean to hurt her.'

'SHUT UP!' Frank shouted, taking a step towards Macklin and flushing with anger.

'Ignore him, Frank,' said Neil. 'Jim, get into your scuba gear. We're going to put the new propeller shaft in.'

When Jim went forward to change, and Jeanne and Olly began transferring the food from *Lucy Mae*, Frank sat down and put his face in his hands. Neil remained facing Macklin.

'I panicked,' Macklin went on quietly, his eyes as expressionless as always. 'Jerry was convinced that without food you were going to kick us off the boat before we cleared the Chesapeake. When I got back with that tool he'd already taken over the boat without me. Ask Jim.' He looked up at Neil with an anguished expression which Neil couldn't quite believe. 'Take me with you. I can help.'

Frank erupted from his seat and grabbed Macklin by the throat, sending his head crashing back against the mizzen mast. 'SHUT UP! YOU STUPID BASTARD!' he shouted. 'You say another word and I'll kill you!'

Neil pulled Frank away. 'Help Olly and Jeanne,' he said to him quietly.

For a moment Frank stood looming over Macklin; Neil could feel him trembling.

'I can't stand that kind of talk,' Frank said, finally moving away. 'A man steals my boat, hits a woman in the face, has his crony almost kill Lisa, and expects us to forgive him. Jesus!'

As he led his friend over towards the *Lucy Mae*, Neil

couldn't respond. He was disturbed to remember that he himself had been perfectly ready to steal a boat to go chase after *Vagabond*. And would he have let Macklin and Jerry stay if they'd got no additional food?

Now left alone with Macklin, Neil knelt down to remove the large section of the floor to get at the engine. He took a flashlight out of the tool chest lying on the shelf above the engine to examine the state of the repairs.

'You need me, Captain Loken,' Macklin suddenly said to him in a whisper. 'You need my medical skills. You need someone else aboard this ship with your cold will to survive. You can use me.'

Neil pushed himself back up to a kneeling position to look at Macklin in the dim light. Macklin was staring at him serenely.

'The others have too much heart to survive in this world,' Macklin went on. 'You can use me, you know it. I didn't want to take this boat. I can't sail. Without Jerry I'm no threat to turn pirate again.'

Neil looked back at him without expression. 'Despite your cold will to survive,' he said, 'the helpless people with too much heart have tied you to a mast and are about to throw you overboard.'

Jeanne and Frank came into the wheelhouse carrying bags of groceries and disappeared down into the main cabin.

'You know Frank won't kill me,' Macklin whispered. 'That woman wouldn't let him. Only you are strong enough and cold enough to kill me, but you need another man like me. And you need a doctor. You know it.'

'With you around we'd damn well need somebody's medical skills,' Neil said.

When Jim came into the wheelhouse dressed in his wetsuit, Neil stood up. 'If Frank agrees, we're dumping you ashore at the first opportunity,' he said to Macklin.

'I'm a fighter, Loken,' Macklin said in a normal voice. 'You need another fighter.'

'I can use your .45,' Neil replied, nodding to Jim to pick up the new shaft. 'The rest of you, no. Let's get to it, Jim.'

18

Because she felt herself moving in a dream from which she might momentarily awaken Jeanne was partially detached from all she did. The pedestrian act of bringing groceries into the galley was slightly unhinged by having to pass by the dark figure of Macklin bound to the mast whispering greedily to Neil. Later she could hear Neil and Jim grunting and swearing as they worked on the engine shaft, and as she traipsed to and fro between the two boats she became aware that around *Vagabond* was a vast darkness. There were no lights to be seen now in any direction, and although stars shone above them the whole northwestern third of the sky was ominously dark. She had managed to put away almost half the food in the galley when the propeller shaft was finally fixed, the engine tested, and the sails again raised. With the men shouting to each other on the deck above her, Olly poked his head into the galley and said an awkward goodbye. In another moment she felt the steady hiss of water along the sides of the hull at her feet; the anchor was up and they were sailing.

And then, in a casual, almost routine way, the nightmarish side of her dreamworld began again. They had been sailing no more than a minute or two, she still working in the galley, now lit by a kerosene lamp, when the companionway to the wheelhouse, which had been dark, was filled with light. She heard Neil shout: 'Don't look!' and a moment later Frank's voice: 'Get the sails down!'

She felt a wave of weakness and despair sweep over her. She braced herself, expecting the boat now to be hit as her car had been by the force of the blast. She heard and felt feet rushing across the cabin roof and again Frank's voice shouting something to Jim. The sails began to flutter and snap as they did when the boat came up into the wind. She still crouched by the galley stove, her teeth clenched, her hands clutching the counter top.

A screeching sound cut into the flapping sails – the sails being lowered? – and then Neil's face appeared in the cabin entrance.

'Batten everything down!' he shouted. He started to leave but, catching her blank expression, he turned back. 'Big waves may be hitting us from the blast. Store everything where it can't get loose and fly around.'

While she began putting the dishes and remaining groceries away helter-skelter into drawers and cabinets Jim leapt down into the cabin.

'I'll help,' he said and, kneeling, pushed back the carpet and removed a section of the floor. 'We'll store the rest of the food in the bilge for now,' he added.

By the time she and Jim had battened everything down in the main cabin and come back up into the wheelhouse, the glow to the south, over Norfolk Jim told her, was large and growing, but not as bright as the blast over Washington. The sails were tied down and the boat motoring slowly north, its diesel engine barely audible.

When Jeanne checked Lisa and Skippy she was surprised to see that someone had tied them into the berth: two half-inch lines across the top of the blanket attached to fittings in the far wall and at the edge of the berth near the cabin walk space. They couldn't roll out.

'Hold on, Jeanne!' she heard Frank shout and then became aware of a hissing, swishing sound growing closer. She grabbed the handrail of her own berth just as *Vagabond* was struck by a noisy moiling wash of water. The breaking waves threw *Vagabond* forward, swinging Jeanne around and slamming her into the wall beneath her berth.

But that was all. The rushing sound continued and

Vagabond seemed to be surging and rocking, but the blow seemed relatively harmless. Her children didn't even waken.

Back up on deck she saw Frank, looking grim, handling the wheel and looking to his right where she could see another boat, the *Lucy Mae*, easing alongside. With Neil and Jim assisting, the two ships were again tied to each other, both motoring slowly forward.

'I came back for dessert,' Olly said to her from his cockpit and smiled an elfin smile.

Neil returned to the wheelhouse. 'We ought to motor into deeper water,' he said to Frank.

'You think there'll be more waves?' Frank asked.

'In two or three hours there may be some huge waves,' Neil replied intensely. 'The water near the blast area will have been hit with tremendous force and sent rolling up the Bay. These little things that are hitting us now are just from the local shock wave.'

'How much time do we have?' Frank asked.

'If the waves are moving at twenty to thirty knots, probably about two hours. Maybe more.'

'In that time we could get ourselves into the lee of Tangier Island,' Captain Olly said.

'That would be good,' said Neil.

'Let's do it,' agreed Frank.

Neil and Olly were now both frowning over at the *Lucy Mae*.

'Olly,' Neil said. '*Vagabond*'s made for big seas, but the *Lucy Mae* will be swamped and sunk if the big ones hit before we make the lee of Tangier. I think you ought to anchor and come with us.'

'How much warning you figure we'll get?' Olly asked.

'If this light holds we should be able to see big waves coming from quite a distance . . . about a minute's warning,' Neil answered. 'But Christ, Olly, we can't know even that for sure.'

131

Olly nodded. 'Why don't we both motor side by side,' he said. 'I'd like to try to make it.'

'Okay,' agreed Neil. 'Stay close in our lee. If we see danger we'll signal with the air horn and turn due north away from the waves. You motor over and board us. Figure you have about thirty seconds. Why don't we send Jim with you to help you prepare to abandon your ship if the time comes?'

'Sounds fine to me, sonny,' Olly said. 'How big you figure these waves'll be?'

'Too big,' Neil replied.

The two vessels were soon speeding through the rough water thirty feet apart, headed northwest to hide behind the northern end of Tangier Island fourteen miles away. Jeanne could see *Lucy Mae* rolling and pitching in the short steep waves sent northward by the local shock waves. *Vagabond*'s motion was less, since her three hulls made her more like a huge sailing raft, but the waves still smashed into the port hull with ominous crashing sounds.

After becoming queasy while preparing some hot tea in the galley, Jeanne remained in the wheelhouse. Frank was steering while Neil with the binoculars was keeping a lookout south for the anticipated larger waves.

It must have been something like two hours later – Jeanne had fallen asleep on the settee – with the two boats still running side by side, and now only half a mile from Tangier Island and nearing the protection of its northern end, that Frank's shout awakened Jeanne.

When she sat up she saw Neil now at the wheel grab the airhorn and shoot out four loud blasts. Frank, with the binoculars, ran into the cabin to come up beside him.

'It's a WALL OF WATER!' he shouted.

'Help Olly and Jim get aboard,' Neil shouted back, glancing to his right where already the *Lucy Mae* was approaching. 'Jeanne! Get below!'

But she simply took hold of one of the wooden supports of

the wheelhouse roof and looked back at him dumbly.

'Untie me!' Macklin said fiercely, but Neil, ignoring him, slowed *Vagabond* slightly to permit *Lucy Mae* to come up alongside. Jim threw an armful of things into the cockpit and then disappeared for more. Olly handed something to Frank and shouted to Jim to get off. Frank was trying to hold the two boats together as they rolled and smashed into each other's sides while Olly next turned back to his steering wheel, and tied a line to one of its spokes. When Jim had thrown the last of the *Lucy Mae*'s salvageable gear on to the trimaran and boarded, Olly jumped aboard *Vagabond*, tugging on the line. The *Lucy Mae*, still under power, swung away and ploughed at a right angle out into the darkness.

'Damn pretty boat,' Olly commented as he watched her go.

All the hatches and door slides had been put in place earlier and now everyone except Neil crouched in the wheelhouse looking aft through the plexiglas window at the low wall of water growing out of the horizon behind them, the wall made visible by the huge hill of light which filled the low southern sky from the explosion over Norfolk.

'Untie me!' Macklin pleaded to Jeanne who looked past him at the approaching water.

Neil had opened *Vagabond*'s diesel to full rpm and *Vagabond* rushed forward away from the tidal wave at over nine knots, but the wall still grew towards them, a roaring sound now clearly heard as the wave smashed along the shore of Tangier Island. Neil had swung the boat slightly towards the island, but when the wave was only a hundred feet away he turned back to put *Vagabond*'s stern directly to the racing sea.

The first wave was over twenty feet high, a mound of water rather than a wall, a cap of white froth bubbling down its forward side. The roaring noise grew louder, the wave grew immense, and then was upon them, first lifting *Vagabond*'s stern, then burying it as it struck at three times

133

Vagabond's speed into her three hulls, a river of water ten feet high rushing across the whole boat, smashing through the rear of the wheelhouse, hurling the trimaran forward at twice her earlier speed, hurling Olly, Jim, Jeanne and Frank in a heap against the wall and hatch-slide of the main companionway and tangling Olly in Neil's feet where he stood clutching the wheel.

Jeanne, crushed up against the cabin wall by the cold salt water swirling over her, choked and gasped as she struggled upwards in a nightmare of drowning, clawing at the wall as the water seemed still to pin her down. Frank grasped her arm and pulled her sputtering up into his arms, clinging himself to the control panel shelf.

The water was up to her knees and she assumed that they were sinking, but then she saw Neil looking back over his shoulder with a look of concentration devoid of dismay. The roar was still all around and she felt they must be hurtling through the water at some fantastic speed, but even as she thought this, she saw Neil actually increase *Vagabond*'s speed.

'We'll anchor behind Tangier Island just as we planned,' he shouted to all of them. 'It'll take us a while to pump her out and clean up.'

The water had already fallen to her ankles, some of it pouring into the main cabin through the broken hatch-slide and the rest draining out of the holes of the self-bailing cockpits and wheelhouse.

Jim crawled forward to prepare the anchor, while Frank stared at the smashed fragments of plywood, fibreglass, and plexiglas that had been the back wall of his wheelhouse.

'Not too many boats going to be floating after *that* ripple,' Olly said to Neil with an uncharacteristically grim expression.

'Check our main bilge, Olly,' Neil countered.

'Jesus, what's the use,' said Frank. 'Every time we . . .'

'Go check your starboard cabin bilge,' Neil interrupted.

'Jeanne, check your children. 'We've survived.'

Vagabond had had ten tons of water sweep over her, had over half a ton in her three bilges from stove-in windows and hatchslides, and had a wrecked wheelhouse rear wall, but all her rigging had come through intact. In another half hour they had pumped or bucketed out most of the uninvited water and were anchored behind what was left of Tangier Island. They set up a rotation of two-hour watches and, numb, shell-shocked, exhausted to the point of not caring, all at last were permitted to sleep.

19

Neil didn't waken until nine o'clock the following morning and thus had five full hours sleep, a luxury after the previous forty-eight. As he emerged from his damp cabin he could feel anxiety and irritation moiling within him. In the daylight he saw clearly for the first time the extent of the wreckage of the aft wall of the wheelhouse, saw Olly's gaffs, fishing nets, oyster tongs and other gear still sitting unstored in the starboard cockpit, saw the wrecked cabin hatchslide, noted Frank sprawled asleep on one of the wheelhouse settees – it was Frank's watch – and felt a strong breeze blowing now out of the north. The thought that they had been sitting still doing nothing for almost seven hours rankled him and he had to stop on the aft deck to quiet himself.

But as he gazed around the Bay an entirely different emotion flooded him. A house was floating only a hundred yards to the east; on the shore of Tangier Island were the remains of several wrecked houses and boats. On the island itself not a single building seemed to remain standing. Further to the south was another now familiar ghastly grey mass squatting in the otherwise clear blue sky like an ugly swelling toad. Whatever he didn't like about the condition of *Vagabond* she was afloat; she had survived.

As he stepped down into the starboard cockpit to begin work he stopped, fear again slicing through him like an icicle. *Where was Macklin?* He'd been left still tied to the mizzen mast. Neil leapt down into the starboard cockpit, ran into the wheelhouse and then stopped: Macklin was seated non-chalantly in the sun of the opposite cockpit sipping coffee. Jeanne emerged from the main cabin and behind her he saw Lisa at the galley stove.

'Good morning,' she said.

'How'd he get loose? Neil asked grimly.

Jeanne flushed in response to Neil's anger. 'He was free when I got up,' she replied. 'Can I fix you something for breakfast?'

Neil walked further into the port cockpit and saw with a start that the .22 was lying across Macklin's knees.

'Good morning,' said Macklin neutrally.

'May I have the rifle?' Neil asked.

'Sure,' said Macklin. 'It's of no use to me.' He placed his coffee cup on the seat beside him and handed the .22 to Neil. 'But look, Loken, let me sail with you. Putting me ashore would mean death.'

'How did you get loose?' Neil asked quietly, noting that the .22 he had taken from Macklin was loaded.

'Child's play,' Macklin replied with a sneer.

'Why didn't you take the dinghy and escape?'

'Escape, shit,' Macklin snapped. 'There's no escape out there. My only chance – I admit it's smaller than a flea's cock –' he added parenthetically, glancing to his left at the blast cloud over the Norfolk area, 'is on this ship. Don't sentence me to die.'

'Are you all right?' Neil asked Jeanne, turning back to her.

'Yes. I thought you had released him.'

He nodded, grimacing.

'Would you like to eat now?' Jeanne asked again.

'Thanks,' Neil answered. 'Use whatever's in the refrigerator first--bacon, cheese, other things that will spoil when we turn off the propane to conserve it for cooking. Don't cook potatoes, for example.'

'Fine,' she said, disappearing down into the galley.

'Cook for everyone,' he called after her. As he looked down into the galley he was pleased to see that although the area was a mess it was a functioning mess: Jeanne and Lisa had removed all the food from the bilge where some of it had been damaged by the previous night's deluge and were inventorying

137

and restoring it. He noted too that Jeanne and her two children were dressed as neatly as for a quiet summer cruise, their white shorts and blouses seeming out of place with the big bluish bruise on Jeanne's cheek and the bloody bandage on the side of Lisa's head. Skippy was looking shyly up at him, clinging to one of his mother's bare thighs.

'Can you keep an eye on Skippy for me?' Jeanne called up to him.

'Of course.'

But Skippy didn't need an eye kept on him since he remained with his mother down in the main cabin, clinging to her as if she were safe space in a game of tag. He ignored her suggestion that he go up with Neil and look at a comic book and limited his conversation to periodic statements to his mother: 'I'm hungry.'

Lisa came up to where Neil was examining the wrecked wheelhouse wall to hand him a cup of coffee. The bandage on the left side of her face was immense and had a blot of red in the middle, but she told him that though it hurt and throbbed she felt no dizziness.

'Here comes somebody,' she added unexpectedly, squinting off to the northeast.

Following her gaze, Neil turned to see a small skiff motoring at full throttle towards them, a man standing aft, steering. Neil picked up the .22 again and cradled it in his arm. At first he assumed the man was headed towards the village of Tangier, but the skiff kept coming straight in and coasted to a halt alongside the starboard hull. A small, deeply tanned young man about Jim's age wearing dirty khakis and a soiled cotton sweatshirt looked over *Vagabond*'s coaming at them.

'My father here?' he asked.

'Who's that?' Neil countered.

'Cap'n Olly.'

'He's sleeping in the forepeak, I think.'

'Hey, pa! PA! It's Chris!' the young man shouted.

138

After a moment the old man poked his head up out of the forward hatch and then emerged, his sparse white hair askew; he was dressed only in tee-shirt and underpants.

'Well, you don't have to shout about it,' he grumbled, looking aft, and seeing Lisa standing twenty feet away staring at him, he disappeared back below to get his trousers on.

''Pears you had some waves come visiting last night,' Chris said to Neil, nodding solemnly at the wrecked wall of the wheelhouse.

'We did,' Neil agreed. 'How about you?'

'Well, most of the houses on Smith Island are a few hundred feet further north than they used to be and there aren't many people left to give a damn.' Chris glanced to his right. 'Tangier must have really got socked.'

'I'm afraid so.'

'Good morning, ma'am,' Chris said to Jeanne, who had come up into the wheelhouse.

'Good morning.'

'Well, what you want?' Captain Olly asked when he came out on deck a second time, buttoning up his trousers. 'Getting so a man can't even escape his own family out to sea.'

'I was worried about you, pa,' his son said. 'They said you went chasing pirates or something and then the tidal wave last night, and you didn't come back.'

'Well, I'm back,' he said. 'Got myself two pirates. Woulda gotten more, but there weren't none.'

'Where's *Lucy Mae*?'

'I sent her into Crisfield to pick me up some pipe tobacco.' Chris looked at his father uncertainly.

'We had to cut her loose when the big wave was about to hit,' Neil explained. 'I imagine she's sunk.'

'You okay?' Chris asked his father.

''Course I'm okay. I been dying for two years now and chasin' pirates and dodging tidal waves ain't gonna affect it none. What you been up to? You remember the mayonnaise?'

'I'm going in the Navy, pa.'

139

'What do you mean you're going in the Navy?' the old man countered, seated now on the cockpit bench near his son and pulling on his socks. 'Why you want to go in the Navy?'

'Because I have to,' Chris answered.

'How have to? Why have to? What are you talking about?'

'The President ordered us to,' Chris answered quietly. 'Everybody has to go. I'm taking a special bus this morning at eleven from Salisbury.'

'What's the hurry?' Captain Olly said irritably. 'Navy got a ship needs bailing this afternoon?'

'I've got to go, pa,' Chris insisted.

Captain Olly stood up and looked out across the aft deck towards Smith Island. He stood silently for almost half a minute while his son watched him patiently.

'Well,' the old man finally said. 'Give me a goodbye kiss. Ain't every day a son goes putt-putting off to get himself blown to bits.' He took a step towards his son and presented his grizzled cheek. Chris kissed him awkwardly. Captain Olly straightened up but remained looking down at his son.

'One of them H-bombs come after you, you remember to stay below,' he said.

'You know me, pa,' Chris said, smiling boyishly. 'If I know one's coming I'll want to come on deck to look.'

'Know you will, son, know you will. I figure in another week you'll come raining down into the Atlantic.'

Chris stared at him.

'Don't mind me, son,' Olly said, tears glistening in his eyes. 'I just wish you'd stole a boat and sailed into the Atlantic like a respectable son would do. Or at least a live one.'

'I'm going, pa.'

'I know you are, but I'm not going to stop talking. You're just gonna have to go 'cause I ain't letting you go. 'F I had my 'druthers I'd stay here talking to you 'til this boat rotted and sank. I like your face, son, and the damn sky's gonna be empty without it.'

'Goodbye, pa,' Chris said, and gave his skiff a gentle shove away from *Vagabond* and pulled the starting cord on his outboard. The engine purred into life.

'I know you're going, son, but you can't stop me from talking to you. I been talkin' to you eighteen years and I ain't gonna stop now just 'cause you want to go rushing off to become a smithereen. The world's full of smithereens these days and I don't see why you think one more's gonna make the air smell any purtier, 'specially you smelling most the time like a blowfish after flies been at it a week. Why I remember when you . . .'

His son was already fifty feet away, the sound of the skiff's engine buzzing gently back to them across the water and beginning to fade.

Captain Olly, tears dampening both cheeks, turned to look at Neil and Lisa and Jeanne who had been watching the separation from the wheelhouse. After several seconds delay he snorted: '. . . You got breakfast ready yet, lady? I gotta get some eggs and coffee aboard my belly before I swamp us again with my dribble. Got any that whisky left there, Cap'n? I'm eighteen.'

The three stared at him.

'Nine o'clock in the morning and I ain't even pissed yet,' he went on. 'You got a john aboard this boat or can I pee off the side or use a bucket like real sailors do?'

'Off the aft deck is fine,' Neil answered.

'Would you like some bacon and eggs?' Jeanne asked.

''Course I'd like bacon and eggs,' Captain Olly said as he stepped up out of the cockpit to get to the aft deck. 'And toast and juice and potatoes and anything else you got cooking. A dying, orphaned man got to make the most of his last days. Least he can do is eat like a pig.' Turning his back to the ladies, who went below to prepare breakfast, Captain Olly pissed with dignity off the aft deck.

20

It was thirty minutes later, after they had all finished eating breakfast and begun sailing down the Bay that Neil, on his way forward to check the genoa, placed one foot on to the little step built into the cabin wall for climbing forward, and stopped. He stared at the cockpit deck. He felt horror. A thin, barely visible layer of something lay on the cockpit floor. He bent over and ran an index finger a few inches along the deck and looked at it: a grey smudge. He looked up at the sky above him. A thin haze marred the blue summer sky. He went quickly to the opposite cockpit: the same thin layer of ash lay among the fishing gear and other stuff from the *Lucy Mae*.

He felt trapped. To the south lay a thick cloud over Norfolk; to the northwest the closer, more diffuse grey mass from the blast over Washington. And on the decks at his feet the first radioactive fallout.

'Frank!' he shouted.

Still bleary-eyed from weariness, Frank left the wheelhouse to come to Neil.

'We've got fallout on deck,' Neil told him in a quiet voice.

Frank looked down, reached an index finger to examine the ash, and then looked back at Neil.

'Everybody should go below,' he said. 'I'll wash the fucking stuff off the decks.'

Frank and Neil sent everyone below into the main cabin, ordering them to shut all windows and portholes and check for ash, wiping clean and throwing overboard any they found. Since every thickness of material between them and the radioactive fallout would give some small additional protection, Skippy was put on the floor underneath the dinette table and a jury-rigged piece of plywood used as a

142

wall to create a cave. The table was covered with blankets and sleeping bags from the forepeak. Jeanne ordered Lisa to crawl under it too. Olly suggested Jeanne make a space next to the daggerboard well and beneath the cross beam for greater protection. Conrad Macklin went into the forepeak and covered himself with bagged sails.

On deck Frank began washing down the boat with buckets of sea water and a long-handled brush. Neil disappeared for a while and then emerged wearing full foul-weather gear including rubber boots and the hood tied tightly around his face as if he were about to go out in a gale. He handed a full set to Frank and took over the washing down of the boat while Frank put on his gear. Jim had checked the genoa and when he came aft Frank ordered him below with the others. He and Neil would stay on deck.

As they set sail down the Chesapeake for the Atlantic a low-level dread hung over all of them in the main cabin. They talked in low voices as if at a wake. On the horizon to both north and south lay the ugly grey cloud masses seeming to creep up the sky to kill them. One was chasing down from the north and they were sailing south into the one over Norfolk. There was no escape.

When *Vagabond* sailed past Tangier Village Neil looked dully at the wreckage. Two large fishing trawlers lay on their sides among three houses tilted crazily, as if all five were some child's toys carelessly cast aside. One of the buildings must have been the bar they had stopped at the night it all began, but even through his binoculars he couldn't tell which building it was. He saw no sign of life.

To the east the shore was too distant to determine what had happened, but as *Vagabond* sailed out into the centre of the Chesapeake, Frank reported the capsized hulk of some motor yacht a quarter of a mile to starboard. Here also other floating vessels became visible, a boat sailing south like *Vagabond* and two other boats emerging into sight from the direction of Norfolk. With a sense of foreboding Neil realized that on the previous day the Bay had been crowded with boats, twenty-five or thirty being visible when he'd been searching for the sight of the stolen *Vagabond*. Not many ships had survived the explosion and tidal wave.

It was Frank who spotted the first corpse: a limp wet lump of clothing floating face down less than fifty feet from *Vagabond*'s course. Frank's first instinct was to alter course to retrieve the body, but then he quickly realized that the last thing they needed aboard was a corpse. There would be more.

The two ships coming towards them remained close to the western shore and soon disappeared past them heading up the Chesapeake to God-knew-where. That they had survived at all was a surprise. The boat on the same course as *Vagabond* disappeared into a cove or river on the western shore. By late morning they seemed to be all alone on the vast expanse of the Bay.

The fallout still fell. With a sense of dread and impotent anger Neil noted that every half hour enough would accumulate in areas he hadn't brushed down to be visible. He and Frank alternated doing the cleaning work, both of them getting overheated and exhausted in their stifling foul-weather gear on the increasingly hot day. His face dripping with sweat, one of them would plod over the entire length and breadth of the boat with a big plastic bucket and the long-handled brush, dipping the bucket into the bay, pouring it across a deck area, then rapidly brushing, brushing, brushing to push everything back into the water, where it sank. When finished he would stumble back to the other man, at the helm, and, without a break, the other would take up the exhausting work.

At eleven-thirty Frank collapsed on the foredeck. Neil rushed forward to him and dragged him back, loosening his foul-weather gear. He hoped it was only heat exhaustion and carried Frank below where he could be undressed and cooled off. Olly took Frank's place, wearing his own foul-weather

144

clothing. Macklin was ordered to take a turn next.

Forty minutes later Frank reappeared on deck, dressed again in full gear and ordered Neil and Macklin to go below, saying that if they rotated four men none of them would get overheated again. Olly came up again to share the topside burden.

Down in the main cabin Neil was struck by the stuffy, closed heat and by the silence. Wet towels lay draped over the galley shelves where they'd been used to cool down Frank. Lisa and Skippy were squeezed into the jury-rigged 'doghouse' under the dinette table, Jim seated back against the galley cabinets with a styrofoam cooler and settee cushion on his lap, Jeanne huddled beside the daggerboard well with a settee cushion covering most of her. Their efforts at protection from radiation were pitiful. Neil stripped off his foul-weather stuff and wiped himself down with one of the wet towels. Macklin crawled forward into the forepeak cabin.

'Mommy says the rain has radioactive germs in it,' Skippy said, breaking the silence and peeking his head out of his cave. 'Did you see them?'

'One or two,' Neil answered. 'I kicked them overboard.'

'Mommy says you're *washing* them overboard,' Skippy corrected.

'She's right.'

Lisa also peered out. 'Is it still falling?' she asked.

'A little bit probably,' Neil answered. 'But we're keeping the boat so clean you can't tell.' He knew better, of course. The stuff was still falling, although even Neil thought at a slightly slower rate, and though they were a lot better off here than on land, they were still being exposed, especially those who had to work on deck.

Jeanne crawled out from her hideaway.

'You should get under the crossbeam,' she said. 'You've been exposed already much more than we have.'

He glanced at the space, then at her. He wanted to lie down and wanted to feel better protected.

145

'Can we both squeeze in there?' he asked, frowning.

'No,' she said. 'But you go ahead.'

He hesitated, but the thought of being able to lie down won out over gallantry; he realized how exhausted he must be. He stepped over Jim's legs, held Jeanne briefly as he passed her and then crawled into her space. She covered him with her cushion and sat down beside Jim. *Vagabond* sailed on. Below, no one spoke.

It was at about two o'clock, having sailed twenty-four miles down the Bay and to within forty miles of Norfolk that they came upon the floating hulk of a charter fishing vessel and its survivors. There had been no measurable fallout since Neil had gone below about an hour and a half before, so Frank had let Olly remain on duty with him rather than bring Neil up again. But when he saw the derelict he called down for Neil.

Frank had altered course when he saw the survivors waving frantically at him and with a gloomy, doomed expression he now ordered Neil and Olly to prepare to pick them up.

The hulk lay low in the water, its aft deck crowded with fifteen to twenty people – men, women, and children – a seemingly random collection of those who had escaped the disasters of somewhere to motor into the disaster of the explosion over Norfolk.

A large man with a blond beard emerged from the crowd to stand on the cabin roof and shout that they'd been swamped by a tidal wave, and, with flooded batteries, were helpless. The two vessels rolled and pitched awkwardly in the swells, and when at last rafted side by side, their decks sometimes slammed together with a sickening crunch.

Frank surveyed the packed near side of the yacht, the dazed and anxious faces, all looking exhausted, many sick, some people with burned faces and singed hair, two or three women holding children, men elbowing their way in front of them, and he felt the same sense of despair he'd felt when Neil showed him the ash on the deck: he was trapped and being overwhelmed.

'We're headed out into the Atlantic,' he shouted to those crowding together to board *Vagabond*. 'We can put you ashore at Cape Henry or take you to sea.'

Frank saw that most of the fatigued and frightened faces looked at him without comprehension. A ship had come to rescue them; if he'd announced he was sailing to Hell they still would have boarded.

'Bring all your food!' Neil shouted, but no one seemed to pay attention. The men began to clamber over *Vagabond*'s coaming like pirates boarding a ship they planned to plunder. Jim and Neil alone tried to help the women and children and two elderly men dressed only in bathrobes; most of the young male refugees seemed more concerned with their suitcases or knapsacks.

A scream broke from the confusion and a pale young blonde woman was soon led sobbing into the wheelhouse, her right hand bloody, apparently crushed between the two boats. Neil called down to Jeanne and told her to get Macklin and the ship's first aid kit, and he had the woman seated on a wheelhouse settee. Between sobs the woman kept calling for her cat and seemed as disturbed by its not being present as by her mangled fingers.

The big man with the bushy beard was the only man helping people to escape from the foundering *Fishkiller*, and when Frank yelled again to bring all their food and water he ducked down into the ship's cabin and soon began passing cartons of food across to Jim.

A strange dog snarled at Jeanne when she brought up the first aid kit and Neil had an impulse to throw the stupid beast into the sea. Macklin followed, wearing a raincoat. Neil could hear someone retching loudly off the aft deck and smelled vomit.

As Macklin bent to examine the woman's hand, two men

147

began scuffling behind him and one fell against Neil, knocking him into the seated woman, who screamed in pain. The two men, arms around each other in a violent wrestle for control of some object, reeled against a young couple and child seated on the opposite settee and then bounced off them on to the wheelhouse floor.

Macklin jumped up quickly and grabbed them both by their hair, and, yanking, shouted at them to let go.

In another half minute he and Neil had them separated and quiet. It took almost fifteen minutes before the sixteen survivors and skimpy food supplies of *Fishkiller* had been transferred to *Vagabond*. At last the two ships separated, *Vagabond*'s genoa ballooning out to port with a flutter and a loud pop, and the derelict wallowing in the swells behind her.

The new passengers were scattered in listless confusion over the two cockpits, wheelhouse and main cabin. Dressed in suits, slacks, jeans, bathrobes, and bathing suits were two elderly men, five women, three children, one of them an infant, and six able-bodied men. Neil was aware of at least one dog and cat aboard, but in the chaos it seemed like a dozen. Suitcases, knapsacks, and shopping bags were also scattered about.

After *Vagabond* had been sailing on southwards towards the mouth of the Chesapeake for several minutes, the big man with the beard who seemed to have been their leader came up to Frank, who was at the helm. He had removed his foul-weather jacket and boots but still wore the red plastic trousers.

'My name's Tony Mariano,' he announced loudly. 'Where the hell are you heading?' He was dressed in blue jeans and a silk shirt and fancy leather loafers. He was a powerfully built man in his late twenties and he loomed at least a couple of inches over Frank.

'We're headed out to sea,' Frank replied.

'You're not taking us past Norfolk, are you?' the man persisted. 'That's right into the fallout.'

'That's our plan,' Frank replied uncertainly.

As he watched Macklin work on the woman's crushed fingers Neil was aware that two couples in the wheelhouse were listening intently to the conversation; even the woman he was treating seemed to forget her pain for the moment.

'The law of the sea,' Frank went on in a tense voice to Tony, 'says that anyone rescuing shipwrecked survivors can either continue on to his scheduled next port, or land them at the nearest point they find convenient. We . . .'

'I don't give a fuck about the laws of the sea,' Tony broke in. 'We're not sailing into a rain of death.'

'That's right,' another man said, coming up to the wheel. 'Some of us are sick already. We can't take any more radioactivity.' A teenage boy, an older man and two women now gathered near Frank too. Neil moved towards Frank, feeling a rising anger.

'What's going on?' another man asked, pushing his way past Neil.

'This man is taking us south back into the fallout,' Tony answered loudly.

'If you like . . .' Frank began.

'I thought we were going north,' the new man said.

'I did too,' the elderly man said. 'Away from the explosion.'

Several additional voices made noises indicating that they agreed. Neil felt a wave of blind rage surge through him.

Frank stood frowning.

'But in the north too . . .' he began again.

'Who owns this boat anyway?' Tony asked, looking around aggressively as if someone were trying to put something over on him.

'I do,' Frank replied. 'And I . . .'

'Well, get us turned around before it's too late.'

A chorus of 'yeahs' resounded after Tony's remark.

Neil slid away from the crowd and found Olly organizing the suitcases and knapsacks in the port cockpit.

'Go get the .38 hidden in my aft cabin,' he whispered to

149

him, 'and be ready to back me up. Tell Jim to get the .22.'

Olly nodded solemnly, and when he had left to go aft Neil descended into the main cabin. Two strange women and three children were seated at the dinette and Jeanne and Lisa seemed to be waiting on them. Jeanne looked up intently at him as he entered. 'What's happening now?' she asked anxiously.

'Chaos,' Neil answered. He walked past her and took from its hiding place behind a short shelf of books Macklin's .45. After checking the chamber he returned up into the wheelhouse.

'I think we'd better head east, Neil,' Frank said to him nervously as he emerged and went to the entrance of the port cockpit. 'These people think that . . .'

Neil's gun exploded once with a deafening bang. All conversation ceased. He shoved the person nearest him and the others backed away too. Everyone in the wheelhouse and cockpits stared at Neil, who stood for a moment in the centre of the crowd holding the .45 with its barrel just a few inches below his chin – where everyone could see it. He was feeling a strange mixture of desperation, fury, and determination. With his yellow foul-weather gear he appeared, among the newcomers, strangely out of place.

'All right,' he began in a loud, tense voice. 'I want you all to listen and I want you to get it.

'We're in a war and I'm your commanding officer. I expect everyone here to obey me as if I were God incarnate, without hesitation and without question. I've commanded regular Navy ships ten times this size and been sailing boats like this for ten years. If anyone else aboard feels he's better qualified he'd better speak now.'

There was a silence, and when Neil felt some people begin to stir restlessly he plunged on.

'Good,' he went on, still loudly. 'Frank Stoor, here beside me, who owns this boat, is First Mate. You treat him as you would me. Captain Olly, the old fellow standing over there, is Second Mate. And Jim at the helm now, is Third Mate. They

150

are the ship's officers and their word is law. If anyone wilfully disobeys any of our commands I will personally throw him overboard. DO YOU GET IT?'

No one spoke. Most of them were falling back into that listlessness they'd had before Tony stirred them up.

'Good,' said Neil after a pause, aware now of the sweat dripping down his face, of Frank staring at him uncertainly, of Tony looking at him with a mixture of fear and resentment.

'As captain I'm announcing that our course is through the fallout area around Norfolk and out into the Atlantic.'

A few groans greeted this statement but Neil cut them off immediately,

'SHUT UP!' he shouted. 'We're heading south until I feel it's safe to make a landfall. You may feel that we ought to have a democratic discussion of what we ought to do. I don't give a shit how you feel. If you don't like this policy I'll give you a life jacket and you can go in a different direction. You may decide later out in the Atlantic that you wish you'd never left land. Bitch among yourselves all you'd like, but *obey*.'

'But what if . . .' someone began.

'Anyone who wilfully disobeys one of my commands will be thrown overboard.'

When Neil paused again no one spoke. 'You're beginning to understand,' Neil went on more quietly. 'Now for some commands. First of all I want all weapons – guns and knives with a blade longer than two inches – turned in to the ship's officers immediately. These weapons will be returned to you when we part company. Anyone found with a weapon on his person or in his luggage ten minutes from now . . . will be thrown overboard.'

Silence.

'Secondly, I want this area around the wheel and around the winches kept clear. When an officer orders you to go sit some place on the boat you go sit there and don't move without permission. Consider where he puts you to be your battle station.

151

'Thirdly, anyone who brought a stash of food aboard with them shall immediately contribute all of it to our ship's store. If you leave soon it will be returned to you. We are sharing our ship, our weapons, our water, our food and our skills with you, and we expect you to do the same with us. Anyone caught hoarding a private stash of food or eating or permitting his or her children to eat any of the ship's food not rationed out to them will be thrown overboard.'

Again Neil paused, aware of Jim watching.

'What if we have to go to the bathroom?' a woman asked in a frightened voice.

'If a man has to piss he goes to the leeward side of the boat and pisses into the bay,' Neil replied with the same tense voice. 'If you don't know which side of the boat that is ask an officer. Knowing which side of a boat to piss off is what has made him an officer.' Olly chuckled, but the others were too frightened or awed to respond.

'Ladies will piss in buckets provided in the side cabins. A mate will see to it that the contents are tossed overboard.'

'Aren't there marine toilets?' someone asked.

'Yes, there are. But the animal species capable of landing men on the moon and blowing the world apart has not yet developed a marine toilet that doesn't clog if you stare at it too long. While we're so crowded and while we have more important things on our minds, we won't use them.'

This time when he hesitated Neil felt that he was being understood.

'I sound harsh,' he continued. 'I intend to be harsh. I intend this ship and those remaining aboard it to survive. My experience has been that in life and death situations the traditional Navy way of doing things is the only one that works. This policy is not open to discussion. Are there any questions?'

The silence aboard *Vagabond* as she sailed serenely down the Chesapeake in the direction most people thought they

152

didn't want to go was uncanny. No one spoke. Most of those he looked at, Neil noted, looked simply numb.

'What if we have to vomit?' an elderly man finally asked.

'If you feel seasick go to the leeward cockpit and lean over the coaming. Vomit to leeward.' Neil paused. 'Anyone caught vomiting to windward will be . . . thrown overboard. Anyone vomiting to windward will be so covered with vomit, he'll probably be happy to be thrown overboard.'

A few nervous giggles.

'All right,' Neil concluded. 'All weapons and food to the ship's officers. Anyone attempting to resist these commands will be shot. Olly, Frank, get the weapons first . . .'

'Jesus, Neil,' Frank said a half hour later when *Vagabond* was as calm and orderly as a concentration camp. 'Don't you think you were a little hard on them?'

'No,' Neil replied. 'Absolutely not. We're all trying to survive. Everyone on this boat, *everyone*, will lie, steal, cheat, and kill in order to survive. That speech served one purpose: to let their survival instinct know that the first thing it has to consider is *me*, and what serves the survival of this ship.'

'It was nice of you to let me be First Mate on my own boat.'

Neil looked at Frank with total seriousness. 'It wasn't nice,' he said. 'You deserve it.'

Frank stared at him. 'You bastard.'

'You'd better believe it,' Neil said coldly. 'When I said everyone obeys my commands I meant *everyone*.'

'I see.'

'I hope so.'

21

At seven that evening Neil had them anchored off the coast near Cape Charles and began ferrying refugees into the beach with the inflatable. Neil had repeated to them his intention of continuing south, passing within fifteen miles of Norfolk before making it out into the Atlantic where they would remain until fallout conditions and radio reports indicated they dare return to the US coast. Three people asked to remain on *Vagabond*, one the man who had started all the fuss in the first place, Tony Mariano; the second a woman named Elaine with a small child; and the third a middle-aged college professor named Seth Sperling.

Although Neil had the .45 tucked into his belt and had armed both Frank and Jim for the evacuation and the redistribution of food and weapons, the event proceeded more smoothly than had the boarding five hours earlier. Even Conrad Macklin went meekly when Neil, after consulting with Frank, ordered him off with the very first group.

As he helped people down into the dinghy Frank became aware that some of those leaving were now fearful that they were choosing wrong and wanted to remain, but when an elderly man hesitated and was clearly intending to ask to come back aboard, Frank brusquely ordered Jim to take the last group ashore and cast off the dinghy's painter. The beach was only fifty feet away from the anchored *Vagabond*, and so ten minutes after the last trip ashore *Vagabond*'s inflatable had been pulled back up on deck and stored and the ship was underway again.

When the sun set at eight-forty they were still fifteen miles from the Chesapeake Bay Bridge-Tunnel. The wind was dropping and shifting as they neared the Norfolk-

154

Portsmouth area, blowing now out of the northeast at only six or eight knots. With the tide now against them they began motoring.

After the sun was gone and with the half-moon not yet risen, the blackness that descended upon them was depressing. Fallout was again appearing on deck and the only lights they could see were from fires still burning in the blast area, one in particular blazing up sporadically like solar flares from a dying sun. All the navigational aids seemed to have been destroyed; the lights of the Bridge–Tunnel were gone. They had seen no ships except for one tiny sailing boat in the late afternoon; now at night they saw no running lights of any shipping. As they motored south towards the northerly opening through the Bridge causeway out to sea, it was as if they were the last ship on earth, alone and sailing away from a doomed land into the unknown.

Leaving Olly alone at the helm, Neil joined Frank, Jim and Jeanne in the main cabin for a conference. Although he had ordered each of them to try to sleep for a couple of hours, as they sat around the dinette table all looked exhausted. The men hadn't shaved and were dressed in the same clothes as when the war had started. Jeanne's white clothes were now dirty, her eyes red from fatigue or weeping, and her bruised cheek still ugly.

As Neil spoke his voice was noticeably softer than it had been whenever he'd spoken to anyone on deck. He quietly laid out his plan of three-hour watches, with three watch teams, one led by each of the mates. Frank would work with the newcomer, Seth Sperling, a small man with glasses who seemed uncertain of himself, Olly with big Tony Mariano, and Jim with Lisa. The third new passenger, the young woman named Elaine Booker, was to stay with her three-year-old child. Olly and Seth would sleep in Neil's aft cabin; Tony in the forepeak cabin and Jim with Frank in Frank's cabin. He himself would sleep on the aft settee of the wheelhouse, to be always on call.

Neil said that the amount of radiation they'd been exposed to so far was insignificant, but Frank wasn't certain whether Neil really believed that or was speaking for the sake of morale. Jeanne's queasiness, Neil insisted, was simple seasickness.

When the meeting seemed over Jeanne unexpectedly spoke. 'I don't know how serious you were, Neil, but I warn you that I'll try to stop you from throwing anyone overboard,' she said softly.

Startled, Neil looked at her, then his severe face broke into a small smile.

'I'd have to throw you overboard too,' he said. 'Then who would care for your children?'

Jeanne flushed in anger and Frank quickly cut in. 'He'd have to throw me overboard too.'

Neil stopped smiling and shook his head. 'I never said how close to shore we'd be when I threw someone overboard,' he finally replied.

'Is that a promise?' Jeanne asked, looking at him.

'On the other hand,' Neil went on, 'the traditional punishment for mutiny *is* death. I'm afraid that is the way things are done aboard ship.'

'Not my ship,' Frank said.

'Let's agree then,' said Neil quietly after a pause, 'that if there is a wilful disobedience I'll call together a Court of Inquiry composed of all the ship's officers and let them decide on the appropriate response.'

Jim nodded and then Frank did too.

'Jeanne,' Neil went on gently, 'please leave the management of the ship to me.'

'Not when it involves the lives of my family.'

'Your family?' Neil asked uncertainly.

'I consider everyone who comes aboard this boat a part of my new family.'

Neil frowned. 'Then in that sense every decision I make involves your family.'

156

'Then I am involved.'

Frank was amazed at how serenely she gazed at Neil, her eyes glowing in rebellion.

'All right,' Neil finally commented. 'I understand your concern. If I seem cruel or capricious you may complain to me and we'll try to resolve it.'

'Thank you.'

'And if we don't, I'll throw you overboard.' He grinned.

'Not if I have my butcher knife,' she rejoined, grinning back.

'I believe it,' Neil said, standing up to end the meeting.

Back on deck in the darkness Neil realized that the passage through the Causeway or remains of the Causeway was going to be difficult to locate. He had taken a bearing on Fishermans Island just before dark but since then it was all dead reckoning. Even after the half-moon had risen there wasn't enough light to see anything on the horizon except the line of fires to the southwest. They would be able to see objects appearing in the water no more than sixty feet away. Their fathometer confirmed that they were in the big ship channel, but by itself would give little advance warning of the presence of the Causeway or the rocks of its wreckage. *Vagabond* was making towards the Causeway at only about four knots.

Frank was sick from either radiation sickness or seasickness so Neil had Jim take his place on watch with Tony Mariano. When he ordered Tony to wash down the decks again just in case, Tony went to it quickly and energetically, finishing with sweat pouring down his face and into his bushy beard.

'Helluva way to make a living,' was his only comment when he had finished.

'I wish we could see something!' Jim exclaimed a few minutes later as the three men stood sweating together around the helm.

'Alter course twenty degrees to the east,' Neil ordered.

'What's up?' Tony asked.

'We're not going to see anything until we actually reach

the Causeway,' Neil answered. 'This way when we do reach it we'll know we're to the north of the channel. How are your night eyes, Tony?'

'Damn good.'

'Go forward and stand at the bow as lookout. Keep an eye out not only forward but also to port and starboard.'

'Aye, aye, sir.'

Tony crawled forward in the darkness and soon his huge form was visible against the distant horizon like a black sail bundle tied to the forestay. Neil ordered Jim up to wash down the aft sections of the boat and ordered Tony to do the bow again.

Half an hour later they had still seen nothing. Jim wondered aloud whether they'd miraculously sailed through an opening and not seen either side.

'Or maybe the whole Causeway got blown to pieces,' he suggested.

'OBJECT TO STARBOARD!' Tony shouted, and Jim dampened the throttle and put her into reverse, bringing *Vagabond* to a slow halt.

Neil turned on the 12-volt spotlight and swung it to the right where Tony was pointing. A huge chunk of metal and some pilings appeared to be sticking out of the water. Neil swung the light in a slow arc almost in a full circle, but nothing else was visible. Although *Vagabond* was now in neutral, the tide was carrying her backwards away from the strange objects to their right. The depthmeter showed they were in 35 feet of water – most likely on the edge of the big ship channel.

'Ease her over closer,' Neil said to Jim, holding the spotlight on the huge protruding metal chunk, which seemed to get longer as they neared it. Slowly Jim moved *Vagabond* to the right and forward.

'Okay,' Neil said after a while. 'Back her off.'

'What is it?' Jim asked, still not able to put the huge metal object and broken pilings into any coherent pattern.

158

'A sunken freighter.'

'Wow.'

Jim backed *Vagabond* away and put her into neutral at Neil's command.

'She was either sunk by the blast or may have hit the submerged Causeway. All we can do is ease forward some more, but we may be near it or on it.' Neil left Jim to climb up on the cabin roof to see better.

It was ten minutes later that they spotted the Causeway. It emerged in front of them like a long spit of land, which it was, as solid as the rocks that it was made of. Their spotlight revealed, however, that the roadway was shattered and dozens, no hundreds, of burned-out cars gleamed brightly in the ship's spotlight. No living being responded to their presence.

Neil had Jim swing *Vagabond* to the right, and they motored south about two hundred feet from the Causeway, Neil and Tony watching for the break in the wall that separated them from the sea. The air was still, almost windless. The sight of the endless mass of blasted cars, motionless bodies sometimes visible within, made the humid air seem even more oppressive than it was. They were all in full foul-weather gear, except that Jim had pushed back his hood.

Tony spotted the end of the Causeway first and shouted the information back to Neil, who, nevertheless, kept *Vagabond*'s course due south, as if they were going to motor right past it. But when the changes of depth registered by the depthmeter indicated that they were definitely in the middle of the big ship channel, Neil was sure the opening hadn't been created by the explosion.

'Take her through,' he said quietly to Jim. 'And on the other side alter course to due east magnetic.'

'What about speed?' Jim asked.

'Slow her to five knots. We don't want to hit something now that we're so close to being out.'

As they began motoring through the opening – the other

159

end of the Causeway was now also visible with the spotlight on, off to their right – Jim became aware of the gentle swells of the open sea, lifting *Vagabond*'s bow like a mother's gentle hand and then lowering it again, the ship pitching so gracefully it was like a rocking cradle.

'WHAT'S THAT?' Tony shouted, pointing now to his right.

When Neil swung the spotlight in that direction something huge appeared to be thrashing around in the water, sending gigantic bubbles bursting up to the surface of the sea, not far from the beginning of the Causeway. As Neil held the light on it they all stared, until finally Jim realized what it must be: air escaping from some hole in the undersea automobile tunnel over which they were crossing must be bubbling up to the surface. Agreeing, Neil shut off the light with a grim nod.

As Jim slowly altered course to due east, he smiled to himself with the excitement of breaking free to sea. Except for the unlighted buoys, sunken ships, derelict hulks, nuclear fallout, and further explosions, it was all clear sailing, he thought almost gaily. Ahead of him he could see only darkness, even Tony now not visible.

Lisa came up out of the main cabin with three cups of water and handed one to Neil and then one to Jim.

'Thanks, Lisa, we're sweltering up here,' Jim said, smiling down at her. 'But we're out of the Bay.'

'We're in the ocean?' she asked him.

'Yep. And no new fallout either.'

Seth Sperling suddenly appeared in the darkness beside them.

'Where are we?' he asked, adjusting his glasses and staring at the dark shape of the starboard section of Causeway still visible behind them to their left.

'That's what's left of the northern section of the Causeway of the Chesapeake Bay Bridge-Tunnel,' Jim replied, but looking forward to where he could now just make out Tony crouching at the bow. 'We're out in the ocean.'

'And what's that boat coming towards us?' Seth asked

next, as casually as if they'd been in a crowded well-lit harbour.

'What?' said Neil, wheeling to face where he saw the little man staring. His instinctive reaction was fear.

A motorboat without its running lights, which must have been hidden on the seaward side of the Causeway, was barely visible angling in at them from the darkness of the Causeway.

'Get the guns!' Neil hissed at Jim. 'Aft cabin. Lisa, get below. Tony!' He shouted forward at the dim figure at the bow.

'What's up?' Tony asked as he began to amble back aft, stopping near the mast to retrieve the spotlight.

'A boat coming!' Neil snapped back. 'May be pirates.'

Neil squinted into the darkness and suddenly saw the motorboat now only thirty feet away and closing fast, its big outboard engine now audible over *Vagabond*'s diesel. Still seeing no sign of friendliness, he threw the throttle full forward, *Vagabond* slowly responding. Jim emerged with the weapons.

'Keep the .22,' Neil whispered fiercely to Jim, taking Macklin's .45, 'and take the helm. Seth, can you use a pistol?'

Wide-eyed, Seth shook his head: 'No'.

'Then take it forward to Tony. Quick!'

Even as he spoke he could see the motorboat was already beside them only a few yards away, a twenty-footer with three or four men aboard. Neither it nor *Vagabond* was showing running lights and the men on the motorboat had not hailed them. Neil shouted at them but there was no answer.

Crouching in the wheelhouse doorway, and certain now of danger, Neil fired a warning shot above *Vagabond*'s coaming and over the launch, which had now moved so close to *Vagabond* that he couldn't have hit it from the wheelhouse if he'd tried. The thump as the launch careened into *Vagabond*'s port hull was both heard and felt.

'Get down, Jim!' Neil whispered, watching the coaming for the appearance of a figure. He could still hear the roar of the outboard outside the line of his sight less than fifteen feet away. Crouching, Jim swung *Vagabond* sharply to starboard, for the moment tearing the two boats apart. The launch, speeding on in the old course, became visible twenty-five feet off *Vagabond*'s port side and Neil fired a second shot, this time to kill, but Jim had swerved back again, throwing off his aim. Feeling sure he hadn't hit anyone, he watched tensely as the launch quickly closed on *Vagabond* disappearing behind her coaming.

'STAY BELOW!' Neil suddenly shouted, fearful that Jeanne or Frank, awakened by the shots, might emerge right in the line of fire. Then, again acting instinctively, he ran in a crouch across the wheelhouse out into the opposite cockpit and crawled on to the deck beside the entrance to his aft cabin. As he stared through the blackness at *Vagabond*'s port side he suddenly became aware that the motorboat had dropped back into *Vagabond*'s wake and . . .

The bam-bam-bam-bam-bam of the automatic rifle sent Neil rolling off the deck back into the side cockpit, the slugs slamming through the forward plexiglas windows of the wheelhouse, Jim swinging the trimaran sharply in another evasive turn to the right.

Trembling, Neil quickly crept back up to peer aft, but the launch was no longer in the wake; from the sound of the outboard it was returning to the port side.

Two quick shots rang out from forward, sounding like Tony with the .38, and a vicious answering bam-bam-bam-bam from the automatic rifle.

Jim swerved again, this time into the launch, the two boats colliding with a crash that elicited a scream from one of the attackers. Jim held the trimaran at full left rudder, the two boats crashing again, and a man suddenly pulled himself up on to the deck behind the port cockpit and fired two shots at Jim crouched at the helm.

Hearing rather than seeing what was happening, Neil

leapt aft to get around the wheelhouse, saw the man, shot him once, and then kept running across his cabin top to fire his last three shots down into the launch, speeding along joined to *Vagabond*. Then he dived into the port cockpit, rolling away into the wheelhouse. Jim, squatting low, pulled the wheel now full the other way, *Vagabond* sweeping right.

Again trembling and tingling with fear, Neil crawled behind the wheelhouse settee for protection, listening for the sound of gunfire, his shoulders and back waiting to feel the thud and sting of a bullet. He could feel the launch still bumping *Vagabond*'s port hull and then there was silence as the two boats parted. He dared to peer up and out the shattered port plexiglas window, but could see nothing. He ducked around into the starboard cockpit again, staring aft, but again could see no sign of the attackers. Although he knew he must have hit some of those in the boat he was afraid Jim's manoeuvring had disoriented him and even now the attackers might be about to blast him.

'SETH! TONY!' he called forward. 'COME AFT!'

He needed a weapon now that his .45 was out of ammunition. He thought he had hit two of the three dark figures in the speeding boat, knew he had hit the man on *Vagabond*'s deck. Checking, he saw the man still lying where he had been hit.

Tony thumped down into the cockpit beside him.

'The little guy is hit,' Tony said. 'But that boat is buzzing off.'

'Where?' said Neil.

'It's way off the other side,' Tony replied. 'I think I hit a couple of them.' Even in the darkness Neil could see Tony's eyes were wide with excitement or fear. For half a minute he remained crouched, listening for the sound of the outboard, but he could no longer hear it.

'Are you all right, Jim?' he then whispered.

'Yes,' Jim answered, his voice cracking. 'But they really

163

wrecked poor *Vagabond*.' The forward plexiglas windows were shattered in five or six spots. They'd have to check for other damage.

'Head us back east,' Neil said. 'Keep us at full throttle.'

For a minute more *Vagabond* surged through the darkness, beginning, at almost nine knots, to smash into the swells with loud booming smashes, Neil, Tony and Jim remaining where they were. Then Neil walked over next to Jim and turned off the engine.

In a few seconds the noise of both the diesel and of *Vagabond*'s ploughing through the swells had diminished to nothing and Neil strained his ears to hear the outboard. There was no sound of it. Jim suddenly left the helm and vomited into the sea from the port cockpit. Expressionlessly, he returned.

'Okay,' said Neil, feeling for the first time since the action started a measure of calm. 'Get her going again, Jim. Come on, Tony, let's see about Seth.'

In another thirty minutes the sense of danger had passed. *Vagabond* was almost four miles from the Causeway and, with a light breeze, was now sailing. On the dark night with her engine now off, she was both invisible and inaudible to any potential attacker except at very close range. Neil and Jeanne did their best to treat Seth Sperling's bullet wound, but they knew that the wound was beyond their limited skills. Seth had been struck by the first burst of automatic rifle fire, a slug tearing through his left thigh and embedding itself in his right thigh. The artery hadn't been severed so all they did was clean the wound, staunch the flow of blood, and give Seth some antibiotic.

Later, when Neil emerged on deck he noticed off to his left that the man he had shot still lay on the aft deck. He went and knelt beside the body, that of a slender man, and searched the trouser pockets: wallet, a handkerchief, some change, several loose bills, a business card. Then he rolled the man over to look at the face. In the dim light from the aft cabin where Jeanne was still with Seth he could see little, but something looked strange. He asked Frank to shine a light over and then he saw: the man's face was disfigured with recent burns. Neil wondered if the whole boatload of attackers was equally disfigured.

He briefly recited from memory the concluding verses from the Navy burial service and then rolled the man off the deck into the sea.

At dawn Neil, sleeping in the back of the old wheelhouse area, was half-awakened by he knew not what. Lying on his back he had the vague feeling of still being in a dream. He was disoriented. In the dream he was lying where he was lying, and Jim was at the helm, and another figure, also himself it seemed, was seated a few feet away over on the port settee. The third figure in the wheelhouse was both himself and an intruder, and he struggled in his half-wakened state to determine who the other person was. In the dream the figure began to take on a more ominous emotional tone; Neil began to have that nightmarish feeling of struggling to awaken himself in order to deal with a nearby danger.

He sat up with a groan, awake at last. Jim was standing facing forward at the wheel as in the dream, and to his left, seated with characteristic calm, was the thick small figure of Conrad Macklin. He was sipping a cup of tea.

For a brief moment Neil felt himself back in the dream, then realized, with a sinking feeling, that he was facing reality. Conrad Macklin was back on board.

He looked steadily at the man, who gazed back without expression.

'Would you like some hot tea?' Macklin asked.

'Where'd you come from?' Neil finally asked.

'I never really left,' Macklin answered. 'I stowed away in some sort of storage area up front.'

'How did you get back aboard?'

'Swam out, mostly underwater, right after you put me ashore,' Macklin replied. 'Pulled myself up the anchor line as you were loading the last group on to the dinghy.'

Neil continued to look at Macklin coldly, then released a long sigh.

'A man is wounded,' he said. 'I suppose you'd better look at him.'

'Good,' said Macklin.

'I doubt it,' said Neil.

An hour later, awake but with his eyes closed, he realized that all night long, even before the dream of Macklin, something had been missing, something he ought to be feeling but was not. *Vagabond* was cutting cleanly through the blue waters; dead ahead the sun now sparkled like diamonds on the whitecaps. He had escaped to sea; the horrors of land were receding. At such times he should feel elated. But he wasn't. Something within him must be telling him that this time there was no escape: the tentacles of land had reached out and even now lay heavily on his deck. He was at sea, but that ninety-eight-cent lump of land called 'man' was still with him.

Part Two
ASHES

1

The moon, now almost three-quarters full, lit the sea to the left of *Vagabond* like a giant nightlight. It was after midnight and Neil had enjoyed the last hour more than any since they'd fled the Chesapeake three days before. After two seemingly endless days during which they had been mostly becalmed, and gloom from the radio news hung over them like an invisible shroud, *Vagabond* was now rushing through the night at eleven or twelve knots, and Neil was feeling that exhilaration which for him only a sailing boat tearing through the sea at night could give.

Behind were three trails of phosphorescent white bubbling out so fast it seemed *Vagabond* must be doing twenty knots, no matter what the speedometer read. Ahead Neil could see almost nothing. The trimaran charged into the blackness as if totally confident that nothing could harm her queenly being.

They were now about a hundred miles east of the North Carolina coast and Neil held his course at due south by lining up a cluster of stars that made up Orion's belt with the port upper shroud. He had let Jim and Lisa, whose official watch it was, continue sleeping rather than wake them for their midnight to three A.M. watch. *Vagabond*, plunging forward through the night, was just on the edge of being over-canvassed, and Neil kept checking to feel if the wind were getting too strong for the sail area up. So far it hadn't and part of his joy arose from the feeling that he, *Vagabond*, the wind and the sea were in total attunement.

With sea conditions moderate, he had been able to adjust the mizzen so that *Vagabond* was steering herself. He could wander out of the wheelhouse into either cockpit to stare at the stars or watch the moonlight on the sea, and *Vagabond*, like a giant puppy unleashed and glorying in a midnight romp, galloped forward by herself through the night. At moments like this she seemed as human as he, and he loved her, urged her on in his mind, congratulated her when, after an errant wave had pushed her bow off course, her mizzen slowly pushed her rear end around to get her back on course.

All the troubles of the day were flushing away in *Vagabond*'s bubbling wake. Although the familiar grey cloud masses which had seemed to be permanently pursuing them had dissipated two days earlier, Neil, Frank and Olly had all suffered from radiation sickness. Frank was still nauseous and sick after three days and Olly still suffered from diarrhoea. Although the men had told the others it was seasickness, they all knew that none of them was ever seasick except in exceptionally bad seas. Neil himself had been queasy for two days and once – only he knew it had happened – vomited off the aft deck. His sickness frightened and depressed him, but on this third day appeared to be gone.

In addition, listening to reports of the war had been a depressing and divisive experience. Although a Pentagon spokesman that morning had made a long, vague report about the vast devastation wreaked upon the Soviet Union, about a great naval victory in the Indian Ocean, about the grudging way Allied forces gave ground in what was left of Europe; the idea that the US might win the war seemed irrelevant in the face of a report that most of the population east of Cleveland, north of Philadelphia, and south of Boston was fleeing from the effects of the war – lack of food, water, electricity, and the reality and fear of radioactive fallout. It was implied that half the northeast might soon be uninhabitable for all except a tenth of the former population. Other sections of the country were equally endangered. How people were evacuating when all fuel was requisitioned by the military and the public transportation network had ceased to exist was not explained.

'They're jogging,' Frank had commented, not mentioning

that his wife and daughter might still be alive and part of the fleeing millions.

Neil wandered to the back of the cockpit to adjust the drag on the trolling rig jammed in place there. Although they rarely hooked anything at night, especially at ten knots, Neil had asked Olly to try. As he set the drag and checked the feel of it, he remembered that it was Jeanne who had finally got them out of their oppressive moods. Earlier that evening she had browbeaten them into a singalong. It had started out as lugubriously as mourners at a funeral, but ended with giddy silliness. Captain Olly taught them a blatantly obscene sea shanty and, though Lisa blushed, little Skippy sang along loudly, and triggered the last burst of laughter by announcing that he liked songs about pussies.

Pressing the rod back into place Neil smiled at the memory. The world of the last several days was one emotional somersault after another: the gloom of thinking about the war and personal losses alternating with the delights of sailing or of eating their meagre meals or bringing in a fish. He wished he could control the lows. In the Chesapeake they had endured seemingly hourly threats to their survival, but now, ninety miles from land, he felt it was his task to create for them a new world of more order, routine and dependability. As he returned to lean against the entrance of Frank's cabin and look forward, he thought of his watch teams.

Frank and Tony, Olly and Macklin, and Jim and Lisa were now working out well. At first he'd tried Tony with Olly, figuring Olly might need Tony's extra strength, but it hadn't worked. Tony was a huge athletic man of twenty-eight, outgoing, ebullient, used to running things – a former football star and successful salesman. He'd had trouble getting along with Olly. Although Olly never appeared to order Tony, he as naturally assumed control of *Vagabond* as he had of *Lucy Mae*. He treated Tony as a minor tool, a winch handle perhaps, and didn't tend to listen when the winch handle spoke. Once when Tony finished a brilliant analysis of why loosening the genoa sheet and altering course three degrees had increased their speed a half-knot, Olly responded with a brief silence, a puff on his unlit pipe, and the suggestion to Tony to tighten up on the genoa a bit and alter course three degrees back again. At the end of their first day at sea Tony had taken Frank aside to complain. 'The old guy's senile,' he said off in the port cockpit after Olly had retired into the aft cabin to nap. 'I don't think he relates to people any more.'

'Only when he wants to,' Frank had replied.

'He spent an hour on watch today talking about the various positions he used in screwing his third wife. Claimed there were twenty-seven and began mumbling and swearing when he could only remember twenty-two.'

Frank smiled. 'You get a free stand-up comic every watch,' he said.

'I don't want a stand-up comic,' Tony exploded. 'I want to talk with someone who speaks English.'

'I'll take it up with Neil,' Frank said.

'Why the hell can't you change the watches?' Tony went on. 'You own the boat, don't you?'

'I own it,' Frank replied evenly. 'And Neil is captain. I'll speak to him.'

'Let me work with you,' Tony said. 'Macklin is exactly the quiet sort that Olly will love.'

'You're probably right,' Frank had said, smiling, and, when he had reported the conversation, Neil had laughed and changed the watch teams as suggested.

Jim and Lisa were an unexpected gift. Lisa hopped around the boat with the nimbleness of a cat, and although she had to be reminded to wear a life jacket when she went forward to change a sail, she otherwise followed orders quickly and well. Intensely serious most of the time, she seemed to glow when working with Jim, as if the physical work liberated her from her seriousness.

For a moment Neil was brought out of his reverie by the appearance of a light off the port bow but decided it was just

172

the moonlight reflecting off a distant whitecap. He wandered from the starboard cockpit through the wheelhouse with its unattended wheel to the port side to get a better look and to take a piss off the aft deck. As he approached he was startled to see a head and shoulders silhouetted against the reflection of the moonlight on the water. It was Jeanne's profile, silent and motionless compared to the swirling, rushing rollercoaster ride of *Vagabond* through the ocean.

He stopped unnoticed a few feet away and looked with her out over the water, the night breeze stirring her long hair away from her face.

'Oh!' she said, turning her face as she became aware of his presence.

'Incredible, isn't it?' he asked softly.

She turned away again to look out at the river of moonlight that sparkled across the ocean towards them from the east.

'Yes,' she said.

Neil stood close behind her, steadying himself with his right arm on the wheelhouse roof and smiling, in love with *Vagabond*, the sea, the night, the moon.

'Who's steering?' Jeanne asked, turning briefly back to him, her face obscured with her back to the moon.

'*Vagabond*,' he answered. 'She told me she wanted to handle things herself for a while.'

Jeanne rose slightly to stare past him into the wheelhouse and saw the unattended wheel. Then she looked up at the sails and aft at the three white rivers of light bubbling out behind them. Finally she looked back at Neil. 'Amazing,' she said.

'As long as there are wind, sails, and sea, the world won't be all bad,' he said.

'For *you*,' she commented.

'For me,' he agreed quietly.

'I'm still not comfortable out here,' she said. 'The idea that there's a mile of water beneath me and no dry land within a hundred miles is a little terrifying. I'm sorry.'

173

'If it weren't a little terrifying,' Neil replied after a pause, 'it wouldn't be so beautiful.'

She too took a time before commenting. 'For a while I thought you weren't emotional about anything,' she said.

'I guess I'm not,' he replied. 'Except about the sea.'

'Millions can die but a good wind cures all,' she said, not sarcastically but rather questioningly, as if trying to understand him.

'If I can't save the millions,' Neil replied cautiously, 'then I'm willing to enjoy a good wind.'

'But what if you can?' she countered.

'Then I'd like to know how.'

She turned away and stared out into the darkness. 'No, the millions are lost,' she finally said. 'And I have to admit you're good at saving the single digits.'

Neil remained standing behind her, the magic of the moment now lost in the awareness of the world's problems flooding in.

'A ship's no place for children,' Jeanne went on quietly. 'Especially with reduced rations . . . no definite destination . . . people sick . . . their whole previous lives . . . gone forever . . .'

'I know,' Neil said, 'but children who've just . . . lost their father, seen their mother beaten up, been struck on the head with a gun, aren't likely to be comfortable in any new place.' He paused. 'But Lisa's doing great out here,' he went on. 'Skippy will too. Give him time.'

'I suppose so,' she said. 'But the portions of food you're letting us serve are so pathetically small it's frightening.'

'I know,' Neil said, having to grab the back of Jeanne's settee when a swell sent him staggering. 'But just ask yourself how you're going to feed Skippy two weeks from today.'

She grimaced, nodded, and finally managed a small smile.

'I keep forgetting that the next supermarket may be a decade away.'

'If we're lucky,' Neil replied. The radio reports made it

clear that back on the mainland supermarkets had ceased to exist even in the untouched areas. Everything – even in the farm regions – was being confiscated and rationed by the military. Food was going to be their major worry for a long, long time. He and Jeanne had created an emergency food kit on their second day at sea, good for ten days, he figured, at half-rations, but not counting that emergency cache they had enough food even at their present low rate of consumption for only four or five more days. Catching fish was their key to survival.

A random wave slapped loudly at the speeding hull and sent a fine spray up over them in the cockpit. As he stood there he suddenly felt a strong sense of Jeanne's fear and loneliness.

'I'm afraid stability and the familiar are gone forever,' he said quietly.

She was still looking out over the sea. 'Even on land there's no place left to stand,' she said in a low voice.

In a shattering rush Neil was aware of her as a woman, filled with the desire to hold her, protect her, care for her. He released his grip on the wheelhouse roof and took a stride towards her just as an unexpected swell lifted *Vagabond*'s port hull and then lowered it with a slam, sending Neil tumbling forward and down on to Jeanne. After clutching her right thigh to steady himself he ended up seated beside her on the cockpit seat.

'What's happening?' she asked him urgently. 'Are you all right?'

Neil laughed softly. He could see her face clearly for the first time in the moonlight. Her bruise was almost gone and she looked beautiful.

'I wanted to come over and comfort and protect you,' he said, smiling. 'Instead I almost knocked you overboard.'

Gazing wide-eyed at him, she took a while to absorb what he'd said. 'Maybe you'd better get us life jackets,' she commented, smiling.

For Neil the world was reduced to her eyes gleaming in the

moonlight. He pulled her gently against him, holding her head and hair against the side of his face, simply holding her close. He only noticed the stiffness of her initial response when he felt her suddenly sag against him, relax and sigh.

'Oh, Neil,' she said, and he felt her arms tighten around his back, her powerful hug surprising him. After a long moment they released the strength of their embrace and Jeanne pulled back her head to look with her large glowing eyes into his. Their faces then came together as slowly and inevitably and perfectly as *Vagabond* correcting her course; their lips touched, wetted, parted, kissed. Neil lost track of time and place and when the kiss ended and Jeanne gasped for breath he instinctively glanced at the sails and sea to assure himself that his ship was still on course.

Jeanne sighed. 'Well,' she said, blinking her eyes and looking a little dazed. 'Well.'

'How beautiful you are,' said Neil.

She looked up at him uncertainly. 'Hold me,' she said, coming into his arms again, her face against his.

'NEIL! . . . NEIL!'

When Jim's voice invaded their world with cruel suddenness Neil released Jeanne and stood up.

'Over here, Jim,' he said, looking into the wheelhouse and dimly seeing Jim standing at the wheel looking for him.

'Oh, there you are,' Jim said, rubbing his eyes. 'I just came up to go on watch and saw no one at the wheel and panicked.'

'*Vagabond*'s sails are balanced,' he said, remaining near Jeanne. 'She's self-steering.'

'Really? That's fantastic,' Jim said, coming towards Neil. 'Isn't it about time for me to take the helm. I thought you said . . . Oh! . . . Hi, Jeanne.'

'Hi, Jim,' Jeanne said.

'It's about twelve-thirty,' Neil said, glancing at his watch. 'Since *Vagabond* was doing the job by herself I thought I'd let you and Lisa sleep.'

'Thanks,' said Jim. 'Wow. Look at that moon.'

176

Neil turned to follow Jim's stare out to the east, his eye just meeting Jeanne's briefly.

'It's quite a night,' Neil agreed.

'I feel great,' said Jim. 'I think I needed the extra sleep.'

'Do you want me to fix you some coffee?' Jeanne asked.

'Oh, no, I'm fine,' said Jim. 'Besides, Neil says we can't have any coffee at night except under pressure conditions.'

'"Pressure conditions"?' Jeanne inquired, looking up at Neil.

'I think it means no coffee unless we're sinking,' said Jim, grinning.

'I doubt we'll be able to get any more coffee unless we end up in South America,' Neil commented with his usual seriousness. 'It's now a delicacy. Sorry.'

'Our Captain Bligh,' said Jeanne, smiling.

'He was a marvellous sea man,' Neil rejoined.

'But unpopular with his crew,' said Jeanne.

'*I* like Neil,' said Jim seriously, and Jeanne and Neil both laughed.

A sudden violent snapping and flapping from forward sent Neil rushing past Jim over to starboard. The genoa was luffing and *Vagabond* was veering off-course up wind. He turned the wheel to the right and when he saw her swinging back on course realized that the genoa sheet had come loose.

'Winch the genny in,' he said to Jim, who had followed him over to help. As he steadied *Vagabond*'s course, he watched Jim pull in the line controlling the genoa, first by hand and then with three wraps around the winch.

'Far enough?' Jim finally asked.

'A little more,' Neil said.

When the genoa was sheeted to Neil's satisfaction and with *Vagabond* once again contentedly galloping southwards through the night, Neil turned the helm over to Jim.

'I think she'll steer herself still,' Neil said. 'But you may have to adjust the genny or mizzen sheets to get it right. Do you remember how I showed you?'

'Sure. I've got her now.'

'Good.'

Neil turned to see if Jeanne was still there and saw her standing next to the entrance to her cabin. He walked over to stand behind her, just touching, their backs to Jim, looking out to sea.

'How strange it is,' he heard her say softly after a long pause. 'Here my husband is just dead, millions just killed, millions more doomed, and all I can think of is wanting a man I've known for a few days in bed with me.'

Startled he turned to her. 'Jeanne . . .' he said.

'But I can't . . .'

'. . . Jeanne,' he whispered again. 'Life doesn't offer us much these days . . . We should take what we can . . .'

Separated by only six inches, she turned to look up at him, the moonlight full on her face, his in shadow.

'No, Neil,' she said softly. 'There are others. And my God, only four days . . . I think I owe it to Bob, and to . . . Frank . . . to you even, to assume it's just . . . temporary insanity.'

'Would we were always insane like this,' said Neil.

'No, Neil,' she said and, squeezing his hand once, stepped down her cabin steps and disappeared below. Vaguely Neil thought she might also have whispered a 'goodnight'. He reluctantly slid her hatch closed and, exhilarated and alive, turned back into the wheelhouse. Jim was now sitting on the edge of the other cockpit coaming, staring forward.

'I'm going to rest here in the wheelhouse,' Neil said to him. 'And if you fall overboard,' he went on, noting Jim's somewhat precarious perch on the side of the boat, 'remember to leave a forwarding address.'

'An island in the South Pacific,' Jim responded immediately.

Stretching himself out on the cushions, Neil yawned. 'You'd better be in good shape,' he commented.

'Goodnight,' he heard Jim say to him.

178

'That's my impression,' said Neil, smiling to himself, until the sudden image of Frank chilled him.

Vagabond, indifferent to it all, plunged forward through the night.

2

After Neil had fallen asleep on the cushions in the back of the wheelhouse Jim was forced to resume steering. The wind picked up and was heading them more; he wasn't able to get the sails adjusted to permit *Vagabond* to self-steer. Even though he looked forward to her company on their watch he decided to let Lisa sleep a little longer. He wanted time alone to think.

Although he had disagreed with his father at the time, Jim admired him for trying to get back to their home in Oyster Bay to try to save his mother and Susie. Jim knew that Frank had a fierce loyalty to his family, a pride in it that often made him too severe on his children. Now that he himself was all the family that his father had left Jim felt a sense of responsibility towards him he'd never felt before. This sense of caring was increased by his realization that more than any of the others aboard his father appeared still in a state of shock.

Jim knew he had been hurt by Neil's taking over command of *Vagabond* and that of course his radiation sickness must be depressing him. Jim could see that Frank lacked his usual dynamic energy. When he had worked with him tearing down the remains of the shattered rear wall of the wheelhouse and designing a sail-awning that could be raised and lowered, Frank had been enthusiastic about the work for half an hour and then lost interest, wandering away and leaving the project to others. The only person who seemed able to bring him to life was Jeanne. When she'd suggested that all the men be involved in kitchen work he had smiled at her and argued playfully, 'What's the sense of surviving if I have to wash the dishes?' but nevertheless cleaned up the galley more cheerfully than Jim had ever seen. When Jeanne had become impatient with Skippy's clinging, Frank had spent close to an hour playing horsy and card games with him. Since he knew how much his father *cared* for Jeanne's feelings, the closeness of Neil and Jeanne implied by their whispering together earlier made Jim uneasy.

For although Jim had been too caught up in the rush for survival over the first four days to feel grief for his mother and Susie, now, when he was aware of his father's problems, he experienced a sense of loss. He would never be able to express his love of and appreciation for his mother; she had been cheated out of receiving the love that both he and Frank would have given her had she survived to be with them. Jim's caring for his father was reinforced by this sense of having failed his mother. But how could he help him?

Lisa emerged from her mother's cabin out into the moonlight and came into the wheelhouse.

'It's our watch,' she said. 'Why didn't you wake me?' She was wearing jeans and a blue windbreaker, her hair, dark and long like her mother's, tied into a ponytail. Since none of them could wash with fresh water everyone's hair was getting stiff and straggly.

'Until the wind got too strong *Vagabond* was self-steering,' Jim replied in a low voice, motioning towards Neil. 'Careful, Neil's sleeping.'

'Oh,' she responded, glancing to her right.

Jim felt a little burst of happiness at her nearness as she came to stand beside him at the helm. He took her hand in his. Even though they had flirted with each other the previous summer and were even closer now, since the horrors of the war Jim had felt almost asexual, as if anything too pleasant were obscene. But they needed to touch each other and often held hands while on watch.

'Mom's pacing woke me up,' Lisa said softly. 'She was going up and down the narrow floor space like a subway shuttle.'

'I'm glad you're here,' Jim said, thinking of Jeanne and Neil embracing but not wanting to tell Lisa. For a moment they stood silently, *Vagabond* plunging and hissing through the night.

'*Vagabond*'s really moving, isn't it?' Lisa said.

'It's great,' Jim whispered back.

'You want something to drink?' Lisa asked.

'No, I'm okay.'

'Did you check on Seth?'

'Oh, no, I didn't.'

Lisa took a flashlight and went aft to Neil's cabin to see if Seth needed anything. Seth's right thigh had become infected and whether the antibiotic Macklin was administering would kill it wasn't yet determined. Seth had joked to them about the circumstances of his being hit by saying, 'That's the last time I come up on deck to find out what's going on.'

As Lisa pushed back the hatch and started to descend the short ladder she was startled to see a dim light and the figure of Conrad Macklin sitting in the darkness beside Seth, who seemed to be sleeping.

'Oh!' Lisa said, frightened.

'Can I help you?' Macklin asked quietly.

'I . . . I didn't know . . . I was checking on Seth.'

'He's alive,' Macklin stated indifferently.

'What . . . what are you . . . ?'

'You ever tried sleeping up forward?' Macklin answered. 'I was bouncing like someone was dribbling me.'

'Oh,' said Lisa, noticing now that there was a red glow indicating Neil's radio was on and that Macklin had some papers in his lap.

'I'm sleeping back here,' Macklin went on, 'until your boyfriend stops trying to smash my skull against the forward cabin roof.'

Lisa left with a queasiness from the surge and sway below and an uneasiness about her encounter with Macklin. On her way back to the wheelhouse she noticed a light in Frank's cabin and back with Jim she told him that Macklin was with Seth and that his father seemed to be up.

'Dad's not sleeping well,' Jim said. 'He's still sick.'

'I know,' said Lisa, taking Jim's hand in hers. 'Do you think . . . it's . . .'

'I hope it'll go away in a few days,' said Jim. 'Neil and Olly don't seem bad and they were exposed almost as much.'

'Mom thinks he's a little depressed about losing . . . your mother.'

Jim merely nodded, staring forward into the darkness.

'Do you think she's dead?' Lisa asked softly.

'Yes,' said Jim.

'My Dad's dead too,' said Lisa. '. . . Sometimes it seems like he never lived . . . Everything is . . . so changed.' Lisa released his hand and steadied herself against the control-panel shelf.

'It's strange,' Jim said, putting his arm around her waist. 'Everything I used to be interested in, you know, sports, music, cars, seems sort of far away. I tried listening to some of my favourite tapes and I started to . . . you know, I felt like crying. It was pretty funny.'

Lisa didn't reply, gently moving closer against him. She wanted to put her arm around him but felt awkward and left her hands on the moulding.

'I'm glad you're here, Lisa,' Jim went on very softly. 'I get kinda lonely with my Dad . . . sick and Neil all wrapped up in the boat. You're about the only part of the old world that seems . . . all right.'

'I . . . I'm glad you're here, too,' she said, letting her head fall against his shoulder. 'We will be all right, won't we, Jim?' There was a wistful quality in her voice which Jim felt viscerally.

He hesitated, all the horrors, past and still possible, clamouring for his attention.

'Yes,' he replied simply, pulling her more tightly against him, and ignoring the clamour. 'But not unless we take down the genoa and reef the main.'

She looked up at him puzzled.

'The wind's too strong,' he went on. 'I think the number one watch team better reduce sail.'

She smiled and without further command took over the wheel from Jim who, smiling back, left to get his safety harness and go forward.

3

By mid-morning of the following day Neil's midnight romance had become unreal. Reality was upon him in the form of a crowded wheelhouse and thirty-knot winds out of the east-southeast.

After breakfast he and Frank had listened to another appalling news summary. Refugees were flooding southwards all over the world and being resented and rebuffed by the local populations in the traditional ways of treating war refugees. Cuba, the Panama Canal, and Venezuelan oil installations had all been struck by some sort of nuclear weapon; the Caribbean too would be a disaster area. It wasn't even clear which nation had hit Venezuela, since she, like all the rest of South America, had loudly declared her neutrality and was refusing to sell oil to the United States.

And later, at eight A.M., with the wind now beginning to screech through the stainless steel rigging, and Tony injuring a rib in a fall while trying to bring in a torn jib, reality was fully back. In the crowded wheelhouse under an overcast and darkening sky, Skippy was whining about the taste of fish, Lisa vomited her breakfast on the wheelhouse floor, and Jeanne, queasy herself, was trying to deal with them. For Neil, battling the helm, there was no room for romance with a torn jib, an injured crewman, rising winds and seas, and Frank and Tony arguing with him about their course.

By dead reckoning from their noon position of the day before Neil calculated that they were about a hundred miles east-southeast of Cape Lookout, North Carolina, a spit of land that ended the long sand barrier that stretched south of the notorious Cape Hatteras. Without consulting the others, Neil had been maintaining a southerly course, partly because he was considering a run to the Bahamas and West Indies rather than trying to put in again to the US mainland. Frank had complained the previous afternoon that they seemed to be staying unnecessarily far off the coast and suggested they angle more westward. Now with large angry swells sweeping up against them from the south and the wind still rising, a choice was being forced upon him. They could either continue to work their way south, or they could turn and run back towards land.

They had been unable to pick up a radio station in the Morehead City–Pamlico Sound area of North Carolina and thus had no way of knowing what conditions would be like there.

Reports from the Bahamas about the West Indies were discouraging.. The Bahamian government had declared a state of emergency and martial law, warning Bahamians that the food imports on which they had depended for more than eighty per cent of their normal food had been cut off by the war. Foreign ships, by which Neil knew must be meant American ships, were urged to go elsewhere. As panic buying had eliminated most of the island's stores of food, the Bahamians were not welcoming the sudden influx of sick, injured, and foodless Americans fleeing from the two nuclear explosions over Miami and Cape Canaveral.

Radio Nassau had implied a racial incident in reporting that five American 'yachtsmen' had been killed by several unapprehended black Bahamians 'in a streetfight'. If *Vagabond* had to by-pass the Bahamas they would run quite short of food and water before they could hope to reach Puerto Rico or the Virgin Islands. Jim's and Lisa's success the last two mornings hooking three big fish was encouraging, but they were in the Gulf Stream now; if they continued south, in another day or two they'd be east of it and the fishing less dependable.

As the wind freshened further and storm clouds gathered on the southern horizon like thick black smoke, Neil had to admit that he was also worried about *Vagabond*'s being badly

186

overloaded. A good trimaran normally sails faster than a good monohull because of its lightness, which permits it to skip over the water rather than plough through it. But *Vagabond* was now almost two thousand pounds heavier than the ship they had sailed north and was sailing two or three knots slower. It made her pound heavily into the huge seas which were rolling at her.

Although altering course to run before the storm would end the slamming that was the greatest danger and discomfort, Neil knew that even then the wind and seas would continue to drain energy from those aboard. In his own experience thirty-five knot winds and twelve-foot seas were bearable, but for most of the others they represented a danger far more immediate, palpable, and unpleasant than anything on the mainland. All were seasick except Neil, Olly, Tony and Elaine, and since none of those were the types to go cleaning up other people's messes, most of the cabins were beginning to stink of vomit. With Seth's bullet wounds, Tony's cracked rib and general seasickness, their crew was considerably weakened.

But despite the problems, he hated the thought of turning back towards the fallout and explosions and people-evil of the land. A storm at sea was something he could deal with; the effects of man's madness on land were not.

As he made the rounds of the ship before meeting with Frank, Tony and Macklin to discuss their course, he knew that to continue southwards against these seas would create serious morale problems. It might be exhilarating to escape from explosions, pirates and radioactive fallout, but with those dangers now distant and remote, the endless slamming, slamming, slamming, the awful whine of the wind in the rigging, the woeful roll, pitch, and plunge of the trimaran, the seasickness, and worst of all he knew, no indication of any safer haven south than west, was depressing most of the ship's company. Only Elaine and Tony had complained directly, but the averted gaze of Jeanne, and the sardonic humour of

Frank and Seth revealed similar feelings.

He, Tony, Frank and Olly gathered around the dinette table at eleven-thirty that morning, the four of them swaying and bumping in their seats as *Vagabond* plunged and smashed forward through the huge seas. Jim was at the helm while an almost useless Conrad Macklin sat in misery on the little seat in the corner of the cabin. Everyone else was below in a berth. Frank, pale and weakened from vomiting, and Tony, seeming as energetic and healthy as ever, had both been urging Neil to change course for several hours.

Even before they could begin their discussion, *Vagabond* struck a big roller with a savage smash that spilled silverware out of a drawer and toppled half a dozen books out of the dinette bookcase. Neil went immediately up on deck and instructed Jim to bring *Vagabond* around ninety degrees to head due west while they had their discussion. As he watched and instructed Lisa in adjusting the sheets of the storm jib and double-reefed mainsail, Neil felt immediately how much easier the motion of the boat became. *Vagabond* now began surfing along and down the big swells instead of having to plough through them, and though the noise of the water and wind was little diminished, the actual strains on the boat had probably been halved.

When Neil returned to the main cabin Frank and Tony looked pleased.

'What a different feeling,' Tony announced triumphantly. 'Thank God we didn't wreck poor *Vagabond* before we changed course.'

'Yes,' Neil commented dryly. 'How lucky.'

'Are we going to hold course back to land?' Frank asked.

'Not necessarily. That's a decision that I've decided should be made by the four ship's officers,' Neil replied.

'What about the rest of us?' Tony interjected. 'Don't Seth and me and Jeanne count for anything?'

'That's right,' said Frank. 'I'm not sure it's fair not to include all the adults.'

Neil glanced at Olly, who was leaning back with his eyes closed holding his unlit pipe in his mouth, and at Tony, also opposite him, who was flushed with excitement.

'Are you prepared, Frank,' Neil countered, 'if outvoted by Tony, Seth, Macklin, and Elaine, to surrender the ship's fate to majority decision?'

Rubbing his big hands in front of him, his face wet from the sweat of his nausea, Frank scowled.

'No, I guess not,' he answered slowly. 'We should consult with everybody, but the decision should be made by the four officers.' He didn't look up at Tony opposite him.

'Well, Tony,' Neil said neutrally to Tony, who had flushed at Frank's betrayal. 'What do you advise?'

'You know what I advise,' Tony answered angrily. 'That we stop beating our brains out and get back to land. You promised us in the Chesapeake that we'd be landing back on the US coast. You can't go back on that.'

'Would you feel that way if we begin to run into fallout?'

'Of course not,' Tony snapped back. 'But we should try to get back. Especially when the damn boat is getting smashed to pieces.'

'Frank?' Neil asked quietly.

'We should run before the storm and get back to land,' he said, again not looking up.

'Olly?'

'Whatever you want, Cap, is all right by me,' Captain Olly replied promptly without even bothering to open his eyes. 'I like it out here, but if you feel we ought to go unload a few landlubbers it's okay by me.'

Neil smiled and stood up.

'I'll go consult the others,' he said.

Five minutes later he returned. 'Jim and Seth say they'd rather I decided,' Neil announced quietly as he resumed his seat opposite a now dozing Captain Olly. 'I . . .'

'What the fuck is this shit?' Tony exploded. 'You got everybody but me and Frank under your thumb?'

189

'I doubt it,' Neil replied. 'I'm sure that if Macklin here had the strength to comment he'd want to return to land.'

'You're damn right,' Tony said. 'And what about Elaine?'

'She was sleeping, but I'm sure she'd vote the way you do.'

'You're damn right.'

'And Jeanne?' Frank asked softly.

Jeanne's vote would have been decisive for Neil, but fortunately – or unfortunately – she had been as ambivalent as Neil himself. She was miserable with her seasickness and that of Skip, and frightened of the crashes of the waves against the seemingly flimsy plywood of the hull, but she had at first joked by urging Neil to 'take me away from it all', and 'to take her some place where she could die in peace.' But just before he had left she had clutched his arm and said earnestly, 'You've saved me and my children twice already. I'd be a fool to question how you plan to do it a third time.'

'Jeanne essentially left it up to me also,' Neil finally answered Frank.

'None of this proxy shit,' Tony persisted. 'The fact is that most of those with minds of their own know we ought to be getting back to the mainland.'

'Frank votes your way and Jim and Olly abstain,' Neil went on quietly. 'My personal decision . . .'

'I insist you consult those others,' Tony interrupted.

'My personal decision,' Neil went on, 'is that we continue on a course to close with the mainland until the weather moderates or we encounter the danger of radioactive fallout.'

'It's only fair that . . . What?' Tony said, taken aback by Neil's decision.

'Frank, when you and Tony go on duty an hour from now,' Neil said, turning to his friend beside him, 'try the transistor radio every hour to pick up news about conditions along the North Carolina coast.'

'Fine,' said Frank.

'We're about a hundred miles off the coast now,' Neil continued. 'At this rate we'll close on the coast during the night. We've got to find out if the big navigational lights are in operation.'

'They've got emergency generators,' Frank said.

'I know. They *should* be working. However, I'd prefer not to sail on to the Hatteras or Lookout shoals to find out they're not.'

'We're going back to the mainland?' Tony asked, still adjusting to his unexpected victory.

'If the mainland will have us,' Neil replied, rising again. 'I'm going to check with the short wave to see if I can find out more about this storm. See you later.'

After Neil had left, Olly announced that he was going to take a nap and went forward to lie down. Frank poured himself and Tony a tiny amount of whisky in water and sat down again.

'Well, we won that one,' Tony said.

Startled, Frank looked up at him.

'I think Neil realizes,' Tony went on, 'that he can't run this boat without our support. He's made himself captain, but in effect we have veto power.'

Frank sipped at his drink.

'And I want you to know, Frank,' Tony went on, leaning forward and putting one of his hands on Frank's arm, 'that if push ever comes to shove, I'm behind you one hundred per cent. You understand?'

Frank stared at his drink.

'One hundred per cent,' Tony repeated, standing up. 'As far as I'm concerned you already are the captain.' He paused, staring down at Frank, who didn't look up. When *Vagabond* surfed down a big wave Tony staggered forward, steadying himself against the wall behind Frank.

'I gotta take a piss,' he concluded, and left Frank alone. Frank stared at his drink another ten seconds, then, grimacing, tossed the rest of it off. The grimace continued until, looking sick and swearing irritably under his breath, he went hurriedly up the hatchway steps for fresh air.

When Tony came out of the john Conrad Macklin was

seated at the dinette and had poured himself a shot of whisky. Tony sat down opposite him.

'I thought you were too sick to drink,' Tony said.

'I'm only too sick to stand watch,' Macklin answered indifferently, looking coolly at Tony and pouring the other man a drink.

'You hear what I said to Frank?' Tony asked, holding his plastic cup of whisky.

Macklin nodded and took a short swig from his cup.

'But you know, Tony,' he said after a short silence. 'Frank will never be captain of this ship.'

'No?' said Tony, steadying the bottle after it slid a few inches from *Vagabond*'s surfing along the face of a wave.

'He'll be dead in a month,' said Macklin. 'And besides, he hasn't got the guts to be captain.'

'Well, all I know is that Loken makes like a dictator.'

Macklin nodded and sipped gingerly again at his drink, his round owlish face and eyes examining Tony without expression.

'Sooner or later, Tony,' he went on softly, 'he's going to kick you and me off the boat.'

Tony looked up quickly. 'You, maybe,' he countered. 'But why me? I'm as good a sailor as he is, maybe better.'

Macklin smiled and nodded meaningfully. 'That's exactly why he has to get rid of you,' he said to Tony. 'He knows you're the only other man aboard with captain potential.'

Tony looked at Macklin uncertainly, the sway of the kerosene lantern creating shadows that made it difficult to decipher Macklin's expression.

'Sooner or later,' Macklin went on softly, 'either you'll get kicked off . . . or you and I will have to take over the boat.'

'No one's kicking me off anything,' Tony snapped back.

'That's right, Tony,' Macklin replied, nodding. 'That's right.'

Macklin held his half-filled cup towards Tony and, after a pause, Tony understood. The two men clicked their cups together and drank.

4

When the rain began falling that afternoon Neil called out all hands that had strength to come up on deck to catch and store as much water as they could. Because the winds were gusting by then to over forty knots and the double-reefed mainsail couldn't be used as it normally could to channel rain water into buckets, Neil had his crew use instead a small jib and two nylon Bimini covers. They caught as much as they could in these, then channelled the water into buckets and at last into the main storage tanks and their large plastic containers. With the winds making their nylon collectors difficult to control and his crew never having tried the manoeuvre, there was much swearing and quite a bit of spilled rain water. However, Neil had also stopped up the drains holes in the cockpits to be scooped up later. By late afternoon they had gathered almost twenty gallons, more than half of it quite clear, and even that rescued from the cockpits was potable. Because they were at last headed back towards land and many were seasick, Tony and Elaine and a few others complained it was all an unnecessary game, but Neil kept them at it for two hours. By dusk, there were quite a few grumblers.

For Jeanne the day seemed endless. The smell of vomit permeated her cabin, and though the horrifying blasts of the sea against her cabin wall had ended, *Vagabond* still seemed to be thrown around like a tiny dinghy. Elaine, although thoroughly frightened most of the morning, had been reassured by a solicitous Tony for over an hour in the early afternoon and emerged from their *tête-à-tête* quite cheerful, and as oblivious of the rolling and plunging of *Vagabond* as a globecircling sailor. Her daughter Rhoda was sick, but nothing seemed to disturb the bland Elaine, who, unable to concentrate on anything for more than a minute or two, was another source of misery for Jeanne.

A delicate, wide-eyed blonde, Elaine let her child demand most of her time and was helpless at any job given to her. So exasperated had Jeanne become with her when she was sent to help in the galley that she and Lisa had decided to ask her to stay topside. Jeanne had offered Elaine and Rhoda the use of her berth and usually slept on the floor herself, but at night Elaine would wake her up sometimes to ask her to get Rhoda a cup of water since Jeanne 'was already up', namely on the floor. The child was cranky and slept poorly. Her toys and Elaine's clothes and toiletries could never be confined to the cubicles Jeanne asked her to use but ended up around the cabin as if sprayed there by a random explosion.

Elaine was off somewhere with Tony now, and while Skippy, somewhat recovered from his seasickness, played on the cabin floor a few feet away, Jeanne lay on her back staring at the ceiling and wishing she could express her fears to Neil and be reassured and comforted. She hated feeling so helpless, hated being unable to focus her thoughts on the war or on her feelings for Neil or on anything except the dizzying, nauseating motion of the ship.

Frank came down three or four times to comfort her and see if there was anything he could do, but when he tried to clean up some of the vomit he himself became sick again and had to hasten topside.

Neil appeared only twice, once to ask her opinion on their course – an opinion she was reluctant to give since her mind felt like mashed potatoes still being beaten in the blender – and a second time in the afternoon. He suggested she try to come up and assist in the rain catching.

That time she had struggled out of her berth, stood weakly for about thirty seconds and then fallen woozily into his arms. He had to pick her up and lift her back into her berth.

'I hope you're not blaming the captain for this,' he finally said.

'I'm beyond blaming,' she replied wearily, realizing sadly that she wished he would go away and couldn't see her looking like a drowned cat. And smelling worse.

'You'll be over it by tomorrow,' he suggested. 'Get some sleep.'

'I'll never be over it,' she moaned. 'I'll remember this moment as long as I live.'

'Since it's so special I plan to try to see to it that you live a very long time,' Neil said.

She looked over at him, tried to smile and feebly squeezed his hand.

'I'm sorry I'm letting you down,' she said.

'Never,' he said. 'I just hoped the fresh air might help.' Neil released her hand and, with the edge of the sheet, wiped the perspiration from her face. Then he disappeared. Frank came twice more, but she didn't see Neil again until the next day.

The final indignity for Jeanne came that evening as the storm seemed to be getting even worse. Elaine came cheerfully down into the cabin and told her that Jeanne could sleep in her berth that night, with little Rhoda. Elaine was going to be with Tony. So Jeanne, miserable, was left to babysit while Elaine spent the night being 'comforted' by Tony.

She was too sick to be angry. She barely had strength to wonder where the lovers had a chance to become lovers in the crowded boat. Some day she'd have to ask.

They picked up the light at Cape Lookout at midnight. By two-thirty A.M. they had left it on their starboard beam while making for the Morehead City Inlet. The storm, Neil had concluded, must be coming directly at them. The winds, instead of becoming more northerly as he had expected if the storm were passing to seaward of them, were in fact becoming more southerly. The storm centre must be coming right up the coastline. In any case, the winds were still blowing at about forty-five knots with stronger gusts and the seas remained between eight and ten feet. To turn south now would be impossible.

Fortunately the Morehead City Inlet was wide, deep, and well-buoyed. Moreover, immediate protection was available as soon as they got inside and turned west towards the turning basin. Neil had entered the channel on half a dozen occasions, and although he hated approaching land in a storm, he had no strong fears under the present conditions, not with a boat and a crew he had confidence in.

As they neared the inlet it was Frank and Tony's watch. Lisa and Jim, who had just come off duty, remained on deck more out of excitement than necessity. Still sailing under storm jib and double-reefed main they had already picked up the white flashing sea-buoy that marked the beginning of the big ship channel when Neil turned on the transistor radio. He wanted to try again to pick up local news about conditions in the Morehead City area. The best he could do was a station from Charleston, South Carolina. A voice announced that they were going to repeat the President's address to the nation which had taken place at ten o'clock that evening – five hours before.

With Frank handling the helm and the radio placed on the shelf to his left, the other three men and Lisa lined up along the front of the wheelhouse, peering through the plexiglas windows with their half-dozen bullet holes, out into the darkness, and listening to the President's voice.

'Good evening, my fellow Americans,' the voice began, slow, sombre and sincere. 'It is my sad duty to speak to you on this fifth day of this horrible conflict. Our nation, a victim of the unprovoked attack by the Soviet Union, has suffered immense devastation. So many of our cities have been destroyed that, as you know, our communications with each other have been considerably reduced. The ability of your government to deal with the chaos and suffering which is occurring in many sections of our land is extremely limited. It

196

is the task of our military forces to continue to wage war on the Soviet Union, not only to avenge the horror they have inflicted upon us, but in order to try to destroy their nation before the freedom of all peoples is removed from the earth.

'Those of us who have survived the initial Soviet onslaught must keep always in our hearts that we are fighting on now both for our individual survival and for the survival of the very idea of freedom. Mankind is at a terrifying crossroads: whether we shall all fall to the slavery of communist dictatorship or live on with our principles of individualism and freedom. I urge you all to do everything in your power to contribute to this struggle.

'I have unleashed the power of all our military might against the Soviet Union. I am happy to report to you this morning that though more than half of our great nation lies in ruins, even more of the Soviet Union has been destroyed. We have received no further reports of effective enemy action in the last twenty-four hours. The Russian people, like you, are suffering for the evil of their attack.

'However, despite our successes, I'm afraid that this morning I must issue a momentous warning and executive order. I have been advised by our best scientists working with the National Security Council that all Americans still living in certain areas in the northeastern part of our country must evacuate immediately. I am speaking now to the people of eastern Ohio, New York, Massachusetts, Connecticut, Rhode Island, Pennsylvania, New Jersey, Maryland and Delaware. Within ten days to two weeks the radioactive fallout from the war will have accumulated to such a degree that its effects will make life in these areas almost impossible. Residents are to move as quickly as possible either to Canada or areas in the far north of the region, or south at least as far as North Carolina. United States military forces will provide all assistance at their disposal, but airplanes and vehicles are limited. In most cases you will have to provide your own transportation.

197

'Do not be deceived if your area has not yet received significant radioactive fallout. All indications are that radioactivity and its effects will spread and become worse, causing not only direct death to humans, but contaminating water and food supplies, which will render life unsustainable. Thus, I hereby direct all citizens . . .'

The President's voice went firmly on, reporting next on the greatly reduced fighting in Europe caused by the high number of casualties on each side and indicating that he considered the stalemate as a victory for the forces of freedom, although the destruction of most of Europe was, of course, a great historical tragedy.

He also indicated that he had sent a stern note to the governments of all thirteen nations of South America. He indicated grave consequences if they continued to declare strict neutrality in the world conflict. Although most of these governments were fascist dictatorships, they still historically were part of the free peoples of the American continent and their refusal to permit United States military forces to use certain ports, air bases and oil depots for repairs and resupply was hampering the war effort. In particular, the decision of Venezuela and Trinidad–Tobago to cease selling oil to the US was an economic act of war and would not be tolerated. He also condemned the governments of Mexico, the Bahamas, and several unnamed South American countries for their unjust, shortsighted, and sometimes cruel treatment of American war refugees. He concluded his address with the announcement that with Congress unable to meet, he was using powers granted to him as Commander-in-Chief under martial law to order all Americans between the ages of 18 and 45 to report immediately for military service. His last words were an appeal to his fellow Americans to stand tall in this great crisis.

When the President had finished speaking and a comentator began summarizing his address, Neil turned off the radio. When Jim and Tony went and sat down on a settee behind

198

where Frank remained at the wheel, Neil sat opposite them. They all became aware again of the sound of the wind and of *Vagabond* rushing down the seas in the darkness.

'It all seems so impossible,' Frank finally said, still staring forward. 'The President talks about the evacuation of the whole northeast as if it were the abandoning of a small town because of a gas leak.'

'I wonder why the big cities got hit so bad,' Tony mused. 'I thought I read some place that Arizona and North Dakota were the places that were going to get clobbered. You know, our missile sites.'

No one answered.

'I wonder what "standing tall" means?' Tony went on in a low voice.

'It means we're all drafted,' Neil commented.

'Is that true?' Jim asked.

'Except for Frank,' Neil replied. 'We're all in the military now.'

'I may not be drafted,' Frank commented from the wheel, 'but there'll be things for me to do too. Our country needs us all now.'

Again no one spoke. *Vagabond* surged and rollercoastered forward in the darkness, rolled and surged again. The three men behind Frank sat silently staring at the floor between them, swaying with the ship's swoops and swerves. Neil stood for a moment to stare forward and then sat down.

'I'd like to fight,' Tony burst out after a while. 'But where the fuck are the Russians? Are they supposed to invade?'

'I don't imagine either side sees much of value left to invade,' Neil replied after a pause.

'What about Cuba?' Tony asked. 'Are we going to take Cuba?'

Neil didn't answer.

'I hope everyone just stops fighting,' Jim said.

'Not until we've won,' said Tony. 'The Army needs us. They'll find something for us to do.'

'I'm sure they will,' said Neil ironically.

'What's that mean?' Tony shot back, sensing the cynicism.

'It means I can't conceive what use civilians inducted now can be in this war.'

'They can be a lot more useful than running away,' Frank said. After a brief, awkward silence, he added: 'Here's the number three red-flashing bell. We're in the channel.'

Fifteen minutes later, in quiet water for the first time in four days, *Vagabond* had all her sails down and lay drifting on the incoming tide awaiting a launch from the Coast Guard, whose cutter lay idling nearby, with its cannon, manned by three sailors, barely visible in the darkness.

The launch party consisted of a lieutenant and four men, two armed with pistols in holsters and two with automatic rifles.

'Who's captain here?' asked the lieutenant, a short, stocky man with a neatly trimmed moustache.

'I am,' said Neil. 'What's the problem?'

'Where are you headed?' the officer rejoined.

'Morehead City obviously.'

'Your purpose?'

'Get out of this storm, land some passengers, take on supplies,' Neil answered, finding the interrogation bordering on the ridiculous.

'How many draft-age persons do you have aboard?' the official persisted.

'Three or four,' Neil answered.

'They are to report to the induction centre on Main Street within twenty-four hours,' the lieutenant said, looking around at the five men. 'How much diesel fuel do you have?'

'About fifteen gallons,' Neil answered, lying for some reason he didn't yet understand.

'Unless you've got a special exemption, we'll have to requisition that fuel later today. Do you have weapons?'

'Only an old twenty-two,' Neil replied quietly.

'All weapons are requisitioned. We'll take your rifle now.'

The officer stared at Neil. 'Also,' he went on, his gaze not wavering, 'my men will search your boat.' He nodded to the bosun who divided the crew men into two teams and began a search.

'Jim, you can go get the twenty-two for the nice men,' Neil said, then turned back to the officer. 'What's the trouble? Why can't we keep our rifle?'

'Civilians are going around shooting each other for food, fuel, fallout shelters, you name it,' the lieutenant replied. 'The only way the military can regain control is to make unauthorized possession of a weapon illegal.'

'How are we expected to defend ourselves?' Tony now asked.

'That's been the trouble,' the officer countered. 'Everybody's been defending themselves so vigorously the morticians can't keep up with it. Leave the defending to the Army, Navy and us.'

'Couldn't someone authorize us to keep the twenty-two aboard?' Frank interjected.

'I doubt it. If you want to waste time, the district military headquarters for this region is located about six miles outside Morehead City.'

'What's the food and fallout situation here?' Neil asked.

'We haven't had any fallout since a small amount on the third day of the war,' the officer said, peeking down into the main cabin. 'This rain has about fifty millarem per hour, but that's not supposed to be a problem.'

'And food?' Neil asked.

'All food here is controlled by the US Army. If you want to eat you'll either have to be in the military or go to a refugee centre.'

'Nothing special, sir,' the bosun reported to his superior, as he returned with the other three. 'Just a few fishing knives.'

'Good,' said the officer with a tired smile. 'Okay, captain, welcome to Morehead City.' He motioned to his crew to return to their launch. 'And by the way,' he added, turning

201

back to Neil and the others, 'without written permission from Colonel Nelson, no military-age men are allowed to proceed out to sea.'

'What's that?' Jim exclaimed.

'No vessel is permitted to sea without permission of the local military commander,' the lieutenant replied. His eyes narrowing as he looked at Jim, he added, 'We've had to sink three different ships who didn't think we meant it.'

And he left.

Vagabond then proceeded to motor slowly up the channel towards the almost totally dark small town of Morehead City, and in another hour was anchored a hundred feet off the main line of docks, Neil wanting them all to be able to get some sleep before they had to confront the world. Although it was four-thirty and dawn should have been beginning the storm system kept the sky a night-time dark.

As the boat was being anchored Jeanne came up on deck and went down to prepare hot tea for Neil, Frank and Tony, who soon joined her in the main cabin. She was pale, with a grey puffiness under the eyes from her long bout of seasickness, but now that *Vagabond* was merely rocking gently in the gusting blasts of wind and not playing at rollercoaster, she was feeling better. Olly was already slumped asleep in the little corner jumpseat in the forward end of the room.

'I could use a drink,' Tony announced, staring irritably at his tea. 'Aren't we supposed to celebrate a landfall?'

'Do you feel like celebrating?' Neil asked.

'I don't feel a damn thing,' Tony answered, taking the bottle of brandy Jeanne placed on the table. 'I'm too beat.'

'Thank God we've made it back to land,' Jeanne said softly, standing with her back to the seated men. Neil, Frank, and Tony looked up at her and then Frank stood up and went to her. While the other two men looked on silently, he embraced her.

'Will we be able to find a place to live?' Jeanne asked Frank, looking up at him.

202

'They have a refugee camp,' Frank answered.

'Is . . . is that where we're all going?' she asked with a surprised frown.

'It looks that way,' Frank said.

'All the men aboard except Frank and Olly have to report for military duty,' Neil said.

'But why?' Jeanne asked, freeing herself from Frank's arms and again looking surprised. 'What possible use can any of you be in the Army?'

'We're in a war, Jeanne,' Frank replied, sitting back down opposite Neil.

'No we're not,' Jeanne responded passionately. 'This isn't a war. It's . . . it's genocidal suicide.'

They all looked up at her.

'We're in a war, Jeanne,' Frank repeated. 'Our country has been attacked.'

'Neil, you don't believe in this draft, do you?' Jeanne said, looking flushed with anger or excitement.

'I suppose it's like this ship,' Neil answered after a long pause. 'In a survival situation everyone has to belong to a military hierarchy or there's chaos. Drafting everyone is the government's way of keeping us out of mischief.'

'And we'll be needed in the Army too,' Tony said. 'They're not calling us up just to keep an eye on us.'

'They'll need *everybody*'s help . . . if the war lasts long enough,' Frank suggested.

The silence was not a happy one.

'I'm not going, Dad,' said Jim, appearing unexpectedly on the companionway steps.

'What do you mean, Jimmy?' Frank asked, frowning.

Jim came down the three steps and stood near and slightly behind his father. Lisa appeared in the cabin entrance.

'I can't report for military service,' he said nervously. 'I won't go.'

Frank turned to look at his son, and then returned his gaze to Jeanne who had sat down opposite him.

'I'm afraid the President has ordered almost all of us to serve,' he said.

'I know, Dad. But I won't fight in this war. Not unless the Russians land troops.'

'No one likes fighting nukes,' Tony said, 'but we've got to serve.'

'It's not the nukes and radiation any more,' Jim said. 'It's just that I've decided this war is all wrong, no matter . . .'

'What about your country?' Frank interrupted, not looking at his son.

'I just think . . . I don't know . . . I want to sail south with you, Dad. Help Lisa and Jeanne and . . .'

'What about your country?' Frank repeated stonily.

'I know, I know,' Jim said, an anguish on his face unseen by his father. 'I owe my country a lot. I know that. But the war seems so insane, the kind of killing so wrong . . . I don't see how . . .'

'Jim can't save the country,' Jeanne said as Jim trailed off.

'BUT HE'S GODDAMN WELL GOING TO TRY!' Frank spat out angrily, banging his fist on the table and tipping over the mostly empty bottle of brandy. As Tony righted it Captain Olly's body jerked upright and his eyes blinked open.

'Huh?' he said. 'What say?'

Frank swung his head to look at Neil. 'Are you going to report for duty?' he asked.

'What I do isn't relevant,' Neil answered. 'With my naval experience, in theory I can be of service, but untrained teenagers would only be cannon fodder. If Jim thinks the war is all wrong he shouldn't go. And I may not go either.'

Frank felt a strange sinking feeling and glared at Neil. 'I should have known,' he said. 'You've taken wishy-washy positions so long you've forgotten a man's duty to his country.'

'I know my duty to my country,' Neil snapped back. 'I just happen to believe that my country is now located primarily on this boat.'

'That's inconvenient,' said Frank, 'because in that case I'm kicking you out of your country.' He felt both a senseless rage and an urge to cry. 'In other words you're fired.' The words seemed hollow even as he spoke them.

'Are you going to force Jim to enter this war?' Jeanne asked.

'He's in it whether he likes it or not.'

'I'm not going to report, Dad,' Jim said, now more steadily. 'I'd like to help sail everyone south.'

'You need Jim,' Jeanne said softly across to Frank. 'In this world if we've been lucky enough to have any children still with us, the last thing we should do is let them go.'

Frank stared at the cushion between Jeanne and Neil and unseeingly added more brandy to his empty tea cup, his eyes wet. A siren wailing off in the city half a mile away underlined the silence. Captain Olly again awakened.

'Don't recommend telling grown kids what to do,' he said.

'No one asked you,' Frank muttered.

''S okay,' Olly replied. 'I don't mind volunteering good advice. People who ask for advice generally made up their minds anyhow.'

Jeanne rose from her seat. 'I'm going to get more sleep,' she said. 'Goodnight, Captain Olly, Tony. Goodnight Neil.' She paused. 'Goodnight, Frank.' She leaned down and held his head in her arms and pressed her face against his hair for several seconds. 'You're a good man, Frank, a . . . but you're absolutely wrong about Jim.' And she left.

'That's one sweet lady, that is,' Captain Olly said. 'Ain't met a woman like her since my last wife. She married?'

The ship's clock on the forward wall of the cabin struck six bells and Neil glanced at it.

'We should set a watch this morning, Frank,' he said. 'We haven't seen the last of pirates. I'll take the first two-hour watch and wake Jim for the second. We can all get up at ten.'

Frank looked up dully. 'You still trying to run things?' he said, then let his head fall forward.

Vagabond was back on land.

5

The town of Morehead City, over one hundred and fifty miles distant from the nearest nuclear explosion, a small city in the middle of a rich farming and fishing region, had, in a way, like most of the rest of the country, ceased to exist. Its restaurants, bars, drugstores, service stations, movie theatres, supermarkets, grocery stores, gift shops, banks, and most merchandise stores were closed. The only traditional commercial enterprises open for a few hours each day were the clothing and hardware stores, and one bar: all had become unofficial bartering centres.

The town had electricity, at least in theory, but the military authorities were systematically disconnecting electric service to all except businesses or institutions it considered necessary. The town had food, at least in theory, since a few fishermen still brought in catches and neighbouring farmers still had chickens, pigs, cows and a few early summer crops. But fuel was unavailable for either the fishing trawlers or farm machinery, and harvests from both sea and land were diminishing. No food arrived from outside the county and all food within was being requisitioned for distribution and rationing by the Army, much of it being shifted to areas with greater need. More than half the tillable acreage was planted in tobacco.

Since no private vehicles were permitted on the road without authorization, most normal social life had ended. Local draft-age adults had disappeared either into one of the services or into the faceless masses of refugees fleeing even further south. Those remaining consisted mainly of men over forty, the sick and the maimed, and women and children. Few people other than farmers and fishermen were still able

206

to continue the same occupation they'd been in a week before.

All newspapers and most local radio and television stations had ceased operating. Only one radio station operated on a limited schedule, its sole function to transmit official information and instructions from the national government or local military authorities. There was no music. The national networks had ceased to exist, but the government was able to use satellites to transmit messages to all stations at once.

All manufacturing not directly related to military needs had ceased. All large department stores had sold out of basic items in the first three days of the war – flashlights, generators, batteries, coolers, knives, hatchets, tools, guns, fishing equipment, camping gear, cooking fuels, and so on, and now, filled with useless non-essentials – television sets, record-players, cosmetics, fashionable clothing – they remained closed, unguarded, and unlooted.

The churches alone were booming. Most held services of one sort or another every day, and street corner end-of-the-world preachers gathered small crowds around them immediately, people who listened listlessly, and then wandered away.

The little town had received an influx of refugees from the areas of Norfolk and Washington, the first burst arriving by car and truck, those in the last few days by foot, bicycle, horse and cart, and by boat down the Intracoastal Waterway. Many were suffering from burns, blindness and radiation sickness.

When the survivors on *Vagabond* were awakened by Jim at ten o'clock they saw boats jammed into every available space, being rafted two and three deep in places. Neil eased *Vagabond* in against an apparently unoccupied luxury yacht, the only space large enough to take the fifty-foot trimaran alongside.

After a reconnaissance trip ashore in the gusty wind and

207

rain it was clear that most of the boats had either been deserted for lack of fuel or lack of crew or were owned by people determined to get further south. Some hoped to continue down the Intracoastal Waterway, and a few were planning to go out of the inlet. Whether these latter would be carrying men officially called to duty and forbidden to leave was unclear: most people were tightlipped about their plans and personnel.

Posted prominently on several dockside telephone poles were posters, printed by hand and xeroxed, warning mariners that no ships were permitted out of the inlet with any male of military age without written authorization from the district military commander.

Looking out towards the inlet Neil could see two US Navy vessels, one looking badly damaged, moored in the Turning Basin. He had never known warships to use Morehead City, but with the naval facilities at Hampton Roads near Norfolk destroyed the Navy's options were clearly reduced.

As the morning wore on Neil became increasingly frustrated at his inability to get any reports on the fallout situation in the southeast. There were only three stations left on the whole A.M. dial, each broadcasting only sporadically. Official statements never indicated what people in the Carolinas could expect.

He was depressed too by the break-up of his ship's family. Jim was determined not to go in the Army, but had only a few hours to come up with a workable alternative. After breakfast Jim and Lisa had spent forty minutes talking quietly to each other on the docks in the rain. Jeanne said little about her plans. After talking to Frank she seemed to take it for granted that the refugee centre was her only alternative. Although Elaine chatted pleasantly about being back on land – as if they'd just finished an interesting cruise – Jeanne was silent. She finished packing, cleaned up the galley and sat down in the wheelhouse with Skip.

As the boat-weary, war-weary, weather-weary crew of

Vagabond gathered themselves together that late morning the wind moaned through the shrouds, halyards slapped rhythmically against masts, the rain drummed down on the decks and cabin tops. Although the seasick appreciated the lack of motion all were exhausted from thirty-six hours of storm at sea. Tony was the first to leave, escorting Elaine and Rhoda ashore to find the refugee centre. Frank and Conrad Macklin left a few minutes later carrying Seth on a makeshift stretcher made from two oars and the last section of the jib they had used to jury-rig the awning for the new back wall of the wheelhouse. The plan was that they would take Seth to the hospital and that Frank would meet Jeanne later at the refugee centre in the high school. Macklin, ineligible for the draft because of a foot shattered on a mine in Vietnam, had announced he was planning to try to get further south by car. Neil hoped he would simply disappear.

When Olly went down in the cabin to hide the weapons and disable *Vagabond*'s engine Neil was momentarily alone with Jeanne, but Jim and Lisa came in from the rain and stood awkwardly side by side in front of her. Jim's face was partly hidden under the hood of the yellow foul-weather jacket, from which rain still dripped. Lisa seemed lost in the over-sized foul-weather gear she was wearing, and they both seemed to Neil ridiculously young.

'Jeanne,' Jim began uncertainly. 'I . . . I'm not going in the Army and I guess I have to hide.' He hesitated. 'Lisa wants to come with me.'

Jeanne looked at him with a strange serenity and nodded once, glancing briefly at her daughter.

'Where will you go, Jim?' she asked quietly.

Jim looked uncomfortable. 'Neil said last night he thought my only chance was to get a small boat and head down the waterway,' he said. 'I don't know.'

Jeanne now looked up at Neil.

'Well, captain?' she asked.

Neil resented her addressing him as 'captain'.

'I'm beginning to think we were crazy to come in that inlet,' Neil replied almost angrily. 'Jim is trapped. If the Army is rounding up young people sooner or later it'll round up Jim. The only haven from the government is out at sea.'

'Can't he stay with Olly on *Vagabond*?' Jeanne asked.

'Yes,' said Neil, 'but a man on the ketch forward said that the military police came through earlier this morning searching all the boats along the docks.'

'But why?' Jeanne suddenly burst out. 'What possible use can Jim and others be?'

'How do people like Jim eat?' Neil replied gloomily. 'They have to steal to survive. If they have guns they may end up killing. The government is trying to control chaos.'

'Then perhaps Jim should just go in,' Jeanne said. Neil shrugged and Jim stirred uneasily.

'We shouldn't have come here, Mother,' Lisa said.

'What do *you* expect to find here?' Neil asked Jeanne in a low, tight voice.

Startled, Jeanne stiffened. 'I'm not sure,' she replied tentatively. 'A place to help other people, I guess. A safer place for Lisa and Skip.'

'Safer than what?' Neil asked.

'Safer than the Chesapeake,' she answered, looking at him, adding, less surely, 'Safer than the ocean.'

'Land will never again be safer than the sea,' he responded.

'We're here, Neil,' she countered quietly.

'I hate your going . . . back . . . out there,' Neil said in almost a whisper.

Conrad Macklin suddenly burst in from the rain, stamping the floor, oblivious of interrupting anything, and announced that all private housing had already been taken over by either the military or by earlier refugees. There was absolutely no food being sold anywhere. The hospital they'd taken Seth to was so overcrowded it was treating people in tents and garages, or rather not treating them. Hundreds of victims of burns, radiation sickness and retinal blindness were not being

210

treated at all as far as he could see. Frank had remained to try to obtain attention for Seth. There were no vehicles available for going south and there were roadblocks on every major highway. Macklin ended his report and disappeared below to change and dry off.

When he left, Jim and Lisa still stood in the centre of the wheelhouse with Jeanne, face averted, staring at the floor.

'Look,' Neil said, striding forward so Jim and Lisa could see him. 'I'm going to find out from the Army or Navy what the food and fallout situation is going to be here. If I'm needed in the Navy I'll serve. But I don't think, Jim, that you and Lisa should go anywhere by yourselves. Hold up a bit. Stay here on the boat with Olly. Lisa, at least for now, you should go with Jeanne to the refugee centre.'

'Why can't we all stay on the boat?' Lisa asked.

'Because . . .' Neil began.

'Because we can't flee forever,' Jeanne replied. 'Our duty is to find a place here on land to live and work. There's both farming and fishing here. It must be better than most places. And the only way we can get more food is at the refugee centre.'

'What about Captain Olly?' Lisa asked.

'He'll stay here to guard the boat,' Neil answered. 'In case . . . we need it again.'

Lisa looked up at Jim to see what he was deciding.

'All right,' said Jim. 'I'll hide here for a while. Lisa . . . you . . . better help your Mom . . .'

'When . . . when . . . ?' Lisa began.

'We can visit the boat, honey,' Jeanne said quietly. 'We're all just testing what the new world holds for us. Nothing is final.'

Lisa took Jim's hand and after exchanging a look with him, stared at the floor.

'I'll risk helping you take your things to the high school,' Jim said. Together he and Lisa began to gather up the dufflebags and small suitcases and transport them to the docks. After they'd left the wheelhouse Jeanne stood up and went closer to Neil, who was standing with his hands gripping the stainless steel wheel.

'I wish . . . we didn't have to go,' she said.

'You don't,' Neil answered.

'I mean . . . but you too . . . have to leave *Vagabond*.'

'Nor do I *have* to go,' Neil replied quietly.

As Jeanne gazed at him she realized that he was making a subtle appeal to her.

'But . . . what would we all do on *Vagabond*?' she asked after a pause, Skippy holding on to her skirt.

'We would sail south out of the path of the probable fallout,' Neil answered. 'To the West Indies.'

Jeanne visibly flinched. 'They wouldn't let you and Jim out the inlet,' she said softly.

Neil hesitated. 'Cowards and lovers will always find a way,' he said.

Jeanne gazed at him, flushed, and then impulsively came forward into his arms. She squeezed him, burying her head against his chest. She felt his arms tightening fiercely around her. After half a minute, aware of Skippy tugging gently at her skirt and murmuring her name, she looked up, tears in her eyes. 'I don't want to go,' she said.

'Then don't,' Neil whispered to her.

'Everything okay, Jeanne?' came Jim's voice from close behind her. He had returned. Still in Neil's arms, when Jeanne turned and saw him, the image of Frank in his boyish face reminded her of all the complications and uncertainties involved in her staying for Neil.

She looked back up at Neil, saw his feeling for her, but pulled herself roughly out of his arms.

'Goodbye, Neil,' she said and brushed past Jim out into the rain.

After she had gone, Neil turned to see Macklin seated behind him with a cynical smile.

212

'Well, captain,' he said softly. 'Nothing like a little pussy to make a solid upstanding Annapolis man into a deserter, is there?'

Neil went at Macklin, his fists clenched, but when the other man ducked and cowered on the settee seat, he stopped himself and strode to the back of the wheelhouse to watch Jim and Jeanne disappear into the dock area. She was gone. He stood there silently for half a minute.

'I thought you said I lacked heart,' he finally said.

'Oh, you do, you do,' Macklin agreed affably. 'But I never said you lacked cock.'

'Thank you,' said Neil and then went quickly down into the main cabin to find Olly.

He wanted both to be rid of Macklin and also to advise Olly on caring for *Vagabond* before he reported for duty. He had decided to report directly to one of the ships in the Turning Basin and find out what the military situation was and whether he was really needed or not. For him, like Jim, the war was insane and both sides madmen, but the US Navy, insane or not, was his team and if the game were still being played he had reluctantly decided it was his job to take the field.

Even Captain Olly seemed depressed as Neil went over the boat with him. Neil had requested and the others had agreed that the remaining food aboard should stay aboard for at least the next few days. Neil instructed Olly about where he had had Jim hide their emergency ration supply. He also showed Olly where the two pistols were hidden behind the partition in Jeanne's cabin; he showed him the five-gallon Jerry jug of diesel fuel lined up with the water containers and now labelled 'water'. Since pirates were still a threat, Olly had disconnected the battery cables from the engine and hidden both the cables and the two ignition keys, letting only Neil know their hiding place. In addition, Olly decided to re-conceal one of the two pistols in the galley where he could

213

reach it on short notice.

When they had finished going over the boat Olly stopped in the rain in the side cockpit and began chuckling.

'You sure don't act like a man who's leaving his boat forever,' he said.

'I wish I weren't,' Neil said.

'You joining the Navy?'

'If they need me.'

'Who's gonna decide? Them or you?'

Neil shrugged. 'Me,' he answered.

'Then I'll keep the tea water hot,' said Olly, smiling.

'Cynical old bastard, aren't you?' Neil shot back, smiling in spite of himself.

'I figure you got too much sense to get involved in a war where if you don't shoot 'til you see the whites of their eyes, you'll die of old age without firing a shot.'

'I already fought in that kind of war,' Neil said.

'And loved it, didn't you?' Olly said, ducking now into the wheelhouse out of the wind and rain, leaving Neil to feel a rush of gloom.

6

Frank, already depressed by the confrontation with Jim and by his still lingering nausea, was overwhelmed by what he encountered on land. The first confrontation with chaos and panic came when he and Macklin, carrying Seth between them on the stretcher, left *Vagabond* late that morning. Frank, in the lead, had not even got his feet on the dock when a man in a wet, wrinkled business suit, his greying hair plastered to his forehead, accosted him.

'Are you the owner of the trimaran?' the man asked. A woman and three children stood behind the fortyish man watching intently.

'Yes, I am,' Frank replied as he waited for Macklin to lower himself and his end of the stretcher on to the dock.

'I want to book passage for myself and family on a boat going south,' the man said, his drawn face belying the calm tone of his voice.

'I can't help you,' Frank answered dully. 'We're not going south, and if we were, we'd have a full ship already.'

'I have gold,' the man said, lowering his voice. 'Fifteen thousand dollars worth. You'll need it wherever you're going.'

When Macklin put his end of the stretcher momentarily on one end of a bench, Frank rested his on a nearby railing and looked at the man with surprise.

'Well, you're fifteen thousand dollars richer than I am,' he said. 'But I still can't help you. A trimaran can't take the extra weight.' Despite the rain, five or six other people had clustered around and were listening to the exchange.

'Then take just my wife and children,' the man said. 'They don't weigh much and they can sleep on deck.'

'No, Harry,' the woman interjected. 'I'm not going any place without you. I won't.'

'We're not going south, I'm afraid,' Frank repeated, depressed that a man should be so desperate to leave this place he was willing to sacrifice himself to get his family on a boat. Depressed too that he couldn't help.

'Let's go try somewhere else,' whispered the wife.

The man, sensing Frank's sympathy, kept staring, the woman tugging at his arm, the youngest child tugging at hers, the rain streaming down everyone's faces.

'How about me, captain?' another man asked. 'I'm all alone. I'm a good . . .'

'Me, too!' shouted a woman from the back of the small group. The crowd pushed towards Frank shouting and holding up money but, picking up the stretcher, he and Macklin plunged roughly through the crowd and strode away.

At the hospital Seth was put on a mat on a garage floor. No doctor or nurse or administrative official seemed to know who was responsible for the patients in Barnaby's Ford Garage and so none of the seven patients lying about the room, some on mats used by car mechanics to work under cars, were being treated. They were out of the wind and rain: that was their treatment.

After Macklin had quickly disappeared, Frank crossed the street to the main hospital grounds to find a doctor. He saw a bulldozer digging up one whole section of the side lawn area in the rain, an act which struck Frank as senseless. He assumed it was part of some long-range construction programme. There were large tarpaulins covering what he thought were building materials until he saw two soldiers carrying a body on a stretcher out into the rain, across the still untouched section of lawn and then dumping the body unceremoniously in the mud next to the tarpaulin. An hour later, when he left the hospital he saw the cover removed, and a pile of corpses being bulldozed into a muddy hole.

Inside the hospital he discovered there were only three doctors left for all of Morehead City. All other local doctors had been called up by the Army to serve elsewhere. One doctor was asleep, having worked nineteen straight hours after four previous days of working almost as long. The second was a surgeon working in the OR on those with serious wounds, mostly burns. The third was a paediatrician who was acting physician for the other thousand or so patients located either here or in the refugee centre.

Frank appealed to the nurses and physician's assistants for help. At one point when he was exploding in anger at an indifferent and unresponsive nurse he was dragged away by two Military Policemen whose purpose was to maintain order in the hospital. In the end the best he could do was to see a nurse write down Seth's name and location and tell him that Seth was 'sixteenth on Mr Umberly's list'. Mr Umberly, he gathered, was one of two physician's assistants.

On his way back to Seth he wandered by mistake into a room where the authorities apparently were putting those exposed to severe and presumably lethal doses of radiation. About ten people were lying against the walls or on the floor of what must normally have been a custodian's room, some groaning, one screaming and at least two of them already dead. The room reeked of vomit. All of those sprawled out were badly burned and one man, who had no eyes and whose face was hideously burned – the skin dangling down one cheek – begged in a singsong chant for water. Frank fled.

When he finally returned to Seth he found him flushed and breathing rapidly. He explained about the shortage of medical help but withheld the other horrors he had witnessed.

'Well, they warned us,' Seth said in his high-pitched self-mocking tone.

'Who warned us about what?' Frank asked, kneeling down beside him.

217

'Books,' Seth said, bright-eyed with fever. 'The marchers. The protesters. They all warned us that a nuclear war would be inconvenient. Too many sick and wounded, too few surviving doctors. I should have known better than to get involved in a nuclear war.'

Frank stared down at him where he lay on an inch-thick mechanic's mat covered by the sail cloth they had used for the stretcher. He couldn't tell if Seth was delirious or not.

'It wasn't the Russians and their missiles that got you,' Frank said. 'It was . . . an American.'

'I know,' said Seth. 'They warned us about that, too. Someone predicted that the Russians would win a full-scale nuclear war because their citizens were unarmed and thus unable to wipe each other out.' He grinned up at Frank as if it were all a good joke.

'I . . . ah . . . I'd like to go to the refugee centre and check on Jeanne,' Frank said. 'You think you can . . . ah . . . handle yourself okay until the doctor comes?'

'Of course,' Seth replied, still smiling. 'I have exactly those qualities which in this world make me safe.'

'What's that?' asked Frank.

'I'm useless and destitute,' said Seth. 'I'm even less likely to be visited by a pirate than by a doctor.'

'I . . . I've got to go,' Frank said.

For the first time Seth was silent, staring past Frank at the ceiling, his grin frozen and lifeless.

'Will you come back?' Seth asked in a low, totally different voice.

'I . . . sure,' Frank answered. 'I'll come back this evening.'

'I'd like that,' said Seth, still looking past Frank at the garage ceiling.

'So I'll be seeing you,' said Frank.

'Please come back, Frank,' Seth whispered desperately through gritted teeth, and Frank, sombre, rose and left.

7

Jeanne had no illusion about the difficulties she would encounter as a war refugee in a strange town, but as she had told Neil, the sea was no home for her; every moment she'd been aboard *Vagabond* her heart had been eyeing the horizon for land.

Although she anticipated scarcity and crowding, when she entered the long, low, modern high school building she knew that her anticipation wasn't going to make it any easier. The hall she entered with Jim, Lisa and Skip was crowded with people as wet and weary-looking as themselves. The hard floors were covered with mud and water. People were shouting and a round man with a red nose and bloodshot eyes was trying to herd people into line; twenty-five or thirty confused refugees stood or sat against the walls, a few crying, many looking sick. Four or five had visible burns. Skippy was pulling at Jeanne's belt and periodically questioning her about nothing. She could feel a numbness creeping into her as if her life were again being threatened. With all the sick people around she wondered whether Jim had brought her by mistake to the hospital rather than the refugee centre, but on the walls were the familiar official graffiti of a school: 'Seniors taking SATs report on Tuesday to Mr Owens', 'Graduation rehearsal at 3:00 on Thursday', and 'Support your Tigercats!'

'Mother, let's not stay here,' Lisa said, looking frightened.

'There's no place else to go, honey,' Jeanne answered mechanically.

'We should stay on the boat,' Lisa insisted.

'We've got to try this,' Jeanne replied, fighting off the panic she could feel invading her as it had Lisa. The boat was a refuge of last resort – it had only a few days supply of food left. This was now how people lived on land: it was necessary to try.

It took more than an hour before they were 'registered' and assigned to a room. Jim said an awkward goodbye to Lisa, leaving her stricken and silent, and left to sneak back to the boat. They hiked down the hall to find their room; there a large matronly woman welcomed them 'to the third grade'.

Forcing a smile, Jeanne stood tentatively at the entrance and finally urged Skippy and Lisa ahead of her into the room, which was occupied by four other families, only one with a male adult member. Each group had set up a little personal space by arranging the desks as a low wall. Although no mattresses were available, most families seemed to have sleeping bags or blankets, as did Jeanne. The lights were off and with the wind and rain slashing against the big windows, the interior of the room was dark and depressing. Skippy, however, seemed to relax in the presence of desks and toys and began to play by himself with some blocks not far from another child his age, the other occupying his family's walled-off space. There were seven children in the room.

In the next few hours, leaving Lisa to stay with Skip, Jeanne toured the building and got to talk with half a dozen or so of her fellow refugees. She began to realize how lucky she had been. Many had been a hundred miles from the nearest blast yet been overtaken by radioactive fallout and taken sick. Whether ill or not, most of those she talked to seemed confused and numb rather than terrified, and manifested a debilitating passivity. They accepted instructions, food, friendship and hostility with a numb equanimity which was a symptom not of spiritual maturity but of giving up.

She was appalled when told by a young woman who was caring for those with radiation sickness that only one doctor was available to come to the centre and he could come only for an hour each day. Most of the sick were too weak to go to the hospital and had been instructed to stay in the school

220

where conditions were, in fact, better.

'Are you an official here?' Jeanne asked the young woman, almost afraid to look at the line of ashen, slumped figures propped up against one wall of the large fifth-grade classroom.

'No,' the woman answered. 'I'm just doing what I can to help. My name's Katya.'

Katya was a petite, ashen-haired woman in her early twenties wearing jeans and a sexy peasant blouse with a deeply scooped neckline that seemed strangely inappropriate for treating a roomful of sick and dying people. Wearing no make-up she was not so much pretty as she was striking, especially her dazzling green–blue eyes.

Although Jeanne could feel herself shaky from the after-effects of her seasickness, she worked for almost two hours with Katya, lugging buckets for potties, cleaning up vomit, relaying messages, bringing water and food, and answering questions. At first she was disturbed at Katya's indifference and even disobedience to various officials who appeared sporadically throughout the afternoon – one even ordering them to leave the room because 'you aren't sick or dying' – but she soon came to feel that the only worthwhile things getting done were being done spontaneously by volunteers rather than through any official system.

After they had fed those of their patients who wanted to eat anything, at six o'clock Jeanne went with Katya to get Lisa and Skip and go to the school cafeteria to eat a meal themselves with the other refugees. A tall, skinny young man with spectacles, apparently Katya's boyfriend, joined them at their table.

The food was fried fish, onion soup, and water. The cafeteria was packed and the refugees elbowed into line as if after first run theatre tickets.

'I've been here almost three days,' Katya said when questioned by Lisa about the food. 'We had some meat the first day, but since then it's been all eggs, fish, and a few

221

vegetables, mostly onions. I think we had some apples the second day, but otherwise no fruit.'

'And the portions keep getting smaller,' commented the young man, whose name was Sky. He cleaned his plate of fish away with amazing rapidity and eyed Jeanne's plate with interest.

'I'll give you a joint for half your fish,' he offered.

It took Jeanne a moment to absorb the suggestion. 'No . . . thank you,' she replied. 'What I don't finish I plan to save for my children.'

'That's cool,' said Sky, although clearly disappointed.

'Where are you working?' Jeanne asked him, more to make conversation than out of interest.

'What do you mean?' asked Sky.

'Katya and I are working with the people in the fifth-grade classroom,' she explained. 'I wondered . . .'

'Oh, no. Katya likes to keep busy,' Sky said. 'I like to take things easy.'

'Oh,' said Jeanne.

'Actually I volunteered to help in the kitchen,' Sky continued brightly. 'But they had enough people there already.'

'What . . . what about military service?' Lisa asked.

'Medical disability,' Sky answered.

'Oh.'

'My mind's all screwed up,' Sky explained.

Katya was eating quietly as if indifferent to the conversation.

'Do you plan to stay here?' Jeanne asked, trying to address her question as much to Katya as to the young man.

'Long as the food holds out,' Sky answered, grinning.

'Not me,' said Katya, her eyes flashing. 'The first two days I felt safe here. No more. I'd be out in a second if I could figure a way.'

'Where would you go?' Jeanne asked, scraping the last of

222

her fish from her plate on to Lisa's. Skippy was having trouble finishing his.

'As far away from where the bombs are going off as I can get,' Katya answered. 'If it's like this now,' she went on, motioning at the crowded cafeteria and by implication at the whole refugee centre, 'I hate to think how bad it will get.'

'Perhaps we've already seen the worst,' Jeanne suggested.

'All I know,' Katya countered, 'is that the *alive* people seem to leave this place after only a day or two. Most of those who stay have already given up.'

'What about me?' asked Sky with a sly smile.

'You gave up so long ago you can't even remember when.'

'Thanks.'

'But . . . then why do you work so hard here?' Jeanne asked.

'When there's work to be done, I do it,' said Katya.

'Where there's work to be done, I avoid it,' said Sky, grinning.

Frank appeared suddenly at their table, on his face a look of relief at having located Jeanne.

'Jim's drafted,' he announced, standing behind Katya and across from Jeanne. 'No punishment, but they were marching him through the street when I was on the way here. I ought to be happy . . . I feel like shit.'

'Where will they send him?' Lisa asked, looking up wide-eyed.

'No one knows,' Frank said. 'He's alive, he's being fed, eventually he'll be able to serve: that's all that counts.'

'How can we see him?' Lisa asked. Frank glanced at her painfully and shrugged.

'Sit down, Frank,' said Jeanne, standing. 'I'll go get you something to eat.'

'It's too late,' said Sky. 'They're closed up for the night. You've got to get here early.' He turned to grin up at Frank.

Frank walked around the end of the table and came up to Jeanne.

223

'You okay?' he asked, after a cold glance at Sky.

'I'm tired,' she said. 'I'd like you to meet the woman I worked with most of the afternoon. This is Katya. Katya, this is Frank.'

'Glad to meet you,' he said.

'You own the trimaran, right?' Katya asked immediately.

'Yeah, I do. How'd you know?'

'Jeanne's been telling me her adventures,' Katya replied. 'If you decide to sail again I'd like to join you.'

'I'm afraid I don't think we're sailing.'

'You plan to stay here?'

'It seems that way,' said Frank neutrally.

'I'm getting out of here if I have to crawl,' said Katya, her eyes again seeming to flash angrily.

Lisa and Skip now stood up too, Skip pulling his mother's hand to lead her away. As they started to leave, Sky looked up at them glowy-eyed and grinned.

'Never knock a place that serves free food,' he said.

8

The two US Navy ships moored to the deepwater pilings in the Turning Basin had both been disabled on the first day of the war. The larger of the two, a destroyer, looked like it had felt the effects of a not-distant-enough nuclear blast. Its paint was blistered, portholes shattered, struts and rigging broken. The second, an anti-submarine vessel about two-thirds the size of the destroyer, was less visibly damaged, but it was listing to port like an old man with a bad back. Two Navy men, a Petty Officer and his messenger, stopped Neil at the gate. Both wore side arms.

'Captain Neil Loken reporting for duty,' Neil said.

The Petty Officer eyed him sceptically. Neil was still dressed in his jeans and boat shoes.

'You have a pass, captain?' the Petty Officer asked.

'I've got nothing,' Neil replied. 'All my papers were destroyed in Washington. Let me speak to the Officer of the Deck.'

'You say you want to report for duty?'

'That's right.'

'Where's your regular unit?'

Neil shook his head.

'I'm presently unassigned,' he answered. 'Let me speak to your Duty Officer.'

The Petty Officer stared a moment longer at Neil and then went back into a small makeshift guardhouse and spoke into a walkie-talkie phone. When he emerged he said to the other man on guard duty: 'Take this guy . . . Captain Loken . . . to Lieutenant Margolis.'

Neil was then forced to proceed with the guard across the open dockyard area to the boarding ladder of the anti-submarine vessel, the *Haig*. It felt strange to be boarding a combat vessel in jeans and a tee-shirt rather than regulation Navy attire. The ship seemed in good order, and the messenger guard, as was proper, turned him over to the Petty Officer on Watch, who walked Neil briskly forward. The Officer of the Deck, Lt Margolis, was on the foredeck supervising the unloading of munitions from the large forward hatch.

'What is it, Mr Haynes?' he asked the Petty Officer. Lt Margolis, a slight, pinch-faced man, looked at Neil with distaste.

'This man asked to speak to you, sir. He says he's reporting for duty.'

'He does, huh?' Lt Margolis said. 'Well, sailor,' he went on to Neil. 'What's your story? Where have you been the last five days?'

'I'm Captain Neil Loken,' Neil replied. 'Annapolis, Class of 1971. I just got in from sea. I want to be of service.'

Trying unsuccessfully to mask his surprise and uncertainty, Lt Margolis continued to stare at Neil. 'Were you on active duty when the war began?' he asked.

'No,' Neil answered. 'I resigned my commission in 1975. I haven't served since.'

'Then what are you doing here?' the lieutenant asked with careful neutrality.

'I served in CPBs in Vietnam,' Neil said. 'I believe I can be of more use on a combat vessel than anywhere else.'

Lt Margolis frowned. 'That's hardly your decision to make is it?' he said. 'Certainly we have no authorization to take in men . . . officers . . . from the street.'

'No doubt,' said Neil. 'Still, I imagine this war is going to necessitate quite a bit of improvisation.' Neil could sense the officer struggling with the paradox of having to address a civilian in canvas shoes who claimed to be his superior in rank.

'I'm sorry, Mr Loken,' Lt Margolis finally said in a cold

voice. 'We have no authorization to receive you. You'll have to leave the ship.'

'May I have permission to speak to your Captain?'

'You may not. Escort this man off the ship, Mr Haynes.'

Discouraged and angry, Neil was led back to the boarding ladder and down off the *Haig*. But in the open dock area he noticed and accosted another lieutenant and, with Mr Haynes looking on uncertainly, explained his situation again to this officer.

'The class of '71, is it?' the officer asked. He was a tired-looking, sloppily-dressed man about Neil's own age from the severely damaged destroyer.

'Yes, sir,' said Neil. 'If you have anyone aboard from '70, '71 or '72 they'll probably know me . . . or know of me.'

'Know *of* you, huh?' the lieutenant said, eyeing Neil speculatively. 'Are you famous for something?'

'It was a suggestion,' Neil said, side-stepping the question. 'I have none of my papers with me.'

'There are . . . were half a dozen Academy boys aboard this ship, but none that I can think of during those years. Maybe Captain Cohen. You know him?'

'No, I don't.'

'Then you're out of luck, I guess.'

'Could I see your commanding officer?' Neil persisted.

'I'm afraid Commander Bonnville wouldn't appreciate being disturbed by something as . . .'

'Bonnville?' Neil interrupted. 'Greg Bonnville?'

'That's right,' the lieutenant said, looking surprised. 'You know him?'

'I served with him for eight months in 'Nam.'

The lieutenant hesitated, his exhausted face in a frown. 'Maybe you should see him.'

'I'd like to.'

In ten minutes Neil had been escorted up on to the destroyer *Arcady*. The *Arcady* was a mess. All its topside paint was blistering, its portholes and bridge windows shattered, bloodstains still evident, damaged weapons and debris everywhere. The Petty Officer who received him aboard looked sick, exhausted, or both. It took almost another ten minutes to complete communication with the Duty Officer and receive permission to see Commander Bonnville.

Greg Bonnville had been Neil's group leader for ten months in the South China Sea off Vietnam. He had been a fierce, dedicated, by-the-book officer who had made Neil for that first year in Vietnam a believer in going by the book. Two years later when he'd learned that Neil planned to resign his commission he had telephoned from Manila, where he was then stationed, to urge Neil to change his mind.

As Neil was being taken to the bridge to see him again he felt a pleasant excitement, an excitement that was sickeningly dashed the moment he saw Bonnville.

His old friend seemed to have aged twenty years beyond Neil rather than the ten years of their age difference. Slumped behind his desk in his cabin, he was grey-faced and hollow-eyed. His once eye-catching mane of dark hair was gone; he was almost bald. Scar-tissue marred his forehead and one cheek. He trembled when he stood to greet Neil, his lanky body badly stooped. 'I'm afraid I can't say "welcome aboard", Neil,' Greg Bonnville said. 'The *Arcady* is a deathship.'

Neil stood facing his friend uncertainly. Around him Greg's captain's quarters were strewn with clothes, books and papers. The ship's logbook lay on the floor propped up against a leg of the desk. Greg sat back down with a groan.

'What happened?' Neil asked.

'Wrong war,' Greg answered gloomily, not looking up. 'We were steaming south fifteen miles off Cape Henry, probably thirty from Hampton Roads when "boom", we got . . . permanently decommissioned.'

'Did you . . . personally get hit?'

'I look it, don't I?' he replied. 'I got some mild burns and cuts from the initial blast, but it was the radiation all that

228

morning that clobbered us. The only healthy men who may come through were the engine-room crew. Anyone who had to be out on deck or on the bridge that night is probably . . . not going to live.'

'Including you?' Neil asked softly.

'Obviously including me.'

Neil turned and paced over to the shattered porthole and stared out over the waters of the Turning Basin towards the ocean.

'Is the ship still contaminated?' Neil asked quietly.

'It's pretty clean except in the aft hold, which we've closed off,' he said. 'They almost wouldn't let us put in here 'til they got their own geiger counter man aboard and cleared us.'

'May I sit down?' Neil asked.

'Please,' Greg responded. 'You make me sad standing so erectly.'

Neil sat down on the edge of Greg's berth. 'What are your orders?' Neil asked hesitantly.

Greg looked up blankly and then snickered. 'Stay here and die,' he replied.

'You're kidding.'

'Absolutely not,' Greg countered. 'And damn good orders they are. This ship is dead and the engine-room crew has been transferred to the *Haig*. The rest of us will work with our little individual timebombs by ourselves. Whoever can walk off in a week will be reassigned.'

'Living Jesus,' Neil muttered.

'Quite an end to a distinguished career.'

'There's nothing you can do?' Neil asked, looking up at his friend as if appealing for himself.

'Remain on standby and if, by some miraculous stroke of luck, a Soviet sub should amble up the Morehead City Inlet, go down with my ship.'

'I see,' said Neil, standing and again passing to the porthole, where pieces of shattered glass were resting like a cache of diamonds on the circular sill. 'Look, Greg,' he went on, turning back to his friend, who was slumped forward on his desk, staring down. 'What do you know about the overall military situation?'

Greg lifted his head and the two men gazed at each other. 'All I know is what I can read between the lines of the radio communiqués and orders.'

'That's something,' said Neil. 'What do you think?'

'I think we're planning to evacuate all remaining Naval personnel from the whole east coast. I think it's rapidly becoming a war of individual initiative, just the type we always wished we could be in.'

'But where's the enemy?'

'Ahh,' said Greg, straightening himself with a grimace. 'That's the new twist. The enemy is in the sky, in the food chain, in the rain, in my bloodstream.'

'And the Russians?'

'They've shot their bolt,' he said. 'There've only been two or three incoming missiles since the second day. Their Mediterranean and Indian Ocean fleets are gone. Their population has been decimated – which probably means wiped out. Any warfare still going on is only the last twitching of two corpses. The Russians and ourselves will probably fantasize to our last breaths of snatching victory from genocide.'

Neil looked at the sunken face of his friend and saw no sense of triumph.

'We . . . ah . . . we've won?' Neil asked, feeling feeble and foolish.

'If we've won, it's as the *Arcady* has won . . .' He looked dismally around the room.

A third time Neil walked away to look out of the shattered porthole. Outside he saw the Coast Guard patrol launch begin its turn to sweep back out of the channel in its systematic guarding of the inlet.

'I've been ordered to report to duty,' he announced with his back still to Greg.

'Here?' Greg asked, astounded.

'No. To report somewhere. All men are supposed to report.'

'How'd you happen to end up *here*?'

Turning back, Neil briefly explained his voyage on *Vagabond*.

'And you're all leaving her for *here*?' Greg asked in a low sad voice.

Neil shrugged. 'The law . . .' he began.

'Neil, I told you,' Greg said, leaning painfully back in his chair and almost glaring at Neil. 'This has become a war of individual initiative and . . .' He grimaced and groaned once. '. . . And the enemy,' he continued after a pause, 'the sole enemy . . . is death.'

'And the US Navy?' Neil asked softly.

Greg slumped forward again.

'Wrong war,' he replied in a low voice.

After Neil had left Captain Bonnville he searched out the infirmary and drug dispensary. There he found a sailor kneeling in front of two open drawers and a clutter of bottles and little cardboard cartons strewn around him on the floor. When the sailor looked up at him Neil saw that he was stoned. He was probably searching for some sort of dope – morphine or codeine or barbiturates, from the dull look in his eyes. Slowly a look of bewilderment made its way on to the young sailor's round face as Neil stood stiffly over him but dressed in jeans and a tee-shirt.

'All right, sailor,' Neil said firmly. 'I don't have to ask what you're doing here, but I want you to find me any antibiotics that are still around.'

The small, weary-looking young man, his face pale and his eyes bloodshot, hesitated, still in confusion, still stoned.

'I'm Captain Loken, sailor,' Neil barked in the traditional manner. 'And I gave you an order.'

'Aye . . . aye, sir,' the sailor finally replied, wobbling to his feet. 'Uh . . . antibiotics don't work against radiation sickness.'

'I know.'

'Nothing works.'

'I know. Find them.'

The man stared around the room and then walked over to the opposite wall and began going through drawers. Neil came up beside him and began searching also. Eventually he found two vials containing liquid penicillin and a bottle labelled tetracyclin with a hundred capsules. He located two syringes in a glass cabinet. The sailor was now staring dreamily into an empty drawer.

'Is there still morphine available, sailor? Neil asked loudly.

The man lazily shook his head and smiled. Neil made a further search for pain-killing medication, found a small amount of codeine, and left.

He decided that since weapons had been officially removed from the *Arcady* his only hope was to search the quarters of the Petty Officers. There he encountered, in the four separate staterooms, one corpse, two dying men, and two men listening lugubriously to a newscast. He asked these two about weapons, but they stared back at him as if he were mad or they stoned. In the last stateroom, empty of its occupants, he discovered in a bureau drawer a nine-millimetre pistol – the official Navy sidearm – and a half-full box of ammunition. From this same room he also stole a bottle of aspirin, matches, razor blades, suntan lotion and a small cache of cocaine. When he found himself tempted to steal Kleenex he felt he was becoming a kleptomaniac and hastily left.

Later, as he was leaving the dockyard, Neil ran into the Petty Officer who had originally heard his story.

'Well, Mr Loken, are you going to join us?' the Petty Officer asked.

Neil hesitated only a moment. 'It doesn't look that way,' he replied. 'It appears I've been given . . . an independent command.'

And he left.

9

At ten P.M. that evening, after he had filled out forms, had a perfunctory physical exam from a corpsman, and been issued a uniform, Jim and other recruits of the last three days were rounded up and marched to the Rialto movie theatre. There about one hundred and fifty new soldiers, some even without uniforms, stood at attention between the rows of seats, most sweating profusely in the stuffy theatre, no longer cooled with air conditioning. Jim stood at the right rear, uncomfortable, resentful, curious. For fifteen minutes the men were kept standing thus. Finally a major marched out on to the stage in front of them.

'At ease, men,' he shouted down at them, and a great groan broke from the group as the soldiers relaxed, many of them collapsing into their seats. The relaxed hubbub lasted for less than five seconds.

'ATTEN-SHUN!' the major unexpectedly bellowed.

Surprised and confused, the men struggled back up to attention, a few, not hearing the new command, having to be urged up by those near them.

'At ease, men,' the major shouted at them after less than twenty seconds.

This time the relaxation was much less pronounced, almost all of the men remaining standing, looking at the major suspiciously, not talking this time as they had the last. Jim stood exactly as he had when he was standing supposedly at attention, staring up at the major with resentment. About twenty seconds passed this time, then thirty, and a few of the men began to whisper to each other, one or two to sit.

'ATTEN-SHUN!' the major bellowed again, and again the men responded, many sullenly, until the non-coms spread out

233

around the auditorium began reinforcing the major's command.

'ALL RIGHT,' the major shouted, pacing now off to the left of the platform, his compact body moving with suppressed power, his dark face and neatly trimmed moustache accentuating his neatness and correctness compared to the ragtag bunch of men down in front of him. He glared down at his audience.

'You've just demonstrated the single most important attribute of a soldier: obedience. I don't give a fuck if you don't know your right foot from your left foot, an anti-tank gun from a twenty-two, or a platoon from a spittoon, but if you know how to obey, you'll make one helluva soldier.'

He paused and paced back to the centre of the stage.

'In this war, especially with the losses we've sustained already here on the mainland, it's absolutely necessary that everyone pull together, that we all work to get the country back together again. And the only way that can happen is for the President to point, the officers to lead, and the rest of you to fall in line . . .'

The major wiped sweat from his brow, his bushy eyebrows and trim moustache still glistening under the row of bright lights even after the wipe.

'The Russians haven't landed yet,' he went on in a loud voice that seemed just on the verge of cracking from his effort. 'We hope they never land, but there are already enemies loose in this country and it's our job to stop them. The enemy is anyone who thinks they know better than the President, anyone who selfishly puts his own interests above those of the whole nation. It's the Army's job to keep our country functioning, keep the food, medical and military supplies flowing. Your officers will determine how this can best be done, and then you and they will do it.

'And I don't want any of you assholes to try thinking you know better than your officer. There's only one right way to do things in the Army and that's the way it was ordered done . . . And don't you forget it . . .'

234

He paused, glared, sweat again pouring down his face, and Jim watched him with a feeling of dull dread and hopelessness. He felt trapped in a small room.

'Any day now some of you may be sent on assignments that involve our using our muscle against misguided bastards who think their personal asses are all that count. I don't want any shilly-shallying. If you are ordered to shoot someone, you shoot him. There's no time for you to complain that you haven't heard the guy speak Russian. Anyone who disobeys an order from a superior officer is a traitor and deserves to be shot. Don't you forget it . . .

'All of you men here have just become part of this Army. You are idiots, ignoramuses, assholes, nobodies. Don't pretend you're anything else. We'll teach you to be soldiers. You'll learn. But right from the beginning I want you to know that there's really only one lesson: obey . . . And don't you forget it . . .'

Later that night as Jim spread out his sleeping bag next to Tony's on the floor of a double room in the Moonlighter Motel – their temporary barracks – the other six men in the room, all of whom had been 'in' since the second day of the war, were loose and joking. There were three blacks, two of whom were big men and the third a little runt of a man, and three middle-aged whites. They had all been at the theatre and heard the major's talk.

'Sheet, man, we're the *kings*,' one of the big black men said as he spread his sleeping bag out on top of one of the double beds. 'Ain't no way you gonna get me outa this Army. In here they look out after your ass. Out there it's everybody's ass for hisself. Ain't no way.'

'I don't like shootin' no *people*,' the little black man said sullenly as he prepared to crawl into his sleeping bag, also on the floor. 'You shoot anybody they ask you?'

'Sheet, I shoot my *muther*, man, if they says to,' the first black man countered. 'That's the way it *is*, man. This is *wah*!'

235

The other three men, the older whites, remained silent, two of them preparing to sleep on the second double bed and the third, a plump, redfaced man, bedding down near Tony and Jim.

'If they ask us to shoot somebody,' Tony announced loudly in the brief silence, 'you can be damn sure that guy deserves to be shot.'

Jim, uncomfortable, unconvinced, was quietly unlacing his GI boots.

'Well, at least we won't starve to death in the Army,' the plump man said with a hesitant smile.

'They feed us, they give us guns, and when a bomb comes, they tell us to duck,' one of the other white men said. 'Compared to what I was facing four days ago this is heaven.'

'You're damn right,' the man next to him echoed.

Jim placed his two boots and his fatigues in a neat pile at the head of his sleeping bag and, in his underwear, crawled into his sleeping bag.

'What this wah is, is a great big muther-fucking urban renewal programme,' the big talkative black man said as he undressed. 'Now Manhattan and Washington and Boston all get to look like Harlem.' He laughed.

The others were silent. Jim linked his hands behind his head and closed his eyes. He could feel the floor swaying underneath him, its motion the counterpoint to that of *Vagabond* during the last two days at sea.

He felt isolated, alone. Tony appeared to feel at home in the Army; Jim felt he would be lucky to last a single day. He tried to think about what he could do and where he could go if he escaped, but he was tired, the three blacks were laughing about something and the two white men in the other double bed were whispering. He became conscious of Tony getting into the sleeping bag beside his.

'Don't mind these shits,' Tony whispered to him. 'Tomorrow we'll be assigned to a platoon and it'll be a whole new ballgame.'

Jim didn't reply. He didn't think the league he was now stuck in was going to be getting any better for a long time.

10

For most of his fifty-eight years George Cooper had thought that he would defend his country to the death. He had fought in the Korean War; two of his sons had fought in the war in Vietnam. So it was with some degree of confusion that he found himself behind a barricade of farm machinery, oil tanks, and hay with eighteen other farmers and a few of their teenage sons, preparing to fight a company of soldiers from the Army of the United States. Each decision he had made during the week following the outbreak of war had seemed logical, but there was nothing logical about what was happening now. His own government seemed about to kill him and his sons and friends because they felt they ought to be able to keep some of their farm animals and produce for their own families and friends.

When four days earlier an officer had come and told him the Army needed all his eggs each day and all his spring corn, George had still been too much in shock to resist. But when some of his neighbours began to complain that the Army was taking everything, and then yesterday a new officer came to requisition the rest of his spring vegetables and forty chickens, George began to feel that his country had already been invaded; it was just that the uniforms weren't the colour he'd expected them to be.

George understood that food was now gold and that he and his neighbours were now millionaires in a poverty-stricken world. He understood that with real money now almost meaningless he would have to give away most of his food wealth without any compensation so that others wouldn't starve to death. What he couldn't understand and couldn't accept was that he had to give up *everything* to the government and depend on feeding his own family on what the government planned to give back to him.

Eggs and corn he could spare. But his chickens, or Bart Hasler's cows, or Fred Lapp's hogs, these they couldn't give up without endangering their own families' survival. Taking their animals away was like tearing down small factories.

The officer had arrived that morning for the chickens and George had refused to surrender them. The officer had left, announcing he would return with force. He had. About sixty soldiers were standing with automatic rifles around three lorries parked two hundred feet away on the road. The chickens were in the henhouse behind them. About half of Bart's herd of sixty cows and most of Fred's hogs were in the big barn to their left. A large store of recently harvested vegetables was in the cellar of the main house. The women and smaller children were staying over at Fred's farm a mile away. All the young men were in the service some place, one of them, John Simpson's son Cal, standing with an automatic rifle among the sixty soldiers confronting them.

When the officer shouted at them through a bullhorn, the men chose George to go out and speak to him. The soldiers began to spread out around the barns and henhouse, and Bart, who was in charge of the military tactics, sent men into various defensive positions in the barn and henhouse to keep the soldiers at a distance. Their orders were to shoot to scare if any soldier got within fifty feet of the barns.

The officer in charge was a Captain Ames, a tall, skinny fellow with a nervous twitch on one side of his face. He didn't seem too sure of himself. George wasn't too sure of *him*self. He'd left his shotgun back with the others and ambled slowly out to talk to Ames.

'We've come for your chickens, Mr Cooper,' Captain Ames said in an unnaturally loud voice. 'My orders are to confiscate all edible farm animals in this area.'

'*All* of them?' George asked in surprise. In the morning the order had been just for forty of his chickens.

'All of them.' Captain Ames held out a piece of paper presumably containing written authorization for the confiscation.

'Can't give 'em up, Captain.' George replied, staring unseeingly at the paper but not taking it from Ames's hand. 'Until people are starving to death, I figure I can best take care of 'em here.'

'You're not the one to do the figuring,' Ames countered. 'The Army knows what's needed and we need chickens.'

'Can't do it, Captain.'

'I've got sixty men here that says you will.'

'If that henhouse catches on fire, and that barn,' George replied, squinting back at his buildings and watching the circle of soldiers grow tighter around them, 'then nobody's gonna eat the chickens. Or the hogs or anything else. Why don't you go back and talk it over with your general or with whatever asshole sent you out here.'

'My orders were clear and irrevocable,' Ames said nervously. 'I am to bring back the requisitioned food supplies from this area this afternoon and use whatever force is necessary to do so.'

'You can't bring 'em back if we burn down the barns.'

Ames flushed. 'Why would you do that?'

''Cause we don't like having our property stolen.'

'Your country's at war,' Ames shot back. 'The President has declared martial law. If the Army orders something taken, that's not stealing.'

'I don't figure the President had my chickens in mind when he declared martial law.'

'But he did,' Ames countered. 'He had everyone's chickens in mind.'

'Well,' George said after a pause, 'I'm not too good at arguin'.' He stared off at a group of soldiers behind the barn. 'Fact is, though, if your soldiers get within fifty feet of our barns bullets will hit three feet in front of them, and if they get within forty-five feet of the barns then they'll bump into our

239

bullets. And if they get into the barns then our boys will set the barns on fire. We figure there ain't no way you can carry out your order.'

Captain Ames, seeing that his men were within seventy or eighty feet of the barns in some places, shouted out an order to halt and the non-coms passed on the order. Ames then told George to wait where he was and went to the back of one of the trucks and placed a radio call back to headquarters in New Bern. When he returned to George five minutes later he looked pale and shaken.

'Look, Mr Cooper,' he said with an anguished appeal. 'The colonel says to get what food I can no matter who gets hurt. He says radioactive fallout is coming this way and all our animals will be useless as food in less than a week. The army will be evacuating the area and we've been ordered to take all the food we can find with us. You people should evacuate too. We'll leave you plenty of food for your families, but most of it we'll have to take.'

George Cooper squinted at the officer. The fallout bit might be an excuse or it might be true.

'You plan to kill us for a few chickens and pigs?' he said after a pause.

'I will have to kill you if you disobey the orders of the military commander of this region.'

'For a few chickens?'

'You seem to plan to destroy your barn for a few chickens.'

'My barns are useless without anything to put in them,' George said slowly. 'I figure that you and your colonel can survive without my chickens.'

'Ten minutes, Cooper,' Ames said with a grimace as he glanced at his watch. 'If you don't put down your weapons and let us take what the local military commander has ordered requisitioned, my men will attack.'

George Cooper looked angrily back at Captain Ames. 'Seems like a pretty shitty thing to do,' he said.

'Maybe,' said Captain Ames, flushing. 'But I'll do it.'

George turned and walked slowly back to his friends behind the tractors, examining as he walked the positions of the soldiers around his farm buildings. A few of them behind the henhouse seemed awfully close to within fifty feet of the buildings.

Bart, Fred and two others of the older men met him next to Fred's harvester and he began explaining to them his conversation with Ames. He had just got to the Army's claim that fallout was coming their way when a shot rang out. Then two others. George wheeled to see Captain Ames crouched down next to one of the trucks and the soldiers near him throwing themselves down into the grass. Off to the left two soldiers were running away. To the right, a squad of eight or ten soldiers, in a crouch, were running towards the henhouse. A fusillade of shots erupted from the teenagers there and one of the soldiers fell. Then the real firing began.

11

As he sat exhausted in his aft cabin and fiddled with the shortwave radio Neil was feeling baffled. The day and a half since his visit to Greg Bonnville and making his separate peace had been frustrating. He'd found it easy enough to bluff his way out of the two confrontations with authorities challenging him about his not being in uniform – he pulled his captain's demeanour and Navy lingo and said he was on special assignment from the *Arcady* – but found it difficult to learn what was really happening in the world.

Official radio announcements indicated that Morehead City was a safe area. Army policy was that refugees should stay put. They were offering no assistance to people wanting to move further south. As long as there was no threat in staying where they were he didn't feel he had any right to take Jeanne and Frank to sea, much less to help Jim desert. Although he himself no longer felt an obligation to serve his government, the transformation of Greg Bonnville was not something he could use to persuade others. It was too personal. He himself felt the only safety lay in escaping the mainland to sea; to others it seemed simply his mania.

Conrad Macklin had disappeared while Neil was at the *Arcady* and, since he had stolen some food from *Vagabond*, Neil assumed that he'd seen the last of him. But he'd returned thirty hours later – just four hours ago – to inform Neil that though the Army was maintaining roadblocks to prevent the civilian population from fleeing south, a caravan of Army vehicles containing both military and civilian personnel had been streaming south on Route 17. Macklin had hung around and learned that the Army was having problems with its roadblock units because some were panicking at the sight of so many others going south while they were being ordered to stay put. Macklin urged Neil to take *Vagabond* to sea immediately whether Jeanne and the others came or not.

Neil knew that if he didn't take *Vagabond* to sea soon Macklin would find somebody else who would. Thus he had not only to worry about a correct course of action but again about Macklin's trying to take *Vagabond*. With Olly often aboard alone there wasn't much to stop him. Neil had tried to delay any precipitous action by Macklin by telling him he planned to decide tonight his plans. He had visited Jeanne, Frank and Lisa at the refugee centre briefly late that afternoon and been depressed that they seemed to be settling in; they were working hard, making friends, feeling they were making a contribution. Lisa had spent much of the day trying unsuccessfully to see Jim and had just returned in tears so Jeanne was in no condition to make decisions. Her response to Neil's announcing that he wasn't going back into the Navy was a brief stricken look, as if frightened at the implications for her. Frank told Neil that he could take *Vagabond*, as if for Frank the struggle were over and the Morehead City High School was now home. Neil had left frightened and depressed at their state.

'There was more fallout today. The total's more than an eighth of an inch since we first got some four days ago. Some of the farmers are trying get it off the leaves of the corn and squash and beans, and Pat Nerron reports the wind blows it off the wheat and rye, but it's killing some of the plants even lying in the soil.'

The voice over the shortwave radio was that of the ham radio operator from eastern Tennessee to whom Neil had last listened the evening the war started.

'Henry Tickney says his geiger counter shows it's up to three roetgens in his soybean fields which isn't healthy for either him or his beans, but supposedly it'll drop off each day unless we get more. Like most of us Henry says he only goes out for a half hour a day.

'Three new shelters were started yesterday and one's already finished. Eight people moved in with enough food for two weeks. We put in Jesse and Marge Williams and their two kids, Gor and Hilda Lafson and their son Leo, and the Barletts' sick girl, Tina. The Williams run the Exxon station east of town and are sick and don't have anything they can do, and the Lafsons paid for all the material and labour on the shelter. Like I said, the Williams and Tina Barlett are pretty sick from the radiation and we figure they need the protection. 'Course I guess we all do.

'Martha Peterson died yesterday. After her sons went away we couldn't get her to stay in the cellar.

'The Linkletters and Potts moved south today, using the Linkletters' team of workhorses and a wagon Tim built out of an old truck flatbed. They're the sixth and seventh families to leave. Most all of the young people are gone, of course. Most of the old people have chosen to stay. We don't know whether we'll make it or not, but most of us decided it'd be better to die here than live in those camps they've set up in northern Louisiana and Arkansas. I suppose if we had kids it might be different. That's why we help those who feel they have to go.

'It's kind of sad, though. You know you'll never see each other again. The people leaving feel kind of like traitors and the people staying feel kind of like fools . . . Still, we do what we got to do . . .'

After the channel went dead Neil turned off the set and continued to sit in the darkness of his aft cabin. He became aware of the faint glow of his wristwatch lying at the base of the radio. It was almost midnight. They were dying in east Tennessee, what? – perhaps six or seven hundred miles away. Not even that far.

Sighing, he turned the set back on, adjusted the earphones and began a slow sweep of the ham frequencies. The first voice he brought in reported increased radioactive fallout and radiation sickness in southern Mississippi, with thousands fleeing out into the Gulf of Mexico. Military authority had

244

ceased to exist; soldiers as well as civilians were fleeing, stealing boats, commandeering barges, using helicopters to get away. The voice speculated that west to New Orleans and Galveston there were few survivors. Those fleeing east across the Florida panhandle would probably be overtaken by the lethal fallout. He mentioned some towns whose names Neil didn't recognize, but when he checked his small atlas he concluded the broadcast was from somewhere less than a hundred miles east of Pensacola, Florida, on the Florida panhandle.

Neil moved the dial on, bringing in a ship, the *Athena*, three hundred miles out of Boston, asking for medical advice on the treatment of radiation sickness.

He brought in a station in Bermuda warning of starvation facing the islanders there.

Then his ear caught 'Raleigh, North Carolina' on a frequency filled with static, and he tried to bring it in more clearly. Raleigh was about two hundred miles west of Morehead City. The voice, clearer now, a woman's with a strong southern accent, was announcing that she was taking over for her husband, who was sick but who wanted her to keep up his daily reports. The radioactive fallout in the last day had increased tenfold, and now everyone was trying to stay below ground. Those who ventured out more than half an hour took sick quickly. Those who stayed in cellars or shelters did better. The ground was getting covered with ash, thick, black, ugly. They were drinking only stored water, but most had only a limited supply. Electric pumps could no longer be used. They couldn't figure why the fallout was so great, where it was coming from, and it was scary. They hoped it would stop raining soon.

When Neil switched off the radio this time he was trembling with a great, deep dread, almost a hopelessness. They were all doomed. Shelters, fleeing to sea, joining the Army, being in the Navy, all seemed equally futile.

No, that was a lie. He knew it was a lie, and knowing that

245

all people were not equally doomed frightened him, covered the heavy dread with a sharp layer of fear. Safety lay far to the south and out to sea. He knew that, could see that for a certainty now. Morehead City, bucolic, innocent, unimportant Morehead City, was doomed. In a few days it would be overtaken by the fallout. So too with the rest of the east coast. But the ocean and a run to the south represented hope for life, for him, for Jeanne, for Frank, for Olly, for all of his remaining friends. Only out there, where the fallout was swallowed by the insatiable sea, was there hope for survival, and he knew it was up to him to get them all to act, and to act now. The Army was lying. There was no safety left on land.

The decision made, he stood up, shut down the radio carefully, disconnected the batteries, and went up on deck. Captain Olly was sitting in the darkness of the wheelhouse talking in a lively monologue to the ever-quiet Conrad Macklin. Olly stopped talking when Neil appeared.

'I'm taking *Vagabond* back out to sea,' he announced quietly after sitting down opposite the old man.

'Good,' Captain Olly replied. 'Been wonderin' how long it would take you.'

Neil turned to Macklin.

'To escape out the inlet we'll need another boat to act as decoy,' he said. 'A boat with just enough fuel to get to the inlet and create a diversion. I want you to locate one, devise a plan for stealing it, and, when the time comes, steal it.'

Macklin stared back at Neil. 'You want me to be on one boat while you and the rest are sailing out the inlet on this?' he asked, scowling.

'One of us will be with you,' Neil answered. 'And, if possible, create a plan that doesn't necessitate your hitting or killing anyone.'

'If possible?' Macklin said with a sneer.

'Olly, about how many gallons of diesel fuel do you figure we'll need to get two boats out into the ocean?'

'It's three miles from here?' Olly asked.

'Yes,' Neil answered.

'Six or seven.'

'That's what I was afraid of,' Neil went on. 'Since they took all but five gallons of our fuel this afternoon we'll need more. Macklin, keep an eye open for another three gallons of fuel. Or more.'

'Like everyone else in the world,' Macklin commented.

Neil, staring past Captain Olly with his eyes half-closed in concentration, ignored the comment.

'We leave tomorrow night at ten,' he finally said.

'Who's coming with us?' Macklin asked.

'We'll see,' said Neil, and he rose to return to his aft cabin to sleep.

12

Neil arrived at the refugee centre and located Frank at one o'clock the next afternoon. As he moved through the halls he became distressingly aware that he was entering a little world that, no matter how dislocated, was permitting people to assume that they and this little world could continue to exist. This was a centre where people came to be safe and to be taken care of, and those in the halls had the look of men and women who saw danger as something they had survived in the past rather than something that might still be looming over them.

Neil himself was anxious and tense. He strode down the hall with the feeling that every moment they delayed might be fatal, that even now lethal clouds of radioactivity might be only hours away.

Frank was in the old principal's office supervising the location of some of the refugees. A harried-looking Army lieutenant was standing behind Frank looking alternately commanding and bewildered. As Neil paused in the doorway he watched people come up to Frank for instructions, saw him examine the chart on the desk before him and then send the person running off to perform some duty, Frank carefully putting a chalk mark on the chart.

Neil pushed his way through three or four people and stood in front of the desk. Frank looked up abstractedly as at an old college friend appearing out of place and unexpectedly.

'Fallout is approaching,' Neil said as quietly and unemotionally as he could. 'We've got to leave, sail – go south. You and Jeanne have got to come.'

Frank emerged from his abstracted state and looked at Neil with a tired frown. 'You're running?' he asked.

Neil flinched. 'Everyone in Morehead City will probably have to relocate,' he replied, aware of the half-dozen faces watching him attentively.

'Says who?' Frank asked.

'Frank, let's talk this over in private,' Neil appealed.

'Look, mister,' the Army lieutenant cut in abruptly. 'If there's danger to this area the Army will let people know.'

Neil looked up at the man coldly. 'You'll be lucky if they let *you* know,' he said.

'You think we should all evacuate Morehead City?' Frank asked. He seemed heavy, as if the thought of moving again depressed him.

'Yes. Everyone.'

The crowd around the desk began murmuring.

'No one goes nowhere,' the stubby lieutenant burst in a second time, 'unless the Army says so.'

'I want you to help me save Jeanne and her children,' Neil went on desperately, ignoring the lieutenant.

'Another ocean voyage?' Frank asked. He gazed at Neil a moment more and then turned to look at the refugees around the desk who were looking at him as if for a verdict on their fate. Then he peered sullenly down at his chart. 'It's up to Jeanne,' he said in a low, husky voice.

'Frank, please.'

'No one's going anywhere,' the lieutenant said.

Neil found Jeanne working alone in a small room with a dozen elderly women. She was serving them cups of water and giving them instructions on the routine of the camp, the location of the bathrooms and so on. She looked tired, her hair, tied back in a bun, was damp with perspiration. She had on jeans and a green sweatshirt. Surprised and smiling, she came out into the hall with him.

'What's the matter?' she asked, sensing his urgency.

'There's massive fallout coming,' he said in a low voice. 'We're sailing out the inlet tonight. You, Lisa and Skip must come.'

As she looked up at him he could see the fear and uncertainty in her eyes. She slowly shook her head. 'I . . . can't believe it,' she said.

'Jeanne, it's a life or death decision. No one in this camp will be alive in another two weeks.'

'You . . . Isn't it illegal for you and Jim to leave?'

'Everything is now illegal except staying here and dying.'

'How are you going to get past the Coast Guard?'

'I don't know,' he continued in a whisper as two women passed by. 'I just know we have to do it.'

'But . . .' she began, gazing down the hall after the women as if for help. 'Why . . . tonight?'

'Because the sword may fall at any moment.'

'If fallout's coming, they'll warn us, won't they?' she asked him next, resisting the decision that would force her to run again. 'They'll bus us south, or train.'

Neil grabbed her fiercely.

'They won't,' he hissed at her. 'There *are* no buses or trains except for the Army.'

'Oh, Neil,' she said, twisting in his grasp.

'Don't you trust me?' he said sharply, still holding her. 'Do you think I'm lying to you?'

She searched his face for certainty and saw with a shock that if she didn't leave she would die.

'Oh, Neil, of course I trust you,' she said, suddenly trembling.

'Then come,' said Neil with relief, taking her arm. 'Let's get the others.'

Together they went to get Frank and then the three of them began walking back to Jeanne's room to get Lisa and Skip.

'What about Jim?' Jeanne asked Neil as they hurried along.

'We'll get him,' Neil answered.

'Tony? Seth?' she asked.

'If they want to come.'

250

'How about Elaine?' Frank asked. 'She's here in the building.'

'No,' Neil said firmly. 'I'm exercising triage. Having her on the boat might mean that sooner or later someone else might have to die.'

'You don't know that,' Frank said.

'No, I don't. But she can't come.'

'There's another woman who wants to join us,' Jeanne interrupted as they began walking again.

'No. No one else,' Neil replied promptly, striding on.

'But I promised her . . .'

'No,' Neil repeated as they entered the third grade classroom. Lisa and Skip looked up at their mother. 'Where's your suitcase?'

'It was stolen,' Jeanne replied as she went to Skip and gave him a hug. 'Get our stuff together, Lisa, we're going back to the boat.'

'What about Jim?' Lisa asked, not moving.

'We'll get him,' Neil said.

'Go!' Jeanne said sharply to Lisa, who hurried away to where she had been reading. 'Neil, you must speak to this woman,' Jeanne added.

'No more,' said Neil. 'Come on, let's get going.'

But as the five of them were leaving, Neil's path was blocked by the small, defiant figure of Katya.

'I can sail, sew, cook, and I'm tough,' she said without introduction. 'I want to go with you.'

'We're overloaded,' Neil replied automatically, looking down at her, stopped by her almost comical fierceness.

'But Neil . . .' Jeanne began from beside him.

'I weigh a hundred and six pounds,' Katya countered. 'Pound for pound I'll be the best crew member you've ever had.'

Neil smiled in spite of himself, then shook his head. 'Look . . . we simply can't begin to take any stranger who

251

wants to join us,' he said. 'If you're tough you'll understand that.'

'I understand that,' she replied. 'But you need another woman aboard. Jeanne can't handle everything expected of a woman.'

Neil hesitated, thinking of Jeanne's seasickness, of Elaine's not going with them.

'I can sail, I can sew, I can cook, and I can fuck,' Katya went on firmly, looking Neil in the eye.

'A Renaissance woman,' he murmured, wishing she hadn't alluded to her sexuality, since he knew he'd already made up his mind when Katya had reminded him that Jeanne needed another woman's help.

'All right,' he said firmly. 'Jeanne needs you; therefore, we need you.'

'Thank you,' she said, reaching up on tiptoe to kiss him quickly on the lips.

'But try to remember that it's your first three skills we're taking you for and not the fourth,' he said, moving on past her.

'Please, let's get Jim,' Lisa pleaded.

And they hurried on.

13

'The Battle of Cooper's Henhouse', as one rather stoned corporal had dubbed it, had a gloomy effect on the C company that had fought in it. None of them had been killed and only three of them wounded, but Captain Ames had made it all seem like a mistake. Four of the farmers had been killed – three of them teenagers – and seven wounded before the officers got the shooting to stop. The henhouse had burned down, but most of the chickens had escaped. The soldiers had had more trouble rounding up the chickens and hogs than they had had winning the battle. Ames had radioed for an ambulance for all the wounded but was told to bring them back in the trucks. With the farm animals and wounded taking up two of the trucks, most of the company had to march back the fifteen miles to Morehead City.

Tony Mariano was a member of C company and he was goddamn angry at Ames and some of the others. He knew the farmers had started the shooting because the first shot had hit five feet away from Tony himself. And even before the soldiers had fired a single shot, one of the men in his squad had been hit as they were running forward to hide behind a big fallen tree trunk about thirty feet from the back of the henhouse. So if a few farmers had got killed they had only themselves to blame. Ames going around trying to find out who had advanced without orders was a waste of time.

But though Tony thought his company's actions were justified, he still found the whole business as unpleasant as most of the others. Tony himself had been wounded in the left side, but was laughed at by the other soldiers when the corpsman who examined the wound and extracted the bullet announced that it was a pellet from a pellet gun.

'Hey, Mariano,' his corporal had shouted at him. 'Aren't pellet guns outlawed by the Geneva Convention?' and the whole squad had laughed. Tony had seen the fifteen-year-old who had been killed: the young body and face chewed up by at least three slugs from someone's automatic rifle. Tony hadn't killed him – at least he didn't think he had – but he had sure blasted the henhouse pretty good before Sergeant Collins had yanked the gun out of his hand and shouted at him to stop.

By the time he had marched back to Morehead it was almost seven o'clock and he, like the rest, was exhausted and starved and filthy from wrestling with the hogs and chickens. In the mess-hall they were served another meal of fish and eggs, but with two or three cans of beer for each man, thank God. Jim Stoor was there and he told Jim about the battle, trying to show that it was a serious and necessary business, but he could see that Jim was appalled. God-damn it, there was a war on!

At eight, when a soldier told Jim that Frank and Neil were outside, Tony went along to see what was up.

Frank and Neil were standing in the dusk at the side of the restaurant that was their evening's mess-hall. Frank quickly explained to his son about their decision to try to take *Vagabond* back out to sea.

'I'm coming,' said Jim.

'What the fuck,' Tony burst in. 'You're deserting? And you, Neil, how come you're not in uniform?'

'Wrong war,' said Neil, echoing his friend's words. 'Do you want to join us?'

Tony looked at Neil uncertainly, his loyalty to his country battling with the fear aroused by seeing others fleeing an approaching danger. 'I'm no deserter,' he finally said sullenly.

Neil turned away. 'Let's go,' he said.

'Hold it!' Tony shouted. 'If you take Jim now I'll be an accessory or something.'

The other three stopped and turned to face him.

'If everyone acted as selfishly as you guys our society would be doomed,' Tony continued aggressively. 'It's my duty to report your plans to my superiors.'

'Come with us,' Neil said gently.

'You won't make it,' Tony countered. 'The Coast Guard won't let you out to sea. Don't go, Jim. They're shooting deserters.'

'I was going to desert even if there weren't fallout coming,' Jim said. 'Im going.'

'I'm not letting you guys . . .' Tony began, but then Neil's fist slammed into the side of his face. He staggered backwards into darkness.

14

The night was overcast as Neil had hoped, although on the northern horizon a few stars could be seen indicating an approaching high pressure system. With the wind blowing out of the east at fifteen knots the passage out of the inlet would be rough.

By midnight they were putting the plan they'd developed into execution. Conrad Macklin had stolen a small abandoned fishing vessel named *Moonchaser* and stolen enough fuel to get it to where Neil wanted. They had tied and tacked *Vagabond*'s blue carpets along her white port sides and decking to reduce glare and the chances of being seen by the Coast Guard's searchlight. They had even packed mud on the left side of the lower masts to cut down reflection there.

Neil and Jim were aboard the fishing smack, which was towing *Vagabond*'s inflatable dinghy with its outboard motor tilted up. Frank was in charge of the trimaran, with Olly, Macklin, Jeanne, and Lisa as crew. Skippy was asleep in the port berth, Katya was on call, and Tony was tied up in the forepeak.

Neil had taken Tony back to the docks because he'd feared that he *would* get the authorities to investigate *Vagabond*. He had planned to leave Tony behind at the last minute, but Macklin had argued vehemently that Tony might still have them chased, and, besides, was the best sailor they had for a long voyage. When Frank agreed, Neil decided they could abandon Tony in the Bahamas if he wanted off or didn't work out.

The escape plan was for Neil and Jim to scuttle *Moonchaser* on the eastern side of the inlet – at Shackleford Point – to draw the patrol launch over, while *Vagabond* would motor along the western side of the inlet a quarter of a mile away, pick up Neil and Jim who would motor the width of the inlet in the dinghy to join them, and rush out to sea.

As Neil steered the sluggish *Moonchaser* towards the inlet a light rain began to fall. Neil had decided that he and Jim should take the decoy vessel both because he had confidence they could do the job and because if *Vagabond* were seen and stopped, without him and Jim aboard the Coast Guard might let the ship proceed to sea, simply removing the deserter Tony. Of course he hadn't told Macklin or Tony this line of thought.

As he brought *Moonchaser* to within three-quarters of a mile of the patrol path of the cutter he realized that with the rain falling he could no longer depend on seeing the unlighted buoys and stakes that he'd planned to use to stay out of the main channel to avoid being spotted. He'd have to stay in the main channel, hoping the rain would so cut visibility that he could get the old fishing smack scuttled before the Coast Guard came close enough to see them motoring off in the dinghy.

Jim stood beside him in the little wheelhouse, his face wet with rain from peering around the salt-streaked window trying to pick up the channel buoys and look for signs of shoal water. He could barely make out the flashing red light of the next channel marker, and beyond that he could see neither the running lights nor searchlight of the Coast Guard patrol. Neil was keeping *Moonchaser* to the left of the main channel, motoring slowly forward against the incoming tide. Then, at a little after one, he opened up the throttle and headed for Shackleford Point and the planned scuttling.

Jim still saw no clear sign of the Coast Guard except for brief flashes of white which Neil said were the searchlight. The wind had picked up and seemed to be blowing the rain and seaspray directly into his face. Although it was a warm rain he was shivering. He had on a foul-weather jacket, but his legs were bare and cold beneath his swimsuit. Then he saw what Neil had said would be the last two lighted buoys before the Point: 'a flashing red and a flashing green'. He had to yell now over the noise of the engine to tell Neil.

'I'll take us just to port of the red one,' Neil shouted back. 'Get its number. And watch for the cutter.'

They seemed to approach the blinking red light on the red bell with aggravating slowness, but once there Neil steered to within a few feet of the loud mournful gonging and Jim verified that it had '16' painted white on its red. Almost the moment he looked forward again after they'd passed the bell, he saw the green starboard running light and sweeping searchlight of the cutter. It seemed to be a quarter of a mile off in the blackness and wet wind, almost dead ahead. It was moving west across the channel – away from Shackleford Banks.

Jim shouted this to Neil who brought *Moonchaser* to a complete halt in the water, waiting while the cutter moved further west away from them. Once the light swept in their direction and over the smack, but rapidly, without pausing. Though the glare temporarily blinded Jim, the cutter apparently didn't notice the black hull. Jim saw Neil look at his watch, grimace, and increase the ship's speed. The rain was becoming sporadic, but the wind was gusty and blew in sweeping bursts of spray against the windshield. Ocean swells were now creating a pitching motion in the boat as they approached the open water of the ocean.

In another two minutes the cutter was a little more than halfway across the inlet and still heading for the far side. Neil gave the boat full throttle, his face in tense concentration, and *Moonchaser* pounded forward at seven knots into the tide and ocean swells. The ship rose and smashed down on one big swell that seemed to emerge out of the darkness like some living sea mammal to lift them momentarily and then toss them back into the water. Jim was thrown hard against the control panel and Neil was swung around – still holding the wheel – to bang against the ship's coaming.

'We may really need that Mayday,' he shouted with a grim

smile. Jim, shivering, felt a fearful exhilaration. He peered ahead and could see two flashing white lights one after another – the lights of a range that normally guided ships down the centre of the channel, but that Neil would use to guide them on to the sands of Shackleford Bank. The Coast Guard cutter was off to the right some place, but Jim couldn't pick it up.

'Bring the dinghy up closer,' Neil shouted to him, and Jim stumbled aft, falling against the stern coaming when *Moonchaser* plunged into another swell. Righting himself, he hauled in the towline to the dinghy until it was only a few feet off the stern of the fishing smack where he re-cleated it. Returning forward he stared again into the rain and blackness, and realized Neil was easing the boat towards shore.

'Hold on!' he shouted. 'Here we go!'

With a harsh grating sound, the fishing vessel ran aground, slowing at first and then, as Neil killed the engine, stopping abruptly. Jim grabbed the deckhouse shelf and held on, looking to Neil for orders. As *Moonchaser* seemed to sit contentedly in the sand, Jim turned to get into the dinghy; a wave smashed broadside into the ship with a tremendous crash. Jim was flung to port into Neil and the two men smashed into the side of the deckhouse, then against the coaming, and then they were in the sea.

It happened so suddenly and the chill water of the ocean was such a shock that Jim didn't at first realize clearly what had happened. He was standing in four feet of water that suddenly became seven feet of water when a swell surged past.

'Get the dinghy!' Neil shouted from off to the left. Jim could barely make out the ship heeled over in the surf a few feet away in front of him, but he struggled to her stern and felt for the rubber dinghy. It was there, bobbing and tearing at her towline like a wild horse. As he reached for it, the end of the protruding outboard struck him on the shoulder. He swore, reached again to control the dinghy and was submerged by a huge swell that slapped him in the face like a lazy porpoise flipping its tail. He spat out salt water and felt a sudden panic. He couldn't *get* the dinghy. It danced away from him, then swung its engine shaft at him like a club.

'Cut the line!' Neil shouted, appearing beside him and handing him a knife.

Jim swam the few feet to *Moonchaser*'s stern and pulled himself up and slashed the towline. In an instant the inflatable pulled its line out of Jim's grasp, surged away on a breaking wave and was swallowed up into the darkness.

'GET IT!' Neil screamed, and Jim plunged away after it.

'Mayday! Mayday!' Olly's voice crackled urgently into *Vagabond*'s radio-telephone as Frank stood by, operating it. 'Damn engine went and killed himself. I'm aground on Shackleford Point. Mayday! Mayday! Do you read me? Over.'

Frank switched to receive, deciding that Captain Olly's unprofessional way of sending a Mayday was probably more credible than the scenario he himself had planned. He leaned backwards to look up at Macklin in the wheelhouse who was assigned to hold *Vagabond* motoring steadily into the tide barely inching forward. He nodded at him in reassurance.

'Roger, Mayday,' a distant static voice said from the radio. 'This is the Coast Guard station at Fort Macon acknowledging Mayday. Identify yourself and your position. Repeat: identify your vessel and your position . . . Over.'

Frank switched the button and nodded at Captain Olly.

'This is Cap'n Olly,' he said irritably. '*Moonchaser* is banging on the beach here at Shackleford Point and getting swamped. I'm at Shackleford Point just south of the range. My ship is beginning to . . .' Captain Olly banged his fist down on the radio table and shouted: 'Jesus! Help! We're foundering! Help!'

Frank cut the switch and they listened for the Coast Guard response.

260

'This is Fort Macon Coast Guard calling *Moonchaser*,' the voice said with more urgency. 'Please repeat position and clarify position. Over.'

Frank shook his head 'no' to Captain Olly and kept the button switched to receive. After twenty seconds, the voice came through again.

'This is the Coast Guard calling the *Moonchaser*. We have received your Mayday. Will send assistance. Do you read me? Over.'

Frank shifted the dial on his receiver off the frequency reserved for distress calls to the one he knew the Coast Guard usually used for routine transmission among their vessels. For twenty seconds there was nothing, but finally the same voice crackled out calling the cutter, *Avenger*. After they had established contact the voice said:

'A vessel named *Moonchaser* radioed a Mayday. Ship reports being aground and foundering off Shackleford Point. Can you provide assistance? Over?'

'Roger, Macon. Affirmative. Are you sure it was a genuine Mayday? Over?'

'Affirmative, *Avenger*. Sounded real to me. Over.'

'Okay Macon. *Avenger* headed to Shackleford to provide assistance . . .'

'I'm going up and get us moving full speed to the rendezvous,' Frank said to Captain Olly. 'Keep listening.'

After Frank had disappeared up out of the cabin Captain Olly lowered his head to the radio. For a minute or so there was nothing. Then: '. . . *Avenger* now only about three hundred yards off Shackleford. No sign of a vessel aground . . . Okay, Macon, we've got our light on a black-hulled fishing smack aground and partially submerged . . . She's taking a pounding . . . *Moonchaser*? . . . It's *Moonchaser* . . . No sign of men aboard. We're sending the small launch to investigate. Stay tuned. Over.'

As the seconds ticked away Captain Olly became aware of *Vagabond* beginning to pitch and smash into the ocean swells

261

as she rushed at full speed towards the inlet. He heard Frank say something loudly to Jeanne but couldn't hear what. Two minutes passed before the voice spoke again from the radio. 'This is *Avenger*. There's no one aboard the *Moonchaser*, Macon . . . When was your last radio transmission from the vessel? Over.'

'Just before we radioed you, *Avenger*. Over.'

Another long silence ensued, broken once by Fort Macon Coast Guard Station asking *Avenger* if it 'read me'.

'Affirmative, Macon. I'm waiting for my launch crew to report . . .'

Another silence. Captain Olly realized that *Vagabond* had slowed and become stationary again. She was pitching and slamming more steeply into the swells. They must be at the rendezvous point. After another minute, the voice: '*Avenger* to Macon. Something strange going on here. Launch reports there's no radio aboard the *Moonchaser* . . . How could she send a Mayday? . . .'

Bewildered by the nightmarish suddenness of being pitched into the ocean and having the dinghy torn out of his grasp into the turbulent darkness, Jim had dived clumsily into the water and begun swimming in the direction the inflatable had disappeared. He took six or seven strong strokes and saw no sign of the dinghy when a rubber part of it bumped him in the back of the head as if teasing him. He grabbed a line on it just as another wave rolled indifferently over him. He found he could stand and, holding the dinghy and bracing himself for the next wave, called out into the darkness.

'I've got it! Over here!'

There was no answer and Jim could now see neither the boat nor Neil. He shouted again.

'NEIL! I've got it! Over here!'

'. . . Jimmmm!' came an answering yell from off to his left and slightly closer to shore. Jim began struggling through the surges of water towards where the voice seemed to come from and was startled when a huge fish splashed almost on top of him.

'Help me,' he heard Neil's voice say, and realized that the fish was Neil. He reached out with his free hand and grabbed hold of him. After a wave passed, Neil suddenly stood, choking and gasping for breath and clinging to Jim.

'My arm,' he said, grimacing. 'My elbow's killing me. I can't use it.'

The two men stood in three feet of water and braced themselves as another hill of water swept over them, slamming them a foot closer to shore.

'I'll hold it now,' Neil gasped out. 'You get in. GET IN!' he shouted.

In the ebb of a wave Jim quickly hauled himself over one side of the inflatable and plopped into the middle. It was filled with five or six inches of water. As he got on to his knees, he heard Neil shout: 'Start the engine!'

He turned aft and groped for the release lever that would lower the prop into the water. A wave smashed into the dinghy, jerked it sideways and spilled Jim against the left side nd almost out. He struggled up and groped again for the lever. When he found it, the engine fell with an abruptness that pinched his first finger and he gasped out a Frank-like oath even as he retrieved his hand and grabbed the starting cord. He pulled once but the engine didn't start.

'Start the engine!' Neil shouted again from somewhere in the water near the bow.

Jim remembered the second time to pull out the choke and pulled again. No catch. Again. The engine sputtered and died. Again. No catch. Again: sputter, sputter – he pushed the choke in – roar: the engine was alive.

'Help me in!' Neil shouted, now emerging right beside the dinghy, one arm only over the bulge of inflated rubber. 'Grab the back of my belt!'

As Jim throttled down the outboard, another wave broke over them and smashed them into even shallower water. Neil was then in only two or three feet of water and his whole torso now collapsed across the starboard side of the dinghy, permitting Jim to grab his belt and haul with all his strength to get him up and in. The next wave seemed to scoop Neil up and splash him down in the pool of the swamped inflatable. Jim shifted into forward and pulled out the throttle.

The outboard roared and the dinghy exploded against the next wave, ploughing partly through it like a submarine rather than over it, then surged through fifteen feet of calm water before exploding through the next wave. Even with two men aboard and six inches of water, the boat was able to smash forward at four or five knots. Jim had no sense of direction except to get out of the surf and back into deeper water. Low in the plunging dinghy he couldn't see any channel lights and had only the vaguest idea of which way was west.

'Steer by the swells,' Neil shouted to him, kneeling beside him in the middle of the dinghy, one arm limp and held awkwardly in front of him. 'Keep them coming at you on the port beam.'

Jim had been heading into them but as soon as Neil spoke he realized that their destination of the other side of the inlet was simply across the swells at a right angle. He swung the dinghy to the right, squinted into the rain and spray, and steered at full throttle towards where he hoped to find *Vagabond*. A giant white eye suddenly peered at them from almost dead ahead, then swept away to the right. The Coast Guard cutter was coming directly at them.

'. . . strange going on here. Launch reports there's no radio aboard the *Moonchaser*.'

Captain Olly heard shouts from up on deck and felt something thud against one side of *Vagabond*.

'Okay, Fort Macon,' the voice from the *Avenger* went on. 'We're leaving our small launch here to check ashore for survivors, but *Avenger* is now returning to patrol. Something's

264

not kosher about this. Over . . .'

Captain Olly hurried up the cabin steps and bumped into Frank scrambling across the wheelhouse to get to the controls and get *Vagabond* moving. Jim and Neil were visible in the darkness hauling up the dinghy into the starboard cockpit.

'Coast Guard's coming back,' he said to Frank, who simply gave him a wild look and put *Vagabond* into full speed forward. Neil stumbled into the wheelhouse and collapsed with a groan on the cushioned seat. Jeanne followed and knelt beside him, then called Macklin over.

Captain Olly went to help Jim with the dinghy. He was pulling it off the open deck aft up over the cockpit seat into the cockpit. After the two of them had got it down into the cockpit Jim asked:

'Can we leave it here for now?'

'Sure. I'll lash it down,' Captain Olly said. 'Go help your dad.'

Jim took a long stride over the slightly squashed inflatable and went into the wheelhouse and stood beside his father. Jeanne ducked past them into the main cabin and then Jim leaned out to peer ahead into the rain.

They were motoring at full speed south along the western side of the inlet headed directly out to sea. They were already far to the right of the big ship channel and pounding into the steep swells that rolled directly at them. Jim's glance at the depthmeter showed it reading 'four feet' which meant they were in only seven or eight feet of water. *Vagabond*, with her dagger board up as it now was, but heavily loaded, probably drew a little less than four feet. There was a terrific slam and shudder as a big breaking wave smacked into all three hulls at once. *Vagabond* slowed seemingly to a halt and then surged forward again.

'Have we passed the point yet?' Frank shouted at Jim. 'Look out your side!'

Jim stared out into the blackness off to his right, remembering that the point on which old Fort Macon and the

Coast Guard station were located was the last land to starboard before the open ocean. He thought he could see a few lights, probably the Coast Guard station, slightly aft of their starboard beam.

'I see lights at about four o'clock,' he said to his father. 'I can't see anything directly abeam.'

Another breaking wave crashed into the trimaran, slowing her almost to a halt before she recovered and made good headway again.

'Two feet, DAD!' Jim cried at his father when he saw the depthmeter flicker at two feet, then zero, then three, then zero. 'Zero feet!'

White-faced and grimacing, Frank swung the wheel to bring *Vagabond* around towards the channel and deeper water, but also back towards the Coast Guard cutter.

'It's just turbulence!' Neil shouted from behind them. 'Does it stay steady at one or zero?' he asked.

'It says "zero" now,' said Jim, frightened. 'And just occasionally a "two" or "three".'

'It's turbulence,' Neil said, staggering up between Jim and Frank at the controls, Jeanne seeming to be trying to hold something against his arm. 'We should swing her southwest now. Away from the cutter.'

'I'm not running her aground,' Frank said urgently, holding his course back towards the channel. He stared down first at the depthmeter, which fluctuated erratically between zero and now four and five feet, and then the compass, which showed them on a southeast heading.

'We're free, Frank!' Neil insisted, grimacing in pain. 'We're out of the inlet. Head her southwest, even west. They'll *see* us if we stay on this course.'

Frank, frowning, his face, like each of the others, wet with rain and sweat, looked once briefly, fearfully at Neil.

'Are you sure?' he asked.

'Head her west!'

'Six feet!' Jim announced.

Frank turned the wheel back to the right and *Vagabond* swung to starboard, first heading south, then southwest, where Frank straightened her. As they surged into the blackness, taking the swells now on their port side, Jim took a long look aft and saw the light sweep along the Fort Macon Point, then out towards them. A white eye blinded him as the wheelhouse filled with light, and then the light moved away out to sea.

None of those standing in the wheelhouse spoke and Neil joined Jim in watching the subsequent movement of the light.

'They didn't see us,' Neil said quietly. 'Take her full west, Frank.'

'I'll keep her on southwest,' Frank said, not looking at him.

'I tell you we're free!' Neil shouted.

Frank didn't answer.

'Five feet,' said Jim. All three men now looked at the depthmeter, which held at five feet for a few more seconds and then went on to six, seven, then ten feet. Frank eased the wheel a little to the right and slowly the boat swung more to the west until, after a half minute, Frank steadied her at 260 degrees, ten degrees south of west.

Yet again the light, less bright now, exploded into the wheelhouse as the distant cutter swept the sea with its searchlight. Again it did not hesitate or return to *Vagabond*, which, at full rpm, sliced and ploughed away. For two or three more minutes the depthmeter read between ten and twelve feet, and then began climbing rapidly through the teens. Indeed, they were free.

Part Three
WATER

1

Free. Except for the threat of radioactive fallout, of storms, of pirates, of their overloaded trimaran breaking apart, of death by thirst or starvation or disease, of mutiny, of the antagonism that the whole rest of the world now felt against the white people of America and Russia, both of whom they blamed for the war, those aboard *Vagabond* were free to do as they pleased. They sailed south.

The war sailed with them. Although they increased their distance from the coast as they moved south, and the threat of fallout receded, its consequences in the bodies of Frank and Olly and possibly others remained. Frank looked much more haggard than anyone else, had lost ten pounds and was sick again after a three-day remission. Olly was 'better' but still feeling 'poorly'. Even Neil still felt unaccountable nausea once or twice.

Nevertheless, at sea after a whole day of adjusting sleeping accommodations, meal times and rationing, they settled into a routine. Their watches remained the same except that Katya sometimes spelled Lisa with Jim. Macklin and Tony were berthed together in the forepeak, Katya in with Jeanne, and Olly slept either in Neil's aft cabin or on the dinette settee.

Tony, in his big, bluff, self-confident way, had made himself thoroughly at home again. Although he spoke loudly the first day or two about his being forced to let his country down, after they heard a report about heavy radioactivity at Morehead City and the mass evacuation south of all who could move, he ceased to raise the subject. He flirted with both Jeanne and Katya, helping them in the galley more than any of the other males and turning out to be an excellent cook,

271

especially of fish – their principal food. He was also, Neil admitted to himself, the best all-around sailor of his crew.

Katya and Jeanne got along well together, and though Katya wasn't a cook she let Jeanne, Lisa and Tony instruct her. She was, as she had advertised, a good sailor and tough, usually volunteering to help with sail changes on any watch when she was awake. When Tony and Macklin began to come on to her she handled each of them in his own style. With Tony she was casual and playful; with Macklin quiet and direct. Neil never knew precisely what passed between her and Macklin their second evening at sea, but he saw him speak to her in the side cockpit with a tight smile, saw her flush and speak angrily at him. He sneered, said something back, and wandered quietly away. If Katya was good at 'fucking' she apparently was in no hurry to prove it, at least with Macklin.

Macklin himself rarely said or did anything to draw attention to himself. He blended in. On land he had stolen a case of canned fruit, a carton of cigarettes, and five six-packs of beer. Though the fruit was relegated to emergency rations, they worked their way through the beer at two a day, dividing it up and sipping at it as if it were a rare champagne. When asked where he had got these items he had simply shrugged and said he'd 'stumbled across them in some guy's cellar'.

Their destination was the West Indies, initially Puerto Rico. But with the southeast wind forcing them to sail directly south by the end of the third day Neil felt they were already so close to the Bahamas that they should make a landfall on Great Abaco Island. There they might barter for more food and water, even, if they found the right conditions, try to settle. However, radio Nassau reported debilitating food shortages throughout the islands, and Americans were not welcome. If the principal food was fish, they might as well continue at sea.

Fishing was, in fact, the focus of each morning and evening's effort. They had two ocean rods and reels with good line, but only five lures, one of which they lost on their second day. At dawn and dusk they usually trolled with both rigs, one from each cockpit. The rods were usually jammed into place with a strong drag on the reels so that no one had to sit and hold them all the time. When a fish was hooked the helmsman would bring the boat up into the wind to slow it down, and someone would stand by with both a gaff and a large net while the other man on watch duty, who was responsible for the rods, would begin to reel in the hooked fish.

Because such fishing was new to most of them and because their lives depended on it, the bringing in of a fish was a major community event. They caught three bluefish their first evening, a twenty-pound tuna the next dawn, two dolphin and a tuna that dusk, then inexplicably lost two hooked fish and a second of their lures during the next dawn. The third evening, however, they recouped with two more dolphin and a barracuda.

Neil himself, with his arm in a sling from cracking his elbow on the *Moonchaser*, couldn't help with the fishing, but it interested him to watch the different styles his crew had in bringing in and gaffing the fish.

When Frank was in charge of the gaffing there was shouting and confusion and irritability before Frank could get the man controlling the rod and reel to position the fish properly for gaffing or netting. Once the fish was flopping around in the cockpit there was always a delay and more shouting before Frank, looking pained, would knife the fish out of its misery.

When Olly was in charge everything proceeded as quietly as if all were in a silent movie, the only sound being Olly's soft talking to the fish. Olly never told the man at the rod or at the helm what to do, but by talking to the fish – 'Come on in a little closer, fella, my back hurts and I don't like leaning down none' – the man at the rod would know exactly what to do. When he had gaffed the fish, Olly would say something like 'Up you go, sonny, easy does it', as if the fish wanted to get aboard and all of them were involved in a co-operative enterprise. Then, after the fish was aboard and flopping, Olly would take a minute to praise the fish to all the onlookers. 'Look at those colours, will you? I ain't seen anything as pretty as that since my second wife bought herself that new dress', or 'Now isn't that a big fella. Must weigh twenty-five pounds and not an ounce of fat. Bet he was an Olympic champ down below . . .'

And when Olly killed, he always began talking to the fish again. 'Okay, big fella, afraid we got to quiet you down. I gave you time for your prayers but if you got anything else you want to say better say it now . . .' The fish would flop violently in response to this, or once, so everyone agreed, made some distinct grunting sounds, and then Olly, with one neat slice, would quiet the fish forever.

'Don't he look beautiful?' Olly would conclude. 'Just hope I look half as good when the Big Fisherman hauls me in and lays me out. I'm damn sure I won't taste as good.'

Conrad Macklin on the other hand gaffed and killed a fish with a fierce scowl as if involved in a life-or-death combat with a life-long enemy.

When Jeanne participated in the fishing Neil found himself focusing more attention. Her glistening dark skin and full lithe body distracted him considerably from the problem of boarding the fish, especially as she wrestled with the rod and reel or stuck her behind in the air to lean down to gaff, clad as she usually was only in shorts and a bikini top. She and Katya seemed to have the same effect on Tony, Macklin and Frank. Lisa's budding body, perhaps because of her shy dignity, was less observed, except by Jim.

They were adapting to a world of scarcity. Neil restricted the use of their remaining two gallons of diesel fuel to the charging of the three batteries. Oil was now everywhere unavailable except to the military. To avoid having to charge the batteries any more than necessary, Neil used them solely for the shortwave radio. For illumination they used kerosene lamps, and, when necessary, flashlights. They had only four gallons of kerosene and that too might never again be easy to obtain. The two dozen candles aboard Neil stored as light of last resort. Even matches were scarce. Fortunately, no one smoked except Jim, who smoked marijuana and was abstaining, and Macklin, whose cigarettes had been confiscated by Neil to use in the West Indies as barter.

But the bleakness of the land world and of shortages Neil and Frank and Olly kept to themselves. For all of them the sea represented a haven, a relief from the terrors and suffering they had experienced on land, and Neil wanted to try to keep it that way. For the first time there began to be casual joking among them that had been lacking before.

On the second afternoon Neil had overheard Captain Olly teasing Frank about *Vagabond*.

'Yep,' Captain Olly was saying. 'You gotta good ship here, Frank. All you got to do is take off those two side boats you got, and the masts, and put a bowsprit on her and paint her black and she'd be right pretty. Might not even have to paint her.'

Frank laughed as he sat down in the wheelhouse with a small cup containing his daily ration of beer.

'Thanks,' he said to Olly, who was at the helm with his own cup.

'Don't be embarrassed your boat don't look like a boat,' Olly went on. 'Brazen it out. Pretend you got yourself a beginner's boat. You know, a three-wheeler so you won't tip over.'

Frank laughed again and even as he did, Neil realized that it was the first time since the war had begun that he *had* laughed. 'I tell people I got a special three-for-the-price-of-one deal that I couldn't pass up,' Frank said.

'Yep. Good story. Good story. Got to tell them something, that's for sure, so they won't know you're nuts,' Captain Olly concluded.

While Neil assumed responsibility for the sailing of the ship, Jeanne began to assume responsibility for how they interacted with each other. At dinner their second day at sea she suggested that at every evening meal they observe a half-minute of silence before eating, and if anyone wanted to offer thanks for the food or for life, he or she might. Jeanne usually spoke, occasionally mentioning some specific individual she wanted to acknowledge. Often Katya or Jim or Frank would also add a brief word. More rarely Tony or Neil.

That night too she embraced and kissed each of the others still topside before she went below to her berth. Although all she said to each was 'Goodnight' and the person's name, Neil could see that the physical contact loosened the isolation each tended to feel. Even Conrad Macklin flushed and looked pleased. Among the men, at Jeanne's prodding, there were more 'good job, Frank', and 'thanks, Jim', and 'that's good, Tony', where before there had been either cold correctness or nothing.

Captain Olly had the most trouble adapting to the more affectionate routine which Jeanne kept urging upon them. When Neil relieved him at the helm at the change of watch and said 'Nice job, Olly', he testily replied: 'Can't expect me to run aground in five thousand feet of water.' When Jeanne gave him a goodnight kiss the second time he grimaced and grinned. ''T warn't much of a kiss,' he said. 'If you want to get laid you got to do better than that.'

Jeanne looked surprised and then smiled, 'Don't worry,' she had said, her eyes flashing. 'When I want to get laid, the man will know it.'

Most of them found the meals repetitious and skimpy. They were rationing themselves severely on the last of their canned foods and some remaining fruits and vegetables, and salting and drying some of their fish steak for later. They were cooking in salt water and had cut their fresh water intake to a quart per person per day. The six adults were all experimenting with drinking a cup or two of sea water each day.

To help avoid unnecessary gloom Neil became a censor. He permitted only Frank and Olly to listen to the shortwave and

276

transistor radios with him. The violent, anti-white, anti-Americanism he was picking up from stations in the West Indies they kept to themselves. The probability of mass starvation on many of the islands within a month they did not mention. Officially they were sailing for the islands untouched by the war. In his heart Neil knew that no place and no one and nothing would ever be untouched by this war.

Shortwave and transistor reports from the US mainland raised on the third day at sea a new spectre. A summer flu seemed to be afflicting many people in the west and southwest with an unusually high number of fatalities. One ham operator speculated that a biological warfare laboratory had been destroyed and that one of its germs had been responsible for the epidemic. In any case it now seemed to be killing more people than fallout. Typhoid had also become a problem. Of the fighting itself there was little news. The superpowers were still technically at war, but now like two exhausted and glassy-eyed fighters who had landed such devastating blows in the first round that they seemed barely capable of standing, much less hitting each other. Thus it seemed that each day the ramifications and elaborations of the world disaster spread a little further, like a spilled bottle of black ink slowly soaking along a paper towel. Cuba had been heavily bombed by conventional means early in the war and when the Cubans tried to take the US Navy base on the eastern tip of their island, the US had used a tactical nuclear weapon to destroy much of the enemy force. Cuba's Air Force and Navy had allegedly been destroyed, but no effort made to invade. Guantanamo was being evacuated.

Although nuclear explosions had destroyed the Panama Canal, Miami, Cape Canaveral, American forces in Central America and oil refineries in Venezuela, the Caribbean area had been spared nuclear explosions since the third day of the war. Some rich Americans were flying to Puerto Rico and this influx of the privileged was being resented. Despite the presence of the US Navy, which, with the losses of its other

Caribbean bases, now had its largest facility outside San Juan, pirate attacks were occurring on both private and commercial ships, both small and large. Food riots occurred on a regular basis in San Juan and smaller cities although officially there was as yet no starvation.

It was to this island that *Vagabond* was supposedly heading, but in the new world that all had experienced over the last ten days no one aboard expected anything. Neil set a course, they sailed on. In this new world the future was something that could only hurt or terrify or kill. To look beyond the next wave was dangerous. Neil set a course, they sailed on. To hope for more could only be done in whispers.

2

On their third night at sea Lisa and Jim had the ten to two watch, with Neil awake in the wheelhouse. Near midnight Jeanne fixed some hot tea, one bag for three cups. *Vagabond* was still sailing due south with a good easterly breeze. An afternoon squall line seemed well behind them. With Jim now at the helm and Lisa watching the trolling rig in the side cockpit, Neil and Jeanne sat kittycorner from each other a few feet apart in the unlit wheelhouse, sipping at their weak tea.

'Do you think about where we're going to end up?' Jeanne asked him unexpectedly.

Neil did think about it, frequently. It made for depressing thinking.

'Yes,' he answered.

'Will we be able to settle in Puerto Rico or the Virgin Islands?' Jeanne asked after she saw he wasn't going to go on.

'Perhaps,' Neil replied, doubting it very much. As he looked at her he wished he could share his fears but wanted to spare her the burden. Even with the mostly overcast sky the nearly full moon gave light to *Vagabond*'s decks and allowed Neil to see the outline of Jeanne's face and body. She was very still, her teacup held in her lap. The afternoon squalls had dampened the seas and, for a change, *Vagabond* wasn't pounding but rolling gently through the water.

'I suppose, ultimately, it has to be South America, doesn't it?' she went on. 'Some place untouched, where the . . . infrastructure of civilization is still solid.'

Neil sipped at his tea. He'd heard a report that half a dozen South American countries – all of whom had by now declared their neutrality – had set up internment camps for American refugees. The threat of the mysterious plague-like disease which was spreading from the western US was increasing their fear of and resentment of Americans.

'Yes, I guess it will,' he said, without elaborating.

'That was a strange time we had that other night, wasn't it?' she said unexpectedly in her low, intense voice. Neil became aware of Jim at the wheel eight feet away, able to hear. Of Lisa too not far away. 'That other night' in the side cockpit had been . . . my God, almost a week before.

'It was a lot more than that,' Neil answered.

'Yes . . .' she replied in a soft voice.

For half a minute, as Neil stared at Jeanne's indistinct face, neither of them spoke.

'There aren't any rules any more, are there?' she said after a while. 'We have to create our own.'

'There are rules,' Neil said. 'Blowing up the world doesn't end rules.'

'I mean . . . some of the old ones can't be applied any more.'

Like what? Neil wondered. Like widows and a period of mourning? Love leading to marriage? Love leading to bed?

'Like what?' he asked. He noticed Lisa coming in from the port cockpit to talk to Jim.

'The old rule that you could go to bed with a man for enjoyment,' Jeanne said in a low voice.

Startled, he waited for her to go on. It wasn't an old rule he had expected her to come up with.

'In the new world,' she continued softly, glancing towards where Jim and Lisa were also talking in low voices. 'In *our* new world, in this small world of *Vagabond*, that rule won't work. My sleeping with . . . a man would transform our universe.'

'Yes, it would,' Neil said.

'Frank wants me to sleep with him,' she announced.

'I see,' he said in a voice so low he wasn't sure she could hear it. Then, louder: 'Rather popular, aren't you?'

280

For a moment the only sound was of the water rushing past *Vagabond*'s three hulls. In the darkness Jeanne was only a vague silhouette.

'. . . Neil . . .'

The sound of anguish in her soft voice made Neil move to the edge of his seat and, leaning towards her, he started to speak, but knew that even whispers would be heard by Jim and Lisa. He slowly lifted his right hand in the darkness to touch her unseen face. When it reached her cheek, she held it against her face with both hands, turning to kiss his palm with her lips.

'I see,' Neil said in a normal voice.

'I hope you see,' she answered in a low voice, but still one that Jim and Lisa could hear.

'What I see,' Neil said slowly, smiling in the darkness, caressing her face with his hand, and aware of the absurdity of the conversation, 'is that you are still temporarily insane. Am I correct?'

'Yes,' she said softly.

'And you see that I am still temporarily insane. Correct?'

'Yes. I hope so, yes.'

'And now you're telling me,' he went on in a low voice, barely able to contain his joy and laughter, 'that Frank has become temporarily insane, too. Is that right?'

'Yes.' She giggled softly.

'How about Jim? Is *he* insane?'

She laughed again. 'I don't think so,' she said.

'Well, *I* think so,' said Jim suddenly from the wheel. 'I can't tell *what* you two are talking about. You sound *nuts*.'

'Mother, you *are* being silly,' Lisa added with a childlike primness that Jeanne thought she'd lost since the war began.

As Neil and Jeanne stopped laughing, Neil could feel Jeanne tense, her hands still gripping his.

'Oh, Lisa,' she said. 'You missed it all. We're joking about the insanity of trying to create a new world in South America; yet that's where all of us – Frank too – think we have to end up.'

'Not me,' said Jim. 'I think we should head for the South Pacific.'

'See,' said Neil, grinning in the darkness. 'You were right, Jeanne. Jim at least is still sane.'

'Thank God,' said Jeanne.

'Right,' said Neil.

'Around Cape Horn,' said Jim, and Neil and Jeanne's laughter burst out again into the wheelhouse, Jim and Lisa turning to stare at them in slight bewilderment.

'Christ, how do you expect me to sleep?' Frank's voice cut into Neil's giddy world like an executioner's sword.

Pulling away from Jeanne, he turned to see behind him Frank's gaunt body outlined in the opening of the wheelhouse. He had come up from his cabin where he'd been sleeping.

'I'm sorry, Frank,' Neil said quickly. 'We got a little silly, I guess.'

'You sure as hell did,' Frank said, still looming in the entrance ten feet away, his face haggard. 'It sounded like a couple of loonies out here.'

Jeanne stood up. 'It was thoughtless of us,' she said. 'Forgive us, Frank.' She walked over to him and put her arms around him. Neil saw him respond stiffly at first and then put his arms around her and lower his head to the top of hers.

'You make it kind of tough to hold a grudge,' he said.

'I hope so,' she said softly.

'What were you doing anyway?' he asked.

There was a brief silence. 'Flirting with Neil,' she answered. 'I'm trying to get out of even-day garbage detail.'

'Try flirting with me,' Frank said. 'I *own* the damn boat.'

Jeanne stretched up and kissed Frank on the cheek. 'Goodnight again,' she whispered and moved away towards her cabin.

'You might pay a little attention to the boat,' Frank said to Neil. 'Every now and then, for appearances.'

Neil felt a rush of anger. 'I pay attention to this boat every second of the day and you know it,' he snapped back.

Jeanne had stopped at her cabin entrance and Jim and Lisa, withdrawn through it all, stood at the wheel.

'Yeah,' said Frank after a strained silence. 'I guess you're right. I'm sorry, Neil.'

Neil waited a moment before responding. 'Don't worry about it,' he said. 'I'm sorry about the noise.'

'Yeah. Goodnight. Goodnight, Jim. You too, Lisa.'

Frank moved away again to his cabin, sliding his hatch closed behind him. Neil walked over to where Jeanne was still standing at her cabin entrance.

'I'm sorry, Jeanne,' he said to her softly.

She looked up at him in the darkness and then away.

'I . . . think I love you, Neil,' she said in a low voice. 'But it's no good. We're a family. Our . . . love would be . . . a kind of incest.'

'You're not my sister,' he replied, almost sharply.

'Ahh, but I am,' she said softly, looking up at him. 'Don't you see, you and Frank are brothers, and Frank and I are brother and sister, so you . . . we're all too close, Neil.'

'I see that Frank would be hurt by our love-making,' he said after a pause. 'And I don't want to hurt him. But he'll be hurt by our love whether we . . . act on it or not.'

She turned away her face, barely visible in the dark.

'In this world . . . in our new world, no one must be alone,' she said.

'Does than mean no two can ever be together then?' he asked, pulling her gently against him.

She turned to look at him, then again turned away. 'Oh, Neil, I don't know,' she whispered. 'I've got to get things right with Frank. You must see that.'

Neil stared down at her shadowed face. 'I'm not sure that's possible, Jeanne,' he suggested quietly.

When he tried to lift her head to look at her she pressed it against his shoulder, refusing to budge. He could feel the wetness of tears on his bare shoulder. He held her, caressing her hair against her back, his smile fading, a sudden awareness striking him of being on a ship racing through the night away from a universe of death to the north. The image of Frank angrily looming in the wheelhouse entrance returned to him and he felt a great sadness.

'It's no use, Neil,' Jeanne finally whispered. 'We're not free.'

In the wheelhouse after Neil and Jeanne had parted to their separate cabins Jim and Lisa continued the task of keeping *Vagabond* moving on course. For many minutes neither of them spoke. Lisa left Jim to check again on the trolling rig and spent two minutes reeling in the lure to check for seaweed. She cleaned off the lure and let it back out again, adjusting the drag. When she returned to Jim at the helm they were again silent. They didn't touch each other.

A woman's muffled crying from Jeanne's cabin cut through their silence, both of them stiffening. After another minute in which every groan of a line stretching, slap of a halyard, luff of a sail, whine of wind in the rigging seemed for a brief second to be the sound of a woman moaning, Jim finally spoke: 'Are you all right, Lisa?' he asked quietly, touching her briefly on her shoulder, then letting his arm fall.

'It's so sad,' she said in a small voice.

'It's hard on my father, too,' Jim replied. 'He . . .' He stopped, silent.

'I know,' she said.

'Everyone seems so alone,' said Jim. 'It makes me feel lonely.' He had to put both hands on the wheel as *Vagabond* slid off the face of a swell.

Lisa took his arm and hugged it, then put her arms around his waist and pressed her head against his shoulder. 'Don't feel lonely, Jim,' she said. 'Don't ever feel lonely.'

Jim released one hand from the wheel to put his arm around her. Still facing forward he hugged her to him. He

284

was grinning. 'Hey,' he said, looking down at her until she raised her head to return his gaze. 'I wish I could kiss you.'

'Why can't you?' she replied, looking up at him seriously.

'I thought you wanted us to be the best watch team Neil has?' Jim asked.

'I do,' she said. 'But a good helmsman should be able to steer and kiss too.'

Joy-filled, Jim bent and kissed her, *Vagabond* almost immediately racing slightly off course and, after fifteen seconds, slamming into a wave with a boom and shudder, effectively breaking the kiss.

As Jim wrestled the wheel with both hands to get *Vagabond* back on course, Lisa clung to him, her head buried now against his chest.

'I love you, Jim,' Lisa whispered and, still burying her face against him, went on: 'Please love me, please love me.'

Jim squeezed her against him, his heart pounding, his eyes forward seeing nothing.

'I do,' he whispered down at her.

'And I want you to make love to me,' Lisa said. 'Before we die I want you to make love to me.'

'We're not going to die,' Jim said.

'Yes, we are,' Lisa said. 'Oh, Jim, hold me, hold me. You're the only solid thing left in the world . . .'

Jim hugged her to him with his left arm and held *Vagabond* roughly on course with the other.

'Make love to me, Jim,' Lisa whispered hoarsely. 'I so want us to make love.'

'We will,' he said. 'We will.'

'We're so alone . . .'

3

Frank lay on his berth staring up at the white ceiling where the reflection of sunlight off the water danced like cold white fire. He'd been sleeping since half an hour after coming off watch at six that morning and figured it must now be getting close to noon.

He didn't feel rested. He felt bone-tired. His lower back had a dull ache which had bothered him off and on over the last several days. His belly ached. An occasional wave of nausea swept over him like a pestilential breeze. He wanted the voyage to be over. He loved *Vagabond* and was completely at home on her but his ship, like the rest of life, was slipping out of his control. As long as he had owned her – three years now – he had loved her partly because she was *his*, his creation and his to control. Now she was no longer his. She belonged to . . . to everyone, who needed her. If he didn't like Skippy's comic books lying about, or Jim taking over half his cabin or playing his guitar up on the foredeck, or Neil's always sitting or standing in the wheelhouse as if it were his personal command post, he was no longer free to say so. It was their boat too. If he tried to have everything run to please him everyone else would be miserable. So instead he had to be miserable.

Vagabond was getting junky. No matter how often he and Neil spoke about it, no one ever seemed to clean the blood and fishscales from the side cockpits, never remembered to pick up the lures and leaders and line that always seemed to be lying about. The wheelhouse was cluttered every day with comic books, towels, paper cups, books, food particles, or some-body's shirt or socks. Bullet holes in the plexiglas. The aft wall now a sail. The blankets and sheets stinky. Jeanne and Katya kept the galley and dinette in good shape when they were about, but at other times, Olly, Tony and Jim left little

286

messes. Neil and Macklin were neat, he supposed, but Neil didn't seem to be trying to control the others.

And he hated the way Neil made all the decisions without even the pretence of consulting him. He felt like a passenger on his own boat. He knew he didn't have Neil's experience or instincts but he knew his boat, had handled her more than Neil, and resented being shunted so totally aside. He felt he had the right at any time to override any of Neil's decisions, but hadn't yet found an issue that was right for reasserting his control. Neil didn't even seem to be aware of the ways he was ignoring his skills, advice and rights as owner. And Neil seemed to be starting to flirt with Jeanne.

Jeanne. There was the fucking rub. Frank wanted her closeness, needed her closeness to protect him from the shocks that were bombarding him, felt that she needed his closeness and comfort, but suddenly, out of nowhere, there was Neil. He himself had known Jeanne for ten years, since the early years of her marriage, and in the past few years had . . . become damn fond of her. It wasn't so much sexual feelings, except occasionally, just strong feelings of warmth, affection, longing even that he found hard to express to her, but which he felt she sensed. Shit, maybe he was in love with her, and had been for a couple of years.

And now Bob was dead, she needed a man, he needed her, and suddenly there was Neil. It wasn't fair. He rolled from his back to his stomach and wrestled angrily with the pillow.

When he'd finally told Jeannie of his feelings two nights before, he'd felt subtly rejected. She'd admitted that she'd sensed his affection and appreciated it, and said she admired him over the last year for not creating conflict for her by approaching her overtly and asking her to respond. She seemed to think it was okay now for him to express his feelings, but wasn't at all sure about herself. Events had moved so fast that she didn't think she could depend on *any* of her emotional responses. But now he wondered if it was all just bullshit to cover the fact that she was turned on by Neil.

287

'Turned on': Jesus, that phrase turned him off. His feelings for Jeanne went far beyond just being turned on. So Neil was younger and had muscles like a gymnast and always stood looking like Patton in his shorts: what kind of a relationship could you have based on that?

But what could he do about it? What could he do about anything? *Vagabond* hissed and plunged forward as if an independent creature fleeing for herself southwards through the sea, he and Neil her obedient servants. Would Puerto Rico solve his problems? Neil's disappearing into the wild blue yonder of the Navy again would certainly solve one problem . . . but even the idea of Neil's leaving saddened him. Although Neil had become self-absorbed lately, normally he was the only one he'd ever sailed with that appreciated *Vagabond* the way he did, could communicate with a glance what a blast it was sizzling along at thirteen knots or swinging at anchor in a squall . . .

But even sailing these last few days didn't inspire him with enthusiasm. Nothing did. A part of himself felt he was dying and he needed someone to talk to, but she always seemed too busy. He felt lonely and alone, his two best people, Jeanne and Neil, beginning to sail away from him on a different tack. He wanted to alter course, stay with them, sail with them, but in the nightmare world he was inhabiting he couldn't find the sheets, or, finding them, had no sense of whether they should be pulled in or eased. Rudderless, his life raced through the night and he, its captain, no longer knew his position or his course. He was lost. And his fucking back ached. And he wanted to puke. And it was ten: his and Tony's watch again.

The nice thing about Neil's insisting on a tight, rigidly maintained watch schedule was that every six or eight hours it forced you to stop thinking and act.

Frank pushed himself heavily up off the berth and lowered his legs to the floor. Action. Action. Slowly, painfully, he began putting on his boat shoes.

4

That night in the forepeak Jim and Lisa finally found a place and time to make love. Olly and Macklin were on watch, and Tony, who also had a berth forward, was talking with Katya up in the wheelhouse. The others were asleep in their various cabins. For Jim and Lisa it was the only place they could find to be alone.

The motion of *Vagabond* into and over the swells alternately accented and interfered with the motions of the lovemaking in ways that made Jim and Lisa giggle. Everything – even their awkwardness – was a delight. The few couplings Jim had known, burdened with the pressure of performance and the absence of love, hadn't prepared him for the unexpected joy of being with Lisa, who, inexpert, shy and passive, made him feel that his every touch and kiss was a miracle of perfection. His first entering her had been painful for her; his first climax a disappointingly minor event soon forgotten in the midst of rising pleasure and excitement of the continuing play of their hands and lips and words. They were naked and sweating, suppressing their noises and giggles, and enraptured with the discovery of so much happiness. When Jim had climaxed a second time they lay side by side facing each other, grinning, laughing, trying half-heartedly to raise their conversation above the idiotic.

'You did too squeal,' Lisa insisted. 'And it was nice.'

Jim shook his head, smiling. '*I* didn't hear a thing,' he countered.

'Do I make noises?' Lisa asked.

'I was too busy to notice.' Again they laughed, until a noise in the main cabin curtained off only a few feet away sobered them. They lay quietly, staring at each other, listening. They heard Tony swear and Katya laugh.

'Do you think they might come in here?' Lisa asked.

Jim grimaced and nodded. 'They might,' he said.

'Should we let people know?' Lisa asked. 'You know, about . . . what we're doing?'

'No,' said Jim. 'Our parents have enough to worry about without . . .'

'I know,' said Lisa. 'After Frank and Mother had that long talk after dinner tonight I found her crying in her cabin.'

'Really? I don't understand what's happening with them all, do you?'

'I thought she . . . liked Neil, but now . . . I don't know.'

'My father said . . .'

Katya abruptly ducked up from the curtain and appeared only a few feet away. 'Oh!' she said. 'Hey, I'm sorry. I must have the wrong room.' She laughed briefly and as quickly stooped down to disappear back into the main cabin.

As they heard her and Tony begin arguing Jim grabbed his swimming trunks and pulled them on and Lisa scrambled for her shorts and blouse.

'What is this?' Tony said, suddenly emerging into the room. 'Neil gives me the worst berth on the boat and even then it's not mine.'

'I'm sorry,' said Jim, whispering. 'Would you please keep your voice down.'

'I can't even *talk* in my own cabin?' said Tony.

'Oh, shut up,' Katya whispered from behind him. 'Leave them alone.'

'We're leaving,' said Jim. 'And I'm sorry we . . . used your bed.'

'It's not mine, it's Connie's,' said Tony. 'But it's the principle of the thing.'

'Tony, you've got as much principle as an eel,' said Katya.

'Come on, Lisa,' said Jim.

'Do your parents know you're screwing?' Tony asked.

'Not yet,' said Jim. 'And I'd like it if they didn't know.'

'Sure,' said Tony. 'I dig it. I don't imagine your Dad would be too hot about your fucking with Jeanne's baby. Hey, you know, it's statutory rape! How about that?'

'Go,' said Katya to Jim and Lisa. 'Tony, you're an ass.'

'Statutory rape. Army desertion. I'm witnessing all sorts of crimes.'

'You witness a crime every time you look in a mirror,' said Katya. 'Goodbye, kids. I'm glad you're lovers.'

Jim and Lisa left, the shame and uncertainty stirred by Tony not erased by Katya's blessing. They stopped for a drink of water in the galley and then soberly climbed the steps into the wheelhouse.

Olly was snoring on a settee while Macklin stood at the wheel, the light of a cigarette casting a brief reddish glimmer to his face. Jim was aware that Macklin had been ordered not to use any of the cigarettes and he automatically stopped, looking at him.

Macklin didn't speak, simply returning Jim's gaze, then looking at Lisa, then back at Jim. Lisa left to go to her cabin with Jeanne. Macklin exhaled a cloud of smoke towards Jim but the rush of air from the port entranceway blew it aft.

'Have a good time?' Macklin asked.

Jim returned his stare a moment longer and then walked past and out of the wheelhouse towards his own starboard cabin. His futile rage at Tony and Macklin had him trembling.

Down in the cabin Frank was awake, staring at the ceiling.

'Where you been, Jim?' he asked.

Jim went to the little sink to wash the sweat off his face.

'With Lisa,' he answered after a moment. '. . . Talking . . .'

His father didn't say anything for a while. Jim wiped off his face and chest, the salt water leaving him still sticky.

'I'm glad, Jim,' Frank said. 'I mean your and Lisa's getting together. Being friends. It's good.'

Jim, his back to his father, felt a wave of emotion flood him

– gratefulness to his father, love of Lisa, sadness at his father's troubles.

'Thanks, Dad,' he said, wiping his face and chest.

'You know,' said Frank, still invisible on his berth, 'Jeanne and Lisa and Skip are really part of our family now. We've got to take care of them . . . take care of them just as we would . . . your mother and Susan.'

In the darkness Jim put the washcloth and towel down on the sink and went to his narrow berth forward of Frank's.

'They . . . they're good people,' Jim said as he climbed up on to the foam mattress.

'They're family,' said Frank. 'Lisa's your sister.'

Jim pulled the sheet up over his damp, sticky body and pulled off his swim trunks. He felt a chill at his father's describing Lisa as his sister, fearing that Frank was thinking in terms of himself and Jeanne and not seeing Lisa as separate, as . . . a woman.

'Goodnight, Dad,' he said.

'All of us . . .' Frank seemed to say softly, but Jim didn't know what he meant, and in another minute he could hear the heavy rasp of his father's breathing in sleep.

Lying in her berth beside Katya the next morning Jeanne thought about Neil and about Skippy's not eating enough and of how gaunt Frank was beginning to look, and of Neil's thighs and Skippy's fascination with fish guts, and of Lisa and Jim, and of the planet withering with the plagues unleashed by the war, and of her weariness in dealing with it all, and of Neil and of her happiness. At times their voyage seemed hopeless; at other moments selfish and narcissistic. Part of her felt that she ought to be suffering and dying on the mainland with the rest of the world, not alive with love. She wanted to be a nun administering to the suffering victims of this war horror; she wanted to be naked in Neil's arms. She wanted to devote her life to bringing up her children so that the world they created would be free of the evil that her generation had unleashed. But she wanted a house, a big double bed, with a supermarket and restaurant next door. She wanted Frank to stop loving her and Neil never to stop. She wanted the world to stop surprising her with its ability to kill people; she wanted to die. No, she wanted to live, to live, to live.

She slipped briskly out of her berth and, though it was still forty minutes to go before she was due to feed the two watch teams, she began to dress.

'Hey, what's the problem?' Katya asked her unexpectedly. 'You've been tossing and turning as if trying to solve the entire world's problems in one long think.' Resting on one elbow, Katya was looking sleepy-eyed at Jeanne, who stood a few feet away buttoning her blouse. Katya spoke in a low voice so as not to disturb Lisa and Skip, still asleep in the adjoining berth. At five, the light was just gathering in the east.

'Restless,' Jeanne answered.

'Men *do* have that effect, don't they?' Katya countered, not accepting the evasive answer. Jeanne stared back but didn't reply. 'Frank and Neil are both coming on to you,' Katya went on, 'and you're interested in Neil. Where's the problem?'

Jeanne leaned down to put on her boat shoes. Although she liked Katya, she was unused to confiding in another woman, especially one she barely knew.

'I don't think my personal emotional problems are worth talking about,' she finally said in a low voice.

'They're worth talking about if you plan keeping me awake every night thinking about them,' Katya replied. 'Hey, come on, I'm exactly the person you should talk to.'

Jeanne walked softly to the forward part of the cabin to check that Lisa and Skip were asleep. When she returned opposite Katya a gentle swell rolled under *Vagabond* making her three hulls tip, slide and roll with a queasy sideways motion that always made Jeanne feel a mild dizziness.

'Have you slept with Neil?' Katya asked after the silence continued.

Unused to such bluntness, Jeanne remained turned away.

'If you'd like me to vacate this berth and take Skip off your hands today so you and Neil can be alone, I will,' Katya said. 'I mean getting it on with a lover on this boat is getting to involve a major logistical effort. It's worse than a girls' dorm.'

Jeanne turned back to Katya.

'You . . . and Tony?' she asked.

'Oh, me and Tony are the types that could make it in Grand Central Station . . . if that's what I wanted,' Katya replied, smiling sleepily. She sat up and stretched, the sheet sliding off and revealing her small breasts with long nipples.

Jeanne looked away. 'It's not a problem of privacy,' Jeanne said softly.

'Well, tell me what it is,' Katya said. 'I promise to give you bad advice which you can ignore. It's the telling that will help.'

Jeanne glanced again at her sleeping children and finally, with a sigh, began talking. She explained that in the wake of the personal losses all had suffered, those aboard the ship now formed a kind of family, one which took precedence over any single person's desires. Nothing should be done which might divide the family. Although she and Neil might be attracted to each other, she felt that if that meant the unhappiness and bitterness of Frank then it wasn't worth it. In the telling she somewhat played down her feelings for Neil, an action which, when she'd finished, left her vaguely dissatisfied with her explanation.

Katya, now sitting up and leaning back against the partition between her berth and that of Lisa and Skip, was brushing out her curly, ashblonde hair. When Jeanne stopped talking, Katya frowned. 'So don't sleep with either of them,' Katya concluded, looking puzzled. 'Most men survive. Or they find someone else they can bury their sorrow and other parts of their anatomy with.' She looked at Jeanne questioningly.

Jeanne was depressed by the advice. It was excellent advice, but had the flaw of asking her to give up Neil.

'Or sleep with both of them,' Katya went on, watching Jeanne carefully.

'No, I can't do that,' Jeanne said simply.

Katya swung herself out of bed to begin dressing. As she reached into a cubby to get her shorts she became abruptly irritable.

'You think too much, Jeanne,' Katya said. 'If you and a man love each other, that's it, that's first. The rest of the world doesn't count. Family doesn't count. A woman friend doesn't count. Grab it.'

She stepped into her shorts, then grabbed a yellow tee-shirt and pulled it over her head, shaking her hair and brushing it down when her head emerged.

'Everyone else does,' she added, and, with Jeanne staring after her, she climbed the hatchway steps, slid back the hatch, and left.

5

According to Neil's noon sunshots *Vagabond* was now about fifty miles north of the reef and cays lying off the northeast coast of Great Abaco Island. Sailing at about seven knots, *Vagabond* might come within sight of land a little before sunset.

The thought gave Neil little exhilaration. He found himself approaching this landfall warily. Already he and Frank had argued that morning about whether it was definitely necessary to obtain additional food and water before sailing on for Puerto Rico. Frank was concerned at having to halve their food intake for up to two weeks, while Neil himself felt that starvation was not their primary danger. The Bahamian government had announced that it was confiscating any foreign vessel that landed in Bahamian waters without first clearing Customs at Freeport or Nassau. All weapons aboard any ship were being confiscated. The rash of pirates that were afflicting Bahamian waters could be stopped only by the rigid enforcement of these rules. All food was strictly controlled and rationed by the authorities. Foreigners unable to pay with gold, silver, or barter for their food, were being forced to join work forces or – those who had them – give up their boats as exchange.

Had not the wind direction made a landfall on Great Abaco Island a logical course Neil would have preferred to stay at sea, away from the dangers he foresaw closing with the land. The sun was shining brightly, the sky a deep blue, and the sea sparkling with small whitecaps from the twelve-knot breeze still blowing perniciously out of the east-southeast. Frank, at the helm, was pinching *Vagabond* a bit east of south because when they came to the reef they would have to

296

proceed southeast along it until they decided if, where, and when to take *Vagabond* into land.

It was a little before the changing of the watch at two o'clock that Jeanne, using binoculars, spotted a ship. At first this was all she could be sure of. Ten minutes later she and Neil, alternating use of the large pair of binoculars, had determined that it was a sailing boat heading north, but without any sails up. A minute later, when the boat altered its course to the west, Neil thought that it, like the only other sailing ship they had seen on their trip south, was starting to flee. Then he realized differently.

'What is it?' asked Jeanne.

'It's a drifting boat,' he replied, handing her the glasses. 'Probably abandoned, a derelict.' As she began studying the mysterious ship, Neil walked out into the port cockpit where Frank and Tony were looking through the smaller glasses.

'Alter course,' Neil said to Tony at the helm. 'We're going to take a look.'

'What the hell for?' Tony asked.

'There may be survivors,' Neil replied. 'If not, there may be supplies we can salvage.'

'Anybody still alive on that boat we can do without,' Tony commented. 'This close to land the ship's probably been sacked already.'

'We're going over,' Neil said.

In half an hour *Vagabond* had arrived within a hundred yards of the derelict. The ship's white paint was blistered and peeling, fragments of the mainsail lay loosely along the boom, and a halyard was loose and swinging idly back and forth with the rocking of the boat. There was no sign of life.

'Ahoy, *Windsong*!' Neil shouted as Tony brought *Vagabond* so close to the wind all three sails luffed and she became almost dead in the water ten yards short of the forty-foot ketch.

'Hit the horn,' Neil said to Tony, who gave one loud blast from the air horn on the control panel shelf.

297

'Are you going to board?' Frank asked Neil.

Just then a figure emerged from the cabin into the ship's cockpit. Crouched and blinking into the bright light, a small, unshaven man in his forties wearing only a bathing suit stared at them.

Neil and the others, stunned, stared back.

'Can we assist you?' Neil asked loudly after the shocked silence.

'Water,' the man said hoarsely. He was hollow-eyed. 'Water,' he repeated more loudly.

As Jim ducked below to get some of their precious water and the man peered down into his own cabin, Frank came up to Neil.

'What are you going to do?' he asked.

'Take him off,' Neil answered, staring glumly at the stricken *Windsong*. 'Back her off a bit,' he added to Tony, 'then bring her up to the port side. Get the fenders.'

'There must be others aboard,' Jim said, arriving with water. 'He can't be alone.'

'The guy's practically dead,' Tony said, easing *Vagabond* alongside *Windsong*. Neil and Frank moored the two boats side by side with the fenders cushioning their impact.

'Do you want to abandon ship?' Neil asked. 'We can take you aboard.'

The man, the bones of his rib-cage protruding grotesquely against the skin of his emaciated body, lowered his head and stared at the water.

'We're all dying,' he answered. 'I don't know.'

'Radiation sickness isn't necessarily fatal,' Neil said. 'You may recover.'

The man looked back up at Neil.

'I know,' he said. 'That's what's hell. But my wife and daughter . . . are almost dead. They'll never make it.'

Jim now handed a plastic jug of water across to the man who, with sudden agility, grabbed it and hugged it to him.

'Let me go below and – decide what we'll do,' he said and

298

less nimbly made his way down into the cabin of his boat. Neil, Frank and Tony were left in the side cockpit waiting.

'What is this shit?' Macklin suddenly said, appearing beside them, looking sleepy, the hair of his chest glistening with sweat. 'You bringing more people on to raid our food and water?'

Neil didn't reply.

'If they're all dying,' Tony said, 'it'll just be a waste. You said yourself that prospects of finding food in the Bahamas don't look good.'

'I know,' Neil said.

'What happened to your fucking principle of triage?' Macklin interjected.

Neil didn't answer. The four of them stood silently in the gently rocking *Vagabond* awaiting the reappearance of the dying man. What had happened to triage, thought Neil, was that at sea you didn't abandon a fellow sailor.

The man emerged from his ship's cabin. 'I'd appreciate it if you could take us off,' he said. When they stared at him, he finally added, 'I'll need help.'

'Mac,' said Neil. 'Go aboard and give the man a hand.'

'Go yourself,' Macklin said and stalked away.

'I'll go,' said Frank. He boarded *Windsong* ahead of Jim but suddenly noticed along the coaming and in the cockpit a fine grey ash. He first took it to be sand, but with a stab of fear realized it was radioactive ash. He clambered quickly back on to *Vagabond*, pushing Jim back ahead of him.

'Jesus Christ,' he told Neil. 'There's fallout on deck.'

Neil looked and frowned.

'This is ridiculous,' said Tony. 'Let's get out of here.'

Neil hesitated again, then turned to Frank. 'I'll board and help them abandon ship,' he said.

'I'll help you,' said Jim.

'You stay here,' Frank said gloomily to Neil, grabbing his shoulder. 'With your bum arm you're the wrong man for the job.'

When Frank boarded *Windsong*, Jim quickly followed. Ducking below into the main cabin Frank saw that there were two women lying under dirty sheets on opposite sides of the main salon on what normally would have been settees. The cabin was a jumble of pails, towels, open cans of food, dirty dishes, clothing, blankets. The stench of sweat, urine and excrement was stifling. The small hollow-eyed man stood apologetically next to his wife.

'They can't walk and I can't lift them,' he said.

Frank pushed himself forward to the older woman, bent over and tried to force himself to smile. But when he saw the grey-faced, frozen apparition that stared up at him the 'Hi' he had been about to speak froze in his throat. He gasped. Without further effort at sociability he leaned over and picked her up and headed back towards the gangway. The woman was almost dead. She was wearing nothing under the sheet and the contact of his hands with the naked flesh after seeing death on her face horrified and disgusted him. He wanted to run up the stairs, but Jim appeared, descending.

'Bring the girl and get out quick,' he said sharply to him.

Teeth gritted, his face showing his fear and disgust, Frank climbed the cabin steps, went quickly over to *Vagabond* and, refusing Jeanne's offer of assistance, thrust himself from one boat to the other.

'Where are you putting her?' Jeanne asked.

'Frank's cabin, I'm afraid,' Neil interjected. 'All three.'

Frank carried the woman down.

Jim meanwhile suffered the same sickening shock at the sight and smell of *Windsong*'s cabin as, with face averted, he gently slid his arms under the daughter and lifted her up. She was small and light. As she came into his arms, he noticed her turn her face away from him.

'Come on,' he said to the man, and began his return to *Vagabond*.

'Are there things we can salvage from *Windsong*?' Neil asked Frank, who was coming out of his cabin after placing the

300

woman up on his double berth and instructing Jim to put the girl beside her. Macklin stood nearby, glaring.

'No,' Frank snapped back. 'Let's get away now, fast.'

The skeleton of a man, standing slightly bent over in the starboard cockpit a few feet away, grimaced.

'We've got a few emergency rations that you can have,' he said. 'It's stored . . .'

'Let's go!' Macklin said sharply to Neil. 'That ship's contaminated. Everything on it may be carrying death. Let's go.'

He himself brushed past the man and untied the aft line that held *Vagabond* rafted to the other ship, and then hurried forward to get the other. In just a few seconds, *Vagabond* fell away, her sails filling, then surged forward and past the stricken *Windsong*.

The owner turned and looked at her as *Vagabond* steadily but slowly sailed away, then the man moved slowly to the hatchway to go below.

Frank stepped trembling into the wheelhouse to deposit the fenders Macklin was bringing back under the settee seats.

'Take it easy, Frank,' Neil said.

'We've brought death aboard,' Frank said grimly.

Neil, staring forward past the little transistor radio which lay on the control panel shelf, was as tight-lipped as Frank.

'I know,' Neil replied. 'But when was he *not* aboard?'

The presence of the three apparently doomed refugees upset the occupants of *Vagabond*. Having three dying people aboard was a disturbing reminder of their own danger and created among some a guilty resentment of the new burden of stricter rationing and more limited space. Frank now had to sleep in the wheelhouse, Jim aft with Neil. Frank found himself resenting mild Sam Brumberger as if he were a boorish guest who'd crashed a previously enjoyable party. He was naturally appalled by his resentment. He realized that if they had abandoned Sam and his family, he would have felt badly.

He was annoyed too with Jeanne for showing so much solicitude for the refugees, seeming to spend the whole afternoon in endless trips down into the hellhole of his cabin to minister to their needs. None of the men had any appetite for such service, although Olly went down and spent an hour talking with Sam.

'Wife's just about dead,' Olly said to Frank when he emerged. 'The daughter's not going to make it either. Sam now thinks he should have scuttled his ship.'

'Sam looks pretty bad, too,' Frank commented.

'Yep. Tough way to go,' Captain Olly said. 'Prefer a quick sinking myself.'

'Me too,' said Frank.

The rescue of the Brumbergers had cost them more than two hours so that when the wind fell away to nothing at dusk they were still fifteen to twenty miles from land.

Sam Brumberger told his story after dinner that night.

Sam, his wife, and daughter and two male friends had left Miami to bring their boat north for the summer. On the night the war started the ship was shaken by a tremendous blast. With his two friends on watch, Sam was with his family below. He was thrown off the settee berth on to the floor. Recovering, he staggered up and hurried topside. Although there was a terrifying brightness to the southwest which lit the night he couldn't at first see anything wrong. He called to his friends and got no reply. Then he saw one of them lying across a seat in the rear of the cockpit. His friend's body was smoking. He had been literally fried to death.

The other friend had disappeared, presumably thrust overboard by the blast. His wife, sleeping in an upper berth forward, had been badly burned in the stomach region and upper thighs. He and his daughter had escaped direct injury from the blast.

That morning when fallout began to fall on to his deck he got his engine going and motored northeast for eleven hours skirting north of Grand Bahama Island until he ran out of fuel. Meanwhile, he, his wife and daughter had begun to vomit.

On the fourth day Sam spotted a fishing boat and fired a flare and the boat motored over. It was a beat-up, twenty-five-foot runabout with an outboard on its last gasp. There were two black Bahamian men aboard and one white man. They looked shocked at the sight of Sam and his boat and Sam's wife. At first Sam was afraid they were just going to motor away. But they decided to stay. They locked Sam in the forepeak, looted *Windsong*, and took turns raping his daughter on the settee berth three feet away from her dying mother. Since then *Windsong* had been drifting helplessly.

Listening to Sam tell his story, Frank found it strange to listen to a man who knew he was dying, accepted that he was dying and who handled everything with emotionless objectivity. He was also strangely apologetic in what he said and did, as if the needs of a man who was going to die were futile and irrelevant. Commenting on the war, Sam seemed to speak from some other world that he alone, because of his condition, had moved into. 'I never thought we could spend a trillion dollars on something without sooner or later demanding our money's worth.'

Later that night, after everyone but Neil, Frank and Jeanne were in bed and *Vagabond* was wallowing in a dead calm, there was a strange scene. Jeanne, having just returned from another visit to Frank's cabin to clean up after one of the sick, had stopped, after washing out a towel in salt water, to take a look at Neil's elbow. Frank was steering, and Jeanne sat beside Neil on the wheelhouse settee and adjusted the kerosene lantern in order to get a good look.

The swelling of Neil's elbow had gone down considerably. He could move his lower arm about forty-five degrees without pain, although there was still redness over a three square-inch area. They had not used antibiotics and were depending on Neil's body to handle the infection by itself.

Neil, happy to have Jeanne near him, tried to joke lightly

with her about his arm and her ministrations, but she seemed solemn and withdrawn.

'You're sure you want to keep trying to do without the sling?' she asked after they'd finished the examination and wrapped the elbow again with gauze.

'Yes. I think that's the best way to put pressure on myself to use the arm more normally.'

'All right. But the infection's still there.'

'For Christ's sake,' Frank suddenly interjected. 'Put some mercurochrome and a bandaid on it and let him be. People *dying* all over the world and you're worrying about Neil's sore elbow.'

Jeanne looked up towards Frank, who kept his back to them, and then glanced fearfully at Neil. She moved away from him and stood up.

'She also spent half the day with the Brumbergers,' Neil said to Frank's back.

'At least *they*'re dying,' Frank shot back, half-turning. 'Can't you take care of yourself anymore?'

In the awkward silence that followed, Jeanne gathered up the medicine kit and hung the lantern back from the roof.

'I promise either to heal myself or to reach a dying state as soon as possible,' Neil finally rejoined.

'And you, Jeanne,' Frank said, ignoring Neil's remark and stopping her on her way down to the main cabin. 'Don't waste so much time with the Brumbergers. You've got your own life to live.'

'I thought I *was* living it,' she replied coolly.

'You're not,' Frank countered loudly. 'You're spending all your time with Lisa and Skippy and cleaning up vomit and mothering Neil and not a second on yourself.'

Neil saw Jeanne watching Frank closely, seeming to study him.

'I'm sorry, Frank,' she said. 'I suppose I am compulsively *do*ing things whether they need doing or not. I'll try to relax.'

304

Frank stared at her, seeming as surprised as Neil by her abrupt acquiescence.

'Well . . . It's just that I want you to be happy,' Frank finally said.

'I know,' she replied. Then she stepped down into the main cabin.

Later, after she'd gone over to her own cabin to sleep, Frank stopped Neil as he too was headed to bed.

'That's one incredible woman,' he said to Neil.

'Yes,' said Neil.

'If I don't achieve anything else in the rest of my life except see to it that she's taken care of, I think I'd be satisfied.'

Neil looked into Frank's intent, confiding face and felt a distant stab of fear.

'She . . . She's a fine woman,' he said.

'I hate to see her martyring herself,' Frank went on. 'She's working much too hard.'

'Maybe it's better for her now than thinking,' Neil commented.

'Maybe,' Frank said and took a deep breath. 'Jesus, what a world. Just when things were beginning to look good we get three breathing corpses.'

'I know what you mean.'

'You think it'll ever end?'

Neil looked at Frank's now less intent, somewhat distracted face and, without thinking, answered simply: 'No.'

And he went to bed.

6

At dawn the next day Sam came up from his cabin to report that his wife and daughter were dead. He announced his news to Neil apologetically, as if announcing that he'd broken someone's tea cup. He and Neil discussed their deaths briefly and concluded that they should be immediately buried at sea. Land was visible four miles to the south and Neil was worried about both pirates and Bahamian government boats.

By six-thirty everyone except Jim and Katya, who were in their berths after an early morning at the helm, had finished a spare breakfast and was ready for the burial. Jeanne, concerned about the effect on Skippy of seeing bodies tossed casually into the ocean, asked Lisa to keep him occupied in the forepeak.

The adults gathered self-consciously in the cockpit outside Frank's cabin and looked morosely at the covered bodies of the women, which lay the length of the cockpit seat. Jeanne had wrapped them together in a clean sheet and Neil had weighted the bodies with an old dinghy anchor. He'd tied it and the sheet to the body with light twine.

Sam Brumberger was Jewish but his wife was not, and he had told them he had no strong feelings about how she should be buried, only that he wanted to speak publicly over them before they were committed to the sea.

As he watched and listened, Neil was struck by the grotesqueness of this funeral. Everyone, including Sam, was dressed in bathing suits or cut-offs or jeans, and was either bare-chested or wearing a tee-shirt. *Vagabond* was sailing forward under cloudless blue skies, through sparkling blue water. Only an unpleasant odour – from either the bodies or

Frank's cabin – and everyone's increasing thinness reminded him of death.

Sam spoke again with that almost painful objectivity that his own death seemed to give him of the troubles he and his wife and daughter had had, her weaknesses, his, as if they were traditional parts of a eulogy. He was like an historian summing up a doomed civilization. Sam seemed to be not just burying his wife, but himself also. He was summing up before the Lord his being, offering it without apologies.

'Human beings don't plan to die,' he was saying. 'They get picked, incredulous and protesting, and leave the stage like a vaudeville performer getting the hook. In some ways Ingrid and I've been lucky: we got to say our goodbyes, sing our final song, and walk off the stage under our own power, knowing precisely where we were going.

'So, Lord, we commit Ingrid's body to the sea. I thank you for her life. I thank you for her death.'

At first when Sam ceased speaking, Neil was uncertain that indeed he was finished. Then he nodded at Frank, and Neil joined Frank in lifting the linked bodies up, first to the edge of the coaming, and then, with a quick thrust, into the sea.

Sam had stood with lowered head during this act and he did not raise it to watch the bodies swirl aft, slowly sinking. Jeanne came up and gently embraced him, held him for five or six seconds, and then wordlessly went back into the wheelhouse. Neil, surprised at his mild revulsion at seeing Jeanne hugging the dying man, then went up and put his hand on Sam's shoulder.

'That was fine, Sam,' he said, feeling awkwardly that he sounded as if Sam had just done a good job hauling anchor.

The others, too, after saying a brief word to Sam, moved into the central part of the boat. It was Neil who, turning back to adjust the mainsheet, saw Sam Brumberger climbing up out of the cockpit. Neil *saw* him, one leg already over, straddling *Vagabond*'s coaming, moving clumsily and weakly,

307

knew what he was doing, *knew* he could stop him, but didn't.
As he watched, Sam pulled his other leg up on to the coaming,
looked down into the water rushing past, then pushed himself
off into the sea.

'HEY!' Frank shouted from behind Neil, and then rushed
past into the cockpit.

Sam's head bobbed up briefly in the wake of *Vagabond*'s
starboard hull, then disappeared. Frank stared aft.

When Neil turned into the wheelhouse, he saw Captain
Olly steering *Vagabond* as if nothing had happened.

'Good man, Sam,' Captain Olly said, staring forward. 'Got
himself a good death, too.'

For Neil, Olly's wisdom made only the smallest dent in the
horror.

7

The low smudge of land lying on the horizon dead ahead grew
slowly towards them through the hot, still morning. They had
listened at eight to news of destruction and starvation
throughout the world that made their recent deaths and
present rationing seem insignificant, yet Neil sensed his ship
approached this land reluctantly, with more fear than hope.
They'd had no rain and foresaw none through the next day
anyway and Neil felt they had to try to duck into an outer cay
for water if an opportunity arose. Jim was reading a Guide to
the Bahamas trying to determine which islands had fresh
water and which didn't, but the writers of the Guide had
never anticipated anyone's wanting to get water on uninhabited islands when it was available at any port. Neil
doubted that any of the small islands would have springs or
wells. Any hope they'd had earlier of sailing into Hopetown or
Marsh Harbour for supplies had been dashed by the government edict that all foreign vessels had to clear Customs and be
disarmed in Nassau or Freeport.

At eleven that morning they observed a small plane flying
south. Its circling low around *Vagabond* had made Neil
uneasy, and he called everyone together to discuss tactics for
repelling pirate attacks. They had only three weapons, the
nine-millimetre pistol with four dozen bullets, Macklin's .45
with two dozen bullets, and the .38 revolver with two bullets.
They were 'short on artillery', as Olly had described it. They
decided their flare gun could appear to be a fourth weapon.
They talked about the possible ways they might be attacked,
and Neil assigned them to various defensive positions with
standing orders on how to respond in various contingencies.

By one o'clock they were only about half a mile off from

where the surf was breaking against the outer reef. They were sailing south-southeast along this barrier, low islands being visible across the emerald lagoon beyond the reef. When they came within clear sight of an abandoned lighthouse Neil was able to verify their landfall: they were off Man-of-War Cay. The next opening in the reef was six miles down, into Marsh Harbour, the most populated town on Great Abaco Island. Neil knew that it was desirable to land for food and water, but before he decided on whether to try to sneak in for supplies, or sail to Nassau, or bypass the Bahamas completely, he hoped to be able to talk to someone on one of the local boats.

An hour later the gloom which had accompanied the first hours of their fresh contact with land deepened when they sailed past the buoyed channel leading into Marsh Harbour. They could see the town and a few boats anchored in the cove and at the dock. They sailed past. They were outcasts.

After another mile Neil ordered Jeanne to bring the ship about to head offshore to avoid the reef. As soon as they had tacked he noticed a launch speeding towards them from the Marsh Harbour Inlet. Neil ordered them to take their prearranged defensive positions: Jeanne, Lisa and Skippy below amidships with smoke flares; Neil standing in the aft cabin hatchway holding Macklin's .45; Frank in the forepeak hatch with the .38 revolver; Jim in the starboard cabin hatchway with the Navy nine-millimetre pistol; and Tony in the port cabin hatchway with the flare gun. Captain Olly was with Katya at the helm. They all kept their meagre weapons momentarily out of sight, their intent being to create the illusion of having four heavily armed men on guard at four widely separated points.

Neil, standing on the second step of his aft cabin, with his head and shoulders sticking out above the cabin opening, clutching the .45 in his right hand, watched the launch speed up to them from the left. It had a machinegun mounted on the foredeck, manned by two black men. As the launch slowed, he saw in the cockpit two additional black men, one studying *Vagabond* through binoculars. When the launch swung up behind them Neil saw the second man in the cockpit, who was wearing white shorts and shirt in contrast to the khakis and jeans of the others, smile a big, white-toothed smile at *Vagabond*. Neil had the momentary absurd idea that he was about to shout 'Welcome to the Bahamas!'

Instead the launch pulled up parallel to *Vagabond*, holding off about thirty feet. For perhaps fifteen seconds the men on the two ships contemplated each other, their two vessels slicing serenely through the water side by side at five knots. Captain Olly broke the silence.

'Hi, there, fellas,' he shouted amiably. 'How they hanging?'

As far as Neil could tell the launch was manned only by the four black men already visible, all of whom looked back at Captain Olly blankly.

'We need some food and water,' Captain Olly went on. 'You fellas know where we can get some?'

'Where you headed, Mahn?' the officer whom Neil had seen grinning shouted back.

'Puerto Rico,' Captain Olly replied. 'Where you fellas headed?'

'You have permit for Bahamian waters?' the officer asked.

'Shit, no,' Captain Olly replied. 'We're heading Puerto Rico.'

'No weapons permitted in Bahamian waters,' the officer shouted. 'You have weapons aboard?'

'No weapons,' Captain Olly replied, heading *Vagabond* into the wind and slowing her up some.

'We will board you then for routine inspection,' said the officer, grinning.

'You try to board us,' Captain Olly replied in the same easy-going tone, 'and we'll blast you all to kingdom come.'

The white-toothed smile disappeared from the man's face.

'We ain't got no weapons,' Captain Olly shouted as the two

vessels continued slicing through the water side by side. 'So you don't got to inspect us.' Olly grinned. ''Course if you *do* try to board us we'll have to sink all four of you fellas.'

The officer turned to the shorter man at his side and they whispered together urgently. The two men at the machine-gun were staring back looking for orders.

'What you have to pay for watah, Mahn?' the officer shouted.

'Got a good Johnson outboard,' Captain Olly replied. 'Got some cigarettes.'

'You have gold? Silver? Jewellery?'

'Maybe,' said Captain Olly. 'You selling water?'

'We sell you fifteen gallons of watah,' the officer replied. 'You pay in gold, silver, or diamonds.'

'Can't we sail in to one of these here little islands and get some water?'

'Not without permit,' the officer replied, grinning. 'For permit you must go to Nassau and surrender all weapons.'

'Need a permit for water, huh?' said Captain Olly. 'Seems a little shitty to me.'

'You have gold? Silver?'

Olly frowned and looked aft at Neil who shook his head slightly in the negative.

'Not a drop, sonny,' Captain Olly said. 'Got some fancy clothes, though, you fellas might like. You like fancy clothes? Also got a bottle of whisky.'

'I think maybe we trade, right, Mahn?' the tall officer said and flashed his smile.

'Right, sonny, but you tell those two fellas with the peashooter to point it forward, okay? I get indigestion staring at the open end of a barrel.'

After the two men manning the gun moved aft, the two ships eased in closer to each other, Captain Olly bringing *Vagabond* up into the wind so that the two boats could tie up to each other. He instructed Jeanne to come up and help Katya

312

prepare the fenders, the four other men maintaining their defensive positions.

When the two ships were secured, Olly went down into Frank's cabin and brought back up two of his dress suits while Jeanne brought two packs of cigarettes and a half-full whisky bottle from the main cabin. After the goods were spread out on the cockpit seat, negotiations began. The launch crew had brought up on their deck five three-gallon containers of water. While the grinning officer came aboard to finger the material of Frank's suits and hold them up to his body to check size, Captain Olly dipped a finger into each of the water jugs to see that they were fresh and potable. They all tasted heavily chlorinated but drinkable. Olly grimaced each time he sampled the water.

'Worst water I ever tasted, sonny,' he said to the Bahamian officer. 'This horse piss or what?'

The black man just grinned.

'Two suits, whisky and cigarettes for nine gallons watah,' he said.

'No sale,' Captain Olly replied. 'I'll give you that blue suit there for all fifteen gallons, including the jugs.'

The black officer laughed and slapped his bare brown thigh below his clean white shorts.

'You crazy, Mahn,' he said, glancing at Katya with a grin. 'Watah is gold. This suit's just pretty shit. No way it's gold.'

'Take it or leave it, fella. We got to get on to Puerto Rico.'

The black man glared. 'I sell you good watah, Mahn. You pay me whisky, cigarettes, and suits. You want me to arrest you?'

'Now, now, fella,' said Captain Olly, his wrinkled face breaking into its toothless grin. 'I got an army of sharp-shooters in all four cabins. Unless that there peashooter can shoot in four directions at once you ain't arresting nobody, least not on this boat.'

The black man still glared, puffing out his chest and

breathing heavily. The other three men looked on from the cockpit indifferently. The officer's eyes abruptly narrowed and he scrutinized Captain Olly carefully.

'I sell you fifteen gallons with*out* the jugs, for this blue suit, the whisky, and the cigarettes.'

'*With* the jugs.'

'With *two* jugs, Mahn. I cannot give you more.'

'Okay, fella, you got yourself a deal.'

Captain Olly grinned and stuck out his hand. The officer grinned back and they shook hands heartily. The three men in the other boat began laughing and talking, the whole atmosphere abruptly changing. Olly asked Katya to bring up three empty plastic containers to take the water from the three jugs that had to be returned, and the Bahamian officer called one of his men over to admire his beautiful suit. Both men took a slug of the whisky and then handed it over to the last two blacks still aboard the launch.

'Well, now, tell me, Cap,' said Captain Olly to the officer, after taking a slug of whisky himself when it was handed to him. 'Why's your government so fussy 'bout our landing and getting a little water.'

'I don't know, Mahn,' was the reply. 'Too many you Yahnkees, s'pose.'

'But you got plenty of water here, don't you?'

The man frowned. 'Watah, yes, Mahn, but not food. Ships want food and can't pay for it. They take our women, too. You bettah keep your guns, Mahn, or you won't have your women.' He looked over at Jeanne and Katya and grinned.

'Your government have other boats southeast of here likely to bother us?' Captain Olly asked.

'Doan know, Cap'n,' the officer answered. 'But it's not us you 'av to worry about, it's *pirates*. South of here the pirates so thick, you can walk across their decks all the rest of the way to Puerto Rico. You ought to get to Nassau quick, Mahn. Pirates stay clear of Nassau.'

'Who are the pirates?' Olly asked, frowning.

'Everybody, Mahn!' the officer shot back, grinning hugely. 'Everybody who's got a boat. 'S only way a mahn can make an honest living.'

Olly frowned again.

'Well, thanks, Cap,' he said, and stuck out his hand again to the Bahamian officer. 'We 'preciate your help.'

'That's all right, Mahn,' said the officer, shaking hands and then getting back on to his launch with his other men. After placing his new suit neatly on a seat he turned and gave Olly a big grin. 'Welcome to the Bahamas, Mahn!' he said loudly, spreading his arms out wide, one holding the whisky bottle. 'Right?'

And the two vessels parted.

As the Bahamian launch receded towards the entrance to Marsh Harbour, Neil emerged from his cabin, ostentatiously wielding his pistol. The others soon joined him in the starboard cockpit next to Olly at the wheel.

'Well,' Neil said. 'We've just survived our first pirates.'

'Shall we go to Nassau?' Frank asked, shaking his head and pursing his lips in disgust.

'We can't risk it, Frank,' Neil replied. 'It's still on to Puerto Rico.'

'With only twenty gallons of fresh water?' Frank said, startled.

'If we go to Nassau we'll never get out. They'll take our weapons, make us barter away our equipment for food, and all we'll gain is extra water and two hundred extra miles to have to fight off pirates. It's not worth it.'

'But who knows if it's any better in the Virgins or Puerto Rico?' Tony asked, joining them.

'Puerto Rico's a lot larger,' Neil answered, 'and they're both presumably more friendly to Americans.'

'Isn't there a chance Puerto Rico will become involved in the war?' Jeanne asked. 'We've got naval and air bases there.'

'And we can sail to either of them from Nassau almost as

easily as from here,' Frank added.

'Not if they've taken our weapons,' Neil countered, tight-lipped. 'We'd be sailing a thousand miles through a sea of pirates armed with Olly's gaff and a boat hook. I'd prefer dying of thirst.'

Frank shook his head and paced away past Olly into the wheelhouse and then turned around and came back. 'In Puerto Rico you'd be a draft dodger and Jim a deserter,' he reminded Neil.

'In a war in which all fighting will have ceased,' Neil replied, 'I doubt that by the time we get there anyone will care.'

'But can we go on much longer with so little food and water?' Jim broke in. 'You told me yesterday we've got enough dried fish and water left for only three more days.'

Neil frowned, frustrated at facing three unacceptable alternatives. 'I suppose we could try sneaking into one of the out-of-the-way cays,' he mused aloud.

'And if they catch us without clearance, they confiscate the boat,' Frank said. 'There's no way we should try that.'

'Can't we land on an island at night, get water and get away before daybreak?' Jeanne suggested.

'All the cays are buffered by reefs,' Neil replied. 'We can only get in and out during daylight hours when we can see the shoals and find the channels.'

'And we'd be spotted during the day,' Frank added. 'The Bahamians probably have air patrol as well as cutter patrol.'

No one spoke. They seemed to have reached an impasse. Frank again paced into the wheelhouse, this time sitting down. Jeanne looked at him and then at Neil, finally at Olly, who stared forward humming lightly to himself.

'We should keep going,' she said quietly. 'God's put us in the middle of the biggest supermarket in creation and if we can't learn to eat and drink what's out here we don't deserve to live.'

When she stopped speaking Frank ran his two hands

316

through his thinning grey hair and stood up. He stared absently at Neil.

'The West Indies,' he said almost to himself. 'Jesus, I bet by the time we get there, we'll decide we have to go to Brazil.' He smiled mournfully at Jeanne.

Neil moved for the first time since the discussion had begun. He lifted up one of the new water jugs.

'I think we might begin planning on it,' he said.

'Well, Mac,' said Tony, a few hours later. He loomed over Conrad Macklin, who was seated in the side cockpit at the rolling rig. 'How do you feel about our captain's latest decision? You enjoy starving to death?'

Macklin looked up at Tony neutrally, then idly tested the drag on the nylon line. 'Yes, I am,' he answered quietly.

'You are?'

'I enjoy starving,' Macklin replied, causing Tony to stare at him uncertainly. 'Considering the alternatives.'

'I still think we should try to dock in here and try to get some food.'

'Be patient, Tony,' Macklin said, looking up at him and smiling. 'The thing you don't understand is that sometimes retreat and lying low are the best strategy. Our Loken's no fool: he's not afraid to do that.'

'Yeah?'

'Just like us, Tony,' said Macklin, still smiling. 'Just like us.'

8

And so they sailed on, past the white sand beaches and gleaming emerald water of the eastern Bahamian cays and out to sea to the east, having to make long tacks against the southeast wind, Neil wishing it would shift, hoping he could guess which way it would shift, and sailing on to either San Juan or the Virgin Islands, whichever the wind and the radio reports made appear a more feasible haven.

A new intensity came into the voyage. After their first escape from the mainland a certain exhilaration and hopefulness had accompanied them southwards. They had food and water, and though they rationed themselves for both, it was something of a game, merely 'contingency planning'.

But now they had been turned away from a place they had seen as a source of supplies; now they had been sailing almost a week without a landfall and the contingency had occurred. There was no way to buy new food; no sure way to obtain water. For at least another week the ocean was the only store doing business and the skies the only water depot. Now they would sail successfully to Puerto Rico or the Virgins within two weeks or perhaps die. Now the billowing white clouds that flowed lazily above them represented not beauty but potential moisture; the colour of a dawn was watched for signs of an approaching low pressure system that might mean rain or a shift from the trade wind pattern heading them.

Now the fishing was as serious an undertaking as war, and when some huge fish snapped through the wire leader and took off with Jim's best lure leaving them with only three, he was left as pale and shaken as if he'd lost an important platoon

318

in battle. Now that they were out of the Gulf Stream the fishing was much less dependable. In the first five days after picking up the Brumbergers they caught only two fish.

Now they began the monotonous, unpleasant, bone-jarring bashing to windward into the seas that the tradewinds seemed to be building malevolently against them. Neil, since it was his decision that they sail on past the Bahamas with insufficient food and water, became obsessed with the battle to sail *Vagabond* to windward as fast as possible. Although one of his basic principles was never to criticize the wind, he found himself cursing quietly each time he awakened to find it still on their nose. He began to view the wind and waves as opponents he was fighting, an uncharacteristic attitude that he tried to check. Noting Lisa's thinness, Frank's weakness, recognizing a certain lethargy about everyone's movements – including his own – filled him with a rage to drive *Vagabond* eastward to a safe landfall where they could rest and eat and replenish their depleted stores.

He searched out the boat for useless weight as he might have sought out spies. Overboard went the portable television set, overboard some rusted chain, overboard two dozen of the ship's trashy novels, old magazines, half-finished cans of paint, some junk wood, and nine or ten heavy bolts that Frank didn't have the slightest idea how they could be used.

They also discussed removing *Vagabond*'s diesel engine, both to lighten the boat and to create a private berth for Olly to ease the over-crowding. With Frank concurring, Neil decided that its possible future usefulness in a world mostly devoid of fuel didn't match its burden of six hundred pounds extra weight. In a six-hour operation that involved all the men, Frank and Olly supervised the unbolting and winching up of the heavy engine. By the time they were done they had had to use half a dozen jury-rigged pulleys hanging from the main boom, wheelhouse roof and mizzen mast. When the engine, from which they had removed the alternator, finally rolled off the aft deck into the sea, the men let loose a long cheer and, dirty and sweaty, confiscated a beer each as their reward. It was the first successful mutiny on *Vagabond*, and Neil, clutching his own bottle, accepted it with a smile. The trimaran gained an inch on her water line aft, and her trim was now much better.

With the engine gone and no generator aboard, the batteries were unhooked from everything except the short-wave radio. Olly and Jim began to try developing a man-powered generator out of the diesel alternator, but with three batteries aboard it didn't seem pressing.

However, after the camaraderie of removing the engine, the smashing to windward began to take its toll.

All were being weakened by occasional seasickness and their diet. They were now eating primarily the fish steaks they had dried from a week before. They opened one can of fruit a day – for ten people. They boiled or baked two potatoes a day. For liquids there was only occasional tea, powdered orange drink. Except for one six-pack kept for 'an appropriate occasion' the beer was gone. They drank water.

The tensions among them built. Everyone needed more private space than was available and the small ship became for some a claustrophobic trap. Tony exploded at Neil for assigning equal rations to everyone, arguing that a big man like him needed twice the food that Lisa and Skip needed. Neil replied that Tony still had twice the body fat and that until someone manifested symptoms of malnutrition the rations would remain the same. Both Tony and Macklin complained about sleeping in the forepeak and Neil gave them permission to use his aft cabin or the dinette settee when either was free. Macklin complained continually of seasickness, but still somehow managed to eat his share of rations. Katya sometimes took his place as crew for Olly.

When Jeanne reported that a can of peaches was missing, Neil did nothing, but when she discovered a small can of chicken spread had also disappeared, Neil laid down the law: if someone were caught stealing food he'd be put on half rations and abandoned at the first landfall. Tony became angry again when Neil seemed to be directing his remarks primarily at him and Macklin, claiming Neil kept singling them out. Neil said the rule applied to everyone.

Neil felt increasing irritation at such scenes, but he knew that if he'd worked things out with Frank and Jeanne his other burdens would be more manageable. But he hadn't. Although he and Frank treated each other with politeness, Frank's jealousy of Neil and Jeanne remained fierce. By words and glances he showed his anger or gloom at any closeness between them, while himself showering Jeanne with attention – in the galley, helping with Skippy, inviting her to crew with him and Tony. Although Frank was less sick than during the first ten days – he was now keeping food down and showing more energy – he still *looked* ill and Neil couldn't bring himself to do anything to hurt him.

But his relations with Jeanne, already sobered by the depressing deaths of the Brumbergers and the by-passing of the Bahamas, and dampened by his obsession with getting *Vagabond* east to a safe landfall, were further curtailed by Frank's jealousy. Neil could feel a barrier building between himself and Jeanne.

He longed to be with her, touch her, speak gently, but somehow such opportunities never seemed to arise. The few times they'd managed to be alone had found Neil absorbed in some boat problem and unprepared for intimacy: tongue-tied, abstracted, the barrier between them.

The claustrophobic mood of the boat affected Jim and Lisa too. Depressed by the invasion of their privacy by Tony and the leers of Macklin, they withdrew from the others on the boat, becoming an island unto themselves.

Vagabond sailed on, the mood of her ship's company heavy. The meagre meals – unvaried, repetitious, sparsely seasoned; the stink of the fish steaks drying in the sun; the stiffness of clothes washed always in salt water; the seeing of the same familiar grizzled faces and unkempt hair day after day;

the constant surge, sway and smash of *Vagabond*; the constant hunger and suspicion that others were somehow eating more; the depressing reports from the outside world indicating war, disease, starvation and violence spreading faster than they could flee – all these oppressed them. Olly, who usually spent an hour each day telling stories to Skippy, now puffed violently on his unlit pipe. Katya and Tony were lovers; then fought bitterly; then were lovers again. Lisa and Jim, like two aliens from some other planet, moved gingerly among them, doing their work, then retreating to Jim's guitar, Lisa's diary, long whispered conversations on the foredeck. Neil, Frank and Jeanne, caught in a tense tangle that couldn't last, lived each day according to the rules of routine and decency, then retired each alone to loneliness.

They sailed on. The squalls that hit them four days after leaving Great Abaco Island eased the water problem. To gather water all the self-bailing cockpits were stoppered and even the inflatable dinghy was brought up on the foredeck and partially inflated to catch water there. They gathered two and a half gallons in the first ten-minute downpour, and close to six additional gallons in the two heavier showers that followed.

After the squalls the wind shifted to the south, the seas lessened and *Vagabond* began a long tack directly towards San Juan. With the reduced weight of both man and material – the ship's company had already shed almost a hundred pounds – *Vagabond* began to race towards San Juan at almost a hundred and eighty miles per day clip.

For Jeanne, Frank's anger at even the most casual warmth between herself and Neil, and Lisa and Skip's recurrent symptoms of hunger, contributed to a heaviness that nothing could relieve. When she initiated quiet conversations with Neil, hoping to re-establish their warmth, Neil was polite, but somehow withdrawn. Once she had felt like throwing herself into Frank's arms and sobbing out her longing for Neil, only to smile bitterly at the double folly of such an act.

As *Vagabond* ploughed forward, even the next wave seemed to Jeanne to be a future too distant to consider. She slept, awoke, cooked breakfast, stood watch, read to Skip, ate two mouthfuls of fish at noon, helped Neil with his sextant sunshots, played with Skippy, perhaps helped gaff a fish, cleaned the galley, checked the dried fish, napped, helped with the third meal of the day (the word 'dinner' was too grandiose for the tiny snack which each meal had become), lay on her berth staring at the ceiling, and slept. Sometime in the future, perhaps, she could live again.

A week after leaving the Bahamas, when they were less than eighty miles northwest of San Juan, the outer world, the one they were trying to escape, the one they were trying to rejoin, paid them a fresh visit. It was after one A.M. when a sudden glow lit the distant horizon ahead of them, bloomed briefly like a bright flower, and warned the watchers that man had again unleashed his madness on man.

They reacted to this explosion over San Juan not with terror but with a kind of bewildered mechanicalness. It seemed somehow so wrong, so unjust, that after fleeing for almost three weeks and for over two thousand miles they should find, *ahead* of them still, *more*, that they could feel no emotion except dull dread.

Jim and Lisa, on watch, turned *Vagabond* off the wind to sail away from the explosion, Lisa going crisply to the winches to let out the sails – as if responding to this explosion were a normal part of their nautical duties. At Jim's call Neil came hurriedly up on deck, saw the light, now behind them, and went to the helm to check the course. Disoriented, he took a half minute to realize that it was probably San Juan that had been hit. After calculating their approximate position, he ordered Jim to alter course back to east. They would have about two hours before a tidal wave would arrive; only then would they turn to run before it. Because of the immense depth of water he guessed that the wave wouldn't be breaking and would probably be less of a threat than the wave in the shallow Chesapeake. Meanwhile they would continue east, towards the Virgin Islands. When Neil took out the transistor radio and tuned it to their usual station in San Juan, they found it was no longer broadcasting.

A tidal wave came rolling in at *Vagabond* in the early-morning hours on schedule, a wave a little less than twenty-five-feet high appearing among the three-foot seas that had been running. Frank, at the helm in the darkness, with Tony, Neil sleeping in the wheelhouse behind, saw it at almost the last moment, a huge wall of water glistening in the light of the moon. He swung *Vagabond* away to run before it, but the gigantic unbreaking swell instead hit him on the aft quarter. *Vagabond* lurched violently, skidded along the wave at tremendous speed as it was carried like a toy for forty or fifty feet, and then lurched again as it toppled back to starboard at the crest, the wave rolling under her like the back of a mammoth whale. The huge sea was followed by several other large waves in the fifteen- to twenty-foot range, but by then Frank had swung *Vagabond* downwind running before them, surfing down their faces sometimes for half a minute and setting him to grinning with incongruous exhilaration at *Vagabond*'s speed and grace under pressure. Neil came clambering up awake after the first smash and, groggy from sleep, shouted seemingly contradictory suggestions, but Frank, having survived the first awful wall of water, was not much concerned with *Vagabond*'s handling the puny little fifteen-footers. He just grinned at Neil and kept doing what he was doing.

The sunrise the following morning provided a terrible beauty. The whole southeast became a glowing sweep of bright reds and oranges such as none of them had ever seen before at dawn. Already above them high dark clouds were spreading out across the sky, tinged now with the most delicate pink, but, as the sun rose higher, shading to tannish yellow, then brown, then a brownish grey, and finally and simply to the all-pervading thick dull grey which they had so hated and feared in the Chesapeake.

By nine A.M. San Juan was about seventy miles to the southwest. Sailing east, they were moving in the opposite direction from the high altitude flow of radioactivity, which was westerly. Yet even sailing at eight knots they didn't gain on the expansion of the cloud; it spread outwards from its centre faster than they could flee. When the familiar terrifying ash first again appeared on their decks Neil once more ordered everyone below and had Tony dress in foul-weather gear to sweep the decks clean. By the time he had finished just the first clean-up he was collapsing from the heat and, calling weakly, had to be helped down into the main cabin. Neil had developed a technique of steering *Vagabond* by compass from down below in this emergency since the steering cables passed down from the wheel at the rear of the main cabin and could be pulled alternately to adjust *Vagabond*'s course. The decks could be swept down every twenty minutes or so by someone as well protected as Tony had been, but no one dressed for the arctic had to be on deck to steer.

By noon, three hours after the first discovery, they were no longer able to see any evidence of additional fallout. The dark cloud was mostly west and south of them, only a thin grey layer being directly above.

It was Captain Olly who seemed most disturbed by the latest explosion. Neil discovered him late that afternoon sitting forward on the starboard hull, staring blankly out at the grey water to the southeast of them. Neil realized he must have been sitting there for hours.

'What's happening, old fellow?' Neil asked him, standing nearby, holding on to a stainless steel shroud for balance. *Vagabond* was rolling and plunging uncomfortably as she reached eastward in the southerly wind.

'Feeling a little poorly,' Olly answered after a brief pause.

'Your stomach?' Neil asked, concerned about radiation sickness.

'My heart,' said Olly.

'My God, what's the matter?'

'Not *that* heart,' said Olly irritably. 'I mean . . . I mean that dust gets me down.'

'I know.'

'I don't mind explosions or tidal waves or fires or big winds. A sailor's meant to have to deal with those. But when it *rains* death, how do you reef for that?'

Neil didn't answer. They stared together out at what seemed to be an ugly grey sea beneath the cloud bank to the south.

'And the ocean . . .' Olly went on in a low voice. 'For fifty years I been figuring that no matter how much man ruined the land, the one thing he'd never destroy, no matter how hard he tried, and I *knew* he'd try his damnedest, would be the sea . . .'

Neil let the silence hang briefly and then said softly: 'It's not destroyed yet.'

Captain Olly removed the unlit and perpetually empty pipe from his mouth and tapped it idly on the deck.

'No,' he said after a while. 'It ain't. But I seem to have underrated man's talent for making a mess of things. All these years I been depending too much on man's weakness and stupidity. I figured he was just too dumb to mess things up totally.' He looked up at Neil, his grizzled face and red eyes looking tired and old. 'I just pray the Lord God will save us from man's intelligence.'

Neil looked at him a long moment and nodded. 'Amen,' he said.

Part Four
LAND

1

Jeanne had slept while the men anchored *Vagabond* during the early morning hours, so that when she came up on deck a little after six, she looked upon the boats floating nearby, the quiet, waveless harbour, and the white buildings of the town blossoming up the hillsides in the distance as a child might at her first big city. For more than two weeks she had known only the constant motion of the sea; now, *Vagabond* lay as still as if embedded in concrete. In all that time they had seen no more than four ships, one at a time; now as she slowly swept the horizon with her gaze she could see twenty, thirty . . . more. For the last two days . . . since the explosion over San Juan – she had felt continual low-level fear; now, surrounded by motionless white hulls, with white houses sleeping in the early dawn light less than a mile away, she felt that fear disappear. There was no exhilaration, no joy: simply a sense that here, for the moment, at last, was a safe space.

She moved into the wheelhouse and saw Neil stretched out on the cushions asleep, his bearded face and tousled hair showing his exhaustion even as he slept. She wondered if he'd collapsed there too tired to bother to go aft to his own cabin. He must have fallen asleep after the anchoring only hours earlier.

She slipped quietly down into the galley to prepare herself a cup of tea, then remembered that they had no more tea or coffee. She poured herself a small cup of water. Back in the wheelhouse, sitting opposite the motionless, leaden body of Neil, seeing the slanted rays of the early morning sun sparkling on the golden hairs of his thighs and legs, she felt a wave of longing, tenderness and pride: they had come through; they had made it. But as she felt love welling up within her she thought too of Frank, and then the beautiful body of Neil, so still before her, made her sad.

It was too much for her. They were too much for her. There was no way she could create a world where all of her loved ones could be happy. Although she herself was beginning to feel at home at sea, her children needed land. But the men, all of them really, seemed unenthusiastic about any of the alternatives that they might find for living on any of these Caribbean islands. Here they were in Charlotte-Amalie in the American Virgin Islands, as far as she could tell as safe and unhostile a place as there was within a thousand miles, and four of the men had spent two hours the previous evening discussing the supplies necessary for another two-week voyage and getting depressed because it seemed hopeless. She had tried to talk about what they could expect from St Thomas and though Frank had shown interest, Neil had done no more than give her a book to read.

'What's that, Mommy?' Skip suddenly asked, coming up from his cabin and standing in front of her in his tiny red swimming shorts and staring out at the fleet of anchored boats and the distant houses.

'That's . . . that's land, honey,' she answered in a soft voice so as not to disturb Neil. For a week now Skip had been asking 'When are we going to get to land, Mommy?'

'That's land?' Skip asked, looking puzzled.

'Yes. That's the city of Charlotte-Amalie on an island called St Thomas. We may live here for a while.'

'On a boat?'

'No, on land, in a house.'

'Like the one in Washington?'

'No. Smaller. But nice.'

As Skippy pulled himself up on to the cushion beside his mother he was silent, still staring at the distant town. 'They don't look like real houses,' he said.

'They don't? Why not, honey?'

After a pause he said: 'They just don't.'

330

Neil stirred, adjusted a forearm under his head and chin and then resumed his deadman pose. He had begun to let his beard grow and was in that halfway land of looking scraggly and down-and-out. As she looked at him, affection and desire mixed with her sadness.

'Do they have a MacDonald's?' Skip asked.

'What?'

'Can we go to MacDonald's today?' Skip repeated.

'Oh, no. I'm afraid not. I don't think they have a MacDonald's.'

'What about a Big Whopper?'

'I don't know, honey. We'll see.'

Hamburger: it too will have disappeared. On the islands there would be no beef or lamb, perhaps a little pork and fowl, but mostly fish. She smiled to herself as she realized that she was imagining herself having to announce to Skip the death of the hamburger. Could he take it at such a young age?

Maybe she should sleep with both of them. She had to sleep with Neil, but with Frank the outsider, could not do so 'publicly', could never in that way slap Frank in the face after his fondness for her over the last two years. Perhaps she could become a seafaring camp follower, available to whichever officer was officially on watch, the way Katya seemed capable of being.

But she knew she couldn't, and the tension that existed between Frank and her and Neil was painful. This landfall might represent escape from waves and starvation and fallout, but it was no escape from themselves.

When a Customs launch arrived at eleven, Neil was up but the other men had to be awakened. Most joined Neil and the others topside, all haggard and grizzled or bearded, even Jim. They looked like the collection of war refugees they were. Katya's hair was tangled; she had lost several pounds from her already small frame, but still looked healthier than the men. Lisa, though now a woman, looked, because of her frailness, more like a child than she had a month earlier.

Although they were nervous about the arrival of the Customs launch, they had heard a radio report that the local island government had simply ignored the US military. Apparently any effort to draft the mostly black islanders would have led to an instantaneous revolution. Even as it was, the local government, controlled by blacks but greatly influenced by white interests, was on shaky ground.

The senior Customs officer was a nervous, pudgy white man and his two-man crew was black. They searched *Vagabond* for weapons, asked detailed questions about their previous voyage, seeming to want to be certain they had been at sea nine days since the Bahamas, and, without explanation, insisted on taking everyone's temperature. Just before the Customs men left, Neil asked how he and his friends could expect to get food if they had no gold or silver or much else to barter with.

'Then you fish,' the pudgy officer answered. 'New immigrants aren't eligible for food assistance unless they surrender all their belongings and live in the refugee centre out in Capo Gorda.'

After the launch had motored off, and their guns and ammunition hidden behind a false partition at the back of Jeanne's berth had not been discovered, they prepared to go ashore. Jim got out the dinghy and he and Macklin began to inflate it. Jeanne and Katya were talking about the chances of finding a home on St Thomas when a man and a woman suddenly appeared beside *Vagabond* in a little eight-foot rowing boat.

'I say, you chaps going ashore?' the man asked. He was a round, red-faced man, his big chest and belly heavily matted with dark hair, although the flesh sagged on him as if he had recently lost weight. Both he and the woman, a bleached blonde, were in their forties and were wearing rather spare black bikini bathing suits.

'We are,' Frank replied. 'Why?'

'We own the little blue Wharram catamaran over there,'

the Englishman said, pointing. 'Always willing to lend a hand to a multihull sailor, you know.'

'We appreciate it,' said Frank.

'Philip felt you might need some advice before you go ashore,' the women said, smiling. 'He's very good at advice.'

'We've been at sea for more than two weeks,' said Frank, feeling an unexpected pride as he spoke. 'I guess we can use some advice about what the landworld is like these days.'

'It's a bloody mess is what it is,' Philip countered, holding on to *Vagabond*'s coaming with one of his big hands. 'I know it's a bit presumptuous of me to come over here like this, but the world's become awf'ly small, and where there's a chance to find a friend I like to take it.'

'I see,' said Frank, his mood wavering uncertainly between suspicion and acceptance. He moved aside to let Olly take over helping Jim pump up the dinghy.

'Fact is,' said the Englishman, 'if you're going ashore for food and petrol and water there's a bit you might know first, right?'

'Would you like to come aboard?' Frank finally asked.

'Don't mind if I do. Take the oars, Sheila.'

The large Englishman and his petite and pretty wife climbed nimbly up on to *Vagabond* and introductions were made all around: they were Philip and Sheila Wellington of the catamaran *Doubloon*. A beer was brought up from *Vagabond*'s 'wine cellar' (the bilge) and passed to those who seated themselves around the wheelhouse.

'Bloody marvellous,' said Philip. 'Haven't had a good warm beer in more than two weeks.'

'Supplies are tight here, too?' Frank asked.

'Tight?' Philip snorted. 'If your whole wealth consists of your bare boat then your food consists of seaweed, shellfish, rain water, and fish.' He looked at his wife with a warm smile. 'We had no gold or silver and pawned Sheila's jewellery ten days ago to buy sailcloth and a week's worth of food. And beer doesn't exist here these days.'

'Can food be bought?'

'Some, I suppose – with gold, silver, diamonds, jewellery,' Philip replied. 'And, ah, with pot and pussy. Such are at present the six coins of your nation's former realm.' Frank and Neil looked at him uncertainly. 'You'll have to barter first with the precious metal dealers, then with the individual merchants. Very few shopkeepers will barter themselves, except a few will deal in dope and a lady's favours.'

'Is there much chance we can stay here, make a home here?' Jeanne asked.

Philip looked at her, grimaced, and looked away. 'Not bloody likely,' he replied. 'I'm afraid the world here is becoming a bit of a black and white thing, you know? Blacks don't seem to appreciate the fact that whites are blowing up the whole world and . . . uh . . . then the survivors running to the blacks for help.'

'But the Russians started it,' said Tony from the port cockpit.

'Ah, well, I'm not certain too many blacks are sure of that.'

'St Thomas is all black?' Jeanne asked.

'Pretty much so,' Philip replied. 'And most of the refugees are white or now Puerto Rican. The rich whites who live here are holed up in various enclaves – those that haven't left, that is.'

'What are *your* plans?' Neil asked abruptly from his seat in the corner of the wheelhouse.

The big Englishman frowned. 'The bloody war's got too close,' he said slowly. 'I suppose you know San Juan got hit? . . . We've decided to leave. We want to be part of a fleet.'

'A fleet?' Neil asked.

'Pirates. You can't go twenty miles in any direction without having them all over you. Bloody trouble is you can't know who to trust. A friend of mine sailed off with another ship four days ago and yesterday his ship turned up stripped and foundering while the other ship is reported sailing happily onwards a hundred miles from here. The world's not a nice place these days.'

'But where are you going?' Neil persisted.

'Thought we might try Australia,' the Englishman replied softly, staring at his hands.

'Australia!' Frank exclaimed.

'My boat's too small, I know', said Philip, looking up intently. 'But I have a friend who's got a fine old wooden sloop, fifty-five-footer, she is, and . . .'

'But Australia . . .' Frank said again. 'Jesus. That's quite a sail.'

'It's quite a world, Frank.'

'Yes. I guess it is.'

'England doesn't much exist any more, you know,' he went on intently. 'And since they bombed Puerto Rico and Venezuela and the whites were massacred on Dominica, no one feels too bright about this whole area. Everyone who can afford it is getting out. Food was short before on all the islands. Now it's almost non-existent here. Things can only get worse, right?'

'Have you stocked much food?' Neil asked.

Philip snorted out a half-laugh in reply. 'There are two types here: those who've got their gold and silver and those who haven't. The rich are selling all to fly out of here now. And the rest of us fish.' He laughed and, though his belly shook, his eyes weren't twinkling.

'What are you people planning to do?' asked his wife suddenly.

Frank didn't answer and a strained silence ensued.

'Survive,' Macklin finally growled.

'Oh yes, I know . . .' said Sheila. 'But . . . well . . .'

'I'm sorry, Frank,' said Philip. 'But I suppose I've got to ask also whether in this new world you're rich or poor.'

'We're poor,' Jeanne said. 'We have little food left, and none of the mineral wealth that passes for currency. We could never barter for enough food to go to Australia.'

'Bit sticky for us all,' commented Philip.

'I'm glad you're poor, Jeanne,' Sheila said. 'Anyone who has gold on his boat seems to have a lead anchor in his heart. Phil was saying as we rowed over here, "Hope to Christ they're not hoarders." '

'It's a paradox I guess you'd say,' commented Philip. 'The way things are, if you had plenty of gold you'd be the type that doesn't share, whereas since you, ah, haven't gold, we're likely to help each other.'

'How do you figure to help us?' Frank asked.

'Well, for one thing, give you advice on what you can and can't sell. For another, I've been here for almost a month and know not only St Thomas but what's been happening throughout the Antilles. For example, when the war started a few ships left for some of the islands south of here, but later starvation and revolution and civil war devastated two or three of the islands, and a lot of ships came back. And now after the explosion over San Juan, a lot of ships have departed again.'

'There seem still to be quite a few,' Jeanne said.

Philip looked briefly out at the ships at anchor around them. 'About a third less than on Thursday,' he said. 'And half of these ships here are motor yachts. Almost all of them lack fuel to go anywhere even if they wanted to. Some came in yesterday from Puerto Rico.'

'Is it possible to rent a house?' Jeanne asked.

'I suppose anything is possible if you have the means to pay for it,' Philip replied. 'But you won't be welcome.'

'Can we at least get water free?' Neil asked. 'We've less than three gallons left.'

'Water's rationed. You'll get some, but not enough for a voyage.'

'Jesus, what's happened to traditional Caribbean hospitality?' Frank asked, frowning.

'It was obliterated, Frank,' Sheila replied, her face as gloomy as those of the others, 'the day the white man began

336

bringing disease and death south with him instead of tourist dollars.'

Her husband frowned too. 'And of course the other reason we're feared is the plague,' he said.

'The what?' Frank exclaimed.

'You'd best watch where you get your water from,' Sheila explained. 'There's some sort of mysterious disease on the islands, not many cases yet and worst on Capo Gorda, that kills about half the people it strikes.'

'Is that why the Customs people took our temperature?' Neil asked.

'Yes,' Philip replied. 'It seems the disease is carried by Americans from the mainland, or so they say.' He was frowning and didn't raise his head to look at the others. There was an awkward silence.

'Rain water's safe,' said Sheila.

There was another silence.

'When it rains,' Philip added gloomily.

2

It only took them a few days on St Thomas to realize that
conditions were appalling. Black antipathy to all whites was
palpable in glances and gestures at every moment. In the
month since the war the food shortages had already taken
their toll. People looked gaunt, walked slowly, squabbled
violently over the tiniest disagreement about food or water.
They soon realized that the black men fishing at every bridge
and breakwater and along most docks were not fishing for
leisure, but for survival. The street vendor haggling over the
price of two oranges was haggling not because of 'cultural
tradition' but from economic desperation. The voluptuous
black mother spending twenty minutes in the private office of
the store manager was not coldhearted or neurotic but only a
human being spending thankfully her last discovered
economic asset. In this world there were no luxuries, only
necessities.

Human society on St Thomas was falling apart. The
government was still paying its employees in paper dollars,
which were no longer being accepted by the few farmers,
fishermen and merchants who had things worth selling.
Consequently, government employees, once the island's élite,
were now working for nothing, whereas most other workers –
half the population was unemployed – bargained to be paid in
food and water. Pot-smoking and prostitution were now
public and open since there were no facilities to jail offenders
in, no food to feed them with, and only unpaid, disgruntled
policemen to arrest and guard them. Bicycles and mules were
the popular vehicles of the new world. The airport was
usually deserted of both planes and people since most private
planes had flown south and regular commercial flights to

anywhere had ended through lack of fuel or the piracy of the commercial aircraft. The sight of a plane over St Thomas two days after *Vagabond* arrived had sent such a rush of people from town to the airport that when Neil saw it he thought he was witnessing some annual island bike race: over a hundred people pedalling out to the airport as if their lives depended on it.

Everyone who could afford to leave either had left or was trying to. With food inadequate on all the islands, the poor, with nothing to lose, were beginning to demand forcefully their fair share of the little that was still left. On their first walk through the streets of Charlotte-Amalie Neil, Frank, and Jeanne had seen the broken and unboarded windows of supermarkets and grocery stores, all of which were now empty and deserted. Some downtown blocks had so many looted and abandoned stores it seemed 'the revolution' must already have occurred, and yet the local whites they were able to talk to still spoke as if they feared a black uprising and takeover. There were tanks parked all along the waterfront. Except for the three white enclaves outside of town and the St Thomas Hilton, Neil didn't see that there was much left on St Thomas of value to 'take over'.

Settling on St Thomas began to seem increasingly unlikely. In their first few days Frank was offered houses in exchange for *Vagabond*, but the desperation and hopefulness with which the two different owners advanced their offer sobered Frank considerably. He discussed with Neil the possibility of selling *Vagabond* to raise enough gold to fly most or maybe all of them to Brazil, but the prospect of arriving destitute in Brazil was unpleasant, and worse, they would have to sell the boat before they could have any sort of an assured flight.

And to complicate their situation more, the news from the other Caribbean islands and from the rest of the world was dismal. Although the war seemed no longer to be being fought, conditions worldwide were still getting worse. No one dared pronounce the war over; no government proudly announced victory or abjectly offered surrender; but reports of new fighting had ceased – at least among the major powers. Battles for food and between refugees and neutral countries trying to keep them out were increasing. US government officials, still speaking from some unidentified underground headquarters, now, after three weeks of exhorting its citizens to rally to defeat the Soviet Union, spoke only of steps to be taken to save the surviving population. Although the government spoke, there was no evidence that anyone was listening. From what could be gathered from the shortwave radio and an occasional newscast on the local A.M. station, the country seemed to be divided up into areas and pockets, each struggling independently of the others to survive their particular problems. Reports seemed to imply that more than two-thirds of the US population was already dead.

Starvation on the mainland of the US was not yet reported. It was July, and survivors had plenty of natural growing things for nourishment – if they lived in areas uncontaminated by radiation – but throughout much of the rest of the world it was *the* problem.

Other diseases were now beginning to claim as many victims as radiation sickness and burns. Dysentery, typhoid and cholera were increasingly appearing throughout those areas of the world where loss of electricity and overcrowding meant reduced and polluted water supplies. Worst of all, the mysterious disease from the western United States was spreading to places untouched by missiles, as it had to the Virgin Islands. Colombia, Venezuela and four Central American countries had outlawed all immigration from the north, quarantining or exiling anyone caught illegally within their borders. The 'flu' virus that had been talked about weeks earlier was now definitely more than a flu, but the etiology of the 'plague' remained unknown. All that had been established was that the incubation period was between a week and ten days; that transmission seemed to have to be oral – through ingestion of contaminated food or water, or

340

through mouth contact with someone infected. Flies going from the sweat of an infected person could contaminate food.

The prognosis was known now too. The disease began with stomach cramps, then a fever, then a high fever which might last five or six days, followed by either death or a remission of symptoms. Treatment was to try to reduce and control the fever – medication, ice packs, fluids, etc. Unfortunately, none of them was very successful. Although about a quarter survived with no ostensible permanent damage, and a similar number survived but seemed to be debilitated by the disease, lacking in energy and endurance, about half died.

As a result, international travel and trade had almost ceased. Jeanne and Neil listened to a report that the Venezuelan Air Force had threatened to shoot down a Boeing 747 that wanted to land in Caracas after an eight-hour flight from Toronto. When the plane was almost out of fuel and circling outside the city the Air Force did shoot it down. No one survived.

For the first time those aboard *Vagabond* discussed returning to the US mainland. It appeared that there they could still find sufficient food. The radioactive fallout would be diminishing eventually, or so they hoped. But the problem of avoiding the disease, and of avoiding the violence of those who feared they were carriers of the disease – this was frightening.

Any area of the country untouched by the epidemic would be erecting the same kind of total and deadly barriers to possibly infected outsiders as were other areas of the world. Moreover, most of the stored and growing food would already have been confiscated and controlled by previous survivors in each area, and when winter came these sources would be barely enough for them. Outsiders would not only be feared and kept away because of the 'plague' but because of the burden they would place on the already limited subsistence of those already there. Neil had listened to one shortwave report of a small renegade group of soldiers and a band of survivalists fighting a pitched battle for the food and shelter the survivalists had prepared. The broadcaster didn't know who had won, but it wasn't a game that any of those aboard *Vagabond* had any heart for.

Thus, although their stay in the harbour at Charlotte-Amalie permitted them to recover from the weariness of being at sea for almost three weeks, by the end of a week a new kind of weariness was afflicting them: the fatigue of searching endlessly for some end to the threat of starvation, and finding none. Olly, with help usually from Jim, Lisa, and Katya, spent most of every day fishing, sometimes with hook and line, at others with a net along the shore, or raking for shellfish. Frank, possessive of Jeanne, took on with her the task of bartering for what little food was available in the city. Over the week they bartered away dozens of 'useless trinkets': watches, shirts, shoes, necklaces, blouses, a transistor radio, the rest of Macklin's stolen cigarettes, Jim's remaining small supply of grass. Yet during the week they ate no better than they had at sea and had no more reserve food supply than when they had first dropped anchor. They were running to stand still.

So almost from the first day, on the torpid streets of Charlotte-Amalie Jeanne felt lost and uneasy. She arrived wanting to find a home for herself and Neil and the others, for the alternative seemed an endless sailing from one hostile place to another. But as she talked to government officials, to shopkeepers, as she pushed her way through the devastated and littered streets or along the waterfront bartering for food, she could feel no connection with anyone, black or white, mostly only a powerful, sullen hostility. She felt herself out of sync with the island and its people. By the third day she was just going through the motions. She wanted to leave.

It wasn't simply that she was white in a world mostly black. It was more than colour. She sensed that for those who had lived on the islands for a few years anyone who had arrived after the holocaust – black, white, or Puerto Rican – was an outsider, an intruder – even, she realized with a start, a coward. To have fled one's homeland was to be guilty of selfish betrayal, even if that home had been blown off the earth and the homeland become a vast crematorium. And the anger and contempt with which most of the longtime residents responded to her and the other refugees was undoubtedly intensified by their own fear and their own desire to flee to some ultimately secure haven. A black woman whom she casually tried to befriend at the fish stall turned on her with unexpected hatred: 'Go way, rich lady,' she said fiercely. 'You best fly while you can!' The woman's rebuke acted to re-stir Jeanne's own fear; made her begin calculating if she *were* still 'rich' enough to flee.

It hadn't taken long to learn beyond any doubt the commonness of the currency Philip had called 'pot and pussy'. Marijuana joints were traded as cigarettes had been during earlier wars. Bags of it were the big bills of island currency. And some women, if they were young and attractive and otherwise destitute, went to buy necessities from certain merchants quite reconciled to paying with the availability of their mouths or bodies. One merchant they'd heard about had, out of his own physical limitations, resorted to selling water or fruit or fish to certain women for 'IOUs.' – payment to be upon future demand of the bearer of the IOU, the bearer not necessarily being the merchant himself. He, in turn, used the sexual IOUs to buy things he wanted from other merchants.

The second real estate agent Jeanne had called upon, a dignified black man her own age, had offered her a month's free rent in a cottage he controlled in return for her 'friendship'. The suggestion seemed to her not so much insulting as irrelevant, but it contributed to her feelings of uneasiness about St Thomas.

So too did what was happening to Lisa and Jim. On their second trip ashore the two had discovered in the downtown city park a gathering of teenagers, black and white – the only part of the local life that seemed comfortably integrated – playing guitars and ukuleles and drums, singing, smoking pot, even laughing, and often gathering around the latest street-corner prophet, haranguing about doom or salvation or both. Almost every day after they'd worked with Olly fishing or gathering shellfish they went ashore and spent time with new friends. Katya sometimes went with them.

Lisa, although younger than most of the others, seemed determined to fit in with this society, one which disturbed Jeanne mainly because she knew so little about it and had no control over it. She could feel Lisa pulling away from her. Lisa and Jim would answer her questions about the Park Square people with code word replies: they were 'cool', 'loving people', were 'non-violent', but Jeanne felt only a dull dread at what seemed an aimless passivity in their response to the threats of starvation and disease. Katya didn't help matters when she said that Jim and Lisa were just trying to hold on to a little more of their normal lives before existence became again solely devoted to day-to-day survival.

And finally the other thing that made her feel out of place in Charlotte-Amalie was the absence of Neil. With him staying so often on the boat or off on other people's boats she had no heart for the land. Neil was a major part of any new home, and if he were rejecting St Thomas then she must too.

And so, after six days, she felt herself back where she had been on day one: on a ship without sufficient food to leave and without sufficient food to stay; unable to live with the man she loved because it would destroy the family that was her new world. And her children, whom she had vowed to save, to whom she felt she wanted to dedicate her life, grew steadily thinner, and Lisa steadily more remote. The climax came one afternoon when Lisa was preparing to go ashore with Jim to visit their Park Square friends.

She confronted Lisa down in their cabin as Lisa was changing from the wet clothes she'd worn earlier seining for bait along the shore with Olly, Jim and Tony.

344

'Lisa, sweetheart,' Jeanne said to her. 'I hardly see you these days. What do you *do* in the city every day?'

'We don't do anything, Mother,' Lisa answered, slipping out of her one-piece suit and into panties and shorts. As she did Jeanne noticed that Lisa seemed to be trying to show that she was unaffected by her own nakedness, not hiding her breasts as she'd done for most of the last two years.

'For seven or eight hours?' Jeanne asked, regretting her accusatory tone.

'There's not much to do, you know,' Lisa replied, not looking at her mother. 'This isn't exactly Washington.'

'I know, I know,' Jeanne said, trying to get away from the confrontational mood. 'What do you talk about?'

'Lots of things,' Lisa answered, pulling a blouse over her head. She no longer wore a bra, partly because the only one she'd had with her was worn out.

'But what are some of them, sweetheart?' Jeanne persisted. 'I'm interested in your life, remember?'

'Oh, Mother,' Lisa said with a sigh. 'It's hard to tell you. About lots of things. The way you adults messed up the world. About how to scrounge for food. About what we want to do with our lives.'

'How do most of your friends manage to get food?' Jeanne asked, handing Lisa the brush she knew she was glancing around for.

'Some of them fish,' Lisa answered, beginning to brush her hair. 'Garbage cans outside rich white people's homes. A few go house-to-house begging.'

'Your friends beg?' Jeanne asked.

'Certainly, Mother,' Lisa snapped back. 'There are no jobs and no food. What do you expect?'

'Don't their parents manage to provide food?'

'Sometimes,' said Lisa. 'But most of us want to be independent of our parents.'

'By *begging*?'

'It's better than blowing the world apart.'

345

'I don't see how parents here are responsible for the war,' Jeanne responded, feeling annoyed with Lisa's self-righteousness.

'Some of them are white, Mother,' Lisa said, as if that explained it. 'And Robby says all whites started it with their super-rationality.'

'Ah,' said Jeanne, knowing she was too annoyed to enter reasonably into an abstract discussion. 'I see.'

'That's why music is so important,' said Lisa.

'Yes . . .' said Jeanne, standing uncertainly in front of Lisa, who was ready to leave. 'Tell me, sweetheart, is Jim your lover now?'

Lisa, who was about to escape, stopped, her eyes on the floor. In front of Jeanne she slowly raised her eyes and faced her. 'Yes, Mother,' she answered quietly, without defiance or apology.

Jeanne, who'd been holding her breath, let out a sigh. 'I see.'

'You and Neil . . .' Lisa began.

'It's all right, honey,' Jeanne said, biting her lip and averting her face to look out the window. 'I . . . Jim . . . Jim is . . . a fine man.'

'I love him, Mother,' Lisa said in a low, uncertain voice.

'I know, honey,' Jeanne said and went forward and hugged Lisa to her. 'I know.' They held each other for half a minute until Jim's voice called Lisa from the dinghy alongside *Vagabond*.

'But Lisa,' Jeanne said releasing her daughter but blocking her path. 'I don't want you abandoning the boat. Stay here. Make love here if you must.'

'It's not that,' she said, and, inexplicably to Jeanne, she became irritable again. 'You don't understand. There's no life for us on the boat. Nothing but more of the violence that Neil and Frank seem to believe in. Some of the people in Amalie are different, and Jim and I are interested in finding a better world.'

Jeanne felt herself stiffen again at Lisa's oversimplified

rejections and a frightened sadness at her daughter's need to escape from the boat and the adults on it. Their world was falling apart. 'But, honey . . .' she began.

'I'm going,' Lisa announced and brushed past Jeanne and left the cabin. Jeanne followed and as Lisa climbed down into the dinghy she wanted to call her back or issue some warning, but couldn't articulate even to herself what she feared. 'Lisa,' she called down to her. 'I . . . I want you to find a better world, but . . . just be certain it *is* a better world.'

For a moment Lisa pretended to busy herself with helping Jim get an oar in the oarlock, but then she looked up at her mother defiantly. 'It can't be any worse than the one that's sent us here to starve to death,' she said.

Jeanne, feeling she had nothing better to offer Lisa, could only look down in shocked silence. Jim, smiling up at her awkwardly, shoved off and slowly rowed Lisa away.

3

For Neil, after a week on St Thomas, land was again enemy territory. After their first few days anchored in the harbour he let any or all of the others go ashore to try to find food or a house or whatever it was they thought they wanted. He believed that each of them would soon conclude the hopelessness of finding here a haven. Every time he left *Vagabond* he was ill-at-ease, constantly looking back at the water towards the white tri-hulled form of his ship, his home. Except when he was with Jeanne; together they carried home with them.

The idea of settling on St Thomas was against his instincts. He feared *Vagabond*'s being pirated; feared the plague; feared putting himself under a governmental authority that itself was little better than piracy. His reaction to the appalling conditions on St Thomas was ambivalent. While he sympathized with the native islanders and resented the rich whites flying or sailing off to other havens, he knew full well he was one of the lucky ones who had a vehicle to flee with and knew he'd be happy to use it. Indeed, was constantly scheming to be able to use it.

Yet that alternative, *all* the alternatives, were, as always, heartbreaking. Somehow, some way they had to get in sufficient food for a voyage even longer than the one they had just completed. Somehow, some way they had to obtain more weapons to protect themselves against pirates and eventually, Neil speculated, against foreign navies and air forces. Somehow, some way they had to find a place on the planet where they could feed themselves and be free of the great leaning grey weight of the nuclear holocaust. Somehow, some way. It was life.

He talked with as many sailors as he could and although many said they wanted to flee, all were as stuck as he. The only difference was that many of them had lost confidence in themselves or in their boat and were waiting, waiting, stuck in their own stuckness.

Philip and Sheila Wellington were exceptions. They were determined to get away, and since their thirty-foot catamaran's mast was cracked they were trying to work out a deal with a man named Oscar White who owned an old fifty-five-foot sloop but had little skill or experience at sailing. Philip had become increasingly edgy over the week Neil had known him; he was convinced that St Thomas was about to explode and that they had to get away.

On their eighth day on St Thomas Neil met Philip again, this time on Oscar's sloop, *Scorpio*. The ship was an old racing boat, once queenly, now old and unmaintained, still solid it seemed to Neil, but with much gear in need of repair and all its varnish and bright work needing attention.

The three sat in the huge airy open cockpit in front of the beautiful mahogany wheel, alone polished and gleaming. Oscar was an intense, smallish man in his thirties, with wild long blond hair, a big handlebar moustache and narrow blue eyes. A former real estate broker he had left his job, wife and family for a fling in the Caribbean on a cheap yacht he planned to fix up and sail off into the sunset. The war had interrupted his idyll after less than two months.

His crew consisted of two young men who'd latched on to him in Fort Lauderdale. Gregg and Arnie were both wiry young men, much more laid back than Oscar, and apparently happy to go along with whatever he decided. They were also friends of Jim, Lisa and Katya. There were usually two or three young women aboard *Scorpio* but none showed up for the conference, nor did Gregg and Arnie, content to remain fishing off *Scorpio*'s stern.

Philip and Oscar sat on one side of the cockpit and Neil on the other.

'It's no use, Neil,' Philip said as each of the three sat holding a tall glass of water as they once would have held gin and tonics. 'There's no non-violent way to do it. Believe me, I've tried.'

Neil stared gloomily at his drink of water. Philip was one of the few men he'd met who saw the situation since the war as he did: a struggle to the finish for individual survival. Or rather group survival, for Neil was committed not simply to himself but to Jeanne and to all who sailed on *Vagabond*, and now, although the commitment was unspoken, indeed perhaps unconscious, he was committed too to Philip and Sheila. But much as he liked Philip he was less enthusiastic about getting involved with Oscar and *Scorpio*, although if Philip were to become *Scorpio*'s captain he would go along.

'So what dishonest ways are there?' Neil replied. 'I haven't seen much on St Thomas worth stealing.'

'I've been thinking about our situation a great deal,' said Philip. 'As Samuel Johnson said, the prospect of hanging concentrates one's mind wonderfully.'

'And?' asked Neil.

'Both of us have two basic necessities: a large supply of food for a long voyage and weapons and ammunition,' said Philip. 'Without these two there's not much hope in setting out.'

'Especially food,' said Oscar. 'We're already starving.'

'Weapons as well,' said Philip, flushing slightly but continuing to address Neil opposite him. 'To get south we're going to have to run the gauntlet: the twenty or so islands of the Antilles, each of them having a pirate ship or two operating out of them.'

'How can you know that?' Oscar asked.

'I've been listening to the shortwave for a month. I've witnessed ships arriving stripped of everything but one sail. I've heard Maydays from vessels under attack. I haven't remained here because I'm afraid of the sea or of starving. I'm afraid of the land, of the men who come from it.'

'All right,' said Neil, 'but where in God's name can we get

350

weapons? I thought you told me there wasn't even a black market for them.'

'We get weapons, old boy,' said Philip, brightening as if at last he'd come to what he wanted to talk about, 'from the pirates.'

Neil examined Philip's glowing face.

'How?' he asked simply.

'I've discovered one of the pirate ships,' he answered, becoming serious again. 'It's a forty-two-foot Hatteras docked at Martin's Marina. Knowing what ships have been hit and when, and where *Mollycoddle* was at the time, I figured it out. That plus rumours in town and the unexplained wealth of her captain and crew.'

'*Mollycoddle*?' asked Neil.

'Bit of a larky name for a pirate ship, what? Yet Forester and the others, with no assets other than that ship, never lack for petrol, food, liquor or barter goods necessary to buy women. They live like kings in a large estate they've taken over outside the city. Their sudden prosperity has only occurred since the war began, since the breakdown of government has made piracy almost a risk-free crime.'

'You plan to get weapons from them?' Oscar broke in.

'Precisely. We'll hit their ship,' Philip replied.

'Is this Forester – Michael Forester? An Englishman?'

'I believe so.'

'Jesus Christ, count me out. That guy and his gang are killers. I mean they've shot people on the streets of Charlotte-Amalie and no one does a thing. Even the blacks are afraid of them.'

'I can understand your concern,' said Philip, flushing, 'but when you hear my plan perhaps you'll change your mind.'

'You plan to raid their ship?' Oscar persisted.

'Yes.'

'They'll outgun us three to one,' said Oscar.

'Not when there's only one or two men aboard.'

'When is that?' asked Neil.

'Every night that the ship's in port,' said Philip, again looking at Neil. 'They live on their estate. They always leave a guard on the *Mollycoddle*, often two, I think, but I don't consider one or two overconfident guards an insurmountable obstacle.'

'Do they have radio contact with the estate?' asked Neil.

'I believe they probably do, yes, in fact,' agreed Philip.

'You think they keep their weapons aboard?'

'Some certainly,' said Philip. 'Some on the estate. But the ship will be much easier to hit.'

'Food?'

'I'm sure the *Mollycoddle* is kept well-stocked.'

'You steal the ship's weapons and food and then what?'

'We sail off into the sunset!' said Philip triumphantly.

Neil frowned, considering.

'You're crazy,' said Oscar. 'There'll be a dozen well-armed pirates with a twenty-two-knot Hatteras chasing us to give us a cheery goodbye.'

'We scuttle the Hatteras,' said Philip confidently.

'They have other boats,' suggested Oscar.

'They're not certain who hit them,' countered Philip.

Oscar shrugged, scowling.

'Let's hope so,' said Neil.

'Also, we are now two ships, both armed to the teeth, sailing side by side. A rather undelectable target.'

'Not when someone's mad,' said Oscar.

'True,' said Philip, flushing, 'There *are* risks involved in piracy, my boy.'

Philip was looking at Neil, his face glowing with excitement, while Neil watched the two young crew men aft become agitated as one of them reeled in a fish.

'It's too dangerous,' said Oscar.

'There *are* risks to piracy,' Philip repeated, looking at Neil, 'but not as many as in being the victims of pirates.'

'Screw it,' said Oscar. 'Those guys won't bother me. I haven't got anything worth attacking.'

Grimacing, Philip continued to look at Neil. 'I'm depending on you to iron out the military wrinkles in my little plan,' he said to him. 'I but point the way.'

'Any particular time-frame?' Neil asked after a silence.

'Ah, yes, that,' said Philip, suddenly frowning. 'I'm afraid we may decide there's a bit of a rush. Three things. First – I heard a rumour today – just a rumour so far – that quite a few cases of that plague have appeared right here in the city.' Neil stared at him in dismay.

'Not too pretty,' Philip went on. 'Secondly, let's face it, we're none of us getting any fatter. Our larders are already bare. I believe we should strike as soon as we can.'

Neil nodded. 'And the third thing?' he asked.

'The luxury cruise ship, the *Norway*, is scheduled to arrive here later this afternoon.'

'My God,' said Oscar. 'How do you know?'

'Fred Turner on the *Spright* told me an hour ago. The *Norway* had been hung up in Santo Domingo since the war began but the US Navy has given her a huge supply of diesel fuel from its supply on Vieques, and the *Norway* is now carrying about 500 Navy personnel.'

'What's it doing here?' Oscar asked.

'Well . . . that we can only surmise. But clearly it will be taking on passengers. The sight of more rich people sailing off on a lovely white cruise ship is not likely to be greeted with enthusiasm.'

'Maybe we could get aboard?' suggested Oscar.

Neither Neil nor Philip commented.

'It would be a lot safer than messing with Michael Forester,' Oscar persisted.

'I wouldn't count on it,' said Philip.

'Well, all I know is that if it's a choice of starving or warring with pirates, I'll choose starving,' said Oscar, standing up.

'I understand, Oscar,' said Philip. 'I respect your decision. But . . . if things work out, do you still want me to assume command of *Scorpio*?'

353

'You get me food and guns, Buddy, and you can sail *Scorpio* for the rest of your life.'

'Good,' said Philip.

Oscar wandered aft to check on the fishing.

'Well, Neil?' inquired Philip, leaning forward.

Neil shrugged, then smiled and raised his now empty glass. 'I'd like to see both the *Mollycoddle* and their estate,' he said. 'Is that possible?'

'Oh, absolutely,' said Philip, grinning and standing up quickly with surprising grace for such a bulky man. 'Sheila spent the morning casing the estate, and the *Mollycoddle* is moored at Martin's Marina. We've borrowed three bikes for the occasion.' Philip was grinning triumphantly.

'Rather sure of me, weren't you?'

'You're a sailor, Neil. This hunk of filth called St Thomas could no more hold you than a cinderblock could hold *Vagabond* at anchor.'

'You think I'll drag out to sea, do you?' asked Neil, smiling and standing.

'Drag, old boy?' said Philip, coming forward to clap Neil on the shoulder. 'No, sir. You'll *fly*.'

'From the sound of your plan,' he said, 'I'd better.'

4

That night Neil explained to Frank, Jeanne, Tony and Macklin the plans he and Phil were developing for raiding the *Mollycoddle* for food and weapons. Although Macklin indicated approval, Tony, irritable, found half a dozen weaknesses in the plans. Frank, looking fatigued, simply didn't feel the possible gains justified the risks. After Tony and Macklin had gone down to the main cabin to prepare a small meal for themselves, Neil continued to pressure Frank.

'No, Neil,' Frank said, 'I just can't see it. Someone would get killed. Your whole plan scares me.'

'Frank, we've got to leave,' Neil insisted. 'There's nothing for us here. St Thomas is close to exploding. Hundreds of people will leave on the *Norway* . . .'

'There's St Croix, there's Puerto Rico . . .'

'Don't bullshit yourself!' Neil exploded. 'In these islands there's only chaos, revolution, starvation, madness and war. That's all we've found, that's all there is. It'll only get worse.'

'And you think pirating another man's ship will improve things!'

'I want all of us to survive. And without food and weapons we won't make it.'

Frank strode away from Neil and glared out across *Vagabond*'s foredeck at the few distant lights on the hillsides of Charlotte-Amalie.

'I'm not sure I want to contribute to a world of pirates,' he said.

'Then you'll be contributing to a world of starvation and radiation sickness and death.'

'We're still alive so far,' he said huskily.

'By outsailing the fucking war! And that's what we've got to do now.'

'And what about Jeannie and the children? They can't take the ocean. They need a place on land.'

'I know that,' said Neil, shaking his head and grimacing. 'I know that, Frank. Believe me, I know that dragging everyone out to sea again isn't going to bring happiness, but this is probably our best chance. Philip's going to try to take the *Mollycoddle* whether we join him or not. Sailing in a fleet with him improves our defences against possible pirates. It would be nice if we could wait a week or a month, but we can't.'

'You're acting too fast, Neil,' Frank said, shaking his head wearily. 'Our food supplies are nil, our water low, and you want to solve all our problems, pirate a boat from pirates, raid their estate, load our supplies, and fly to sea all in the next couple of days. It's too much. It's too sudden. I can't do it.'

'But you, yourself . . .'

'No! Leave me alone. I'm done. I'm sick. I'm exhausted. I'm going to my berth and sleep. I'm too tired to argue with you and too tired to agree with your plan. I'm sorry.' And he left Neil for his cabin.

Neil stared after him angrily until Frank had slid the hatch closed behind him. Fists clenched, he walked to the opposite cockpit and was surprised to see Jeanne's hatch open and Jeanne standing there looking calmly up at him. Her face showed her fatigue. She was wearing Frank's bathrobe. The two of them looked at each other expressionlessly.

'So we have to leave again . . .' Jeanne mused softly.

'Apparently not,' commented Neil, anger still in his voice.

'But you feel we should . . . steal some food and weapons and sail.'

'Yes,' Neil answered quietly, realizing that she had listened to the whole loud argument. 'I'm sorry. I just don't see how we could make a home anywhere in the West Indies.'

Jeanne still stared up at him, absently pulling the top half of her bathrobe closer to her neck. She glanced across to Frank's cabin on the other side of the boat.

'Come down into my cabin,' she said, turning and walking down the ladder. Neil swung himself into the opening and descended after her. She stood facing him halfway down the narrow floor area of her cabin between her berth and that of Skip and Lisa, Skip's bare foot just sticking out off the edge of the furthest berth. Being alone with her here sent something warm through Neil, although the present situation was distinctly non-erotic.

'Frank's a gentle man,' Jeanne said.

'I know.'

'And Jim's withdrawal from the boat and his . . . relation with Lisa has upset him.'

'I don't blame him.'

She hesitated. 'And . . . us . . . that upsets him,' she went on. 'He . . . he's in no condition now to make such an important decision. Especially on such short notice. He's an awfully good man, but at this moment . . .'

'Yes?'

'I think you should go ahead with your plan without him,' Jeanne concluded quietly, looking up at Neil. 'I'd like to help in any way I can,' she went on. 'And I think it's important that Jim be part of it. And Lisa. And Katya.'

'If they'll come,' Neil said sullenly.

'They'll come,' she said.

Neil watched her carefully. She stood there, clearly weary, with the same regal authority she always seemed able to maintain.

'It'll mean a long two-, three- or even four-week ocean voyage,' he said. 'A lot of it like the one we had from the Bahamas, slamming, slamming, slamming. There won't be any escaping it.'

She looked back at him and smiled. 'I'm used to it.' But then she shrugged a tiny shrug, her chin falling down, 'But some day . . .' Tears had formed in her eyes.

Neil took her in his arms and held her close with one hand

and caressed her hair with the other. 'Jeanne . . .' he said, holding her tightly. 'When an animal is being chased, after a while all it wants to do is lie down and let the dogs take it. It wants it all to end.'

At first she held herself stiffly in his embrace and then collapsed against him, her arms returning his hug, her hair pressed against his cheek. Although she made no sound, in her fierce hug he could feel the tiny tremors of her crying.

'. . . Run . . .' she said.

'You keep running,' Neil said. 'Later, if you make it, you can have the leisure to worry about what *kind* of a life you want to lead. Right now, for us, the dogs are still at our heels.'

Jeanne nodded, but she looked sad and beaten.

'I love you,' he said softly in her ear. When she didn't respond he bent to lift her up and place her on her berth.

'It's too . . . no,' she said, speaking mechanically. 'Please . . . no . . . Skippy . . .'

He climbed up beside her on the berth, not able to see much, wishing he could see her face, her eyes. Groping at the head of the bed he found a flashlight and turned it on, letting its light fall against the far wall. She was staring at the ceiling, seeming to refuse to look at him. Her expression was tense, withdrawn.

For a long time, resting on one elbow he stared down at her.

'Hey,' he finally said. 'My name is Neil. I'm in bed with you.'

Tears welled up in her eyes, which she closed, a grin appearing on her face. 'I guessed as much,' she said.

'The least you can do is say hello,' he continued, loving her smile and bending to kiss the tears in the corners of her closed eyes.

'Go away,' she said, reaching up to put her arms around his neck and hold him close.

'Never,' he replied, coming over on top of her. 'Never,' he whispered. And they made love.

From the moment Jeanne drew Neil down on top of her and opened her mouth to his kiss, their desire, so long restrained, exploded in a series of passionate caresses and couplings that followed one another without words, thought or conscious intent. The necessity of silence imposed by their unspoken concern for the sleeping Skip and the more distant Frank seemed to add to their sensual intensity. Occasionally they would emerge from their sexual universe to find themselves nose to nose staring at each other as if each had awakened from some unbelievably joyous dream. Their eyes would speak a brief acknowledgment of their jointly created miracle, but their mouths, as if afraid to break the spell, remained wordless. Then they would lose themselves again in fierce intertwining.

'Living God, Jeanne . . .' Neil finally whispered when exhaustion finally left them, sated but still joined, back in a more normal world.

Jeanne, again beneath him, simply smiled up at him.

'Yes . . .' she said.

Up in the wheelhouse Tony and Macklin sat alone, Macklin smoking, Tony sipping at some rum he'd bartered for earlier. Frank and Olly were below sleeping. Although Katya had returned, Jim and Lisa were still ashore. Tony and Macklin had seen Neil follow Jeanne down into her cabin, but for a long time talked about Neil's plans for a raid.

'The trouble is,' Tony complained in the dim light falling from the kerosene lamp, 'even if we raid the pirates and get some decent food it just means more endless sailing.' In the month since the war Tony had lost all his fat and was now tall, muscular and slender. His boisterousness had given way to almost daily irritability. He and Katya had fought again a few minutes before and it didn't help matters that she had compared him unfavourably with Neil. To give Jeanne and Neil privacy Katya had gone aft to sleep in Neil's cabin.

'That's all there is, Tony,' said Macklin quietly. 'We'll never be safe until we're into the southern hemisphere.

Vagabond's the only way for outcasts like you and me to get there.'

'Maybe,' said Tony. 'But I'm not sure I want to spend the rest of my life as a cabin boy.'

'Oh yeah, that,' said Macklin, grinning. 'That we can probably change.'

'I'm getting a little tired of waiting,' said Tony, pacing back and forth in the dim light.

'As long as Neil and Frank are together you and I will be cabin boys,' Macklin went on. 'Let's face it, right now no one needs us. They have Neil. He's hardass enough to get them to save themselves. Without him they'd flounder.'

'Without him they'd need me . . . us,' said Tony.

'Yes, without him.'

Tony stopped in front of Macklin, who sat with his accustomed heavy composure.

'I don't notice us doing much about it,' Tony said.

'They'll do it for us,' Macklin replied quietly, 'if we give them enough time.'

'Do what?'

'Split the boat apart. Send Neil packing. You don't think Frank is going to let Neil stay aboard once he finds out he's balling Jeanne, do you?'

Tony looked uncertain. 'I don't know,' he said. 'Frank likes Neil, and if Jeanne went with him . . .' He paused. 'He'd sure enough be pissed though.'

'Unfortunately,' said Macklin, 'Frank seems determined not to see what's going on.'

'Why don't we tell him?' asked Tony.

Macklin sat very still. Then he took out a cigarette, lit it and took a long toke. 'Beats me,' he replied.

Frank, bone-weary, nevertheless staggered out of his berth when Tony told him there was some trouble between Neil and 'a woman'. Confused, half-asleep, he had felt an instant anger that Neil was bothering Jeanne, but before he could ask further Tony had disappeared.

Slipping on a pair of shorts and taking a flashlight, he stumbled up out of his cabin and went aft to Neil's cabin. He knocked on the hatch, then slid it open. Flashing his light down to descend the ladder he was startled to see Katya's bare legs and then her questioning face. She pulled a cover over the rest of her body.

Frank's first hit was pleasure: so Neil was balling Katya, he thought. He was glad. But when he saw that the man in the berth was Olly, snoring peacefully, Frank blinked uncertainly. 'I'm . . . ah . . . looking for Neil,' he said.

Katya blinked up at him.

'He . . . went topsides to check on . . . the anchor,' she replied.

'Oh.' Frank closed the hatch and walked into the wheelhouse.

'Have you seen Neil?' he asked Macklin, who was seated against the mizzen mast with his feet stretched out on the settee. 'Tony said something about some . . . problem.'

'He's in bed,' said Macklin.

'No, I just checked there,' Frank said.

'In bed with Jeanne,' said Macklin indifferently.

Frank remained where he was, turning the light off to leave himself in relative darkness. He felt fear. Unexpected and powerful fear. He walked reluctantly to the port cabin, hesitated, and then banged his fist down three times on the sliding hatch, like a judge gavelling for order. From inside came no response. In a small burst of breeze *Vagabond* swung slowly off to port in the darkness, swinging on her anchor. Frank hammered again three times on the hatch.

'What is it?' he heard Jeanne finally say.

'I'm looking for Neil,' Frank said harshly, even as he had a strong momentary hope that Macklin was wrong, a hope that sunk, dragging his heart with it as a silence returned to the cabin. Then he heard the sound of someone landing with a thump on the cabin floor.

He waited.

In another few seconds, the hatch slid forward away from him, a figure came quickly up the ladder steps and stopped at the top, three feet away. It was Neil. After a hesitation he came out into the cockpit and stood before Frank. In the wheelhouse behind them Macklin was turning up the kerosene lantern and its dim glow now fell across Neil's bare chest. He was wearing only his swimming trunks. Frank stared at him; Neil returned his gaze steadily without expression. Then Frank saw on his shoulder a long black strand of Jeanne's hair.

'You goddamn son-of-a-bitch,' he said automatically.

'No, Frank,' said Neil. 'I'm . . . sorry . . .'

Frank swung his fist with the same instinctive rage that he had uttered his profanity. The blow struck Neil solidly in the side of the head, sending him reeling to his right and tumbling into the cockpit seat. There, stunned, he sat for a moment turned sideways to Frank, touching the left side of his face.

'You heartless, selfish son-of-a-bitch,' Frank said, his fists clenched at his side, looking down at Neil. Neil looked up, anger in his eyes too.

'Selfish, Frank, not heartless,' he said.

'How *dare* you take advantage of that woman when she . . . she . . .' Frank wanted to say 'she's mine' but the words stuck in his throat and he felt an urge to cry.

'I'm sorry,' Neil said. 'But sometimes something becomes more important than loyalty to a friend.'

'A GODDAMN FUCK?' he shouted at Neil.

Neil looked up at him coldly. 'Yes,' he answered quietly.

Frank lunged at Neil to grab him by the throat, but this time Neil fell sideways to avoid the charge and grabbed Frank's left arm to pull him past and send him crashing into the back of the cockpit seat. Frank turned and reached for Neil again, but he pulled himself up and away. Blindly, Frank rose to come at him a third time.

'Look, Frank, this is ridi . . .'

As Frank swung at him Neil ducked under the blow and slammed into Frank's chest, sending them both a second time back against the cockpit seat, Frank being crushed hard against it by Neil's weight. The wind was knocked out of him, leaving him momentarily stunned. He felt Neil push himself

362

to his feet and step back again into the middle of the cockpit. Both men were gasping for air.

Frank looked up at him, feeling both a hatred that seemed unwinding out of control and a sad, little boy urge to cry, as if Neil were the neighbourhood bully picking on him.

'Look, I know . . .' Neil began.

'You ever go down in her cabin again and I'll kill you,' Frank said, expressing his inconsolable rage.

Neil remained uncertainly a few feet away, his fists clenching and unclenching at his side, sweat matting the hairs of his chest.

'Don't say that, Frank,' Neil said softly. 'You don't : . .'

'I SAID IT! I MEAN IT!' he shouted back. 'STOP BETRAYING ME!' he screamed.

Neil flinched at those words. Jeanne appeared behind him in her cabin entrance, looking past Neil at Frank with a pained, frightened expression. Frank's heart ached for her: how he wanted to protect her, care for her.

'It's not Neil you should be angry with,' he heard her say to him.

'Damn it, Jeanne, how could you?' he asked huskily. Again he wanted to cry.

'Get below, Jeanne,' Neil said, pushing her back with his left arm. Frank saw now that Katya, wearing Neil's robe, was standing in the wheelhouse beside Macklin and Tony, watching. And Jim and Lisa had now returned too; staring at him. A greater sense of sadness and humiliation flooded through him. He felt beaten.

Slowly he brought himself to a standing position. 'Have . . .' he began, but had to clear his throat. 'Have I made myself clear?' he said to Neil with as much coldness as he could command, the sounds coming out huskily, like those from a dying man.

'Yes,' said Neil.

'Good.'

Unseeingly, the images of people blurred – later he realized that he must already have been crying – he moved past Neil, shoved himself between Katya and Tony and returned to his cabin. He had lost everything.

5

Guiltily, unhappily, Jim and Lisa escaped *Vagabond* with Katya, in theory to barter for some additional food out at the commune at Salt Point, but in reality to get away from the ship conflicts they couldn't handle. They sailed with Oscar, Gregg and Arnie and two young women aboard *Scorpio*. One was Oscar's girlfriend Janice, a plumpish woman of thirty with short curly brown hair. The other was a slender, nervous young girl named Mirabai who was vaguely connected with Arnie. Both women – and the men too he realized – struck Jim as frighteningly passive and apathetic. None of them seemed to have any ideas about how they might survive what was happening. They were vaguely hopeful that the commune might feed and take care of them, and only Oscar seemed interested in joining *Vagabond* and sailing further south. Gregg and Arnie, often stoned on grass, seemed indifferent even to the prospects of the commune.

The old racing ship moved sluggishly and Jim noticed how tentatively Oscar and his crew handled her. He became concerned at the small anchor they threw overboard, especially when they payed out so little scope that a fresh breeze might well blow them out to sea. Oscar explained that their big anchor had been stolen. When Jim suggested that it might be advisable to put out another hundred feet of anchor line they thought it was a swell idea.

By the time the three from *Vagabond* rowed ashore at Salt Point with Oscar and Janice it was after four in the afternoon. Then, as they were pulling the dinghy up on to the beach, Gregg's shouts from *Scorpio* indicated that even with the additional scope *Scorpio*'s anchor was dragging in the rising wind. Oscar and Jim left the three girls and began rowing full

364

speed back to the sloop. The three women were left to investigate on their own.

Salt Point was a barren peninsula stretching out from one of the three white enclaves still surviving on St Thomas. It had become an unofficial home for a small group of homeless young whites and blacks who were to varying degrees followers of Big Robby, an end-of-the-world preacher.

As Lisa followed Janice and Katya into the low shrubs to cross the peninsula towards the cove where Janice said the barter boat was reported to come, she moved reluctantly, unhappy at being separated from Jim. On the other hand she needed to be away from the tensions of *Vagabond* and looked forward to checking out the commune. Big Robby preached that the end of the world was upon them – just three more weeks or something like that – and that all should take joy in the last days. All Lisa wanted was joy with Jim, and though she and Jim didn't really believe the actual end of everything was only three weeks away, they both wanted to hold on to and explore the happiness and love they'd found.

When they were halfway across the peninsula they saw in the distance three or four rather dilapidated one-storey wooden structures and some people. As they came nearer Lisa saw that two of the women in one group were bare-breasted and a man leaning back against the wall of one of the shacks was completely naked. Several people were smoking, and when they were in the clearing she could smell the sweet odour of pot. A man with a bushy blond beard and long hair tied in a bun behind his head emerged from a shack near them. He was wearing cut-off jeans.

'Hey, welcome, good sisters,' he said. 'I'm Thunder. Don't think I've seen you around here before.' He grinned at Katya.

'We're just visiting,' she said.

'We heard good things about you,' Janice added. 'Thought we'd check it out.'

'That's great, man, great,' Thunder said, smiling and looking from one to another and then back at Katya. 'We're getting dozens of new people every day. The last days are here and I guess everyone's finally learning to groove.'

No one responded immediately to this and in the pause Lisa introduced everyone to Thunder. A naked white man and black girl walked by holding hands, the girl's long hair falling down her back. Lisa noticed how skinny they both were and that the girl's bony bottom was covered with a light coating of sand.

'We're not much on clothes here,' Thunder went on, smiling. 'Everyone's free to do what they want. Bare-assed or tuxedo, it's all cool here.'

'But bare-assed is cooler,' Katya commented and Thunder laughed and reached out and put a bony hand briefly on her shoulder.

'You're right there, Katya,' he said. 'Especially in this heat. Hey, you people be sure to stay for the party tonight. Big Robby's gonna lay a rap on us and then we'll all have a good time.'

'Is there some place to get something to eat and drink?' Lisa asked.

Thunder's face clouded. 'There's a cistern about two hundred yards past that last house. Just follow the path. But it's getting low so we're having to ration. Our next meal's about dusk – only an hour – but I doubt the girls are back from buying the fruit and fish.'

'We'll survive,' said Lisa, tossing her dark hair away from her face.

'Yes . . .' said Thunder, looking slowly at the three of them with a frown. 'Hey, you know, I don't want to preach, but you cats ought to loosen up a bit, enjoy yourselves. This is the peninsula of love, man, and Robby's message is that we should *joy* in these last days. You folks appear a little down. Loosen up, man. Do what you will, but joy!'

They stared at him.

'We're a little done in by our sail,' said Janice.

366

'Sure, man, I dig that. But you got to know that within a month the whole earth will be destroyed,' Thunder elaborated, his bearded face strangely expressionless as he spoke.

'Things don't look too good,' Lisa agreed tentatively.

'You got to *joy*, man. These are the last days. Let go!' He smiled at them and gave Janice an awkward hug. 'If you want to get stoned the communal pot supply is in this first shack here. I'm afraid it's rationed, too.'

'No thanks,' said Lisa.

'Joy, brothers and sisters,' Thunder pronounced, opening his arms in a belated welcome. 'Joy in all you do. The last days are here.'

'Joy to you, too,' said Lisa shyly in a soft voice as Thunder strode away after two women who were following a path off to the left.

'May the last days find you soon,' said Katya, so low that only Lisa could hear.

'Hey, Oscar asked me to get some pot,' said Janice. 'You go on ahead. I'll join you later.'

Lisa and Katya walked on. When they emerged several minutes later from the shrub oak to the water's edge they found themselves among six or seven other young women and girls and one man, all but two of them black, all watching a long, powerful motor yacht slowly approaching a large mooring about forty feet from shore. The black women were wearing blouses and cut-off jeans, both so frayed in some cases they were close to rags. The hot wind was blowing off the shore at this point and the water, despite the strength of the breeze, was in the lee, calm.

'Excuse me,' said Katya to the one white girl, who was wearing only a bikini bottom, her small, naked breasts a light stripe in her browner upper body. 'Where can we get something to eat?'

The girl frowned. 'The boat,' she said, pointing. 'They bring it on the boat.'

Lisa could see that two men on the big boat had successfully tied their yacht to a mooring and the ship lay at rest about fifty feet out.

'I say, are you girls coming, or not?' one of the men yelled from the bow of the yacht.

'Bring us the little boat, mahn!' one of the black women on shore shouted back.

'Oh no,' the man shouted back, grinning. 'You can swim out today; the exercise will be good for you.'

'Put the boarding ladder down!' shouted a pudgy black girl, slipping off her brightly coloured but tattered blouse and leaving it neatly next to another woman's basket. The woman then ran four or five strides into the water and made a clumsy dive to begin swimming out to the yacht.

'Ah, shit, I can't swim,' one of the other black girls said, as two more black women prepared to swim out.

'HEY!' shouted the white girl to the man standing on the bow watching the swimmers. 'I CAN'T SWIM! How about a lift?'

'Later, sweetheart,' the man responded. 'We'll let these ladies row in with what they buy.'

'Oh shit,' said the white girl to herself. 'By the time we get there, they'll be tough to bargain with.'

'Who cares?' said a black girl. 'We'll eat anyway.'

'Shit, rotten mangoes and fish.'

'It food, I eat it.'

Lisa and Katya stood just behind these two girls listening and watching the three women who had swum out to the yacht, who, one by one climbed up the boarding ladder on the starboard side of the yacht and disappeared into the huge cockpit. From where they stood, the wind, blowing directly offshore, was keeping the yacht with its bow directly at them so Lisa couldn't tell what was happening aboard the boat. The man who'd been on the bow went aft when the women began climbing aboard.

Three of the women still on shore now moved off along the beach and seemed to have lost interest in the yacht, leaving

368

only Lisa, Katya, and the black girl who was desperate for any food. When Lisa next looked at the boat she saw two of the men peering over the top of the windshield high up on their yacht and examining her and Katya through binoculars.

In another few minutes a dinghy appeared from around the back of the ship and a black woman climbed down into it and paddled towards shore. The girl in front of Lisa and Katya walked down to the water's edge to meet her.

'Fucking white pigs!' the returning woman said, throwing the oar up the beach. She retrieved a small cardboard carton half-filled with something from the bottom of the dinghy and came towards them.

'You want food,' she said to Katya as she approached, 'go get it. They tol' me to tell you they feeling generous. They like white girls.'

Lisa began to walk down the beach to the dinghy. As she did she noticed the men had tied a line on the dinghy's stern which was attached at the other end to their yacht. Katya had been slow in following but now she stood beside the dinghy into which the last black girl had sullenly climbed.

'Coming?' she asked Katya gloomily.

Lisa looked at Katya.

'Who are these men?' Katya asked slowly as if calculating.

'They bring food and stuff every few days,' said the black girl.

'Is there ever any rough stuff?' Katya asked.

'Why they use rough stuff?'

'Do they have guns?'

'I never seen none. You, June?'

'Oh, they got guns,' said the woman who had returned. 'They pirates, mahn.'

'Pirates?' Lisa echoed.

'My God, that's the *Mollycoddle*,' Katya exclaimed, suddenly remembering Neil's presentation the night before.

'Sure. They *famous*,' said the black woman.

'You stay here,' said Katya to Lisa. 'I'm going out to take a look.'

'Shouldn't we wait for Jim?' Lisa asked.

'I'll be all right,' said Katya. 'The only thing I've got they might want to pirate can't be permanently removed.' She laughed nervously and then walked down the beach and after a long hesitation dived into the water.

As Lisa watched Katya's slow progress, the last black girl was having trouble pulling the dinghy into the water; Lisa helped her, and, the boat afloat, impulsively jumped in beside her.

Katya had swum past the boarding ladder to examine the yacht's stern – where its name would be – so that Lisa and the black girl arrived before her. When they boarded they were greeted by two white men, dressed neatly in blue Bermuda shorts and clean white sportshirts, and immediately offered a lit joint. The older of the two, a pale white man in his late thirties with side-burns and a baseball cap, paid special attention to Lisa. One of the two black girls still aboard was lounging topless on a cushioned chair in the huge open area aft smoking woozily. She seemed disoriented when the joint was passed to her. When Katya pulled herself up the ladder, her wet tee-shirt clinging to her breasts, the third man looked at her with frank interest.

'I say, you look better clothed than most women do naked,' he said to her. 'I'm Michael,' he added.

Katya shook her curly blond hair and with both hands squeezed the water out of most of its length.

'Hello,' she said coolly, looking carefully around the boat. 'We'd like some food.'

'Why certainly, darling. What would you like?'

Katya took the proffered joint as Lisa had done, and took a distracted puff. 'What have you got?' she asked.

'Over here,' said Michael.

'How old are you?' the older man wearing the baseball cap asked Lisa. He was short and thickset, with powerful forearms, and though Michael and the other man seemed to have English accents, this man was American.

370

'Fifteen,' said Lisa, feeling self-conscious under his frank appraisal of her figure.

'That's nice,' the man said. 'You been in the commune long?'

'No, I'm just visiting.'

'You'll love it,' he said, grinning. 'Everybody loves it.'

With Katya and the black girl on the other side of the boat looking into some cans and boxes there, Lisa became aware of a loud male grunting coming from the main cabin forward. A girl's suppressed little half-screams occasionally accompanied the grunting.

'Sounds like Robert must be selling the whole stock,' Lisa's admirer in the cap joked to her.

'I'd like as much of the fruit as you can spare,' said Katya. 'You can keep the fish.'

'Why certainly, darling,' Michael said. He was tall, slender and clean-shaven with hard blue eyes that glittered happily. 'How much fruit would you say we can spare, mate?' he asked his shorter friend.

'Quite a bit,' said the other.

'I think we might be able to part with all the rest, don't you think?' said Michael.

'Certainly.'

'Thank you,' said Katya. 'May I take the basket, too?'

'I think that might be arranged,' said Michael.

'Fine,' said Katya, abruptly lifting the straw basket of fruit and striding back towards the boarding ladder. 'Let's go, Lisa.'

Michael grabbed her arm in mid-stride, and as Katya spun sideways, a few oranges spilled forward into the cockpit floor. Katya remained half-crouched, holding the basket clutched to her chest staring at the fallen oranges, Michael still holding her arm.

'Payment, darling,' Michael said quietly. 'The matter of payment, don't you know?'

Katya slowly lowered the basket to the floor and then

371

straightened up. She looked slowly over at Lisa. Now the sounds of the woman's gasping screams, whether of pain or pleasure – Lisa, frightened, couldn't tell – came sharply from the cabin forward. In the silence of the confrontation between Katya and Michael the screams seemed horrendously loud and obscene.

'You've got to pay them,' the sullen black girl who'd accompanied them aboard said.

'It's only fair,' drowsily said the other black girl collapsed in the chair.

'Besides, darling,' the man named Michael said, seeming slightly to ease his grip on Katya, 'these are the last days, remember? Nothing matters. Take joy in all you do.'

'That's right,' said the sullen black girl gloomily.

'Of course,' said Katya, shaking her head as if clearing it. 'I'm new here and just didn't know.' She smiled at the man whose big hand still held her arm. And then she added in a voice so soft and husky and sexy it startled and frightened Lisa: 'How do you like it, Michael. You name it, I'm good at it.'

Lisa thought that even Michael looked surprised at the sudden sexual power Katya seemed to be turning on him.

'Don't forget me,' the other man said nervously.

Katya turned to the other man. 'I'll take care of you too,' she said huskily.

The woman's and man's noises from the cabin had ceased.

'But what about these other girls?' she added, still in her new husky voice. 'Don't they get some food, too?'

'Certainly,' said Michael. 'Help yourselves, girls. Take the dinghy ashore with your food. It's been lovely seeing you again.'

'Oh, no,' said the man in the baseball cap. 'I've got a little girl here who wants to pay too, right, honey?' he said to Lisa.

'Go, Lisa,' said Katya sharply.

The older man grabbed Lisa firmly by the arm. 'And miss the fun?' he said, smiling.

With a swiftness that caught everyone by surprise, Katya pulled a short mahogany boat hook from its fastener near the control panel shelf and whacked the older man a vicious blow on the side of his head, forcing him to release Lisa and stagger away.

'SWIM!' shouted Katya, turning to swing at Michael who, crouched, was approaching her.

Lisa took two steps to the yacht's coaming, and, glancing back to see Michael ducking under the boat hook, tackling Katya and sending her sprawling, and the third man with a drawn gun coming at her, she hopped over the coaming and into the water. As she surfaced and began swimming for shore she heard a man shout, then Katya scream.

Lisa slipped once as she staggered out of the water and, seeing two men getting into the dinghy to pursue her, broke into a run towards the shrubs. Even as she darted down the trail to cross the peninsula she wondered if she should turn back to try to help Katya. It was getting dark and she decided to get off the main trail and find a place to hide. She tripped once and fell, immediately springing up to run on. Seeing a small fire and a shack ahead of her she ran, whimpering now, for help.

When she emerged into the firelight an old black man who'd been sitting beside the fire leapt up.

'Git away!' he shouted. 'Go!'

Lisa stood frozen, trembling, almost unable to speak. 'I . . . I need help,' she finally blurted. 'Some men . . .'

'Go way!' the old man shouted, then turned to look at the shack ten feet away.

A young white man and woman were crawling out of the entrance, their eyes red and watery.

'Water,' the man called feebly. 'Please help us. Water . . .'

'Get back in there!' the old black man shouted and brandished a heavy stick at the two feeble crawlers. 'Back! – back . . .'

Lisa gasped as she suddenly realized that the two were sick, feverish. Glancing in terror back for any sight of her pursuers she ran on. She hadn't gone more than forty feet when she came upon the burnt-out remains of another shack, the white bones of three skeletons gleaming in the dim light of dusk.

Whimpering, she ran on, no longer aware of exactly what she was fleeing, only needing to run, to escape the horrors that seemed to explode into her life in an unending series. She had to get back to Jim, to *Scorpio*.

6

At dawn the next morning Jim reported to Neil that Katya and Lisa were missing. Earlier, after he and Oscar had finished re-anchoring *Scorpio* they had begun looking for the three women, but found only Janice. They traced Katya and Lisa to where the barter yacht had been moored and then . . . nothing. A sullen black girl told Jim that the men on the *Mollycoddle* had motored off with 'de sexy white girl' but that she thought the younger white girl must have escaped. Although Janice and Oscar had abandoned the search when it got dark and returned to *Scorpio*, Jim had kept looking another four hours, finally stealing a bicycle to ride the ten miles back to Charlotte-Amalie, and then having to swim out to *Vagabond*.

For Neil and Frank and Jeanne it was clear that now they *had* to raid the *Mollycoddle* and probably the estate too. Katya – if she were still alive – was either on the boat or out at the pirates' estate. Lisa had either shared Katya's fate or had escaped and was already back on *Scorpio* or making her way to *Vagabond*. Through binoculars they soon determined that *Mollycoddle* was moored at her berth at the docks, but that *Scorpio* hadn't yet returned.

Neil and Jim guessed that Oscar was too timid and inexperienced a sailor to try to sail the ten miles back to Charlotte-Amalie Harbour in the dark. Neil suspected that Lisa, fleeing, would try to find Jim and thus have first gone back to try to get out to *Scorpio*. He ordered Jim and Tony to go back to Salt Point, hopefully there to find Lisa. In any case they were to help sail *Scorpio* back to join *Vagabond* in Charlotte-Amalie. After Katya and Lisa were both safe – God willing – and additional food and weapons had been garnered from the raid, the two ships would set sail together to head for the southern hemisphere.

With Jeanne's upset at the disappearance of Lisa mostly assuaged by Jim and Tony's leaving to search for her, Neil next signalled the Wellingtons with the airhorn to begin final plans for trying to save Katya and Lisa and, yet again, themselves.

Eight hours later Jeanne walked slowly along the dock, having to hold a wide-brimmed straw hat on her head with one hand to prevent its being blown off by the wind. Ahead of her and to the left was the *Mollycoddle*, rocking in the rough seas being rolled in by the storm, its stern to her, the wind blowing it a few feet off the dock, its mooring lines taut. She was wearing a black bikini top and a blue denim skirt, the skirt necessary to hide the small automatic strapped to the inside of her right thigh; the brief bikini top was to increase the friendliness of *Mollycoddle*'s guardians. Neil's last stern-faced words to her after he'd helped her strap the gun to her thigh were: 'Don't let anyone feel you up.'

At this moment he was, Jeanne hoped, in *Vagabond*'s dinghy hidden six boats back. Philip was casually fishing from the dock a dozen yards behind her. Olly and Conrad Macklin, with binoculars, were seated in the park area 'admiring the boats' and 'watching the big waves'. Neil had asked Frank to remain aboard *Vagabond*, telling him that if Neil himself were killed, Frank had to be safe to take over leadership. He was to come in only after they'd succeeded.

As she neared the stern of the pirate yacht she saw no sign of life. Neil said they were certain there was at least one man aboard and Philip thought there were two, but whoever was aboard was below. Perhaps the hot wind from the distant hurricane had discouraged them. Or worse, perhaps Katya was there with them . . . and Lisa . . .

Timing things carefully she waited until she was exactly

opposite the open cockpit of the *Mollycoddle* and then released her hold on her hat. It went flying off towards the yacht, Jeanne uttering a little scream. The hat sailed into the cockpit as planned, but then bounced on a seat cushion and flew out the other side, no, hit a metal strut and dropped back into the cockpit. She stared at it wide-eyed. In theory a guard was supposed to come out, rescue the hat, enter into conversation and ask her aboard. Nothing happened.

Glancing up and down the dock and trying to look upset and pathetic, Jeanne next moved to the edge of the dock and contemplated either hailing the crew of the *Mollycoddle* or going aboard after her hat.

'Ahoy in there!' she said in as helplessly feminine a voice as she could muster, the rushing of the wind in the rigging of nearby sailboats effectively drowning her voice.

No one responded There was four feet of open water between the dock and the coaming of the *Mollycoddle*, an easy jump for Jeanne, if only the gun didn't bounce loose. Steadying herself on the dock, gauging her jump carefully, she leapt into the yacht's cockpit, letting herself fall forward with a crash on to her left side, screaming a good loud scream and lying there askew, moaning.

In a few seconds the cabin door opened and a large bare-chested man holding a pistol appeared, staring at her fiercely, then up at the dock and along it.

'What the hell are you doing here?' he asked with a distinctly American accent.

'My hat,' said Jeanne, grimacing in pretended pain but pulling down her skirt and adjusting her legs so that her gun wouldn't show. Then, sitting up, she gestured at the straw hat lying on the other side of the cockpit.

'And you jumped after it, huh?' the big man said, now grinning, his handlebar moustache flicking up at the ends.

Jeanne nodded, rubbing her left foot which she decided she had twisted. But not badly. She didn't want to be carried.

'Need some help?' he asked, stuffing his pistol in between

377

his belly and his shorts.

'No, no, I'm fine,' she said, holding up a hand to halt him. 'I'm just a little in shock, I guess.' She looked up at him and smiled wanly. He stared at her breasts.

'You want a drink or something?' he asked.

'Oh, no, I don't want to bother you,' Jeanne said, standing awkwardly. 'Although come to think of it a drink would be nice.'

'Hey, Mike, can the lady have a drink?' the big man asked, and Jeanne saw a tall, slender man with a neat beige sportshirt and shorts standing in the cabin door. He was eyeing her coldly. She smiled at him. He smiled back.

'Certainly, Bart,' he said. 'We wouldn't want her to leave in pain. She might sue us.'

Jeanne laughed prettily.

'Come in, darling.'

'Said the spider to the fly,' said Jeanne as she limped past Bart and Michael and into the luxurious main salon of the Hatteras. There was no one else there; no sign of either Katya's or Lisa's things.

'Wow, this is something,' Jeanne said as she stopped in the middle of the plush carpet and looked around, still half-hoping, half-fearing signs of Lisa's presence.

'What would you like to drink?' asked Michael. 'Please sit down.'

'Thank you,' said Jeanne, sitting in a leather chair and quickly crossing her legs. 'Gin and tonic?' she asked.

He laughed. 'How about some rum?' he asked.

'That's fine too.'

'Bart?'

'Sure, Mike,' said Bart and disappeared forward into the far part of the galley.

'I'm Michael Forester,' said Michael.

The last name so surprised Jeanne she couldn't decide who she was. 'I'm Jeannie Wilkins,' she said after an awkward hesitation.

378

'And what brings you tumbling into the *Mollycoddle*?'

'Stupidity, I guess. My hat blew on to your boat.'

'A likely story,' said Michael. 'Are you sure it wasn't because you noticed my handsome face in the street and followed me here out of uncontrollable lust?'

Jeanne smiled, again awkwardly. 'If I'd seen you before, I might have!' she managed, smiling more broadly.

'Are you often overcome with uncontrollable lust?'

Jeanne felt a bit overwhelmed. At the rate this conversation was going, Michael would have her in the sack before Neil had paddled halfway here.

'Only on hot, stifling days when there's no wind,' she answered.

'Ahh,' said Michael. 'What disappointing weather then, no?'

Bart entered with the drinks and handed one each to Michael and Jeanne and kept a bottle of beer for himself. He sat down on a second easy chair in the salon.

'Cheers,' said Michael.

'ANYONE ABOARD?' a loud voice came from the dock outside.

'See who it is, Bart?' said Michael, frowning.

Jeanne tensed. This was the proverbial it. She uncrossed her legs and straightened in her chair. She wished she'd practised drawing the gun. Bart arose, put his beer down, adjusted the gun in his belt, and walked up the two stairs into the cockpit and looked to his left.

'What is it?' she heard him say to Philip.

'You have a gaff I can borrow?'

'You seem nervous, Jeannie,' she heard Michael say and saw him staring at her with a suspicious frown. 'What's the matter?'

'That man's voice . . .' she said uncertainly.

'Yes? . . . What about it?'

The yacht lurched as if a sudden new weight had been added. Michael and Jeanne both saw Bart still standing in the

379

centre of the cockpit but now facing away from the door with his arms raised.

'Don't shoot, Buddy,' Bart said loudly.

Michael leapt up, rushed at Jeanne and past her to a drawer from which he drew out a pistol. He then crouched behind her chair facing the cabin entrance. Jeanne, frozen, was stunned by such a piece of bad luck: Michael had chosen the one place she couldn't draw her gun without his seeing her.

Neil and Philip appeared in the cockpit, Neil nudging Bart who, with arms raised and weaponless, was coming down into the cabin.

'He's got a gun on me, Mike,' Bart said when he saw Michael's pistol aimed at them from behind Jeanne.

'All right, lady,' said Neil. 'Go into the galley with your hands behind your head.'

'You move, lady,' hissed Michael, 'and I'll kill you.'

'Go ahead and kill her,' Neil said evenly. 'She's none of our business. MOVE, LADY!'

Slowly, Jeanne stood up and, appalled, terrified, walked slowly towards the galley area.

'What do you want?' Michael asked tensely.

'All we want . . .' began Neil.

'Don't turn around,' interrupted a voice from behind Neil and Philip. 'Throw your guns on the rug.'

Someone Jeanne couldn't see had come into the cockpit behind Philip and Neil and had a gun on them. Neil, after a brief hesitation, threw his gun on to the rug between Bart and Michael. Then, as Philip threw Bart's gun and his automatic into the same place, Jeanne reached down, lifted her skirt, and, hand trembling, pulled out the loaded .38 automatic. She remembered to press the safety as Neil had instructed and held the weapon in front of her, her lower body hidden by the galley bar that separated the main part of the galley from the salon.

Bart picked up the two guns and Michael stood up behind

the leather chair. A third man, black, pistol in hand, appeared in the cabin entrance behind Philip and Neil.

'Who in bloody hell are you two?' Michael hissed angrily, relieved at last from his fear. He thrust his gun violently into his belt and crossed to the couch to retrieve his barely touched glass of rum. He glared at Jeanne, not really seeing her. Neil didn't reply.

The black man, behind Neil and Jim, spoke: 'Okay, mahn, you get over against the wall opposite the galley,' he said. 'Bart, you search them.'

Neil and Philip walked slowly to the wall on the other side of the main salon. Michael, his back to Jeanne, watched. Bart dropped two guns on to the couch behind Michael and ambled over to Neil and Philip. The black man turned slightly away from her too to watch.

Jeanne froze. As soon as she spoke and showed her gun they'd turn and shoot her. Three to one. And later Neil. She was unable to raise her gun.

'They're clean,' Bart announced after his search.

Michael turned to Jeanne. 'Perhaps you had better check the lady, too,' he said.

Jeanne stared at him wide-eyed with fear. As Bart came towards her she reacted instinctively: she crouched and raised her gun to her eye level, aiming it directly at the new man whose pistol was still pointed at Neil.

'Drop it!' she snapped, so sharply it astonished her. Her eyes were wide, hysterical, only her head and the gun visible above the galley shelf to the three antagonists in the salon. Bart stopped and all of them watched her, each motionless and uncertain.

Then the black man swung his pistol at her and fired, and Jeanne pulled the trigger, the gun jumping in her hand, the two shots following one after another in less than half a second. Neil leapt on the man who had shot at her, ripping the gun from his hand, and Jeanne shifted her aim to Michael who still stood only eight feet away, his hand frozen on the

381

butt of his gun still in his belt. 'Don't shoot!' he screamed.

Neil next took Bart's weapon and stood behind him with two guns, one in each hand. The man who had shot at her had been hit and had fallen to a sitting position; he was clutching his shoulder and looking at Jeanne with both surprise and pain: as if she had committed a social *faux-pas* by shooting him. Philip began retrieving the weapons on the couch and rug.

Michael slowly turned to look at the wounded black man now slumping back against a chair, at the bewildered look of Bart, at pleased-looking Philip now holding a .45 aimed at Michael, and finally at Neil, who was smiling at him tensely.

Finally, slowly, Michael looked back at Jeanne. He stared at her with frank hatred. 'You bloody bitch,' he said quietly. 'Are the boobs fake too?'

'I'm afraid that information is classified,' Neil answered, coming up behind Michael to remove the gun from his belt.

'You'd better pray I never get a chance to find out for myself,' Michael said.

Jeanne, feeling at last safe, lowered her gun on to the countertop and leaned against the counter. The big war might be over, but the small wars seemed to be getting worse.

7

In planning their raids on the *Mollycoddle* and the estate Neil and Philip had known of a storm passing south of them but felt it could work to their advantage. Normally the easterly trade winds made it difficult to sail east from the Virgin Islands, but the counterclockwise winds of the storm would give them a southerly wind as it moved westward. What they had failed to consider was the unexpected size of the storm and the slowness with which it moved to the west. Because it was big and maintained a leisurely pace westward into the central Caribbean, the waves it was sending northward were huge, much larger than they had anticipated, as were the winds – thirty knots and gusting to forty-five.

Standing with Philip on the dock beside the captured Hatteras, which Olly, Macklin and Jeanne were busy ransacking for everything of value, Neil could feel doubt and fear blowing through him with the wind. Events were moving too fast, involving too many people, too many variables, too many unknowns to permit him to deal with all that had to be done. The wind and seas were rocking the boats at the dock, and Neil watched with increasing anxiety the size of the swells rolling into the supposedly protected harbour. The noise level from the beating of halyards and lines against masts, the whine of the wind in the rigging, and the slamming of waves against docks and boat hulls was unnerving. As they tried to discuss their plans Philip had almost to shout to make himself heard. 'I don't like this blow,' he shouted. 'I'm not sure we have the time to raid the estate before dark.'

For Neil the initial purpose of the raid – food and weapons – was no longer worth the risk. But there was the question of Katya and Lisa. Neither had been aboard the *Mollycoddle* and

Michael and the others wouldn't talk about who was at the estate.

'We need food,' Neil replied loudly to Philip. 'There's too damn little on *Mollycoddle*.' He was watching the waves rolling in at them, at times froth blowing off the tops in a horizontal saltwater rain. The Hatteras had already produced two automatic rifles, a small shotgun and four automatics, at least two pounds of marijuana, four bottles of rum, but only a small cache of food. Either Michael and his men bartered for food on a daily basis or their food supply was at the estate.

'I know,' said Philip, 'but this wind . . . I don't know. Is it worth it? There's the girl, of course.'

'The girl's worth it, Phil,' Neil answered grimly, feeling a disturbing lethargy and dread. 'And Lisa may be there too. I know we're going to have a helluva time getting out to sea in this, but . . . I *have* to go out there. If you want to . . .'

'No, no. If that's the case, let's get on with it.'

So they went ahead. Bart and the wounded black man were tied up in the forepeak of the Hatteras while Michael was to accompany the raiders to the estate. The plan was to use the *Mollycoddle* right up to the last minute to tow *Vagabond* up over her anchors to get her out of the harbour against the strong winds. *Scorpio*, too, would need a tow if she returned; she was already overdue. Neil only hoped that *Vagabond* didn't drag anchor before they got back out to her. It was already past four-thirty: only two and a half more hours of daylight.

They divided into groups. Frank and Olly were to barter some of *Mollycoddle*'s marijuana and surplus weapons and other 'useless' valuables for food while Neil's raiding party was at the estate. Sheila and Conrad Macklin would remain to guard *Mollycoddle* and continue to try to make radio contact with *Scorpio*, while awaiting her. Going the mile and a half to the pirate estate were only Neil, Philip and Jeanne with their hostage, Michael. They rode bicycles.

Neil felt frail and vulnerable on a bicycle, and the gusty

384

wind increased his feeling that events were moving too quickly, decisions made too hastily. He wondered how many officers had led their forces into battle riding bicycles. Although the three others had ten-speed bikes, Neil rode a cumbersome old one-speed, and had to labour to keep himself just behind his prisoner, Michael. Both of them were periodically blown several feet to one side by a gust of wind.

The estate was a large rambling summer house overlooking the water. It had a swimming pool on one side and a set of swings and slide on the other. Its only landscaping were a few low shrubs and flower beds. The grass was dry and brown from lack of water. In the driveway was an old Ford station-wagon with its hood up.

Michael was ordered to hold his unloaded pistol and pretend that he and Neil, who was armed with a fully-loaded automatic rifle, were guarding Philip and Jeanne, who preceded them up the gravel walk to the front door with their hands clasped behind their heads.

'What is this?' a little man with glasses asked after he'd opened the door, gun in hand, to Michael's knock and hail.

'Some new booty,' Michael answered sullenly.

Philip and Jeanne pushed their way in past the man. Michael, with a tense glare back at Neil, followed.

'I say, who are you?' the little man asked Neil.

'Michael's cousin,' Neil answered, smiling and holding the automatic rifle casually aimed at the little man's stomach. In the living-room were two couches, some handsome carved wooden chairs and a piano.

'Oh, really? Where'd you come from?'

When no one else appeared Neil saw Philip lower his hands, remove the revolver he had wrapped and tucked in as part of his belly, and move towards a doorway at the far end of the room. When the little man, bewildered, turned to watch, Neil struck him in the neck with a karate chop and dropped him to the floor.

Neil crouched back against the closed front door, watching

Philip approach the doorway at the far end of the room. Jeanne came up to him.

'My gun,' she said softly to Neil, and he remembered, and pulled the automatic out of his belt and handed it to her. At the far end of the room Philip disappeared through the doorway and there was a bang that made Neil swivel his gun to the right: the wind had blown a shutter loose and it had banged alongside a window there. As he watched, still tense and fighting off trembling, it banged again. Philip emerged from the far room.

'Kitchen,' he said. 'I'd say it's quite well-stocked.'

'Call your friends,' Neil said to Michael. 'Ask them to come down here.'

Michael glared at him without replying. Neil swung his rifle to point it at his stomach.

'Jeanne,' he said. 'Go into the kitchen and start getting the food into boxes and bags. Michael,' he went on. 'I'm waiting. Call your friends.'

Michael turned and walked slowly to the second doorway leading off the main room. As Neil followed he saw that it led off into a hallway that had a stairway leading to the second floor and a closed door leading somewhere on the ground floor. Michael stopped near the stairway and called: 'I say, Larry! Rick! Tolly!' he shouted. 'Come down and have a chat! It's me, Mike.'

A door opened upstairs. 'Welcome home, old buddy,' an American voice said. 'What brings you back so soon?'

'I brought you a lady, Rick. Tall. Dark long hair. I know how fond you are of long hair.'

'Be right down.'

'Ask who's around,' Neil whispered to Michael, the muzzle of his rifle against his back.

'I say, Rick, who's here today?' Michael yelled up the stairs. 'Is Tolly around?' A silence followed, then Rick's voice, puzzled: 'What d'ya mean, "Is Tolly around?" You know that Tolly . . .' The voice stopped and left only an ominous silence.

Neil raised the butt of the rifle and slammed it into Michael's head, sending him in a heap to the floor. Neil ran up the stairs two at a time and burst into the room from which the voice seemed to have come. Rick was standing at a bureau groping into the top drawer. 'NO! DON'T!' Rick yelled and dropped back into the drawer the gun he'd been after. Neil wheeled and backed himself against the wall inside the door.

'Who else is in the house?' he asked. Rick, a tall, thin young man with glasses, looked with nervous eyes first at Neil, then at the door.

'There's Arthur, I think, and Larry and the Pussycat . . .'

'Arthur's a little man?' Neil asked.

'Yes?'

'Where's Lar . . .'

Two shots rang out from downstairs. Neil ran to the door, then wheeled back on Rick who still stood frozen, but now with both arms stretched towards the ceiling.

'Don't shoot!' he said again fearfully.

Enraged at the delay Neil crossed quickly to Rick and drove his fist into his face, sending him crashing back against the bureau and down to the floor. He grabbed the pistol from the drawer and, carrying the automatic rifle in one hand like a handgun, rushed back to the head of the stairs. 'PHIL!' he shouted down.

There was no answer. Michael's legs were still visible at the foot of the stairs, his torso and head in the living-room. The silence brought forth from Neil a low moan of anguish. Two shots and silence: Philip must have been hit by some newcomer. He edged himself to the banister at the top of the stairs and peered down. Still no sound.

'You down there,' Neil shouted. 'I . . . I . . . I know you got Phil so I want to surrender. I never wanted to be part of this . . .' Neil wanted to get the man – Larry was it? – to talk, to focus his attention on Neil. Perhaps he didn't know Jeanne was in the kitchen. Oh, dear Lord please don't let him have shot Jeanne . . .

'Throw your gun down the stairs!' a deep male voice commanded from some place in the living-room.

Neil took out Rick's gun and tossed it down the stairs. It bounced twice and came to rest near Michael's feet. Neil noticed that the door to the other downstairs room opposite the living-room was now open. Come on, Jeanne, he's talking to me. Shoot the bastard.

'Now come down with your hands held high up over your head,' Larry commanded next.

At what point will I become visible to him? Neil wondered. He took a step down the stairs. Then another. Where are you, Jeanne? he wondered, prayed. A third step. Two more and my legs will be in sight. He won't shoot until he can hit my belly. A fourth step. No more. Something, pray it not be death, must be stopping Jeanne from shooting from the kitchen. He had to get Larry to move. He took a fifth step down, then leapt the last seven steps in two long strides, and threw himself into the room opposite the living-room, rolling away from the door opening. Two shots whizzed past him, pounding into the stairway wall.

Neil got to his knees, glanced quickly around the room and stopped, stunned. Katya was sitting on the bed only six feet away, naked. She looked at him with as much surprise as he guessed he must be looking back.

'Can you see anyone?' Neil whispered. She responded with a barely perceptible nod. 'Is Lisa here?' he asked next.

Katya shook her head and whispered, 'They never got her.'

Remembering the layout of the living-room Neil next asked, 'Is he behind the couch near the front door?' Again Katya gave a barely perceptible nod.

Positioning himself at the edge of the door opening, he adjusted the rifle in both hands, then reached around the corner and sprayed off a three-second blast towards where he remembered the couch to be. He heard a muffled scream, then the sound of movement.

'He went towards the kitchen,' Katya whispered.

Neil stood up, took two quick strides across the hallway to the entrance to the living-room and hesitated. As he started to peer into the room the bam-bam-bam of three quick shots blasted from the kitchen area. He ran into the living-room, rifle at the ready, and crouched behind one of the ornate wooden chairs. He saw two bodies on the far side of the room near the kitchen, one partially hidden behind the end of the second couch, only the bare legs visible. The first, he saw sickeningly, was Philip, and for a horrifying moment the bare legs of the second looked feminine. A movement at the kitchen door caught his eye and Jeanne stood there, her automatic at waist level, her eyes on the man she had apparently shot, blood spreading in a wide red splotch on the white cotton material at the shoulder of her blouse.

8

From the minute he and Olly began trying to barter for food Frank sensed that something was wrong. As they made their way from the docks the streets seemed strangely empty. The few people in the doorways of homes or bars or at street corners all seemed to be standing for the sole purpose of staring at Frank and Olly as if they were enemy agents. Black food vendors with whom they'd bartered half a dozen times were now either gone or refused even to talk to them. They entered the nearest bar to find out what was happening.

Even at five in the afternoon Bosso's was packed. People were standing two and three deep at the long bar running along one wall, and the dozen small tables along the other were all filled. Almost everyone was drinking either water or a special post-war punch spiked with rum. Imported alcohol had disappeared. Frank and Olly stood awkwardly in the crowded space between the bar and the tables. Everyone in the bar was white except at the far end where three black men stood, surrounded by a halo of conspicuous space. Many of the men in the bar kept glancing nervously at the entrance as if expecting an important but feared visitor.

Most who talked spoke in low voices or whispers, as if at a wake. There was no boisterousness or joy. The one loud drunk who made an effort at jollity sounded insane and soon lapsed into gloomy mumbling. Captain Olly wedged himself between customers to press against the bar.

'Say, fella,' he asked the nearest bartender, 'who died?'

The bartender, a big man with thick glasses and wearing a cowboy hat, came towards Olly with a frown. The subdued bar had hushed even more at Olly's loud outburst.

'What d'ya mean, "who died?"' the bartender sullenly asked Olly.

'The way I figure it,' Captain Olly replied, 'everyone's mother just got run over by a steamroller. Never been in such a dreary place. You got a law against talking in a normal voice?'

'You a stranger here?' the bartender countered. The two other bartenders, although still mixing drinks, were half-turned, listening.

'Hell, I've lived here for days,' Olly said. 'You fellas acting as if you'd just learned that your blind date was a Russian missile.'

'You want a drink?' the bartender asked.

'The price of drinks these days being what it is I think I'll make water last into my next incarnation.'

The bartender shrugged his big shoulders and moved away to another customer. Unabashed, Olly turned to the man to his left.

'What's bothering everybody, fella, huh?' he asked the tall, slender man who stood there. The man turned and looked coldly down at Olly. He shrugged.

'The blacks may be going to riot,' he said.

'I see. What's their gripe?'

'I wouldn't know,' the tall man said, looking away and lifting his almost empty glass to his lips.

'You don't seem much bothered,' said Olly.

'I'm leaving tomorrow morning,' the man said neutrally.

'Well, ain't that nice,' said Olly. 'Where you headed?'

The man placed a silver dollar on the bar and then brushed past Olly and left. Olly returned to Frank.

'You give it a try, Frank,' he said. 'I guess I ain't got the personality I once did.'

A big black man, with glittering white eyes and a sweat-covered face, abruptly stood before them. He was dressed in a neat brown suit totally inappropriate in the sweltering heat.

'You want to know why it's so gloomy in Bosso's today?' he asked, smiling, his gleaming eyes either stoned or mad.

'Yeah,' Frank said. 'We'd appreciate it,' and, glancing at Olly, followed the man over to the empty space near his friends. The other two men were dressed in the casual and unpretentious style more usual among Virgin Islanders, white and black.

'These people want to know what's going on,' the first man said, grinning absurdly at his two friends. 'I've promised to tell them.'

The other two blacks, subdued and sullen compared to the man who introduced himself as Mr Sutter, looked at him and then turned back to the bar and their drinks, which were water.

'Everyone's a little touchy these days,' Mr Sutter said.

'Why?' Frank asked.

'Well, you see,' said Mr Sutter, turning his glittering eyes on Frank, 'the obliteration of San Juan has had a certain depressing effect on everyone. We all thought we were safe here and then "boom" we find we're not. Five days ago the small cruise ship, *St Augustine*, loaded with almost a thousand passengers, most of them white, sailed away from the white enclave at Canneel Bay on St Johns. Tomorrow the *Norway* does the same.'

'Where are they going?' Frank asked.

'The *St Augustine* is going to Rio de Janeiro, and the *Norway*, ah, the beautiful *Norway*, is sailing to, ah, yes, South Africa.'

'Jesus,' said Frank.

'This mass exodus of whites to South Africa is having a certain alienating effect upon some of the blacks,' Mr Sutter went on, grinning as if telling a dirty story. 'Certain resentments seem to have arisen. A feeling, as you main-landers would put it, of being screwed.'

'Are most of the people in here planning to sail tomorrow on the *Norway*?' Frank asked.

'All but my two friends here,' Mr Sutter replied, gesturing at the two blacks next to them at the bar. 'They lack both gold and the belief that South Africa is Nigger heaven.'

'You're going?' asked Frank.

'You're goddamned right. Forced to choose between my identity as a live rich man or a dead black man, I've had no trouble in opting for the *Norway* and Capetown. The South Africans may not like the colour of my skin but they've always liked the colour of gold.'

A commotion at the entrance of the bar distracted Frank: the people nearest the door began to talk loudly and, as if a plug had been pulled at the door, everyone in the room began to be sucked towards the entrance.

'THEY'RE COMING!' someone shouted and several men produced guns. A man now stood a few feet away aiming a .38 at the three blacks still at the bar. Mr Sutter, sweating, grinned grotesquely.

'I assure you,' he said to the thickset white man with the gun. 'I am *not* part of the revolution.' The other two blacks were looking sullenly at the white but appeared unperturbed.

'I want you three to turn around,' the white man said, 'and lean against the bar with your arms outstretched. I'm going to check for your weapons.'

Captain Olly had left for the entrance, where the sound of gunshots could be heard, but Frank stood watching the confrontation.

'I'm sailing on the *Norway*,' Mr Sutter insisted, trying to establish his connection with the 'good guys'. 'And although it makes me gag, I must confess that essentially I'm on your side.' None of the three blacks had moved.

'I said turn around,' repeated the white man, looking nervous. 'And get your arms extended to the bar. NOW!' He poked his gun in Sutter's ribs and gave him a shove.

'My dear man,' Mr Sutter began, but even as he spoke, one of the other blacks had leapt forward and grabbed the gun arm of the white and began wrestling with him. The other leapt to help, while Frank stood tensely in surprise and indecision. Within three or four seconds the white man staggered back against Frank, and one of the blacks,

393

crouching, aimed the gun at them and backed towards the rear door of the bar. An explosive roar from the bar sent the man staggering backwards and falling in a heap to the floor, his shirt shredded. The other black fled. Frank turned to see one of the bartenders crouched behind the bar with a shotgun smoking. A distant explosion was heard from outside.

'FRANK! Let's go!' Olly shouted from the front entrance.

'Get out of here, Sutter,' the bartender with the shotgun said.

'Yes,' said Mr Sutter, and, tight-lipped and terrified, he darted out the back exit.

When Frank left the bar with Olly the bright afternoon sunlight blinded him and he could only see a few figures moving rapidly from left to right, towards the docks. The gunfire was from off to the left and from behind the buildings across the street. There was another loud explosion and the ground trembled under their feet. As his vision improved he saw smoke rise above the boutique across the street. As he and Olly turned right to hurry towards the docks Frank saw a huge brown tank rumbling down the street towards them, a handful of soldiers running crouched alongside and behind it.

He and Olly scurried along the sidewalk watching the big tank and the half-dozen soldiers – mostly black, Frank noted in surprise – chug past them in the direction of what Frank thought were the black rioters. A small Datsun heading towards the docks with a cracked windshield careened up on the kerb near them to avoid the soldiers and tank; the white driver, bleeding from a head-wound, looked terror-stricken.

At the end of the first street, still a block from the docks and the marina where *Mollycoddle* was tied, a cluster of white civilians were crouched behind two overturned empty vegetable carts looking up the street where the tank had now stopped and from whence the shots were coming. Most of the men had either a rifle or handgun.

Another explosion rocked the pavement and Frank turned to see that the tank had turned around and its smoking cannon was now aimed down the street at them. Half the soldiers had disappeared, but the others were visible crouched behind parked cars; two were firing at the whites.

'The bastards are firing at *us*!' someone shouted.

'Let's go!' another yelled and two of them began running towards the docks, soon followed by the other four.

A piece of sidewalk popped up in front of Frank as he and Olly followed. It took him two strides to realize that it was a bullet.

They were all running now and within a minute had arrived at the dock area where cars were being overturned as barricades, while a few soldiers – here mostly white – looking bewildered, made half-hearted efforts to direct the flow of people. Along the three blocks of waterfront Frank could see only a single additional tank; it sat with its cannon aimed incongruously and ominously out to sea.

At the marina where *Mollycoddle* was kept were dozens of men, women and children and mounds of luggage. Most were gathered near the small boat dock, trying to get out to the *Norway*, still at anchor a half-mile out in the harbour. There was no crowd around *Mollycoddle*, and as he approached, Frank saw why: Macklin and Sheila stood aboard facing the dock each with an automatic rifle held at the hip and aimed at the dock. Although Sheila looked as if she could probably handle her gun, Macklin looked as if he *wanted* to use his, and his grim look alone would discourage most people.

The ground in the marina parking lot abruptly exploded less than fifty yards away, sending people running in all directions and leaving four or five men sprawled on the ground. When Frank turned back he saw that rafted seaward to *Mollycoddle* was *Scorpio*, so low in the water compared to the Hatteras he hadn't seen her at first. With a surge of joy he saw Jim and Lisa emerge from the main cabin with empty boxes for transferring *Mollycoddle*'s food to *Scorpio*. Jim waved and shouted: 'We found Lisa on *Scorpio*.'

'For Christ's sake don't stand there!' Macklin shouted. 'Get aboard! We've got to get away!'

'Where's Jeanne and Neil?' Frank asked, boarding *Mollycoddle* behind Olly.

'They're not back,' Macklin shouted. 'They'll never get back through this. Get us out of here.'

Frank looked at Sheila who, pale, looked back at him questioningly. Glancing at his watch Frank realized that Neil and Philip were already half an hour overdue.

Oscar ran up to Frank from *Scorpio*. 'Pull us out of here,' he said, his small eyes wider than normal. 'They'll sink us!'

'Tony!' Macklin shouted.

The glass in *Mollycoddle*'s main windshield ten feet away shattered in three neat holes; Macklin crouched and Oscar threw himself to the floor. Frank, standing numbly, now realized there was gunfire all around them.

Tony sprang from *Scorpio* and in a crouching run joined Macklin huddled behind *Mollycoddle*'s combing.

'Get us out of here!' Macklin shouted at him.

Tony crawled over to the controls and, glancing fearfully around, finally stood up and turned on the engine.

'Get the dock lines!' Macklin shouted at Frank and Oscar.

Another explosion boomed behind them and Frank turned to see the dock one channel away burst into fragments and a body go flying off and into the water. Sheila clutched his arm. 'We can still wait,' she said. 'We can't desert them.'

'GET THE GODDAMN DOCK LINES!' Macklin shrieked at Frank and Oscar.

Jim appeared beside Frank, slightly hunched over. 'We're not leaving yet, are we?' he asked. The smoke from the recent explosions, although it was blowing away from them, prevented them from seeing much of what was happening in the streets. Along the docks people were running, crouching, stampeding on to boats to get out to the *Norway*, occasionally shooting with seeming randomness back into the smoke.

'No . . . no, we're not,' Frank said in a low voice.

Macklin, wild-eyed, suddenly jumped and ran forward along *Mollycoddle*'s side and, with a knife, slashed the forward dockline. With the wind blowing the yacht against the dock, *Mollycoddle* remained where she was but when the two aft lines were cut, Tony would be able to motor off. As Frank, Sheila and Jim watched, Macklin next ran aft and cut the two other docklines.

'GO! Tony,' he shouted.

But Frank and Jim both came alive at once, going to the wheel where Tony crouched.

'Not yet,' said Frank.

Tony stared back at him, his usually placid face filled with fear, then looked to Macklin for support.

'Get out of the way, Frank,' Macklin said, loudly, but with the calm coldness he usually manifested. 'I'm saving our lives. Get us out of here, Tony.' Macklin's automatic rifle was aimed directly at Frank and Jim. 'If you're so hot to be with Neil and Jeanne and Philip, get off the boat. You too, Sheila.'

Sheila, still holding her automatic rifle – aimed vaguely shoreward – looked at Frank, then Macklin and finally back to the dock area. 'Oh, my God,' she said.

When Frank let his eyes follow hers he saw emerging through the smoke in the parking lot, one pulling a garden cart, the other pushing a wheelbarrow, Neil and Katya.

9

Escaping from the estate had been a nightmare. Philip had been shot twice, one bullet passing relatively harmlessly through the fleshy part of his side and the second into his back just to the right of the fifth vertebra without exiting.

Jeanne had taken a bullet into and through her shoulder but, amazingly, after they had staunched the flow of blood, worked with one arm to help transport food with Katya, dressed again in her shorts and tee-shirt. When the car wouldn't start, Neil found in the garage a wheelbarrow and a large garden cart. He carried Philip outside and placed him in the two-wheeled cart. Jeanne and Katya brought out boxes, cartons and plastic bags of food and put them gently around the wounded Philip. They put the heavier foodstuffs in the wheelbarrow. With Neil towing the garden cart like a dray horse and Katya pushing the wheelbarrow, they fled. Jeanne, insisting that she was still strong enough, bicycled one-armed on ahead.

On the strangely deserted road into town, an old black couple they passed looked enviously at the food and seemed to conclude that Philip was a rich man being carried by an employee.

As they entered the outskirts of the city they began to hear gunfire but the streets were still mostly deserted, only an occasional bicycle or motorcycle racing away from the violence. When they came within a few hundred yards of the docks the smoke blowing about from the explosions both masked their progress and made it difficult. Jeanne's wound finally had her close to collapse and Neil carried her on his back the last hundred feet.

When he arrived coughing, sweat-soaked, exhausted, but untouched by shell or fragment, he was disoriented, unaware of the conflict aboard *Mollycoddle*. Frank and Jim took Jeanne as she slid semi-conscious from Neil's back, assuring her that Lisa had been found safe on *Scorpio*. Sheila and Tony carried Philip aboard; others brought the food. Five minutes later they motored *Mollycoddle* away from the docks, *Scorpio* first rafted to her side then in tow. Olly, Jim and Lisa were aboard *Scorpio* to help Oscar.

Events were now out of control. *Mollycoddle* plunged and ploughed out against the wind and waves, which careened towards them as if pushed by white demons. Spray exploded aft against the windows, cutting visibility. Philip and Jeanne were placed on the long settee behind *Mollycoddle*'s lower steering control centre and Macklin was trying to examine their wounds. Fifty yards away water burst high in the air making Neil fear waves were smashing against some wreck or uncharted rock – until he realized it was an explosion. A quarter mile off to port the gigantic white *Norway* lay placidly at anchor, surrounded by a dozen small boats all scrambling to get to her side to unload passengers. *Norway*'s wide boarding ladder was packed with people shoving their way upwards. Water spouts burst in the sea around her. When Neil looked back the hundred yards to the dock they'd just left he saw an explosion rock the ship that had been moored behind them, sending its mast toppling over into the sea.

They motored out against the swells to the mouth of the harbour and there cut *Scorpio* loose to sail off to Anguilla, where they hoped to rendezvous the next day. Tony warned Neil that *Mollycoddle*'s fuel gauge registered 'empty', but it seemed trivial. As they continued on back to pick up *Vagabond*, the *Norway*, now ahead of them, gave four blasts of its horn and began hauling anchor. A fire was burning on the aft deck, smoke moiling horizontally shoreward on the fierce wind.

Vagabond, lying to two anchors veed out at about sixty

degrees from her bow, tore and plunged like a maddened horse at her tether. As everyone began unloading the new food and transferring the wounded to *Vagabond* Neil felt unrealistically weary, worried about Jeanne's wound, and burdened with the same nagging sense of foreboding that had been with him since their taking the *Mollycoddle*. The seas were building too high; the sun would be gone in half an hour. Four blasts from the *Norway*'s horn sent a chill through him.

'We can't get either of the anchors up,' Frank, gasping for breath, reported to Neil. Although Tony was motoring *Mollycoddle*, the wind was apparently too strong to let him move the boats where he wanted them to go.

'Cut one,' said Neil. 'Cut it now and let's not waste time. If Tony can't pull the other out cut it too if you have to.'

As Frank returned forward to work with Katya again on the anchors, Sheila brought the clean towels and medicine box Macklin had asked for. Then she went to bring boiled water. As Neil bent down beside Philip where he lay on the wheelhouse cushion aboard *Vagabond*, he was surprised that Philip was still conscious.

'Sorry to impose on you like this,' Philip said to Neil as Macklin squinted and daubed at the wound in his back.

'There *are* risks to piracy, my boy,' Neil said, searching the medicine box for more gauze. Philip managed to grin. *Vagabond* lurched forward as *Mollycoddle* accelerated. Frank shouted. Sheila, at the helm of *Vagabond*, shouted back. The halyards banged faster against the masts. A wave smacked into the starboard hull making the trimaran lurch sideways.

'Tell Frank to get the main triple-reefed and ready to go up,' Neil said to Sheila, standing again.

'I think Frank's done it,' Sheila replied.

'The storm jib?'

'It's hanked on.'

'Where's Olly?'

'You sent him with Jim.'

'Oh, yes,' said Neil, feeling confused. 'Who's helping Frank forward with the anchors?'

'Katya,' Sheila answered.

'Jesus,' said Neil. 'Are the anchors up yet?' Although he could see Frank struggling on the foredeck he couldn't tell what had been done.

'They're pulling one aboard now,' Sheila replied. 'I'm certain they had to cut the other.

'Hand me a towel,' Macklin said to Neil.

While *Mollycoddle*, which let *Vagabond* drop back to be towed behind her, plunged ahead, Macklin finished cleaning the two wounds, telling Neil he couldn't say how seriously Philip had been torn up inside, but with *Vagabond* bucking and rolling, they agreed it was useless to poke around to see. Neil realized for the first time that leaving land might mean dooming Philip, yet neither Philip nor Sheila had suggested they stay to seek a doctor. And now they were committed to sea: ashore were Michael and his men awaiting them.

When he stood up again and peered forward into the wind and spray and saw the size of the waves as they made their way towards the open sea, Neil again felt fear. At any moment a tow-line might snap, an anchor drag, an engine fail, someone fall overboard. As the *Mollycoddle* careened and crashed forward, pulling *Vagabond* out to sea, he watched the *Norway* moving seaward off to their left, her anchor still being hauled, smoke still billowing out aft. Her decks were packed. When Macklin finished checking Jeanne, Neil then carried her down to her cabin and placed her on her berth. She was unconscious. As he was tying both her and Skip into the berth so that they couldn't roll out, he felt a strange new motion and a new sound which at first he couldn't place. As he hurried back up on deck he suddenly knew: *the engine had stopped. Mollycoddle* had run out of fuel.

'GET ABOARD!' Neil shouted to Tony as *Mollycoddle* drifted rapidly back towards *Vagabond*. 'FRANK, GET READY TO CUT THE TOWLINE!'

Neil himself ran towards the mast, stumbling when

Mollycoddle crashed into *Vagabond*, then arising to loose the halyard and begin hauling up the already triple-reefed mainsail. He dimly worried that no one had been assigned to *Vagabond*'s wheel, but someone . . . The triple-reefed main, flogging loudly, went up and he winched it up tight, tied it down and began raising the storm jib. With a loud twang the tow line flew past his leg and *Vagabond* lurched away from the now more slowly drifting *Mollycoddle*. Neil quickly tied down the jib halyard and raced aft.

Sheila was at the wheel, but as he approached, she left it to help Katya sheet in the storm jib which was loose and flogging. They were drifting off on a starboard tack, seeming to be pushed almost sideways downwind. *The daggerboard was up*.

'DAGGERBOARD!' he shouted forward to Frank, pointing.

Frank nodded and staggered to the place just aft of the mast to begin forcing down the twelve-foot-long central dagger-board, five feet of which should be under the boat cutting down leeway. In the two minutes it took to get it down – Macklin had gone forward to lend his strength – *Vagabond* had ploughed and plunged forward, sliding sideways too, towards Smith Point on the left side of the harbour. Land there was less than a quarter of a mile away. The docks behind them were about three-quarters of a mile off. With the daggerboard finally down the ship gained speed and began to point better up into the wind.

'Will she come about in this?' Sheila asked him.

'She'd better,' Neil said, knowing their lives depended on it. 'We'll make it,' he added. 'PREPARE TO COME ABOUT!' he shouted to his crew. Frank was already at the port jib sheet and winch, Katya and Tony ready to release the jib in the opposite cockpit.

'DON'T RELEASE THE JIB TILL I YELL!' Neil shouted.

'You're backwinding the jib?' Sheila asked.

'Yes. COMING ABOUT!' he shouted and swung the wheel full right, *Vagabond* labouring slowly up into the wind, the five-foot seas smashing into her three hulls with loud cracks, spray flying aft into the faces of those in the cockpits handling the sheets.

Squinting forward through the streaming and holed plexiglas windows of the former wheelhouse Neil could barely see the jib in the gathering dusk. *Vagabond* now plunged, rocked and shuddered dead into the wind, both sails snapping as they luffed. The jib, still held close-hauled for the starboard tack, was now beginning to be backwinded, pushing the bow further around on to the desired new tack. *Vagabond* swung right with increasing momentum, Katya releasing the jib the instant Neil gave the command, Frank winching it in on the other side.

With two more tacks they were out of the harbour and heading east a half-mile from the south coast of St Thomas.

Yet Neil had no sense of freedom. The waves outside the harbour were immense; huge, grey, ugly, spume-covered swells, barrelling in at their starboard side, sending them sliding down each one only to be hit broadside by the next with a sickening crash. Philip lay moaning now on the floor of the wheelhouse where he had rolled off when the first angry swell had smacked them into a forty-five degree tilt. Frank had vomited on to the control panel shelf; Macklin had staggered below, useless with nausea. With Sheila tending to her husband, only Neil, Frank, Tony and Katya remained in the central cockpit in the darkness.

It was dark. During their last tack the night had fallen with the swiftness of the tropics and Neil had only his compass to steer by. The sky was totally overcast. There were no navigational aids along the south coast. Only rocks. A breaking wave rolled into *Vagabond* with a shattering crash, sounding as if a hand grenade had exploded against her right side.

'She can't take this,' Frank said to Neil from beside him.

Not hearing, Neil stared at him.

'*VAGABOND* CAN'T TAKE THIS BEATING!' Frank then shouted at him.

Maybe she couldn't, but what the hell choice did they have, Neil thought. To run before the seas meant running into the rocks of St Thomas. Then he thought of the daggerboard.

'BRING THE DAGGERBOARD HALFWAY UP!' Neil shouted to Tony. 'We'll let her slide some,' he explained to Frank. Frank nodded, as Tony snapped on a safety harness and left to crawl forward. Even in the darkness Neil could get some sense of each wave as it approached and he watched carefully as Tony snapped his safety line to a lower shroud and began crawling on his hands and knees across the main cabin roof to get to the daggerboard. Once there he began trying to winch the board up but needed someone to tail the line.

'Give him a hand!' Neil shouted instinctively and Katya left to crawl up on to the foredeck and across it towards Tony. Even as she did so Neil became aware of an unusually large wave bearing down on them, breaking on top.

'HOLD ON!' he yelled and tried to turn *Vagabond* away to take the shock more aft but it was too late. The wave struck *Vagabond* broadside with an explosive crack, a river of water two feet deep swirling across the main cabin top burying Tony and Katya, water crashing into the starboard cockpit, someone screaming. *Vagabond* was jolted left by the blow, wallowing, then sailed on.

Neil could feel water swirling around his feet, felt Frank's arms around him, saw Tony, saved by his safety line, clutching a shroud on the port side of the boat, beginning to crawl again towards the daggerboard: like some persistent insect momentarily pushed away by the intruding finger of some mammoth God. Sheila came up beside him, she too clutching at him for balance. 'WHERE'S KATYA?' she shouted.

Neil searched the port side of the boat hoping to see her clinging to a shroud there, but she was gone. The next wave

404

was large but *Vagabond* appeared to slide away, letting it roll under her, the wave only giving her a playful slap. As the trimaran surged forward Neil turned the wheel to bring *Vagabond* up into the wind to halt her, but she turned sluggishly, unresponsive to the helm.

'No, Neil!' Frank shouted. 'It's no use!'

Even as Neil had swung the wheel his mind told him there was nothing he could do. In the darkness, with Katya having no light, with *Vagabond* not equipped with a marking buoy with light or transmitter, there was no point in trying to find her. Even if she could swim until daylight, there was still no chance they could beat their way back and locate her in the wind and seas still running. He mechanically turned *Vagabond* back on course.

Tony had staggered back to him at the helm. 'Katya went over!' he shouted. 'She's back there!' he added, pointing.

Shaken, Neil looked at him, nodded and held the helm steady.

'We can't help her,' Frank said hoarsely from beside Neil.

'Aren't you coming about?' Tony asked them, still gasping for breath. 'She's a good swimmer. We've got a searchlight.'

'We can't do it, Tony,' Neil said staring forward, aware of an ache in his throat.

'We'd probably kill everyone if we stopped now,' Frank added. 'We've got to get past the point.'

'But we've got to try!' Tony said fiercely.

'She's lost,' Frank said, putting one of his huge, bony hands on Tony's shoulder. 'Katya's gone and there isn't a chance in a trillion we could find her. We've got to sail on.'

Tony, stunned, aware of how close he himself had been to being lost like her, looked briefly at the huge seas rolling at them and then back at where Katya had disappeared and emitted a low harsh groan. He turned back and lowered his head.

'It was my fault,' Neil said, shaking his head, still looking forward, feeling grief and anger. 'I should have gone forward myself. I should never have sent anyone without a safety harness.'

'A stanchion broke off,' Frank said as if in defence of Neil.

'The sea will always break a stanchion if you give it a chance,' Neil replied. 'Never, never, never let her go . . .' he muttered.

For another minute they all stood in the darkness staring forward.

'She's gone,' Tony said softly, flatly.

'I'm sorry, Tony,' said Neil, tears finally falling down his cheek. And then his grief was dampened by sudden fear: *Vagabond's* easier motion meant – that cracking noise when the wave hit –

'The daggerboard's gone,' Neil said harshly, the anger at the forces overwhelming them again mingled with grief. Tony then told them that he hadn't made any progress when the wave hit – the twelve-foot daggerboard must have broken off flush with the bottom of the boat.

'The ocean's way of correcting a captain's error,' Neil added bitterly.

'Will we still clear the end of the island?' Sheila asked.

A minor, casual, life-or-death question. And if we cleared St Thomas there was still St John's and Flanagan Island to clear.

'I doubt it,' said Neil. 'Which anchor did you save?'

'The CQR,' Frank answered.

It would never hold. It didn't matter. Three anchors wouldn't hold in this. And the coast of the islands he was trying to clear he couldn't even see, wouldn't see even at the moment *Vagabond* first began smashing herself to pieces.

'We may not clear the end of the island,' he said, talking as much to himself as to the others, trying to clear his own mind. It was a no-win situation. If you tried sailing more into the wind you'd slow down and make three times as much leeway. If you continued on this reach your course was so close to the end of the island that the waves would still put you up on the rocks. And though they might clear the rest of St Thomas, sticking out further south was Dog Rocks. Dog Rocks: what a place to die.

'I'll shift the battery over so we can use the depthmeter,' Frank said gently to Neil and disappeared below.

'Can you reef the mizzen?' Sheila asked.

'Yes. Why?' asked Neil.

'If we have to . . . to try to tack offshore, the mizzen could help us come about.'

Come about! In this! With no daggerboard! Neil felt like crying.

'I don't think I could even get *Vagabond* in irons, much less bring her about,' he said quietly.

'Then it's in the hands of the Gods,' said Sheila softly.

'He's sure as hell a better sailor than I am,' Neil commented bitterly, thinking again of Katya.

And so they sailed on. Using the depthmeter and a chart of the waters that Sheila had brought over to *Vagabond* with the gear from *Doubloon*, Neil made a guess at when they had cleared the end of St Thomas and what their course needed to be to clear Dog Rocks. He sent Tony forward to listen for the surf breaking ahead. Frank brought up the ship's twelve-volt spotlight to search ahead occasionally too. Neil turned the wheel over to Sheila so that he could concentrate all his weary and spent resources on determining *Vagabond*'s probable speed, leeway and direction, plotting her movements on Sheila's chart and ordering the minor course changes that might let them make a little more progress to windward.

And in the blackness of that night, with the sounds of waves crashing against rocks or reef less than a hundred yards away three times terrifying them into preparations for disaster, they somehow sailed through. At one point with Sheila wielding the spotlight they saw surf shattering itself against a reef less than forty feet to their left. At another point *Vagabond* struck something, probably – since their depthmeter was registering

407

eight feet of water – a little shaft of coral, but she sailed on.

By midnight the storm wind, as Philip and Neil had expected so long ago in their initial planning, moved around to the southwest and the seas and wind began to fall. Having sailed free of the last of the little cays and reefs, they were able to sail easily due east. It was just possible, thought Neil, after he had finished checking Jeanne and Philip again and come up and seen how quickly the waves were diminishing, that they might survive this night after all. They would live to suffer some more.

Part Five
SPIRIT

1

The war – the holocaust war, the war of missiles, bombers, submarines, lasers, satellites and all the sophisticated technology of modern military science – this war between the United States with its western and oriental allies and the Soviet Union with her allies, was, by most measurements, over. No more missiles were being fired; nuclear explosions had ceased. Although death still came out of the sky it fell now gently, subtly, like a soft rain. Although people still died, they no longer disappeared in a flash of light or exploded into fragments like a smashed pumpkin, but died in more natural animal ways: of starvation, of typhoid, of cholera, of dysentery, of fever, of pneumonia, of weariness and of grief. Although no winner had been declared or loser surrendered, the big war was over. Another had begun.

The new war, in that tradition as old as humanity itself, found the former enemies fighting now on the same side against new enemies. The new war was between the devastated nations of the northern hemisphere and the starving but relatively undamaged nations of the southern hemisphere. Those who had survived the first war, finding themselves often with radioactive food and undrinkable water, with diseases known and unknown afflicting them and medical care scarce or absent, fled to those places that they supposed to be safer. The southern nations and peoples were first appalled by the invasion of survivors, then frightened by it, and finally angered by it. If the white nations of the north had blown up the world, let them not try to escape the consequences by fleeing to the south. Thus the new war had begun.

It actually had been going on since the first week of the old war. Venezuela's Navy had forcibly prevented US Naval ships from refuelling in their ports. A sea battle had been fought. Tactical nuclear bombs had been dropped. In miniature, such battles had been repeated throughout the world ever since. American and Russian ships and planes, low on fuel, their home bases destroyed, sought refuge in neutral countries to the south. At first their ships or planes were impounded, their crews quarantined or imprisoned. Later, beginning in the second month of the war, they were sunk or shot down, any survivors killed on the spot. As the warring nations slowly ceased to be nations, so too their armies, navies and air forces slowly ceased to be armies, navies and air forces. Individual units, a plane, a squadron, a company, a tank unit, decided to become a nation unto itself and acted to survive. Often this entailed moving forcibly from a dangerous area to a safe area, and the nations and peoples in the safe areas began to organize themselves to resist these forcible mini-invasions. By the end of the war – and it was over in less than a month – *any* unidentified or foreign ship, plane or person was considered an enemy to be eliminated. When the unknown deadly epidemic disease which became known as either 'the plague' or as 'Nevada X' began to decimate populations as it spread from the American west down through Mexico to Central America, and, in long deadly bursts, to other countries around the world, foreigners, especially Americans, became triply feared, resented, and resisted. To protect themselves, most of the southern nations simply shut down all commercial air and ship traffic with the northern hemisphere. In effect they tried to build a wall and order the war and those who survived it not to enter.

From the point of view of nations like Brazil, all unidentified people, planes and ships, of whatever size or ostensible threat, were, if approaching their territory, considered the deadliest of enemies and treated as such. Untouched by violence, with only a tiny proportion of arriving refugees in relation to their own population or in relation to the masses of refugees flooding elsewhere, Brazil had the healthiest major economy left on earth. It was a shambles. Since those nations to whom they had traditionally exported their coffee, sugar, soybeans, and other goods now lay in ruins, they found themselves without markets for most of their major products. With international trade and travel ended, many stores and jobs ceased to exist. Unemployment had tripled within two weeks of the beginning of the war; it doubled again over the next two months. Without imports, adequate food supplies disappeared. Scarcity, hunger and related diseases became more general each week. Drastic rationing of fuel further curtailed economic activity. Brazil's modern economy ground to a halt. With half the population unemployed food lines and food riots became the norm.

The rich retreated to their luxury homes and apartments and tried to hold the police and military forces in line. In the West Indies and Central America the desperate and starving masses rose up and forcibly took from those who still had something all that they had. Slow starvation and susceptibility to disease thus became shared and universal there. In the countries of South America, where food was still more available and disease less out of control, the rich were able to hold on, while the great masses of people, unemployed and barely fed, became more and more weakened, more and more desperate.

And so, in effect, a third war was beginning: a war again as old as humanity, but exacerbated by the gross overpopulation of the planet by the late twentieth century: the war between those who had enough to eat and those who did not. The number of people who didn't have enough grew greater each day; their need greater; their strength less. The governments of South America held on: shooting all who resisted, shooting all

413

who tried to enter from foreign countries, shooting all who questioned the siege mentality that they hoped would sustain them.

And thus throughout the world the war refugees fought a usually losing battle for survival. Their enemies were legion: radioactive fallout, starvation, polluted water, dysentery, typhoid, cholera, hepatitis, 'Nevada X', the guns and desperation of their fellow survivors, the guns and desperation of their own armies and navies, the guns and ships and planes of the safe countries to which they tried to flee. The war was over. They didn't notice.

2

The 'fleet' of *Vagabond* and *Scorpio* was reunited off the nothern coast of Anguilla late in the afternoon of the day following their flight from St Thomas. Olly and Jim had brought *Scorpio* through the wild, bone-jarring hundred-mile passage despite blowing out two sails, developing frightening leaks that had them pumping almost continuously, and having Gregg's arm broken.

With the wind and seas much diminished and their boats anchored off the lee shore of Anguilla, those on *Vagabond* and *Scorpio* transported supplies, adjusted ship's crews, established radio frequencies and hours of transmission, determined signalling procedures and defence strategies in case of attack, and set their course and rendezvous points if unexpectedly lost to each other. But even as they took heart from their safe passage Lisa reported to Neil something which Katya had mentioned briefly as they were fleeing the pirate estate: Lisa and Katya had apparently smoked a joint with a plague victim aboard the *Mollycoddle.* In Katya's brief, emotional recounting of her capture and imprisonment, she had warned Neil tearfully that a black girl aboard the *Mollycoddle* had been thrown overboard when Michael had realized how feverish she was. Katya had hysterically volunteered to Neil not to sail with them, but in his obsession with getting back to *Mollycoddle* and out to sea, Neil had barely understood. If he had, he still would have brought her.

When Neil informed everyone on both ships and gave orders to use always the same personal cup for drinking and plate and utensils for eating, Oscar and his shipmates insisted that Jim and Lisa be transferred back to *Vagabond.* This was done, with neither one to be involved with food preparation or galley clean-up. Jim joked that it was the best excuse for getting out of doing the dishes he'd ever had. Neil also suggested that mouth to mouth contact should be avoided. If the disease didn't appear in a week or ten days they could assume they were safe and relax some of the stringency of the regime – 'Perhaps permit the holding of hands.' If there was no sign of the disease after a further ten days they could 'have an orgy'. But despite Neil's efforts to lighten the orders, their effect was to make everyone realize that they might be carrying on board the very thing they were at sea to escape.

While anchored off Anguilla Neil sent Jim and Sheila ashore to try to locate the nearest doctor. They returned ten hours later with the depressing information that there were no longer any doctors left on the whole island. They had all fled. Starvation was almost universal. Actually there was one old doctor they'd located in a small fishing village, but he was feeble and indicated he couldn't cope with a bullet wound in the stomach.

Philip, who had been placed on the dinette settee in the main cabin where the pitching and rolling of *Vagabond* would be least felt during their topsy-turvy passage in the storm, had developed a fever. Macklin indicated that an infection had begun in the abdomen. He had started Philip on an antibiotic, was giving him codeine for the pain, and was feeding him only liquids. Philip was urinating normally but had had no bowel movement since being shot. There was still no evidence of internal haemorrhaging. His fever varied between 102 and 103 degrees. Most of his pain was in the back where the bullet had shattered a rib. Jeanne's wound showed no signs of infection and she insisted on being up and about, her left arm in a sling.

Since their southeasterly course towards the eastern tip of Brazil at the mouth of the Amazon would leave them never more than a one-day sail downwind to land, Sheila advised Neil to go ahead with his proposed course and they would see if Philip improved. They both knew that medical skill on most of the islands was probably limited. The further south they got the more likely they'd be to find competent doctors.

Neil made no effort to hide how long and difficult a passage they would have simply to get south to the equator, much less to find a home somewhere along the coast of Brazil or on Ascension or St Helena Islands if that became the decision. By their third day at sea, Oscar and Tony were complaining of the plan. To reach the equator was a voyage of almost two thousand miles, much of which would be against the prevailing winds and along an inhospitable coast. If *Scorpio*'s leaking couldn't be greatly reduced they might not be able to continue as a fleet. Although the leaking was reduced from what it was during the initial stormy passage from the Virgins, it still took five to ten minutes an hour of pumping to clear the bilge. Oscar and Tony were arguing that Barbados might make a possible haven but Neil, happy that the northeasterly wind was letting them head directly southeast towards the equator, refused. Their goal was to cross the equator to escape the fallout and 'plague' of the northern hemisphere and to get to a country not overwhelmed by the effects of the war. Neil also felt it was important to avoid any land until the 'plague' had run its course.

But from the beginning there was a heaviness and conflict to the voyage that was new. The death of Katya, the wounding of Philip and Jeanne, the knowledge that at any moment one or more of them might sicken from disease, the awareness that for all the effort and violence of their raids on the *Mollycoddle* pirates, they were still living on short rations and dependent on the sea for their sustenance – all these created a depression in most deeper than ever before.

Yet on Neil, the effect was quite different and unexpected. Something had broken inside him. Some coiled spring that had him tensely concentrating every moment on the right strategies for survival was no longer there. For him, despite acting with all his skill and energy, the worst had happened: a loved one killed, two others wounded. Some part of him gave

417

up. Or rather, some major part of him now accepted his own fallibility, mortality, inability to deal with the forces attacking them. He still led, but without the desperation that had driven him since the wars began. Instead of feeling his usual rage at the forces of destruction when he realized that Lisa might be infected with the plague he felt strangely tranquil, gentle even. When Tony publicly attacked him for the death of Katya, Neil felt no anger at Tony: he knew himself both to be at fault and to be helpless, and he now accepted both. He was helpless: somehow that new awareness liberated him.

Although he and Frank had had no formal reconciliation, Neil found himself feeling his old affection for him and turning over to him most of the decisions regarding the sailing of *Vagabond*. On *Scorpio* Olly was captain with watch teams led by Tony, Oscar and Arnie: on *Vagabond* Frank, Jim and Sheila were the mates, Jeanne, Lisa and Macklin crewing as necessary.

Neil no longer made any effort to disguise his affection for Jeanne. He touched her, caressed her hair, tended to her wound, spoke to her with love. He made no effort to make love to her, both because of his concern for Frank and his fear of being a carrier of the disease.

When Neil listened now to the shortwave radio and heard of the horrors others were facing throughout the world he felt part of a larger family. On the second night out from Anguilla in particular he listened to two new ham operators, one from Florida, the other from Texas. At first he thought the anonymous voices had revived his Americanism, reminded him of his American roots and citizenship, but when he thought about it further he realized that the larger family he felt connected to was that of survivors.

He felt no connection with the President and his martial law and executive directives and his empty claims of victories. He felt no connection with the heroic pushers of buttons, the pilots of bombers, the submarine captains, the generals

418

generalling from half a mile down inside the earth somewhere. His people were the survivors, survivors throughout
the world, American, English, German, Russian, yes,
Russian even, fleeing this incredible madness that had
somehow come about.

And, strangely, Neil found he could read again. From the
first day of the holocaust until the evening of their anchoring
off Anguilla he now realized that he had been unable to read
fiction or history or philosophy: everything had seemed so
trivial or so irrelevant in the face of his quest for survival he
couldn't get into them. Then suddenly that evening he spent
two hours reading Tolstoy's *War and Peace*, one of two dozen
classic novels he had aboard. The scenes of the adolescent joys
of Natasha and Sonya and young Count Rostov brought tears
to his eyes: the joys that Lisa and Katya were missing – had
missed. The battle of Austerlitz, although totally remote from
their experience of the last month, seemed so real, so human
that his own life and the wounds of Philip and Jeanne again
seemed human, bearable. He knew that his joy in Tolstoy
represented, paradoxically in the light of Katya's tragic
death, his strangely recovered joy in and acceptance of life.
And his acceptance of his powerlessness.

Jeanne seemed to have been affected by Katya's death, her
own wound and her killing a man in a slightly different way.
She appeared more pensive and puzzled. Neil could see that
she too was less desperate than they both had been most of the
earlier time, but could see that as she watched each day for
signs of illness in Lisa, she hadn't quite decided how she would
or could take such another blow. Neil and Jeanne spent more
time talking, not just about the day-to-day details of survival
but also about the blame for all that had happened, both large
and small. Although Jeanne saw that her killing 'Larry' had
been in self-defence she argued quietly that if they hadn't
attacked the pirate estate her life might not have had to be
defended. When Neil reminded her that the pirates had
kidnapped Katya she hadn't replied, and Neil felt grief again:

419

they had retrieved Katya only to sail her to her death.

As they talked on their third afternoon at sea *Scorpio* was visible two hundred yards off to starboard. Both boats were moving smoothly in the brisk trade wind, sailing slightly to windward but not enough to create heavy slamming. Neil was at the helm steering, Jeanne on the port seat of the now open central cockpit. The sky was clear, the day already warm. Jeanne was dressed as she usually was in shorts and a bikini top, Neil in cut-off jeans. She noticed the tendons in the back of his legs showing and became aware again that he had lost weight. His severe face was made more severe by the deep lines that now creased it. It saddened her to see him thus, so near to her, yet so far away.

'We're failing,' Jeanne said to him impulsively. 'We're divided and failing. We're making all the same mistakes that led to the war in the first place.' Like everyone aboard she referred to what had happened beginning in mid-June as 'the war', not the Third World War or anything else. To her, to them, it was 'the war', all previous wars being insignificant skirmishes in comparison. It could take no number because it had no predecessor and couldn't conceivably have a sequel.

Neil turned to look at her but didn't reply.

'We're failing,' she repeated.

'We're alive, Jeanne,' he finally said. 'We're not yet starving to death. We're now sixteen people sailing away from danger. We've made mistakes but we've avoided worse ones.'

'But what's the sense?' said Jeanne. 'To get food for a week or two, Philip and I are shot. To escape, Katya dies. We must be doing something wrong.'

Neil winced. 'I know it seems that way,' he said, easing *Vagabond* slightly away from *Scorpio*. 'But illness, violence and death are the new norm. They can't be avoided.'

'And there's Frank,' Jeanne said, as if the single name summarized an entire problem. She searched Neil's face to see if he had an answer for her and, nodding to her, he gestured with his free hand for her to come to him. She went to his side where he took her hand.

'Frank hasn't asked us to stop loving each other,' Neil went on. 'Although that's the only thing that would change things for him, he's asked us only not to make love. For the time being, with Frank as weak as he is, that's a restraint I'm willing to make for him.'

'I know,' said Jeanne. 'But as you first said, it's really no solution. It doesn't stop him from resenting you . . . us.'

'No, it doesn't.'

'That's what I can't stand,' she said. 'You and he were friends. He and I . . . Now . . .'

When she looked up at him he returned her gaze sternly and removed his hand from hers. He sighed.

'You expect too much of us, Jeanne,' he said. 'Good people hurt each other. It's built into the universe.'

'There were only ten of us,' Jeanne persisted. 'Surely we're capable of creating a happy life for ten people.'

'No, I don't think we are,' Neil countered. 'Not when those ten are forced to live with each other whether they like it or not. Not when those ten are threatened with death every day. No, Jeanne, be thankful your children live, that I love you, that people like Olly and Philip and Sheila have come into our lives. For the rest, conflict and suffering and death will be the air we breathe for a long time.'

3

But if there was peacefulness in Neil's heart there was none in
his fleet. In the late afternoon of the fifth day out of Anguilla
Tony and Oscar, who had asked to come over to have a
conference with Neil, arrived on *Vagabond*. Frank had visited
Scorpio at midday while Neil was taking the noon sunshot, and
he was to be in on the conference too. Although the main
cabin would be hot and stuffy Tony suggested they go below
for privacy, forgetting that Philip was berthed there. They sat
instead behind the wheelhouse area. Actually the wheelhouse
had ceased to exist; only the plexiglas windows forward
remained. Neil had ordered it torn down so that the six-by-
ten plywood and fibreglass roof could be sawed in two, glued
together and fibreglassed over to make a new daggerboard.
The walls had come down, too. *Vagabond* now had open
cockpits running the entire breadth of the boat aft of the
cabins in the three hulls. Two small sun awnings were rigged
up to give protection from the sun over most of the area, but it
was all open now to wind and weather.

Oscar and Frank sat on the aft seat, Neil and Tony next to
each other on the port seat. In their gauntness, and with their
beards and unkempt hair, the four reminded Neil of four
derelicts gathering to share a small bottle of cheap wine. Only
there was no wine. Sheila was at the helm.

'Well, gentlemen,' said Neil gaily. 'This is quite the formal
occasion. You apparently have something you want to
discuss.'

'That's right,' said Tony, looking Neil firmly in the eye.
'This beating to windward is going to break *Scorpio* apart.
We're pumping half the time. It's time to change course.'

'We've already discussed this,' Neil replied quietly. 'Jim, Olly and I all agree the present course is correct. I've been sending Frank, myself and Mac over to help with the pumping and you won't accept Jim.'

'But everyone on my ship except the old guy is in favour of sailing to Barbados,' said Oscar. 'And since Frank agrees we outvote you.'

'Take *Scorpio* and go,' said Neil quietly.

'No,' said Oscar. 'We don't want to split up if we can help it. We want to re-establish the normal order of things.'

'Wouldn't that be nice?' said Neil.

'Tell him, Frank,' said Tony. 'First about the captain thing.'

Frank cleared his throat and slowly raised his eyes to Neil. Great grey halfmoons made deep hollows under both his eyes and the skin around his neck was loose. Sitting hunched over staring downwards had become his characteristic posture.

'When you announced you were the captain of *Vagabond* in the Chesapeake,' Frank began slowly, 'I went along with it. I went along because back then there were twenty or so madmen aboard and your speech shaped them up.' He paused.

'Nineteen madmen,' Tony interjected. 'Remember I was there then, too.'

Frank blinked once, cleared his throat again and went on.

'Now there aren't,' he said. 'Now me, Tony, Jim, Olly . . . even Sheila I guess . . . anyone of us could be captain of *Vagabond* and run the ship. Maybe not as well as you, but competently . . .'

Neil held his gaze steadily on Frank but didn't respond.

'In becoming your First Mate I temporarily gave up my ownership of *Vagabond*,' Frank continued. 'In those times, with an untrained crew, it was probably a good way to do things. Now . . . I'm reasserting my rights as owner.'

'And I'm asserting my rights as owner of *Scorpio*,' said Oscar.

'Oh?' said Neil, choosing to look at Oscar, whose long hair and bushy moustache were tangled and streaked with salt, making him look the least reputable of the derelicts. 'And what does that mean?'

'It means I want Tony as captain and not the old man.'

'And what's wrong with Captain Olly?'

'He never gives any orders except those you give him,' Oscar replied. 'Tony and I run the watches the way we want anyway.'

Neil laughed. 'I'd say he sounds like a perfect captain,' he said.

'I want Tony,' Oscar returned sullenly.

'And what does your reasserting ownership of *Vagabond* mean, Frank?' Neil asked. He saw that Frank's steady gaze did not mask an uncertainty, fear even, that Frank was feeling.

'It means that the captain serves at my pleasure,' he replied slowly. 'It means that I set the course, the captain determines only how to get there.'

'And the same on my boat,' said Oscar.

Neil was surprised that he felt no anger or resentment, but rather a strange calm only slightly tinged with sadness. Very slowly he shook his head.

'No, good friend,' he said to Frank. 'I didn't take the ownership of *Vagabond* away from you. The war did.'

'The war's over, Neil,' Frank replied. 'You don't seem to accept it, but it's over.'

'No, it's not, Frank,' Neil returned calmly. 'At least not the war that cancelled your ownership. And cancelled yours, too, Oscar. No, I'm afraid none of us owns anything any more.'

'That's convenient for you to say,' said Tony, 'since you don't own a boat.'

'Frank doesn't own *Vagabond*,' Neil went on. 'And I don't own my captaincy or my other skills. You don't think I'm free to do what I want, do you? Your lives sometimes depend on my skills, so I'm not free to withdraw them, no matter what my likes or dislikes. Our lives depend on *Vagabond* and *Scorpio*.

You two don't own or possess *them* any more than the man who happens to "own" all the water on a crowded desert island owns the water. By the nature of the situation all who need it own it.'

'Bullshit!' Tony exploded. 'It's Frank's boat. All that intellectual crap doesn't change it!'

'You're right, Tony,' Neil responded mildly. 'My intellectual crap doesn't change it. The world changed it.'

Frank was watching him, his uncertainty more evident. Oscar looked sullen, Tony angry and defiant. Neil rose from his seat, stretched his arms and yawned. 'If you think you own your boats go ahead and think so,' he said and then turned to look directly down at Frank. 'But if you try to *act* as owner, then the world, your friends, your family, will collapse. You can't reinstate the old ways by decree.' He watched Frank a moment – Frank was hunched over looking at the floor – and then turned to Oscar and Tony.

'Olly is an excellent captain because he gives orders only to maintain order,' he went on. 'Tony here is an excellent sailor, stronger and quicker than Olly, and Tony would make an absolutely shitty captain. Tony would give orders not to maintain order but to demonstrate he was captain, and that's a perfect formula for chaos.'

'You conceited bastard!' said Tony.

'The war's over, Neil,' Frank said in a husky voice, looking up. 'You're still running, I believe you will always run, but it's over.'

'It's not over,' Neil replied. 'And I intend to keep running.'

'Dragging us with you,' Frank said.

'No. If enough people want to take a different course then we'll split up,' said Neil. 'The cowards can come with me, and the brave ones return to the West Indies.'

'And who determines which group takes which boat?' asked Frank.

'Not me, Frank. Not you. *Vagabond* should go to those who have to sail to windward. *Scorpio* to those who can best use her.'

'And who decides that?' asked Frank.

'The goddamn owners decide, is who,' snapped Tony in reply.

'There are no easy solutions,' Neil said softly to Frank. 'Think about it, Frank. Would throwing me overboard really solve any of your problems?'

'We're not going to throw you overboard,' Tony interjected. 'Good as the idea may be.'

'Think about it, Frank,' said Neil, still softly. 'Get away from these clowns and see the world as it is.'

Tony's fist caught Neil just below his left ear and sent him stumbling across to the opposite seat where he fell awkwardly, half on his knees.

'What the hell are you doing?' Frank shouted, standing and holding out an arm to keep Tony from Neil.

Neil glanced up at Tony looming over him a few feet away and waited for his head to clear and the ringing to stop.

'This bastard can't keep calling me names and expect me to take it,' Tony barked out in reply to Frank. 'If he thinks he's captain let him show it with his fists.'

Neil's head was slowly clearing and he stood up. He noticed that at the helm Sheila was half-turned, watching.

'I'm sorry I called you names, Tony,' he said quietly. 'I don't blame you for being angry.'

'You chickening out?'

'I made a mistake in insulting you,' Neil went on. 'I apologize.'

'Jesus. What is this?'

'And if you ever pull something like that again I'll smash the nose out the back of your head,' Neil concluded. He brushed past Tony and left, going down into the main cabin.

At the wheel Sheila held *Vagabond* steadily on course.

4

Over the next several days neither Oscar nor Frank renewed their request, and the ships seemed to return to a contented routine. They were proving lucky with the wind: it blew steadily much more northeast than usual and let them sail more southeast than they had hoped. *Scorpio* stopped leaking so rapidly. Other events encouraged Neil.

Macklin had probed Philip's wound and removed the second bullet and his infection seemed to be subsiding. Jeanne's wound was healing perfectly. No one had fallen ill with the plague. A squall left them with a good supply of fresh water.

The only continual source of anxiety was their food situation. Neil and Frank had rationed the two boats for a three-week voyage, rations that assumed they would be catching at least one fish a day. They weren't. Both ships were trolling all the time and hooking nothing. The seas appeared empty. Macklin had machinegunned a porpoise one dawn when he was alone on watch, but the mammal had sunk before he could manoeuvre to it. The bloodstained water had been somehow depressing to Neil and Frank who had rushed up at the sound of the gunshots.

Because they were sailing more southeast than expected they were well away from the danger of pirates. Although *Vagabond* was about two knots faster than *Scorpio* in the trade wind, Neil carried reduced sail and spent a day aboard *Scorpio* helping Olly get every ounce of speed out of her. At night *Vagabond* would sometimes get a few miles ahead of *Scorpio* and then heave to in the early morning.

It was good to see Jim and Lisa looking so happy and well. They were sleeping together now in the forepeak, Jim joking

427

that he was determined to share everything with Lisa, even the plague. Macklin now roomed with Frank. Tony had taken up with a young woman named Mirabai, apparently stealing her from Gregg, the young man with the broken arm. Janice, Oscar's girlfriend, was the only other woman aboard *Scorpio*, a third female crew member apparently having chosen to join the commune at Salt Point just before they left.

They met no ships their first six days out of Anguilla. They passed more than sixty miles east of Barbados and, after a week, were seventy miles northeast of Devil's Island off the coast of Guiana. The fear of the plague was receding. Jeanne was not only regaining her strength but her spirits, standing watch with Frank most of the time, playing more happily than usual with Skippy, even enjoying her food more.

Olly too seemed to have regained his high spirits. Frank sometimes spent a day aboard *Scorpio* as captain and, back aboard *Vagabond*, Olly entertained his friends with exaggerated praise for the 'oldness' of *Scorpio*, claiming nothing became beautiful until it was 'at least sixty'. 'She's as bald and toothless as me,' he said, referring to *Scorpio*, 'but she can still bite.'

Olly was aboard *Vagabond* when they spotted their first vessel. Jim was alone at the helm in an overcast dawn little different from each of the last several days. Neil was curled up on a wheelhouse cushion behind him. In the galley Jeanne had just begun to parcel out the small bits of dried fish and dried fruit which would be their morning meal. Visibility was only about a mile, and Jim, sleepy at the end of an uneventful watch, with *Vagabond* ghosting along at only three or four knots in a light wind, glanced mainly at the compass. There was nothing to see out on the water except the same grey slate they'd been staring at for almost ten days.

And then, after exchanging a few idle words with Jeanne and yawning, Jim glanced ahead and saw, so large and clear and close it was as if a god had that very instant set it down in the sea in front of them, a long grey submarine. *Vagabond* was sailing forward, barely rocking, and there, ahead and a little to port, lay a submarine. With a red star. A Soviet submarine.

For several moments Jim stood staring in disbelief at this grey dawn's apparition. Then, almost unbelieving, he turned to Neil. 'Neil!' he hissed in a loud whisper, as if his voice might reveal the fifty-foot trimaran to the enemy.

Neil sat up slowly rubbing his eyes.

'Mmmhuh?' said Neil.

'A submarine. Dead ahead.'

Groggy, Neil stood up and peered forward. 'Living God,' he murmured.

Jeanne, aware of the suppressed sounds from above, came to the hatchway entrance and looked up.

'What'll I do?' Jim asked in a low voice.

'Hold your course.' Neil knocked on the wheelhouse floor to awaken Olly who slept below.

'All hands!' he called in a sharp but low voice.

'What's happening?' Jeanne asked from the hatchway, then climbed the three steps and looked: ahead and to the left, now only two hundred yards away was the submarine, fully surfaced, with a dozen men on the main deck and several in the conning tower. The boat was immense: almost two football fields long; it was like sailing past an island. Even as she watched, a gun – some sort of artillery piece – emerged from the forward deck. Several men clustered around it. She saw officers in the conning tower looking at them through binoculars.

In his underwear Olly emerged next into the wheelhouse, hair dishevelled, sleepy-eyed, the bones of his ribs showing prominently. He blinked at the grey monster; they were going to pass within a hundred feet of it. He could see two sailors pissing off the bow, but also see the eight-foot-long cannon being swivelled into position to fire on *Vagabond*.

'Raise your arms!' Olly shouted at them. 'Raise your arms! It'll help their morale.'

Neil lifted his arms in surrender as did Jeanne. Jim adjusted his position so that he could steer with his thighs and chest and then he too raised his arms.

'Sheila, get on up here!' Olly shouted. 'And bring Skip. Mac!' He himself, arms raised, clad only in his underdrawers, walked into the cockpit closer to the enemy. When Sheila emerged she took in the scene in stunned silence and slowly raised her arms in surrender.

As quiet and softly as a feather drifting in a pond, *Vagabond* was now gliding past the Russian submarine, less than ninety feet away. Along its deck stood almost twenty Soviet sailors staring in disbelief. In *Vagabond*'s cockpit stood three men, two women and a child, all with their arms raised in surrender, facing the barrel of the cannon aimed directly at them. From the conning tower three Soviet officers were conferring with agitation. As *Vagabond* sailed gently by, the men at the cannon turned a wheel and kept the cannon trained amidships. One of them was looking to the conning tower for instructions. The submarine had quite probably discharged in the past two months up to twelve missiles and presumably killed hundreds of thousands, more likely millions, of people it had never seen. Now it had a puny cannon aimed at seven people it could see.

An officer on the conning tower shouted something at *Vagabond*, seemed angry, and shouted again. *Vagabond* was now sailing serenely away from the submarine and was already a hundred and fifty feet off.

'Shouldn't we heave to?' Macklin asked in a whisper.

'Keep sailing!' Neil replied quietly, his arms still raised.

Again the Russian shouted, this time to his own men, and there was a flurry of activity in the conning tower. A man raced down the ladder to the deck. *Vagabond* sailed on. The cannon swivelled to follow her. A single shot would blow *Vagabond* to bits.

'We'd better heave to,' Sheila said urgently to Neil.

But Neil and Olly were both grinning. 'Keep sailing!' Olly shouted happily.

They sailed on. Slowly, softly, as if tiptoeing past a sleeping giant, *Vagabond* bore away from the great metal whale which, commandeered by ants, threatened to destroy them. For a panicky moment Neil was convinced that the captain of the sub was going to wait until the distance presented a challenge to his gun crew and then blast them out of the water. Then that moment passed. The Russian gun crew, or most of it, disbanded, the men seeming to be working on a different problem. The strange other-worldly meeting of the great grey engine of destruction and the white sailing vessel was ended.

Still Neil and the others stood with their arms raised.

'Can't I put my arms down now?' Skippy complained.

'Yes,' said Neil with strange seriousness. 'You can lower your arms. We've beaten them.'

As they all lowered their arms Jeanne stared at the distant smudge of grey on the horizon and then looked at Neil. 'Beaten them?' she asked.

'No, not beaten them,' he said, correcting himself and still looking thoughtful. 'But we won the only way we could have.'

Olly slapped Macklin on the back and gave Sheila a hug and kiss.

'We showed 'em, didn't we?' he said, grinning wildly. 'They didn't dare fire a shot. Totally bluffed 'em.'

Vagabond ghosted on ahead.

5

All that day they celebrated their 'victory' over the Russian submarine, rafting themselves to *Scorpio* for over an hour to make sure Olly could tell everyone the story. They broke out some of the last *Mollycoddle* rum and partied. They were less than seven hundred miles from the equator and began planning another celebration for that nautical event. They even caught a fifteen-pound fish, their first in four days.

It was nine days since they'd left St Thomas and with the fear of the plague disappearing Jim and Lisa were even accepted as crew members back aboard *Scorpio*, Jim being a welcome fresh hand at the tedious task of pumping. And that evening Neil again made love to Jeanne.

He went to her cabin openly, Macklin and Sheila being up on deck on duty. The lovemaking with Jeanne was more tender than the first time, a long, quiet coming together, that, strangely, left them both in tears.

At eleven they returned topsides. Macklin had gone below to sleep and Sheila was steering. When Jeanne went below to check on Philip, Neil went aft to his cabin to radio Olly. There was something strange in Olly's voice when they made radio contact. After answering Neil's initial question about how badly *Scorpio* was leaking – it was taking fifteen minutes of manual pumping every hour to get it dry – Olly quietly lowered the boom: Lisa was sick. She had stomach cramps and a fever. She probably had 'that disease thing we been worrying about'.

So, thought Neil, after he'd given Olly instructions for isolating both Lisa and Jim in the forepeak of *Scorpio*, this was how it all ended. You could run but you couldn't hide. You could do everything you could think of to flee south as fast as possible and still Death, in unhurried omnipotence, overtook you.

Sitting in his aft cabin in the darkness after the radio transmission he didn't feel like moving. He'd have to tell Jeanne, Sheila, the others. He'd have to deal with the panic here, and probably worse, aboard *Scorpio*. He'd have to decide what to do.

What to do? He wondered how many thousand people, no, million people, in the last two months had looked up into the grey sky watching radioactivity grow all around them and asked what to do, asked it, knowing with horror, dread, gloom, or anger, that there was nothing to do but die.

Had they reached that point? Was Jeanne doomed, even when he felt he'd barely met her? Was Jim, who had gone from boy to man in two months, now literally to burn out at eighteen?

Lisa was sick, cramps and fever. There was an enemy to be fought. They had the advantage of an infinite supply of cool sea water to fight the fever and a good supply of aspirin from the *Arcady*. Lisa, while thin, was not yet weak or severely undernourished from their long weeks of short rations. She would begin her personal battle with youth on her side.

As for the disease spreading, Jim was probably infected, but whether others were or would be depended on luck and their discipline. The standing orders he'd given regarding food, sanitation and personal contacts had been taken with great seriousness . . . until today . . .

And who is to care for and try to save the sick? Olly would do it. He didn't know about the others aboard *Scorpio*. Over here on *Vagabond* Jeanne would do it, would insist on doing it. Frank maybe; the old Frank would have. Sheila would volunteer. Himself? No. It wasn't his type of suicide mission.

Well, time to go to it. He stood up, took a brush to his hair and beard, as if preparing for some formal visit, and left his aft cabin. From the kerosene lantern hanging down in the main cabin Sheila was visible at the helm. He could hear Jeanne's voice below in the main cabin. He stopped next to Sheila and impulsively put his arm around her.

'How are we doing?' he asked.

'Eight knots southeast,' she said, glancing at him quickly, her small grey eyes looking at him slyly, like a cat, the lines of ageing around them crinkling nicely.

'How's Philip?' he asked.

'The same. A hundred and two.'

Neil frowned. 'Well, a hundred and two won't kill him,' he said. 'But it won't have him raising sails soon either.'

'No, it won't.'

'Olly thinks Lisa has the plague,' Neil continued on abruptly.

Sheila looked at him again and then half-leaned against him, taking her left arm off the wheel and letting it fall awkwardly on Neil's, still around her.

'Oh, Neil,' she said, slipping her arm around his waist. 'What a bloody shame.'

'You don't catch Death napping.'

They stood beside each other staring forward another moment, then exchanged a warm look and a brief hug.

'I've got to tell . . . the others,' he said, and went below. Jeanne was there with Frank drinking tea and caring for Philip who, now that *Vagabond* was pounding to windward again, was propped into position on his makeshift dinette berth. He lay under a light sheet, awake, staring at the ceiling. The panelled room had a warm glow from the kerosene lantern which hung from a hook right above Philip. Frank was seated on the edge of Philip's berth, Jeanne standing. Both looked at him intently when he entered.

Seeing them, Neil had the same impulse to embrace each of them. He went up first to Frank, leaned down close to him and put a hand gently on his shoulder. Frank gazed back at him in surprise. Neil smiled.

434

'You're a wonderful man, Frank.'

Frank flushed. 'You're stoned,' he said. 'You've raided *Mollycoddle*'s pot.'

'You still alive, Phil?' Neil asked, then straightened, leaving his hand on Frank's shoulder, gently kneading it. Philip smiled and turned his head slightly to look at Neil.

'I believe so,' he said. 'I just wet my pants again.'

'Good sign,' said Neil. 'Corpses rarely piss.'

When he turned next to Jeanne he saw that she, like Frank, was staring at him in surprise. He went up to her and took her in his arms, caressing her lower back, careful of her left shoulder. Looking down at her he asked: 'How are you?'

'I'm fine. What's wrong? Has something happened?'

Neil, not smiling, nodded in reply. Then he released her, glanced at Frank and paced to the companionway steps before facing them. 'Olly reports that Lisa has cramps and a fever,' he said. 'He assumes it's the disease we've been worrying about.'

All three of them looked at him without immediate response. He realized that his statement seemed so inconsistent with his earlier humour and affection that they briefly wondered if this were a sick joke.

'We . . . I chose this risk,' he went on, feeling embarrassed at the way he had acted earlier though it seemed so appropriate at the time. 'Now we have to pay. I think there's a good chance we can pull her through. But we've got to take absolutely insane precautions to keep it from spreading further.'

'I'll go take care of her,' Jeanne said.

Neil felt his heart sink.

'I'm not letting you go,' he said gently. 'I've already assigned Jim to care for her. I don't think she can give him now anything she hasn't already given him.'

'Is Jim all right?' Frank asked.

'Apparently. Olly said only Lisa is ill.'

'I'm going over to her,' said Jeanne

So this is how it ends, thought Neil again. Modern

technology finding ever new ways to kill brave people and brave people rushing to get their share.

'No,' said Neil. 'Jim will care for Lisa.'

'I CAN SEE MY OWN DAUGHTER, CAN'T I?' Jeanne suddenly shouted at him.

'No, you can't,' Neil replied quietly. 'As you once said, we're all one family now and you can't endanger the rest of us unnecessarily.'

Jeanne turned away against the sink and began to cry. Both Neil and Frank went to her and made comforting sounds and caresses and even as they did, Neil realized they were also trying to comfort themselves and each other as well. But of course there was no comfort or reassurance for any of them.

'NEIL!' Sheila shouted from the helm.

Neil left and hurried up on deck. She was pointing to starboard where a bright red glow was visible off *Scorpio*'s stern.

'A red flare,' she said. 'Doesn't that mean an emergency radio transmission?'

'Yes,' Neil said, hurrying by her. 'I'll go take it.'

In his aft cabin he groped for the flashlight and turned it on to the VHF radio that he used for shortrange ship-to-ship communication. It was already tuned to the correct frequency and in less than half a minute he had established contact with *Scorpio*. The voice that came back at him was Tony's.

'*Scorpio* reads you, *Vagabond*. This is Tony. Lisa's got the plague. Those of us on *Scorpio* can't stay with her. Either she's got to go or we do. Over.'

Neil at first wondered if he had heard correctly, but then knew he had.

'What the hell do you mean?' he shot back nevertheless. 'Over.'

'I mean Lisa should be . . . buried at sea. Now. Before she fucking kills us all. Or . . . or . . . those that are willing to risk their lives for her come stay on *Scorpio* and we'll shift to *Vagabond* . . . Over.'

436

So that's what it's all about.

'Let me speak to my captain over there,' said Neil. 'Over.'

'You're speaking to him.'

'I want Captain Olly.'

When Neil shifted to receive he got nothing. He waited.

'Captain Olly can't make it,' Tony finally said. '. . . Over.'

'I'll speak to Jim,' Neil fired back.

'Jim's locked in with Lisa,' Tony replied. 'He can't talk to you either. Look . . .'

Neil snapped off the radio and stood up. What selfish cowards. Who were they? Tony, Oscar certainly, the two young women . . . Would they be so heartless or frightened? Probably. Gregg and Arnie? They were passive. He went back up on deck and back to Sheila at the helm.

'I'm afraid Jeanne's gone to her cabin to get ready to go over to *Scorpio*,' Sheila reported.

Neil looked at her and then nodded. 'There's been a mutiny on *Scorpio*,' he announced. 'Tony has deposed Olly and wants to abandon ship or toss Lisa overboard.'

'Good Lord,' said Sheila. 'Poor stupid Tony . . .'

'Your poor stupid Tony is a . . .' Neil started to vent his rage with a string of unimaginative obscenities but stopped himself.

'We should head for land, Neil,' said Sheila suddenly. 'There we can quarantine the sick and get the best treatment for them . . . and for Philip.'

So this is how it ends, thought Neil again. The dying rushing to the dying for help. The well murdering the sick. What horrors were next in line?

'We've no right to take our sickness to land,' he said. 'We fight our battle here, at sea. Some of us will live, some die, but we don't carry death to others.'

'But you're forcing those on *Scorpio* to accept the worst risk,' Sheila pointed out.

'No,' he answered wearily. 'I'm ordering Lisa and Jim and Olly returned to *Vagabond*.'

6

Neil radioed *Scorpio* his intention to take off Jim, Lisa and Olly but said that they should wait until dawn to make the transfer. In the six-hour interim Jim and Lisa should be kept isolated in their cabin. Oscar, who took the message, made no comment.

When Macklin came on duty at midnight he was informed of the situation. Macklin grunted, asked Neil if there were anything special he wanted said to *Scorpio* at the regular two A.M. radio contact, and took the helm. Jeanne was down in her cabin with Skippy, satisfied that Lisa would be returned to her. Sheila, off-watch, was down with Philip. Neil took over the helm while Macklin had a cup of tea, compliments of the *Mollycoddle*. The kerosene lantern was hanging in the main cabin entrance, giving light to the area around the helm.

'So what's the use of staying at sea?' Frank asked after a silence from a seat behind Neil. 'The worst has happened out here. There's nothing left to run from.'

Neil was struck with how resigned Frank seemed. He still had expressed neither rage nor grief that his son might soon be ill with an often fatal disease.

'We're still welcome nowhere,' Neil replied. 'And now, carrying what we carry, people are justified in asking us to stay away.'

'The whole world's dying, Neil,' Frank said. 'You'll never find a place that isn't.'

'No, I won't,' Neil answered.

'Then why stay out here?' Frank said with sudden vehemence. 'You're sick. You're becoming some sort of crazy Flying Dutchman dooming yourself and those stupid enough

438

to follow you to spend eternity sailing around endlessly at sea.

'I don't see it that way, Frank,' Neil replied. 'I still see my best defences as being out here, the enemies still bunched mostly on land.'

Frank rose and came up beside Neil. 'So now you're ordering Death brought aboard directly,' he said.

'It's your son,' Neil countered.

'If it were Tony or Conrad who were sick you'd throw him overboard,' Frank insisted quietly.

Neil hesitated, then replied evenly: 'If it had been them at Salt Point I never would have let them back aboard. You're right there.'

'You'd throw them overboard,' Frank repeated.

Neil didn't answer. He knew he wouldn't literally throw them overboard, but he recognized that his response would be quite different.

'And how would you handle things, Frank?'

'Sail to land. Put the sick ashore. Split up. End this fucking running.'

Neil smiled bitterly. 'I'll stop running when He stops chasing,' he said sadly.

'You're mad.'

'Let's just say we'd handle it differently,' Neil commented, turning the wheel over to Macklin, who had returned. 'Zero seventy-five degrees. Keep an eye on the number two jib. It may be too much for her. Wake me up at three forty-five. Goodnight.'

But Neil was not awakened at three forty-five. He was awakened at dawn by the sound of something rubbing against *Vagabond*'s port side. He sat up, instantly awake, listening for the sound again, and angry that daylight was there and he hadn't been called. The sound came again: a crunch and a squeal: something rubbing against her side. It even sounded like fenders rubbing against a dock, but *Vagabond* was hissing through the sea at good speed. The motion: *Vagabond* was sliding down a wave; sailing downwind. She had altered course and was running west. Glancing quickly at the compass he kept aft, he confirmed it.

He stood up, pulled on some cut-off jeans and reached to slide his hatch open. It didn't open. He banged on it several times, almost instantly regretting that he had, as he realized that his orders had been disobeyed and he was probably locked in his cabin. He went to take his gun from beside his berth and saw it was gone. So.

He could hear voices now, one of them Frank's and another Tony's. The peculiar sounds he was hearing must be those of *Scorpio* and *Vagabond* rafted as they sailed downwind together. Neil banged again on his hatch and shouted loudly, calling Frank. He kept it up for a solid minute until finally he heard someone fiddling with a padlock.

The hatch slid open and Oscar, gun in hand, looked down at him warily. Neil climbed quickly up the ladder steps and, even as Oscar began ordering him to stay put, brushed past him to enter the cockpit. On the port side was *Scorpio* tied to *Vagabond*. Tony, Mirabai and Janice were transferring food from *Scorpio* to the trimaran, the two women taking it down into *Vagabond*'s galley. Macklin, with his .45, stood guard. Sheila was at the wheel, Olly at *Scorpio*'s. The two ships, under reduced sail, were sailing downwind in a moderate trade wind. The sun was only a few degrees above the horizon on a clear day. As Neil moved slowly towards the others, Frank, who was standing next to Sheila, turned to face Neil.

'I asked to be awakened at three forty-five,' Neil said to him, going instinctively to the first act of disobedience, as if being locked in his cabin and threatened with a gun were less noteworthy acts.

'It's over, Neil,' Frank said wearily, looking strangely beaten and resigned. 'I . . . I've taken, retaken command of *Vagabond*. We're splitting up.'

Tony had waved off a cardboard carton of food Mirabai was about to hand him and pulled out his gun. He now came

440

cautiously towards where Neil stood just outside the old wheelhouse area on the starboard side. Macklin's gun was now aimed at Neil.

'And what's all this transfer business?' Neil asked Frank, ignoring Tony.

'Lisa and Jim are being left aboard *Scorpio*,' Frank said. 'Those still healthy are all coming aboard *Vagabond* . . .'

'Jeanne's elected to stay with them,' Tony said. 'That's where she is now. So has Olly. We assume you will, too.'

'And you're taking *Vagabond* to Barbados?' Neil asked Tony.

'That's right,' Tony replied, holding the gun at his side. 'And since most people are coming with us and you and Olly think you can supply yourselves from the sea, we're also taking most of the food. Besides, if things don't work out on Barbados we'll have to keep sailing downwind until we find some island or some place in Colombia or Panama where we can make a go of it. I figure the weak little countries of the West Indies or Central America are a lot safer than places like Brazil. There are already a lot more Americans where we're going too.'

'If you're going to land and I'm staying at sea,' Neil said to Frank, 'then you should let me take *Vagabond*. You won't need either her space or windward ocean-going ability.'

'That's settled,' Macklin said sharply. 'We're taking *Vagabond*.'

'*Scorpio*'s not seaworthy for the voyage I recommend,' Neil persisted to Frank, 'but as good for heading west. As soon as she stops having to beat to windward she'll stop leaking.'

'Mac said it's settled,' Tony snapped back. 'If you leave you have to take *Scorpio*.'

'*He* says it's settled,' said Neil with a rush of anger. 'I don't.' There was a newly tense silence.

'Frank also says as the ship's owner,' Macklin replied stonily. 'And this gun says.'

'You're choosing to abandon Jim?' Neil asked Frank.

441

'He chose to go to Salt Point,' Frank replied, looking dully at Neil. 'He chose Lisa. He chooses you. He has to pay the consequences.'

'He's your *son*,' Neil said.

'He's dying,' Frank said softly.

'Jim's already got the disease,' Tony said. 'His temperature's already as high as Lisa's.'

The two boats, rubbing and rolling, suddenly spilled rapidly down the face of a wave and everyone staggered or stumbled to regain his balance. Mirabai spilled a box of food on to the port cockpit deck. As he regained his balance Neil felt a heaviness stealing into him, the heaviness of giving up, the heaviness he'd experienced after long days of battling a storm at sea when the body says 'no more', 'I'll do it later', 'sink the fucking ship'. No matter how fast he ran, the forces of dissolution ran faster. He couldn't believe that the West Indies or Central America would offer anything but slow death; he couldn't believe that any land was as safe as remaining at sea as long as possible. But with *Scorpio* he might no longer have such a choice.

'Sheila and Philip?' he asked, almost to himself.

'Philip's too sedated right now to decide,' Sheila answered. 'I feel . . . his life may depend on getting soon to see a physician. *Scorpio* . . . given the options Tony is giving us . . . I feel that . . . *Vagabond* . . .'

'You're right, of course,' Neil said, nodding.

Captain Olly had turned *Scorpio*'s helm over to Janice and he came over to where the two boats were rubbing.

'Jeanne says she needs more of *Vagabond*'s towels,' he said loudly to all of them. Neil saw now that the left side of Olly's face was badly bruised, his eye swollen almost shut.

'What happened to you?' Frank asked, frowning, as apparently he too was seeing Olly up close for the first time.

'I ain't the ducker I used to be,' he said, sniffing. 'Sorry I let you down, Cap,' he added to Neil.

'Tell her to use old clothes,' Tony responded. 'We're not

parting with any of *Vagabond*'s stuff.'

'Get her some towels,' Frank said to Mirabai, who brushed quickly past Tony to go down into Jeanne's cabin to get them. Macklin started to stop her, flushed in anger, then let her go and didn't comment. In a moment she reappeared with three rather ratty-looking towels and handed them across to Olly.

'You win, Frank,' Neil said loudly. 'I've decided I'm not going on that death ship either. I'm staying on *Vagabond*.'

Mirabai, who was passing from the cockpit to the galley with *Scorpio*'s food supplies, worked on indifferently when he said this, but everyone else who heard stopped and looked at him, Tony and Macklin with suspicion, Sheila and Frank with surprise.

'It's a trick,' said Macklin. 'Don't trust him.'

'It's quite simple,' Neil went on. 'The doomed are going on *Scorpio*, and the winners are taking *Vagabond*. Although I may not be captain I'm still free to choose the winners.'

'What about Jeanne?' Frank asked, looking at him with puzzled surprise.

'Yes, Frank,' Neil replied, staring at him intensely. '*What about Jeanne?*'

'I mean . . . she . . .'

'She's doomed on *Scorpio*.'

'Not with you with her,' Frank said.

'Let's cut this crap,' Macklin broke in. 'Neil's sailing on *Scorpio* no matter what he wants.'

'No, Conrad, no,' Neil replied quietly with a half-smile. 'That would be mutiny and perhaps murder. *You*'re capable of that, but Frank isn't. Can I keep my same aft cabin, Frank?'

'I'm taking the aft cabin,' Tony interjected.

'I'm addressing the owner,' Neil said, continuing to look at Frank.

'You really want to stay?' Frank asked.

'As much as you, Frank. As much as you.'

'Me too,' said Olly, who had been listening from the near side of *Scorpio* and who now climbed aboard *Vagabond* with an

443

exaggerated smile, made grotesque in his puffed face. 'Gotten so I prefer three-wheelers,' he added.

'Get back on *Scorpio*,' Macklin shouted, nervous and angry.

''Course the company ain't as nice here,' Olly said. 'But I'm used to the stink of rotting things so . . .'

Tony instinctively lashed out at Olly with his gun arm. When Olly parried the blow and knocked the gun loose, Macklin swung his gun into Olly's chest sending him back against the cockpit seat groaning.

'Hey!' Frank yelled, rushing forward.

Macklin aimed his automatic and snapped off the safety. 'Hold it!' he snapped fiercely, backing into the corner of the cockpit and looking uneasily at Frank.

Frank stopped only a few feet from where Tony stooped to retrieve his fallen gun.

'The charade's over,' Macklin announced. 'Tony and I are taking over.'

'What's *that* mean?' Frank said, his fists clenched at his sides.

'It means Tony and I are taking *Vagabond* and you can join your friends on *Scorpio*.'

'You little bastard,' Frank growled, 'you couldn't handle *Vagabond* for a single second.'

'Get off the boat,' said Macklin.

'Jesus, you and Tony *are* clowns,' said Frank, sneering. With a suddenness that surprised everyone, he grabbed Tony's gun and tried to twist it free, using Tony's body as a shield from Macklin. Crouching in the corner ten feet away, Macklin swung his gun first towards Frank and then towards Neil, who had taken three quick steps towards him; then he swung his gun back to fire a single shot at the tangle of Frank and Tony.

For a moment that tangle seemed to continue its wrestling unaffected, but then Frank slumped to the cockpit floor. Tony, breathing heavily, straightened and stared down fearfully at his fallen adversary.

Macklin, sweating, turned his gun back on Neil. Jeanne

444

appeared in *Scorpio*'s cockpit next to the young woman at the helm. 'What happened?' she asked into the silence aboard *Vagabond*.

Macklin wheeled towards her with a scowl.

'Get back below or I'll kill you,' he said to her.

'Go below,' Sheila shouted at her. 'He's shot Frank.' A look of shock appeared on Jeanne's face, then she moved slowly past Janice to *Scorpio*'s starboard side against *Vagabond*. She could now see down into *Vagabond*'s near cockpit the bleeding body of Frank.

'Oh, my God,' she said and climbed aboard.

Tony and Mirabai quickly left the cockpit area to avoid the possibly infected Jeanne. Mirabai reboarded *Scorpio* and Tony came into the wheelhouse. Even as Jeanne knelt beside Frank's fallen body, Macklin held his gun on Neil.

'Oscar,' he said to the young man still standing behind Neil, 'put the barrel of your gun in Loken's back and escort him over on to *Scorpio*.'

As Neil felt Oscar's gun press into his back he began walking towards Macklin, who was still crouched back against the far corner of the cockpit, his eyes flicking nervously. The two ships were sailing serenely forward at six knots, still lashed side to side, rubbing and crashing but held off by both ships' fenders.

Neil glanced at Sheila as he passed her at the helm and hoped she might try to help. Mirabai now appeared behind Macklin aboard *Scorpio*.

'That's it,' she said to Macklin. 'I've removed everything you asked me to.'

Macklin glanced swiftly at her, then back at Neil who was now only six feet away. *Vagabond* suddenly swung left, her port bow crashing hard against *Scorpio* and throwing all of them off balance: Sheila had acted.

Neil wheeled and, grabbing Oscar's gun arm, hurled him across the wheelhouse. He crashed into the mizzen mast, his gun ripped from his hand, and slumped to the floor. As Neil

445

turned back to Macklin he saw Jeanne wrestling for possession of Macklin's gun. Neil leapt forward, throwing his weight against Macklin's left side and sending all three of them crashing against the coaming, Jeanne screaming as her left arm struck, then sinking slowly to the deck. Neil grabbed Macklin's gun arm and began banging it against the edge of the coaming. Groaning, Macklin let go of the gun.

Grabbing Macklin by the belt and shirt front, Neil half-carried, half-dragged him past Frank and Jeanne to the rear of the cockpit, lifted him high up over his head and hurled him into the sea. Macklin's head struck the side of *Vagabond*'s deck. He fell between the two boats, bobbed up briefly in the ships' wakes, then disappeared behind a swell.

Neil stood staring after him a moment, then turned back to the cockpit. Jeanne was again kneeling beside Frank, rocking back and forth, almost as if she had forgotten the other violence that had swirled around her. Neil crouched down beside them.

Frank's eyes were open and clear but a thin line of blood trickled from his mouth. He was labouring for each breath, his chest rising, shuddering and collapsing. Neil knew a lung must have been punctured. Jeanne had placed a towel beneath the rib cage and Neil removed it and pushed up the shirt and saw what looked like an exit wound from the bullet. The sight of the immense bleeding gave Neil a sinking feeling: he didn't think they could save him.

Neil groaned, reaching out to touch Frank and letting a hand fall helplessly on his shoulder. Frank managed a grin that was mostly a grimace. 'Christ,' he gasped out, 'have I botched it!'

'Can't we help him?' asked Jeanne, turning to Neil desperately.

'Yes,' said Neil. 'We've got to drain the blood from his lung. Somehow get new blood into him.' He stood up. Tony was in a corner of the wheelhouse along with the still groggy Oscar. For Neil they had no more relevance than bothersome insects.

'We're taking *Vagabond*,' he said to them. 'And staying for the time being at sea. We'll redivide the food after we've tried to save Frank.'

Tony stood with one arm holding the mizzen mast to steady himself, the other still clutching his pistol. He seemed to be groping for an appropriate line of action and not finding any.

'You'll have to tell me when you changed course during the night,' Neil went on. 'I'll plot your course for Barbados.'

'You . . . you're letting us go?' Tony asked, as if Neil held a gun on him rather than he on Neil.

'Yes, ' said Neil, and went below to try to save what still could be saved.

7

Once again *Vagabond* sailed on alone. The two ships had parted. Tony, Oscar and the four others had taken *Scorpio*, planning to sail it downwind back to Barbados. Neil's last exchange with Tony, after he'd checked over the relative food supplies of the two ships and sent some back to *Scorpio* and given Tony one of the two automatic rifles and ammunition, was brief. 'Good luck,' Neil said to him as they prepared to cast off the rafting lines.

Tony, who had been unusually subdued in the two hours since the wounding of Frank, nodded. 'You too,' he said, and as Neil released one line and was moving to untie the next, added quickly: 'Sorry about . . .' but didn't finish.

Neil merely released the second line, signalled Olly on the port bow to release his, and the two ships, free of each other at last, angled out away. Since *Vagabond* was now altering course from west back to southeast the two ships had to cross paths one more time, *Vagabond* luffing her sails and then sailing across *Scorpio*'s wake. For a moment everyone in both ships acted as if the other ship wasn't there, until Olly, still on *Vagabond*'s bow collecting the fenders, stood up and waved heartily.

'Go get 'em, Tony,' he shouted. Tony gave a subdued wave in return, and then the two vessels were speeding away from one another, one to the west, one to the southeast, each to its own fate.

'Always give people encouragement when they're sailing off,' Olly said to Neil after he'd returned aft. 'Otherwise they might come back.'

Philip and Sheila had remained with *Vagabond*. When Sheila had talked to her husband late that morning about whether they should join *Scorpio* Philip had shaken his head.

'I have to have something to live for,' Philip told her. 'With those people I wouldn't. Here . . . I do.'

But his fever was now over a hundred and three degrees; and Neil started a third antibiotic.

Frank, berthed in the dinette where Philip had been, still lived. They had sedated him, drained the blood from the lung, and managed, with great difficulty and uncertainty, to draw almost a pint of blood from Sheila's arm and inject it into Frank. Neil knew that with the primitive syringe he was using there was danger of an embolism but he had concluded that without a transfusion Frank wouldn't survive the first night. Lisa and Jim were quarantined in Frank's old cabin, Philip installed on a wheelhouse settee, with Sheila in the forepeak berth. Jeanne and Skippy remained in the port cabin, but Jeanne began to spend most of her time with Lisa and Jim, planning to sleep on their cabin floor. The disease would reach its climax in the first three or four days so the battle might well be won or lost quickly. Knowing that the disease was not air-transmitted and that cleanliness could have a decisive effect on whether one became infected or not, Neil hoped that they could contain the disease.

Although he had less hope that they could save Jim and Lisa it wouldn't be for lack of trying. All during that long first day Jeanne and Neil tended the two feverish patients. They lay on adjacent berths, only occasionally conscious, sometimes hallucinating, their fevers over one hundred and five degrees. Jeanne worked tirelessly putting on and taking off the seawater-soaked towels and shirts, carrying Lisa's bony, torrid body to the side cockpit to immerse her in the six inches of sea water there. She watched helplessly as the fever raged on unabated and Lisa's breath became faster and faster, shallower and shallower. Neil helped bring water and towels and moved Jim when necessary. Sheila often helped, but most of the burden was Jeanne's.

Neil found it depressing to be down in the heat and stink of

Frank's cabin to confront the sweating bodies, feverish eyes and incoherent words of Jim and Lisa. Jim kept trying to act as if he were only mildly sick, joking about it, inquiring always of Lisa, just out of sight around the partition that separated their two berths, and once even volunteering to help carry her to the seawater bath out in the cockpit. When he found he couldn't even stand, he lost some of his youthful cockiness.

With three of the ship's company close to death and those still healthy feeling almost powerless to help them, the gloom during the day was broken only once, when in late afternoon Olly unexpectedly announced that they should hold a short memorial service for Conrad Macklin, as they had ten days before for Katya.

'He was our shipmate,' Olly explained. 'And besides, burying him might put us in a better mood.' So he, Neil and Sheila had stood awkwardly in a side cockpit and Olly had spoken. 'Well, Lord, we want to pay our last respects to Conrad Macklin,' he began in a serious voice and with bowed head. 'Connie was probably beat on as a kid, and his Mom probably weaned him too early and his Dad kicked his butt so he developed into something of a shit, Lord, pardon the expression, but he didn't work hard at it and was only that way when he felt like it. Still we figure You got the big picture, Lord, and will know exactly what to do with Connie. Us, we got the small picture. All we could think of doing with him was throw him to the sharks . . . Amen, Lord. Over and out.'

Neil and Sheila said nothing.

'Now we symbolically commit his body to the sea,' said Olly, and when he slapped Neil on the back Neil gathered the ceremony was over.

'Funny thing, Death,' Olly announced as they walked back into the wheelhouse area. Neil waited for him to go on with some sort of punch line but he didn't, as if his three words summarized his meagre wisdom on the subject.

Neil was doctoring Frank. When the wounded man spoke

without wrath of Tony and Macklin his tranquillity began to remind Neil of Sam Brumberger. Frank even joked about their triangle with Jeanne, announcing that he was 'retiring' from the field. Feeling helpless in treating Frank, twelve hours after the mutiny Neil made the decision to head for land. Frank's slim chances lay in their finding modern medical skills on the coast of Brazil.

Neil was aware of the dangers involved: the Brazilian government was sinking unauthorized ships trying to land. The day before, a plane had passed overhead, the first they'd seen since leaving the Virgin Islands, and a freighter had passed them heading south. These sightings had disturbed Neil at the time; he feared that *Vagabond*'s presence might be reported to Brazilian military authorities and create the possibility of their being attacked. His hope lay in their being off the northeasternmost coast of Brazil, relatively uninhabited, and in *Vagabond*'s approaching the coast at night and hopefully arriving at dawn. He consulted with each of the others, warned them of the terrible dangers of landing, but they all voted to risk it, Frank alone arguing against.

'I don't think I'm going to make it no matter how many tubes they stick in me,' he said in pain. 'You ought to keep to sea.'

But they turned southwest, heading for one of the coastal towns to the north of the mouth of the Amazon. Neil didn't plan to sail into a harbour but to sneak in, find a sympathetic doctor and only then bring Frank ashore. Even as he searched for a viable plan he knew the risks were great.

At dusk, after looking at the primitive small-scale map he had of the coast he went to fetch their automatic rifle and began planning defensive strategies for their closing with land. The rifle was missing. He asked Sheila if she had moved it and she said no. Nor had Olly. Disturbed, he discovered the nine-millimetre automatic on his aft cabin shelf was missing too. He asked Olly to check for the two other weapons they kept in the main cabin and he reported them gone too. He

451

and Olly were leaving the main cabin feeling baffled when Jeanne met them coming from hers.

'I threw the guns overboard,' she announced quietly, looking frightened of Neil's possible reaction.

Neil stopped in front of her, stunned, staring at her, not wanting to believe her, but knowing that this was the only explanation.

'All *four* of them?' he asked.

She nodded.

'My God,' he commented, turning away from her and staring off aft.

'I know I seem crazy to you,' she said quietly. 'But I don't want to live in the kind of world they create.' Neil still looked away, his lined, bearded face tense and puzzled. 'I love you, Neil. I know you've saved us a dozen times, sometimes with guns, but no more. Now we live or die like the rest of God's creatures, by the strength of our bodies alone.'

Neil still stared stiffly aft, Olly, behind him, stroking his wispy white beard and scowling.

'I can understand what you did, Jeanne,' Sheila said from the helm. 'The guns make us a part of the madness of the rest of the world. I'm glad they're gone.'

Jeanne looked thankfully at Sheila and then fearfully back at Neil.

'Never trusted 'em myself either,' said Olly. 'Only thing I ever killed with a gun was a rabbit, and he died of a heart attack from my missing him so often.'

Neil walked further aft and stared out at *Vagabond*'s wake. He had felt instant anger at Jeanne's acting behind his back, fear too at the unexpected loss of weapons he thought he needed to survive, but with the voices of Sheila and Olly echoing Jeanne, he felt an unexpected peacefulness replace his anger. The guns were gone. They themselves were at sea only a half-day from land and the enemy. It was not possible that the kind of fighting they'd had to do was over, but even if

452

it weren't, the odds were way against their winning even with guns. They'd have to fight the way they'd fought the submarine. We'd better, he thought, smiling ruefully to himself at their being armed now with Olly's gaff and the flare gun. He walked back to Jeanne and held her gently.

'You did what you had to do, Jeanne,' he said, aware of the tension in her caused by the new horrors. He could feel her yielding only slightly in his embrace. 'We haven't had much luck holding off Death with guns, so it can't be much worse without.'

At dawn they were still ten miles off the coast. An hour later land came into sight. Ten minutes after that a jet fighter-bomber, a French Mirage, streaked out of the sky from the west and passed with a roar directly over them.

Neil had long before made contingency plans for both air and sea attacks, and, being weaponless, their plans involved either surrendering or playing possum. They were already flying the Brazilian flag – homemade from a piece of sheet – but it would be difficult to surrender to a jet plane with whom they had no radio contact. As the jet shrieked past and began to climb and turn he shouted at everyone to go down into Frank's cabin. He himself dashed below to prepare the flares. He didn't know whether the jet would return or attack if it did, but as Olly and Sheila passed him carrying Philip they exchanged with him pained glances: the look of people marching to a battle they didn't expect to win.

As he emerged from the main cabin with the flares Neil had a chance to look back: the jet was making a long graceful sweep up the sky to the right, then around, around, and back towards *Vagabond*. Neil was alone at the helm, making no effort to take evasive action, two smoke flares and two fire flares on the control panel shelf, a box of dry matches nearby. The plane flew rapidly at them and Neil experienced the brief image of a man facing a firing squad. Then a brief flash from beneath the jet and almost simultaneously the rush and roar of the missile tearing past the trimaran. The jet shrieked past a second time.

His hands trembling, Neil lit one of the smoke flares and tossed it down into the main cabin. He lit the second and threw it down into the empty port cabin. Dark smoke billowed up out of both of the cabins within seconds as Neil returned to prepare to light one of the light flares. The missile had struck at least a half-mile in front of *Vagabond* but he doubted the pilot had been able to follow it. As the jet rose and swept right a second time the pilot would look back and see his target enveloped in dark smoke. Their hope lay in the pilot's being satisfied with one apparent hit.

But the jet returned. As Neil watched in bitter dread and lit his third flare it came in and fired a second missile. So close did the second shot come to *Vagabond* that Neil thought it might have gone through the mainsail; it burst less than a hundred yards in front of them. The bright flash of the lit flare must have seemed to the pilot – if he could see it, which was doubtful – a direct hit. The jet roared over the smoke-enshrouded trimaran and Neil, coughing and being overcome with the smoke, rushed forward and dropped the jib and mainsail. Then he rushed back through the smoke and down into the starboard cabin with the others. Dark black smoke was pouring out of two of *Vagabond*'s cabins into the sky.

Neil's hands were black and one hand had been burned in lighting the third flare. Jeanne and the others looked at him as if asking for him to announce their fate. He didn't have to tell them they hadn't been hit, and only later did he realize that they didn't even know they'd been fired at.

The jet didn't return a fourth time. It returned to Brazil, apparently confident it had prevailed in its battle with the trimaran.

After five minutes of waiting, with the smoke gradually getting worse even in the closed-off port cabin, Neil and Olly went back on deck. Both smoke flares were going out, but something was still burning in the galley. Neil had to go down and extinguish a smouldering rug. The whole inside of the main cabin was black with the smoke.

The others now climbed out of Jeanne's cabin to survey the wreckage, but there was no wreckage. The multi-million-dollar aircraft had fired two highly sophisticated missiles at the plywood and fibreglass sailing boat but, as Neil explained, the missiles had been metal-seeking or heat-seeking missiles. *Vagabond*, engineless, was without heat and had so little metal in her aluminium spars that the missile couldn't seek it out. The pilot had been trained to fire at a general area and let the missile do the fine tuning. *Vagabond* and her survivors had been saved by modern technology.

Two hours later they raised sails again. After they had discussed their next course of action they decided that they should get as far out of the area as possible: to run directly east another sixty miles and thus fifty or sixty miles off the coast. They would have to do their best for Frank and Philip and Jim and Lisa without the help of the rest of the world. They were alone.

8

As they sailed on towards the equator, the heat and humidity became stupefying; only the recurrent squalls, by keeping their supply of water adequate, kept them alive and sane.

All Neil dared do for Frank was give him a second blood transfusion, but with the plague victims it was an hourly battle to try to cool their bodies. The seawater was twenty degrees cooler than the air and they used it continually. But over the next three days the fevers raged on. Twice Lisa went into convulsions, twice she survived. Jim jabbered on in some otherworldly hallucination about snow and cold and the bottom of the world, sometimes giggling hysterically.

On the third day from the onset, after Lisa had had her second set of convulsions, Neil came down into the cabin to see Jeanne up on the berth with Lisa, her face buried on Lisa's naked chest and neck, sobbing. For a moment Neil thought that Lisa must have died; a wave of sadness immobilized him. Then he became aware of her rapid shallow breathing and realized that Jeanne, who had been driving herself beyond reason, was suddenly giving up. Pressing her face and mouth against the diseased body of Lisa was almost a form of suicide.

Neil could feel rising in him his old rage against the gods or Fate or Death or the war or whatever was pursuing them so relentlessly and now appearing to win. He felt a rage at Jeanne for letting 'them' know they were winning. But then, recalling his helplessness, it passed. He went up to the edge of the berth and gently pulled her off the berth and, as she wailed and resisted, less gently dragged her out of the cabin. With Olly and Sheila watching uncertainly, he took soap and seawater and scrubbed her face, neck and arms. She struggled and cried like a child being punished. Neil even forced the

456

soapy rag inside her lips before finally letting her go.

'Take her back to her own cabin,' he said quietly to Sheila. 'Keep her there. I'll take over responsibility for Jim and Lisa until Jeanne's rested.'

Back below when he felt Lisa's forehead he was horrified: he'd never felt a human body so hot. He dispensed with the side cockpit pool and the towels and instead began throwing buckets of seawater directly over Lisa and Jim and the towels and clothing lying on their naked bodies. For half an hour he lugged the buckets down and poured the cool seawater over them. Later he'd have to bail the cabin's bilge.

Forty minutes later he went to see Jeanne in her cabin. She was there alone and, after asking how she was and receiving a dull reply, he said to her: 'I miss you, Jeanne.'

'Miss me?' she said, looking puzzled. 'Oh,' she added, understanding.

'I know of no law saying I can't love you,' he said. 'Do you?'

'. . . No,' she replied, not looking at him.

'Nor a law prohibiting your loving me,' he went on. 'Is there?'

Face still averted she said: 'Only a law of nature.'

'What law is that?'

'When a mother is threatened with the loss of her child she loses a part of herself.'

'I see,' said Neil. 'That I can't help.'

'Nor can I,' said Jeanne.

'And I still miss you.'

'I know,' she whispered.

'There are no barriers between us now,' Neil said gently, 'except those we erect in our own hearts.'

'I know,' she whispered again, crying softly. 'But I can't knock them down.'

'But what *are* they?' Neil asked gently.

She looked up at him at last, warm tears in her eyes.

'Fear,' she said.

'Fear?'

'We're all doomed,' she said. 'No matter how hard we try, one by one we're going to die. Our desperate acts are only a dancing on a hot griddle before the end.'

For a long moment he held her gaze, searching for words of reassurance, searching for the axe that would smash the barrier. He could find none.

'Still,' he finally managed. 'Dancing is better than nothing.'

'Until you get tired,' she responded.

Although Frank felt better on the morning after the jet attack, some strangely detached part of himself knew he was going to die. It wasn't any rational conclusion based on medical or anatomical knowledge; it was some previously uncontacted part of himself informing him from some unknown world of reality in which, paradoxically, he didn't believe. A mystic certainty had come to him, Frank, the most unmystical of men.

When the heavy sedation Neil had given him began to wear off and his consciousness began to clear, Frank was surprised at the space he was in. His anger at and jealousy of Neil was totally gone. His earlier decision to separate from Jim, Jeanne and his friends seemed that of a total madman. He knew it had come from his resentment and sadness at losing Jeanne, but now losing Jeanne seemed as trivial an event as losing an anchor. The thought of her, even now, made his heart ache, but the ache was somehow amusing, trivial: like hiccoughs.

Even his own death had a somewhat comic quality: wrestling with one big clown, being shot by a small one. Surviving megatons of destruction, to succumb to a tiny piece of lead.

Jim's death, if Jim were to die, was not comic. It was sad. It was the only thing that made him sad. It was the only thing that made him resent the war, resent the holocaust. Jim should live. Lisa should live. Children should live. It was he

458

and Neil and Olly and Philip and their generation which had let things happen: they could die knowing they deserved it, but not their children. We are the single generation in human history to snuff out untold millions, no, billions, of lives of all creatures for untold centuries. We were the assholes that let it happen.

For even as he accepted with equanimity his own fate, he felt a quiet fury at the reality that had been his life. He saw that his joyful playing with money, so dissociated from any human reality, was his personal contribution to the holocaust. He had been a part owner of General Electric and General Dynamics both when he owned some of their stock and when he didn't. He never built a bomb or pushed a button, but he helped pay the men who did.

It made his life pathetic. All his successes and failures seemed now so trivial compared to the Big Failure; all his aspirations so selfish compared to the one he might have had, but didn't. But could men have done anything to stop the flow of events to the ultimate madness? Although he had always thought they couldn't, though his reason even now argued they couldn't, that new voice from that strange detached world announced unreservedly that men could have stopped the flow of events as inefficiently, sporadically and bumblingly as they had set the flow of events in motion. The creative capability of building rockets that occasionally blew up on their pads, was equally capable of tearing them all apart and burying them; and could have done it with the same percentage of errors.

Although it took a lot out of him to talk and though Neil reminded him that every ounce of energy was needed, Frank was thankful that first Jeanne and then Neil let him say a few things he wanted to say.

Jeanne was pale, puffy-eyed, and dishevelled when he saw her thirty hours after she'd begun taking care of Lisa and Jim. It seemed to Frank she was almost a madwoman. When she came down into the main cabin and washed her hands and arms and then sat for a moment beside him, he smiled up at her.

'You look like *you're* the one who got shot,' he said.

She looked startled and didn't smile.

'I'm sorry Lisa's sick, Jeannie,' he went on, aware that his strange lightness was out of place with her now.

'How are *you*, Frank?' she rejoined, finally centring her attention on him.

'Pretty good,' he answered. 'Even dying.'

'You're not dying, Frank,' she said urgently.

'It doesn't matter, dying's not what it's cracked up to be,' Frank went on, aware that he might be feverish. 'And I'm sorry I butted in between you and Neil.'

'That's not important now.'

'I know it's not,' Frank said. ' But I still wanted to tell you.'

'I'm sorry I can't love you as you deserve.'

'Hell, Jeanne,' Frank said, smiling. 'I'd want to be loved a lot more than that.'

Again she looked at him questioningly as if uncertain if he were in his right mind. Then she smiled. 'Thank you,' she said. 'For being the way you are.'

He felt a wave of weariness pass through him and then responded. 'It's simple to become wise,' he said. 'Just get shot.'

The next day he and Neil talked.

'We're only about a day's sail from the equator,' Neil announced.

Frank, whose weariness was increasing and who now slept most of the time, opened his eyes to look at Neil.

'You plan to bury me there? he asked.

'I hope to save you,' Neil replied.

Frank closed his eyes, nodded almost imperceptibly, then opened them again. 'Too late, Buddy,' he said.

'Maybe,' said Neil. 'But we'll try.'

Frank struggled again up into consciousness.

'I'm sorry I won't be rounding Cape Horn with you,' he said.

'Not very likely.'

'The sailing was always great,' he said softly. 'It was . . . the human stuff that messed us up . . .'

As Neil looked down, Frank thought he saw tears in his eyes.

'You, me and the rest of the world,' said Neil.

'Yeah,' said Frank.

For another half-minute neither man spoke and a series of confused images raced through Frank's mind. He became aware of Neil rising to leave.

'Last word,' Frank mumbled and Neil stopped. Frank opened his eyes and felt a strange giddy joy flowing through him. He smiled feverishly up at Neil. 'Advice . . .' he announced to Neil. 'I think . . . the market is . . . at its lows . . .' He felt like laughing. 'Good buying opportunity.'

Neil, like Jeanne, looked down at him uncertainly, then nodded, smiling slightly in return. 'Nowhere to go but up,' Neil commented.

'. . . Right . . .' said Frank, closing his eyes.

9

At dawn two days later, Frank died.

Neil was surprised and unsettled by the grief he felt at Frank's death. He had known Frank was dying and thought he had hardened himself, but when Olly called him down and he saw Frank's stiff body and open mouth, an emptiness and gloom descended upon him which left him immobile. He realized how much unspoken companionship he and Frank had enjoyed even during their estranged period of the last month. The two communicated in a shorthand about the way *Vagabond* sailed as Neil couldn't with anyone else. To realize that he had lost this friend, first to jealousy and now to death, grieved him.

Instead of giving Olly orders about what to do he wandered back out of the cabin and walked aft to stare out at the sea. A distant part of him felt the burden of having to tell Jeanne. But he felt passive, weary. He felt a sad, self-pitying sense that everything was useless, that Death, like a cat playing with crippled mice, could take him and his loved ones at any time He wanted. A tickling on his cheeks and saltiness in a corner of his mouth made him realize that he was crying.

Jeanne came up to him where he stood. Seeing her eyes beaming with happiness he realized that no one had yet told her of Frank's death. She didn't even notice his tears.

'Neil,' she said softly, 'the fever . . . the fever's down. I think . . . it's breaking.'

Neil looked down at her, dazed, trying to absorb her words. 'Lisa?' he asked.

'Both of them,' she answered, softly – as if afraid that if she announced it too loudly the gods would change their minds. 'Jim two hours ago, and now Lisa. Come see.'

Mechanically Neil followed her down into Frank's old cabin. The floor was wet, the room sweltering in the heat of the equator. Lisa lay wanly on the first berth staring at him, a shy smile on her face, beads of perspiration or salt water on all her body. Jeanne adjusted a towel to hide Lisa's nakedness.

'I . . . I'm feeling better,' Lisa said.

'I'm glad,' said Neil simply, feeling tears for Frank and for joy at Lisa's life welling in his eyes again.

'I'm . . . hungry,' Lisa announced uncertainly, as if finally determining the unique sensations she was feeling.

Neil nodded and reached out to put his hand briefly on hers. Then Jeanne, smiling, pulled him further forward to Jim, who was up on an elbow looking at him. Somehow Jim seemed to sense Neil's restrained mood.

'How . . . is Dad?' he asked in a hoarse whisper.

Neil, aware of Jeanne beside him still aglow with the survival of the two young people, couldn't answer.

'I'm glad you came through, Jim,' he said.

But again Jim picked up Neil's unspoken feelings.

'Dad . . . isn't . . . isn't?' he asked Neil.

'Frank died,' Neil said. 'Just twenty minutes ago.'

After hesitating, Jim began to nod slowly. 'He said goodbye to me,' Jim whispered hoarsely. 'He came to me an hour ago . . . his spirit, you know, and told me . . . to live . . . to take care of everybody.'

Neil nodded as Jeanne leaned against him, absorbing the news of Frank's death. He put his arm around her.

'Frank probably saved us all back at the mutiny,' Neil said. 'Now we'll need you.'

Jim now had tears in his eyes. 'But I wish . . .' he began again in a voice weak from three days of little speaking. 'I wish he could be with us when we . . . if we . . . finally . . .'

'. . . Live . . .' Jeanne finished softly.

10

After burying Frank at sea they sailed on.

They kept *Vagabond* well off the Brazilian coast, hoping to reduce the chance of again being attacked by plane or gunboat, their destination still uncertain. As long as food and water were adequate they would continue into the South Atlantic. Nothing they were hearing from around the world encouraged them to try to land. The plague was still spreading. Shortwave transmissions from all of Europe had ceased. Most US broadcasts had ceased. An A.M. station in Uruguay reported that a series of food riots in Rio de Janeiro had been suppressed by the Army and left over three thousand people dead, and the Brazilian Air Force had attacked and sunk a freighter crammed with refugees that had tried, after repeated warnings to turn back, to enter the harbour at Rio de Janeiro. Rio was floundering under the impact of unemployed and starving millions, who were begging, stealing, rioting and fleeing to and arriving from all over Brazil. Thousands had died in the last month from either disease or starvation, many from the newly introduced plague.

But the alternatives to landing in Brazil were equally dismal. The few small islands in the South Atlantic were governed by Brazil or Argentina and their friendliness to American refugees was as doubtful as that of the mainland. Argentina, because it didn't need to import food, seemed slightly preferable. But the last Spanish-language broadcast which Sheila had been able to understand before their transistor radio batteries lost their power, indicated that illegal immigrants were being quarantined and put in internment camps, a gloomy option unless and until they began actually to starve to death. In the meantime they would sail south, hope that the plague would run its course on land, and not reappear aboard *Vagabond*; hope that they could feed themselves from the sea, and wait.

In eleven days they reached the latitude of Rio, passing a hundred miles to the east. Their tentative destination was the coast south of Mar del Plata, two hundred and fifty miles southeast of Buenos Aires in Argentina.

When their shortwave radio broke down they were left with no radios functioning. They began sailing alone amidst a depressing silence from the rest of the world.

And the sea too seemed silent and empty. They saw no other ships. No seabirds accompanied them. Although they trolled all the time, usually with two rods and two lures, the fish, if they were there, usually spurned their offerings. As they grew weaker from their stricter and stricter rationing, they began to dip into their emergency food kit. They established a schedule of rationing that would permit them to reach southern Argentina with an empty larder.

Vagabond sailed now in peace. Their harmony was not simply the result of the lassitude brought on by malnutrition, but rather of the trust and affection that had been forged from surviving together the horrors of the previous two and a half months. Neil and Jeanne were lovers, husband and wife; so too were Jim and Lisa, although she still had not recovered from the disease, being barely able to walk. Sheila and Philip were their benevolent Aunt and Uncle; Olly the grandpop. Neil lived now with Jeannne and Skippy in her port cabin, the Wellingtons taking over his aft cabin.

Jim had slowly recovered his strength. At first Neil and Jeanne had thought that his quiet dignity was only weakness from the after-effects of the disease, but soon they realized that with the nearness of death Jim had developed the same tranquillity that Frank had come to during his last hours. He developed a new low-key sense of humour and was no longer in awe of Neil but able to poke fun at him.

Lisa, although the disease had left her pathetically weak, was childlike in the joy she showed in being alive and in love with Jim. Each morning he carried her from their starboard cabin to the open cockpit areas where she could be with the others. Neil urged books upon her; Skippy urged her to play games with him; Philip began to teach her navigation. She did a little of each. Although her weakness was sometimes heartrending – they had no idea how completely she might eventually recover – her joy in Jim, her happiness in living, made it impossible to be depressed in her presence.

But as they moved further south they moved, paradoxically, into the late winter of the southern hemisphere. They were pitifully unprepared for the cold, especially after having just suffered through two weeks near the equator. Their bodies were lacking in the fat that could be burned off to warm them. Their ship had little winter clothing. With the propane supply exhausted and the kerosene almost gone, they had no fuel to burn to warm a cabin. The three women took the two woollen blankets aboard and began to convert them to clothing. The only cold weather gear they had was Neil's orange float suit and they needed two or three other winter garments so that at least three people could be out on deck at once if necessary. They cut and sewed one small woollen jumpsuit to fit Lisa and Sheila, and another larger one to fit Jim, Neil and Philip. From the remains of the blankets they managed to create a third jacket to fit Olly and Jeanne. Two pairs of sweatpants became winter underwear. Clothing was no longer individual but held in common by two or three similarly built individuals, items worn as the need arose. They were now without soap so clothing began to stink. Their limited number of socks began to disintegrate.

The strangeness of their clothing was only another symptom of their dissociation from their previous lives. Just as they were physically, electronically and geographically detached from most of the rest of the planet, so too they were now in some way detached from the mammoth events which had transformed the earth. The fears and violence of those in the southern hemisphere against refugees like themselves seemed to them as natural and unhatable as the squalls that had afflicted them north of the equator – something to reef for. The destruction of much of the world by the nuclear war seemed like some natural tragedy, as if the earth had been hit by some errant comet.

The plague did not reappear. After two weeks they dared assume themselves free of that danger. They were healthy. They were starving. The bringing in of a single fish was cause for a major celebration. The loss of a hooked fish before boarding it left them limp, empty, afraid. When their emergency cache of food was mostly gone; when they were down to a few days' ration of dried fish; when all their previous stores of food were down to a few rotting potatoes and the last unopened rusted can of spam, they turned, filled with dread, again towards land.

Their lives, which for three weeks had taken on a peaceful, dreamlike quality from their isolation and undernourishment, now, they feared, would once again take on the quality of a nightmare. They approached land feeling themselves aliens about to visit a foreign planet.

But the land came out to them. An Argentine frigate met them thirty miles off the coast and warned them through an electric bullhorn that no 'Norteamericanos' were being allowed on the mainland of Argentina. If they came any closer to the coast their boat would be confiscated and they would be taken to the recently seized Malvinas Islands with other plague victims and illegal immigrants. They turned back to sea.

Yet even as they did so Neil realized that in two or three days they would have to try to land again because they were now almost totally out of food and low on water. They hoped that further south, with the coast often uninhabited, the vigilance would be much less.

And so for two more days, during which they ate only the

last of some rotting potatoes, they sailed southwest another three hundred miles down the coast, remaining seventy miles off. They saw neither another boat nor a plane. A cold front brought with it an overcast sky and Neil was unable to take a sunsight at noon. He had only a rough estimate of his position, but it made little difference. He had absolutely no detailed knowledge of the coast he would be approaching and thus any part of the fifty-mile stretch he estimated himself near was as good as any other. He didn't know whether to expect to crash into towering cliffs or surf up to a sandy beach blooming with tourists.

They made it into the darkness of the night without being stopped or attacked. Neil wanted to close with the shore just before dawn and anchor or tack off until they could determine their next course of action. Approaching at night they would not only avoid detection but also be able to see the lights of any major town and, close to shore, perhaps the lights of individual houses or farms.

At four A.M. with Jim at the helm tightly bundled up in the woollen jumpsuit and foul-weather gear, the depthmeter indicated the depths were rapidly shoaling. They had seen no lights or other signs of civilization. As Neil stood beside Jim at the wheel he felt as if he were on a foreign planet approaching some shore never seen before by human eyes. All he knew of the land he was visiting was that the natives feared and hated aliens. He and his friends were aliens.

'It's eerie,' said Jim. 'I like sailing in the blackness, but not when we're nearing land.'

'The sea will let us know when we're getting close,' Neil replied.

'How far off will we hear the surf?' Jim asked.

'At least a mile.'

Then they became silent. They had both picked up a sound: a distant hum beneath the splash and hissing of *Vagabond* through the water. For two minutes they stood side by side in the darkness straining to clarify the hum. It gradually grew: muted by distance, the crash of the surf on land.

Neil flicked on the depthmeter: thirty-six feet.

'We'll turn and beat slowly upwind,' he said to Jim. 'Ease in towards the shore. At dawn we want to be able to act fast.'

As they sailed slowly towards the shore, the sky in the east grew faintly brighter, and three hundred yards from shore they dropped their sails and anchored.

Jeanne, wearing the homemade woollen jacket over a sweater, jeans and sweatpants, came up to join them. The lightening sky illuminated in front of them the brown, hilly coastline and sand shingle beach. No houses were visible. The line of the coast was more or less straight north and south. Except for a few evergreens the landscape was bleak. They saw no signs of man.

'Not much of a salvation,' Jeanne commented to Neil, putting an arm around him.

'I hope you know some good recipes using bark and pine needles,' he replied. Then he took the binoculars from Jim and began again to study the surf and beach. Although they could paddle a dinghy through the surf to shore, they would risk their lives trying to get back out again and any food they might gather would likely spill out. He concentrated on the debris line along the beach.

'It's high tide or damn close to it,' he finally concluded aloud. 'We're going to beach the boat.'

He had Jim wake the others and order them all into life jackets while he and Jeanne raised sails and tacked up over their anchor and pulled it up. Two hundred feet from shore they would drop it again to act later as a safety line to kedge themselves off. When they came to within fifty feet of where the waves were curling to break into their thirty-yard frothy roll to the beach, Neil turned *Vagabond* downwind.

'It's too rough, Neil,' Sheila said from beside him, her face lined with concern.

'What are the options?' he responded, watching the beach.

469

'Anchor. Wait until the seas subside.'

'We'd be seen,' Neil replied. 'I'd rather take my chances with the surf.' When he glanced at her he saw past her shoulder an unusually large swell coming shoreward and felt that this would be their chance: that big one would be their horse to land.

'WE'RE GOING IN!' he shouted. 'DROP THE ANCHOR!'

He gauged the progress of the swell, shouted at everyone again to hold on and swung *Vagabond* to port. Jim and Jeanne sheeted in the sails and *Vagabond* surged towards the beach. At first Neil feared he had turned too late, but *Vagabond* zoomed landward only slightly more slowly than the swell, which came up behind them and, just as they entered the surf line, lifted them up and hurled them sizzling down its face, water crashing and roaring all around them. They rushed through the moiling froth on the shoulders of the large roller closer and closer to shore and then, just when it seemed like they might sail right up on to the sand, *Vagabond* stopped, sending everyone stumbling off balance.

'DROP SAILS!' Neil shouted and then ordered Jim to take the second anchor ashore.

A second big wave following the one they'd ridden smashed loudly into their stern, sending spray flying across all three open cockpits and inching *Vagabond* another two feet up the beach. A third big wave struck her another thundering smack, water cascading across the aft cabin and into the wheelhouse area. But *Vagabond*'s stern remained directly out to sea and the fourth wave they didn't even notice. Jim had carried the twenty-two-pound Danforth anchor through the low white undertow up on to the sand and pebble beach. After more than six weeks they were again on land.

470

11

Land was a sand and pebble beach, low stunted shrubs and deciduous trees, dry dead grasses, a few low evergreens and low hills. Along the beach was a line of dried seaweed. Except for a single seagull that flew over them and settled on a small rock fifty feet away there was no sign of life.

In the first hour *Vagabond* was thinly camouflaged with pine branches to alter her shape and mute the whiteness of deck and cabin top from air surveillance. As the tide receded she was left in an ungainly position high and dry; at dusk the rising tide would let the surf attack her again.

Their purpose was simple and single: to gather food and water to permit them to proceed again to sea. Water they found in abundance almost immediately: a freshwater stream flowing into a tiny brackish inlet a little less than a mile south of their landing spot. Food was more difficult. Both Sheila and Olly began to search the immediate area for edible herbs and plants but their initial reports were discouraging. The late winter season meant that almost all plant life was dormant. They found a few dry berries, a shrub they didn't recognize with a fruit or leaf-type growth still hanging on its branches, and a variety of dried grasses. They began to gather what they felt they might be able to use.

Olly discovered fish, mostly small, in the brackish pond that their freshwater stream fed into and suggested he take his fine-mesh net and try to catch some. He would need Jim to help. Neil agreed and asked them also to drag five-gallon containers of water back to the boat.

He and Jeanne had also hunted for edible plants but the search had depressed him. He was out of his element, his ignorance of plant life appalling. After an hour he decided

471

that his time could be better spent exploring up and down the beach five miles each way for possible changes in vegetation or signs of wildlife or domesticated animals.

By early afternoon their scavenging for food had produced only berries, grasses, a few possibly edible leaves, some shellfish, a few dozen minnows, and seaweed. Olly planned to use the minnows in the afternoon as bait for larger fish.

Jeanne had seen a herd of cattle on a hill three miles to the south, so, gathering together the ship's two largest and strongest knives, a carrying harness and line, Neil went with her to explore the area, hoping to find not only an animal he could kill but perhaps also stored food, animal fodder even.

As they hiked along the beach he was disturbed at how quickly he was tiring. He hadn't slept since two o'clock that morning and hadn't eaten anything of substance in a day. Jeanne too was weak. They held hands as they walked along, Neil aware of the incongruity of this strangely dressed pair holding hands meandering along the beach only a few weeks from starving to death. By the time they neared the place where she had seen the cattle they were both staggering. The day was still overcast, the sky slate grey, the sun already low in the sky.

Ten minutes later they turned inland towards a second hill, even though no cattle were now visible. As they followed some sort of animal path up a ravine Neil realized that he feared man almost more than he wanted food.

After a forty-minute hike and with the sun within less than an hour of setting, they came within sight of a small herd of cattle high on a ridge half a mile away. By now both Neil and Jeanne were exhausted. Neil wasn't certain he had the strength left to kill a steer. He decided he should sleep near the herd and attempt a kill the next morning. He reluctantly sent Jeanne back to *Vagabond* to report his plans. Exhausted, he sank almost immediately to sleep, the earth seeming to be rolling like the sea beneath him.

When he awoke at dawn and began walking up the barren

hills his purpose seemed strange, unreal. He was intending to kill a steer, butcher it, and drag the usable meat miles back to *Vagabond*, which sat perched on the beach like a ship drydocked for the winter. The cold air and hard earth, both so unfamiliar after months of summer at sea, stung his body. They too were strange, dreamlike. He tried to focus his thoughts on the killing of the steer, its butchering, but the US Naval Academy had never taught him that particular craft.

Weak from hunger he eyed the leafless shrubs and the evergreens in unconscious hope that an apple or orange would be hanging there.

On the crest of a small hill he saw a herd of about thirty cattle feeding two hundred yards off in a small gully with a pond or pool. As he let his eyes sweep the horizon he could see to the east, where bright clouds marked the presence of the rising sun, the distant line of the ocean beyond the hills. As he continued his survey he stopped: to the south he saw smoke – a campfire or house. The sight chilled him. Although he had thought that he would explore for such human habitation in the hope of finding vegetable foods he could steal, his instinct at seeing the smoke was to flee. His interest in exploring disappeared at the first contact with the feared enemy.

So it was to the hunt. Arranging one knife in the deep pocket of his orange floatsuit and carrying the other, he began hiking down to the herd.

When he neared them the individual cattle seemed gigantic. They looked at him out of one eye as if watching a harmless alien from outer space. He *felt* alien. He felt he was on some other planet and these immense bovines were august senators debating what to do with him.

He considered what to do. He would kill the smallest, but there seemed no smallest. They all dwarfed him. To get at a throat seemed ridiculously improbable; his knife now felt no larger or more lethal than a toothpick. Yet kill he must. The thought of his own bony body and those of his loved ones sent a chill through him. The placid beings munching the dry

473

grass represented life. If he had to attack an elephant in order to help his family survive then the elephant had better beware.

The small herd had moved twenty yards further on, a few lingering at the far end of the small pond, most grazing on tiny tufts of dried grasses they discovered in what appeared to Neil to be barren ground. He chose as his victim an especially listless steer that seemed to be daydreaming near the pond. As he walked towards it some of the herd moved slowly away from him, but his intended victim continued to stand in his dreamworld. Knife at the ready he ran the last five strides and leapt on to the steer's back. In nightmarish surprise his frail body struck the side of the steer and slid harmlessly off, collapsing to the earth.

Neil lay stunned. He had been unable to jump on the steer's back. He had made no more impact on the animal than that of a thrown orange rag. He stood up. The whole herd seemed to be eyeing him: strange habits, these orange aliens. His steer had moved ten feet away.

But Neil's failure had aroused some primitive fear and determination. He needed that meat. If he were this weak now, what would happen if he failed? He walked slowly back to the steer and stopped at his side. He considered the angles, his strength, the hand- and footholds. Clenching the knife with his teeth he grabbed the steer's horns and swung himself up on its back.

The animal exploded into life, galloping forward past the others. Holding on to a horn with his left hand and clenching the steer's back with his legs, Neil rode him. He took the knife from between his teeth, pulled himself forward and plunged his knife into the throat area, trying to rip it sideways.

The beast galloped on, Neil cutting and ripping with the five-inch blade, feeling again a sickening powerlessness. The steer finally slowed his gallop, shaking his head and knocking Neil's knife arm down and out away from his throat. The steer swung again, bucking, and Neil was sent sliding off his back, his left hand scraped by a horn.

He lay on the earth and stared up at the steer who stared back, blood spilling down from its neck like an open faucet. Neil slowly arose and backed away, fearing a charge. The rest of the herd had stopped thirty yards off and was circling restlessly, several of them lowing mournfully.

Trembling, Neil waited until the steer finally lay down and died. Then he went to it and began cutting the animal into portable chunks.

He worked for an hour and a half, having to stop to rest at frequent intervals. He chewed greedily on several pieces of the meat and cupped some of the blood in a hand and drank it.

It was three full hours from the time of his kill before he had wrapped some eighty pounds of meat and bone and liver into the jacket, bundled it with line and harnessed it for carrying on his back. It was too heavy for him to carry for long in his weakened condition and he had to drag it up the hill.

He had gone less than three hundred yards back towards the sea when he heard the horses and the voices of men. The sounds came from the direction of the herd. The carcass of his kill would probably be discovered, his trail from there be easy to follow. Sadness and then fear filled him. He was still about a mile from the beach and four miles from *Vagabond*. He had to escape and avoid leading any pursuers to his shipmates. He had to save the meat.

He quickly left the trail to carry the bundle across a ledge and hide it behind a boulder. Returning, he dragged a foot down the trail to imitate the track of his dragged meat and then continued down the trail. He hadn't decided what his next step would be when he heard the sound of hoofbeats and the voices of men approaching. He ran. He ran now devoid of thought or intention. He ran now out of fear.

He plunged blindly off the trail and into the shrubs and low evergreens, but even as he did so he knew he could be spotted from two or three hundred yards in his ridiculous orange suit. The twang of a bullet ricocheting off a nearby rock and the later 'pow' of the sound of the rifle fire only verified his vulnerability. He tore wildly through the underbrush, heading downhill because it was easier and faster. When he came to a ridge he hesitated only a moment and then began skidding down towards the ravine, his chest already aching from his exertion, a part of him wanting to curl up and play dead. His feet went out from under him and he slid the last twenty yards to the bottom. A stream there ran east to the ocean. He staggered up and ran the last thirty feet down to it and began jogging and stumbling along its bank. Forty feet wide and only a few feet deep it rushed and tumbled rapidly over rocks on an incline towards the sea.

Two more bullets scattered pebbles a dozen feet in front of him and he stumbled to a halt. Bent over, gasping for breath, he crooked his neck to look up to the ridge.

Three men on horseback, one with a rifle and two with drawn pistols, were staring down at him. One gaucho pointed and the other two laughed. The man with the rifle shouted to him something in Spanish. Neil wanted to raise his hands in surrender but for the moment hadn't the strength. Finally he got his arms up over his head. The man shouted down at him again, frowning. Neil swayed, hands raised, still trying to catch his breath, barely able to hold his neck back to watch them.

A pistol shot exploded and a bullet plunked into the earth two feet in front of him. The second gaucho raised his rifle. Neil looked dismally to his right where he would have a run of fifty feet before a bend in the ravine would give him protection. A voice shouted down at him again, presumably urging him to come up to them, or perhaps to run. Surrender, if accepted, might or might not save his life but would mean he would never see the others again. He ran.

Or rather he began to stumble along the edge of the stream towards the bend in the ravine, expecting at any moment a fusillade of shots to tear into him. Halfway to the bend, with an instinctive burst of energy, he leapt sideways to throw himself into the rushing water. At almost the same instant the fusillade of gunshots began.

476

12

It was Jeanne who found him. She had been hiking up the trail in the late morning to meet him when she heard the shots. She'd run towards the sound, hidden when three horsemen came up out of a ravine, then gone down into it to search for Neil. Her head told her that he was dead, but her heart hoped. She found no body and began hiking downstream, calling out his name even as she assumed the killers had thrown his corpse into the torrent. After a while she began to see signs of blood and of something dragged, and she forced herself to move faster. Ten minutes later she came upon his motionless body.

His right knee had been shattered – it was a bloody pulp – and he was unconscious. He had tied a tourniquet above his knee. She tried to revive him by splashing water on his face, but even after she got his eyes open he was too weak and exhausted to be coherent. The thought of trying to drag him back the way she'd come was too horrifying to consider. Uncertain of where it led she nevertheless began to drag Neil down the stream. She knew the tourniquet should be loosened periodically but feared for his life. Even at the expense of his leg she couldn't loosen it. She used her sweater as a harness across Neil's chest and under his arms to drag him. Every step pained her as she imagined the pain the dragging must be causing Neil. She thought of leaving him and running for help, but feared she might not be able to find her way back or that he would die while she was gone.

There were places where she had to lift and carry him. How she found the strength she didn't know, but carry him she did. When she had collapsed beside him after getting him past a difficult outcrop of rock he regained full consciousness for the first time. His hands and face were cut and scratched and he looked at her in apparent surprise, disoriented. She put her arms around his neck and hugged him, holding her face against his. When she explained what she was doing he urged her on, assuring her they were near the sea. His alertness gave her new hope.

When she finally reached the inlet half an hour later she saw Olly and Jim fishing near the opening to the sea and called to them. At last there was help.

That night at dusk, at high tide, *Vagabond* was kedged off the beach into the surf and sailed back out to sea to get as far from land as they could before dawn. Earlier Jeanne and Jim had located the cache of meat where the seemingly delirious ravings of Neil had indicated.

With *Vagabond* once more under sail, Jeanne, Philip and an again conscious Neil examined his knee. Their only light was a kerosene lamp and the last of their working flashlights. Neil was now in considerable pain but was insisting they hold off on a big dose of painkillers until he could help decide what they should do. After they had unwrapped the bandage and were all three staring at the bloody, shattered pulp that had been his knee, Neil suddenly spat out: 'Cut it off.'

'No,' said Philip.

'It's useless,' Neil said through gritted teeth. 'Saw it off.'

'I left the tourniquet on a long time,' Jeanne said quietly to Philip. 'The leg may already be lost.'

'Cut it off!' Neil hissed.

When no one responded and Neil closed his eyes and groaned, Jeanne, her own face twisted in pained empathy, spoke again. 'Get the hacksaw,' she said to Jim, who had come to help.

'You're sure it's best?' Philip said to her.

'Yes,' Jeanne said, not looking at him. Then to Jim: 'Please.'

478

Jim left to get the hacksaw. Philip called up Sheila who had been working on the beef in the galley. When she arrived Jeanne explained to her what was going to happen, asking her to relieve Olly at the helm so he could do the cutting. She herself prepared needle and thread to sew up the new wound and possibly the arteries. They needed also to prepare something to cauterize the arteries.

Twenty minutes later, with Neil now heavily sedated but still in great pain, they began the operation. Everyone aboard except Skippy helped. While Jim held Neil down so his leg couldn't move, Olly took the hacksaw, its new blade heated in the kerosene flame and wiped clean with peroxide, and sawed through the skin and bone of Neil's right leg just above the knee and just below the tourniquet. Sheila sewed and Jeanne cauterized the arteries. Philip controlled the tourniquet and soaked up the blood. Jeanne was quietly instructing the others. When they were done and the tourniquet had been removed the bleeding was minor. Neil was unconscious.

When the operation was over Olly took the severed limb over into a side cockpit and dropped it into the water.

'The rest of him will be along later,' he whispered to the sea. As he walked back he frowned and shook his head. *Much later*, he thought, but tried to keep that hope to himself.

13

Their sailing south now seemed an act of madness. They were sailing into winter. They were sailing away from any possible medical assistance for the man they wanted to save. They were sailing down towards the fiercest winds in the world, to the Straits of Magellan, to Cape Horn. They were sailing down to the very bottom of the civilized world, to a land so barren and infertile only the most simple and impoverished of Indians had inhabited it until barely a century before, and even now civilized man had seen fit only to establish a small naval fuelling station. They were sailing away from man.

At the possible cost of Neil's life they had replenished their food and water supplies. In addition to the beef, Olly and Jim had taken twenty pounds of fish and, in the new cold they were experiencing, they were better able to preserve both. They had gathered only a few edible greens, mostly from the sea, and no fruit except a pint of dried berries. They had a large cache of dried grasses and leaves and with the beef and fish enough protein to last a month.

It wasn't clear whether Neil was going to live. He was pathetically weak, sleeping most of the time, sometimes having to be forced to swallow the food which, for him alone, was usually cooked. Jeanne even began chewing up the meat and then feeding him the juices from her mouth. He had lost a lot of blood; his system was adjusting to the shock of the amputation; the constant pain was weakening him. They were giving him the last seven-day supply of antibiotic to fight infection. If it failed they were helpless. On those occasions when he was conscious he seemed frighteningly dazed, and though he tried once or twice to discuss with Jeanne or Philip the ship's plans he seemed to lose the thread of the discussion.

Vagabond sailed on essentially without him.

They had decided to try to sail through the Straits of Magellan to the Pacific. This proposal, which would have seemed so absurd, so impossible two months before, seemed to all of them now inevitable and necessary. They had been driven south by forces beyond their control. Every time they had stopped running and tried to settle they had been driven onward. Although the rest of the planet was now silent, all their radios now silent, they sensed that where men were few and far from the holocaust, there peace might be found. To get to the islands of the South Pacific they had to round the tip of South America; thus they would round it.

Jeanne spent most of her free time nursing Neil in her port cabin. They slept together under the sleeping bags and carpets and life jackets. She had to stand two or three two-hour watches each day but had no galley duties, Philip having become full-time 'cook', while Jim and the women sailed. He and Jeanne had earlier taken charge of the rationing, deciding that they would portion out their food supply over two weeks, planning to replenish it somewhere in the Straits of Magellan.

They had made the decision to feed themselves and hold little back because they knew that all of them were near the end of their strength. Watches had been shortened to two hours because no one had the strength to be at the helm for longer. Each person slept most of the time they weren't needed in sailing the boat. As they got further and further south the seas became bigger, the winds more fierce. Jeanne, novice, and Sheila, veteran, could each take her two-hour watch at the helm alone in twenty- or thirty-knot winds and not have to ask for advice or assistance, but they would leave duty in a state of total exhaustion.

Despite their hardships and the dreary knowledge that they still had to pass through a barren land and endure one more confrontation with civilization before they could begin to sail towards their distant dreamed-of haven, there was no despair in Jeanne's tending of Neil. She had a fierce belief that she could make Neil live, that she would live, that Skip would live. This belief had no more basis than her earlier conviction that they would all die, but it sustained her and in its way helped sustain the others.

For though their food intake was increased, before their landfall and food gathering they had all become perilously weak. Only slowly did they begin to regain a pound or two of weight. As they sailed south the cold became worse, the winds worse, the work more demanding. Moreover, Olly took to his bed. After standing his watch for a day and a half after their departure from land he had collapsed. All he could say was that he was 'feeling poorly' and would prefer a vacation. Although his taking to bed made everyone realize how frail and bony he had become – a laughing skeleton, Philip had called him once – his sickness was a mystery. He had a slight fever, complained of pains in his chest and belly, complained of a toothache, but what ailed him couldn't be pinned down. His illness left Jim and the three women to sail the boat alone, Lisa at last beginning to regain some strength.

Vagabond, scarred and jury-rigged, as tired in her bones as her sailors in theirs, slashed and pounded dutifully forward, her sails tearing more often, fittings coming loose, but still forward.

It took them a full week to sail from their landfall to Cabo Virgenes at the eastern end of the Straits of Magellan, arriving, as Philip had predicted, in a gale. It blew out their working jib; they lost a halyard up the mast; they were blown almost on to a rocky shore before they finally regained control and managed to retreat back out of the Straits to anchor in the lee of a point.

Neil began to get better. Some colour had returned to his face and he was feeding himself now. No infection had shown itself and the best sign of all was when he began trying to give orders on how to run the ship. He still hadn't the strength to leave his berth.

482

They had to remain four days anchored outside the Straits waiting for the gale to blow itself out. During that time they mended sail, tried unsuccessfully to catch fish on the bottom, and rested. They had time to prepare themselves for the ordeal of sailing through the Straits and having to meet or sneak by the Chilean Navy at Punta Arenas.

But when the gale lessened and the wind shifted slightly they sailed on. They were proceeding almost mechanically now without real hope that they would ever see the Pacific, but sailing on because all other options were worse. They averaged only thirty miles a day over the first three days, sailing during the eight hours of daylight, anchoring at night. It snowed at the end of the third day, keeping them at anchor for thirty-six hours. They huddled below in their cabins, Olly joining the Wellingtons for body warmth in the aft cabin.

Neil, although weak and bedridden, although frustrated at being unable to command or participate in the challenge of getting *Vagabond* through the Straits, nevertheless found himself strangely content. Instead of feeling alone and isolated he felt as if he were at home surrounded by a loving family. Jeanne had sawed a hole in the wall separating their cabin from the main cabin so he was able to talk to the others. He had once or twice tried shouting orders from his bunk but even as he did so he realized his contributions weren't needed. Philip and Sheila and Jim were all good multihull sailors. Instead of making him feel unneeded this awareness of his own superfluity was soothing. He could lie in his berth without the sense that unless he got himself up on deck in the bitter cold *Vagabond* was doomed. The only thing that occasionally frightened him about his contentment was the worry that it might be a sign that he was dying.

The loss of his leg left him strangely unperturbed. He stared at his stump with fascination but without dread. He felt he could still be a sailor. Moving about a small boat on one leg presented no great challenge even without crutches or a wooden leg. He was so thankful that he might survive that he looked upon the loss of his limb as a tiny payment he had to make for the privilege of living.

His individual survival had given him hope for the group as well. Although he knew that they would meet man at Punta Arenas, with all the potential for disaster that entailed, he felt that down so far at the bottom of the world the disease called man might have escaped the fear and violence that was destroying the more civilized world.

And so, paradoxically, with the threat of starvation still looming before them; with *Vagabond* being imperilled every other day in the barren Straits; with Neil himself lying in bed with what might be considered a catastrophic wound; with Jeanne still weak from giving up some of her food for weeks to Skip, and having to spend four to six hours a day out in the bitter early spring winds of Tierra del Fuego; he and Jeanne yet found in the tiny haven of their cabin a quiet and calm happiness that had eluded Neil all his life.

It had something to do with life being reduced to eating, keeping warm, and companionship. The violent conflicts afflicting the rest of mankind seemed distant and trivial. A conversation between Neil and Jeanne one afternoon when *Vagabond* was at anchor riding out the snow squalls and forty-knot winds manifested their detachment from their previous world. They were lying under a pile of covers in their berth.

'You know,' Neil said to Jeanne, 'I've been thinking about how the war started.' He paused as if still thinking about it and then went on, 'I'm not sure that the Russians fired the first salvo of missiles.'

Holding his hand as she lay beside him, Jeanne turned to look at him in the grey light of the late afternoon.

'You believed those Venezuelan broadcasts?' she asked, referring to programmes they'd listened to more than a month earlier in which Venezuelan spokesmen had charged that the US had started the war.

'No, not that,' Neil replied. 'The thing that's always bothered me is that the Russians attacked American cities and industries and military bases. We're told they attacked missile sites too, but one station way back at the beginning said something that I've never forgotten: they suggested people flee to North and South Dakota for refuge from fallout.'

Jeanne watched him as he paused, holding his gaze and waiting.

'I can't help concluding that if the Russians didn't hit South Dakota it was because they knew there was nothing there to hit: all our missiles based there had already been fired.'

'If the Russians had struck first,' Jeanne interpreted, 'South Dakota would have been a primary target.'

'Yes.'

'So you think that the President ordered the beginning of a nuclear war?' she asked quietly.

'He wanted his nation to survive,' Neil replied. 'He thought it was sit and get clobbered or strike first. He ordered the first strike for the same reasons that a Russian premier would have needed: fear that the enemy was desperate enough to do it so he'd better do it first.'

Jeanne felt a distant sadness. She hadn't really questioned the assumption of all American radio stations that the Russians had struck first. She realized that she felt it was only natural that they would do it; Americans had been fearing their attack for years. Yet she understood that that very fear, so pervasive, so hopeless, might have led to an American government doing what Neil now speculated it had done. She felt no anger, only the distant sadness.

'The missiles fired at South Dakota targets might have been intercepted,' she speculated, 'or might have missed on the first strike. And then after our Dakota-based missiles had been fired, the Russians ignored the area.' Even as she spoke most of her was accepting Neil's thesis.

'Yes, that's possible,' agreed Neil. 'I'd thought of that. But we know that the very *first* Soviet missiles hit American cities,

485

targets that would always be vulnerable, whereas missile silos are worth hitting only on the very first strike, before they're emptied of their missiles.'

Jeanne looked at him. 'How does it make you feel?' she asked.

'It doesn't make me feel much one way or another,' he replied. 'It doesn't change how many legs I have.' He smiled. 'The two sides had got each other into a position where sooner or later someone was going to hit first. The fact that our government may have succumbed to fear first doesn't really horrify me.'

Jeanne stared out of the cabin window at the almost horizontal line of snowflakes rushing past. She thought of the violence directed at them and other Americans from the nations south of the equator.

'No wonder we're outcasts,' she concluded.

Later that same afternoon their talk brought them to a new subject. When Neil, still huddled under the covers with Jeanne, had talked with her about Lisa's continuing weakness, he had expressed concern that Lisa might be pregnant which, because the foetus might have been damaged by her high fever, would be an added burden on her health. Jeanne had responded that Lisa had had a period a few days before the plague struck her, and then, looking puzzled, suddenly looked with a flush of joy at Neil.

'What are you thinking?' Neil asked, aware of something special happening with her.

'I just realized that . . . *I* may be pregnant,' she said to him, looking half-joyful and half-awed.

Neil felt stunned. Their lovemaking had usually had an end-of-the-world desperation that was outside the normal everyday reality. Pregnancy belonged to the old world, not the ugly, tenuous one they now inhabited.

'My period's overdue,' Jeanne went on, now looking uncertain. 'I suppose it might just be . . . my wound . . . my worrying . . . diet . . .' She frowned as she thought of the possibility of these other explanations for her absent menstruation. But then she smiled again: she and Neil had made love without contraception during her most fertile time. In those days the possible consequences seemed irrelevant. Now they seemed divine. Even the shadow of the possible effects of her exposure to radiation didn't dim her joy.

'Lovemaking does tend to create babies, I suppose,' Neil said to her, still somewhat dazed but with a grin on his face.

'Oh, Neil, I hope so, I hope so, I hope so,' Jeanne said, hugging him.

Bright-eyed, he looked down at her and then out of the window at the snow swirling past. He had a boyishly happy faraway expression.

'Now, we'll *have* to live,' he said dreamily. 'Just to see if it's a boy or a girl.'

But an hour later, as he struggled up on deck for the first time since his being shot, he knew that his puny aspirations would have nothing to do with it. Their lives, even the new one growing within Jeanne, still hung by a thread.

14

By the time they were planning to try to sail past Punta Arenas at night, Philip and Neil had begun to have second thoughts. The absence of any sign of ships or life during their first five days in the Straits had made them suspect that there couldn't be a bustling town of forty thousand people only a little way off. As they neared the place in the Straits where their map showed the city to be and they still had seen no boats, no smoke, no planes, they decided that there couldn't be much of a military presence in the Straits and thus those in Punta Arenas might not be a threat, might, in fact, be helpful and sympathetic. So they ventured to try it by day.

Uncertain of their exact location, they had almost sailed past the town before Philip spotted through the binoculars three miles to the north the charred wreckage of buildings and a few small houses on the hillsides. Nervously they altered course to sail over and have a look. It was a relatively mild day with temperatures in the high forties, but the scene that grew towards them was bleak. All the buildings on the waterfront were blackened shells or burned to the ground. A large freighter and at least a half-dozen smaller ships lay half sunk along the waterfront. As they anchored off a burned-out wharf a few stray dogs scurried like overgrown rats between the blackened timbers of the wreckage. The hills above the town were brown and grey with only occasional patches of white from the recent snow. Nowhere were there signs of human life. So fearful of man had those aboard *Vagabond* become that the abandonment of the city was as much a relief as a source of sadness. Neil, who had joined the others on deck, felt the same sense of being an alien on another planet that he had felt at his last landfall.

They had lowered their dinghy into the water and Jim, Lisa, and Sheila were preparing to go ashore when two, three and then half a dozen people appeared along one small section of unburned bulkhead fifty feet away. There were four men, a woman and a child. Two of the men were carrying rifles. All were dressed in woollen ponchos and several wore the distinctive bowler hats of the Andes. The Chileans stared at the trimaran and its occupants, who stared back. Then one of the men with a rifle shouted something. Jeanne, frowning, shouted back in Spanish a request that he say it again. The man shouted the same thing a second time. Jeanne remained frowning a moment and consulted with Sheila.

'What's he saying?' Neil asked from a cushion in the wheelhouse area.

'As near as we can tell,' said Jeanne with a puzzled smile on her face, 'he's saying – roughly translated – "Hi, where the hell did you get that weird boat?"'

In the next two days, befriended by the few Chileans who still lived in Punta Arenas, they gradually learned that the city had been destroyed in a brief war between Chile and Argentina ten weeks earlier. No one was certain why the war had started, although the two countries had long disputed areas of Tierra del Fuego. It wasn't even certain who had won the war, but Argentinian jets had destroyed the city and sunk most of the Chilean ships during the four days of fighting. With the city mostly destroyed the Chilean government had ordered it evacuated, perhaps as part of a peace treaty, perhaps being unwilling to spend money supplying it with food and fuel during the winter. Thousands of people had sailed off in freighters and Navy ships for Santiago, leaving less than a hundred people who either chose to stay or got left behind out of ignorance. There was no phone, radio, road, or air contact between this part of Chile and the more civilized parts further north. A single Chilean Navy ship had returned a month ago, looked around, and disappeared.

They also learned that *Vagabond* was not the only ship to have arrived since the town's destruction. Six weeks before, an English sailing boat had arrived, made some repairs, reprovisioned as best they could, and then sailed on. A damaged Dutch sloop had arrived three weeks earlier and was beached a mile to the east. A Rumanian sailing boat had arrived only three days before *Vagabond*. The small wiry Chilean man in his thirties who became their unofficial guide joked that Punta Arenas was becoming the 'new French Riviera'.

They met the crews of both ships and for Neil and the others, friendly people were unreal. The absence of threat was vaguely unnerving. The chance to live on land, perhaps in the shell of a house, seemed too good to be true. Food here was very scarce. Spring, although it officially arrived on 21 September, the day they arrived, was still almost a month away. The friendly Chileans had no provisions to spare but they did show the sailors where they might hunt wildlife – mostly rodents and wild dogs – and where they might gather shellfish.

It was unreal, too, to meet the three Dutchmen and one woman and her eight-year-old child who were creating a winter home a mile east of the centre of Punta Arenas while they tried to repair their holed thirty-eight-foot fibreglass sloop. Two of the Dutch spoke good English, as did one of the Rumanians, who, with six others, two of them women, had sailed a forty-eight-foot fibreglass ketch all the way from the Black Sea. It was also anchored east of the wrecked town. Each of the crews was wary and suspicious of the others for a day or two. It wasn't until they had shared the stories of their long voyages of survival that they all began not only to trust but to feel a brotherhood. The Rumanians, like those aboard *Vagabond*, were still in shock at being greeted with friendliness by human beings.

The Dutch had fled Amsterdam on the first morning of the war, landing briefly in Portugal and again in the Canary

490

Islands for supplies. They hadn't experienced the resentment and violence which fleeing Americans had experienced; no one blamed the Dutch for the war. But conditions were harsh in the Canaries, the islands crowded with European refugees and food so scarce aristocrats with millions of dollars worth of gold found it almost useless; food couldn't be easily obtained at any price. The Dutch decided to sail across to Argentina which, they thought, had plenty of food and would welcome them. When they had landed in a small Argentinian fishing village they learned they would lose their boat and be interned. They opted to try for the South Pacific.

The Rumanian story was more harrowing. Working in the Black Sea when the war began, they had all, including the three members of the Communist Party aboard, decided that the war was a meaningless disaster and chosen to run. By the time they got to the Bosphorus a nuclear explosion had blocked the Straits to all big ship traffic but they were able to sail through. They touched on North Africa only once, losing two of their shipmates in an attack by natives, then escaped out of the Mediterranean to the Atlantic. They stopped in Cape Verde to reprovision but found food so scarce they could obtain almost nothing. Sailing on, they'd been dismasted in a storm off Brazil, spent three weeks in a jungle south of the Amazon building another mast, and then sailed on. They too had been fired on by a jet, a Brazilian jet, but it had fired just once, missed by a literal mile and then flown off.

Both the Dutch and the Rumanians seemed surrealistically skinny and bony at first, until Neil realized that he must look even worse.

It took Neil and Jeanne and the others only two days to decide that their plan to sail on soon to the South Pacific was madness created by their desperation. They had no food and little prospect of getting much until the summer season offered a chance to plant and harvest crops; Jeanne was pregnant; Lisa and Olly still in weakened condition, although both now out of bed. Sheila and Jeanne had pulled two of

Olly's rotting teeth a week earlier and his strange low-grade fever and weakness were disappearing. He had recovered sufficiently to pinch Sheila's behind and begin entertaining himself and others again with monologues.

On their third day they moved *Vagabond* east to beach her closer to the other sailing boats. The terrain was desolate: the few trees twisted like grotesque cripples by the fierce westerly winds. Aboard *Vagabond* as Philip and Sheila and Lisa began preparing to cook some of the last of their beef, Olly suggested a barbecue. Philip said that of course that was the easiest way to cook, the only way, but Olly shook his head. 'I mean a real barbecue,' he said. 'With people, talk, laughter. You know, like they do on Smith Island.'

'You mean . . . invite other people?' asked Jeanne.

'Sure,' said Olly. 'Shit, let's cook up *all* the rest of our meat.'

They all stared at him. *Share* all their remaining food?

'Who'll we invite?' asked Jeanne.

'Well, those fellas with the funny round hats for one,' said Olly.

'Everyone,' said Neil.

'What?' said Philip.

'We'll invite everyone,' Neil repeated almost dreamily. 'We'll invite everyone . . .'

'By God, that's a jolly good idea, Neil,' Philip said, grinning. 'To share with friends again, even if it leaves us back with dried grasses and barnacles.'

'Don't criticize barnacles, dear,' said Sheila. 'Lisa and I are concocting a marvellous barnacle salad.'

'Save it for the barbecue,' said Neil. 'Save everything good. Tomorrow we'll share every bit of food we have so we can start from scratch.'

'Bit mad, I suppose,' said Philip, still smiling. 'Still, it beats hoarding . . .'

Jim was the official messenger and he spoke first to their little

Chilean guide, who nodded and looked pleased and hurried away to tell his friends.

But the Dutch were confused and wary. 'You want to share your food with us?' the oldest Dutchman asked, frowning.

'Yes,' said Jim. 'But . . . but we only have a little beef. We . . . don't have much else to eat or drink. It's . . .'

'It's what you call "potluck", no?' the Dutchman said, smiling.

'And "bring your own bottle",' added another, also smiling.

'Yeah, I guess so,' said Jim. 'But you don't have to bring anything . . .'

'Well, we come,' said the oldest Dutchman. 'We come with much thanks.'

The Rumanians were even more dumbfounded. Jim could sense that they suspected some trap. They had greeted him with their rifles at port arms. They whispered together in Rumanian, glancing at him nervously.

'Why do you do this?' asked the Rumanian ship's captain after he finally understood Jim's invitation. 'You have much food?'

'No,' said Jim. 'But . . . we want . . . we decided . . . to share what we have . . .'

'You want us to share our food too, no?'

Jim frowned. 'We want to share our food with you,' he finally said. 'It seems . . . right to us. That's all.'

'We bring our guns?'

'I guess so,' Jim replied. 'We don't have any guns.'

'Ah . . . no guns . . .'

'We'd . . . be honoured if you'd come and eat with us,' Jim repeated.

'Honoured, yes,' echoed the Rumanian, looking puzzled. 'Well, maybe we come. We see.'

'Two o'clock,' said Jim.

'Two o'clock, yes. Well . . . And meat, you say. Well . . . An honour . . . yes . . . Maybe we come.'

And so at two o'clock the next afternoon the five Dutch and seven Rumanians and twelve Chileans came. The Dutch and Rumanians approached as warily as if coming to a minefield. The Chileans, already accepting the weirdness of their latest visitors, came fearlessly. The Dutch brought their last flask of Flemish wine and a specially baked loaf of bread – their first in a week. The Rumanians brought a tiny tin – their last – of caviar, and a freshly caught and baked fish. The Chileans brought a basket of corn and some of their homemade wine. No one brought guns.

And they ate. And though each was limited to a small cup of wine and a single cob of corn, and a few bites of tough, stringy meat, they ate happily. And slowly, very slowly, it began to dawn on each of *Vagabond*'s survivors that they might live. For Neil it was the experience of the friendliness of the Chileans and the Dutch and the Rumanians, expressed primarily in exaggerated gestures of delight at the feast and continual smiles, that made him realize that some deep part of him had begun to feel he would be fleeing and on the edge of death forever. Now the act of sharing the treasured bit of Flemish wine with Jacob and his friends, and a pipeful of tobacco with one of the Rumanians, altered his world view. Running, at long last, was over. The Rumanians and Dutch had decided, like those with *Vagabond*, to remain in the Straits at least through the summer. Although all left in the destroyed city were on starvation rations – *Vagabond* was now in fact totally out of food – fishing in the Straits was good; there were small animals to be hunted, and spring was now only a few weeks away.

To the north the wars they had fled were presumably continuing. Here, at the bottom of the world, a few survivors had gathered. They still struggled to survive, but now with each other rather than against. It was a small first step on the long voyage back.

It was Olly who summed up the new feeling. He came up to Neil and Jeanne after an hour of feasting and mingling and unfolding his monologues with the two dozen strangers, few of whom understood a word he was saying but who laughed giddily anyway. There were tears in his eyes.

'I been feeling funny,' he said to them, 'and I think I finally figured out what it is . . .' He looked up at them, a laughing skeleton. 'I may have to get used to living again . . .'

Author's Postscript

This is a work of fiction. The actual effects of a large-scale nuclear war are so much worse than I have dramatized that no bearable work of fiction can be written about them.